The Great Depression
and the New Deal

ALSO BY FREDERICK E. HOSEN

Unfolding Westward in Treaty and Law: Land Documents in United States History from the Appalachians to the Pacific, 1783–1934 (McFarland, 1988)

Rifle, Blanket and Kettle: Selected Indian Treaties and Laws (McFarland, 1985)

COMPILED BY FREDERICK E. HOSEN

Federal Laws of the Reconstruction: Principal Congressional Acts and Resolutions, Presidential Proclamations, Speeches and Orders, and Other Legislative and Military Documents, 1862–1875 (McFarland, 2010)

The Great Depression and the New Deal

*Legislative Acts in Their Entirety
(1932–1933)
and Statistical Economic Data
(1926–1946)*

Frederick E. Hosen

McFarland & Company, Inc., Publishers
Jefferson, North Carolina, and London

The present work is a reprint of the library bound edition of The Great Depression and the New Deal: Legislative Acts in Their Entirety (1932–1933) and Statistical Economic Data (1926–1946), *first published in 1992 by McFarland.*

LIBRARY OF CONGRESS CATALOGUING-IN-PUBLICATION DATA

Hosen, Fredrick E., 1938–
　The Great Depression and the New Deal : legislative acts in their entirety (1932–1933) and statistical economic data (1926–1946) / Fredrick E. Hosen.
　　p.　cm.
　Includes bibliographical references and index.

　ISBN 978-0-7864-7740-1
　softcover : acid free paper ♾

　1. Industrial laws and legislation—United States.
2. Social legislation—United States.　3. United States—Economic conditions—1918–1945–Statistics.　4. United States—Social conditions—1933–1945—Statistics.　5. New Deal, 1933–1939.　6. Depressions—1929—United States.
I. Title.
343.73'07—dc20　2014
[347.3037]　　　　　　　　　　　　　　　　　92-50306

BRITISH LIBRARY CATALOGUING DATA ARE AVAILABLE

© 1992 Frederick E. Hosen. All rights reserved

No part of this book may be reproduced or transmitted in any form or by any means, electronic or mechanical, including photocopying or recording, or by any information storage and retrieval system, without permission in writing from the publisher.

On the cover: U.S. Capitol (iStockphoto/Thinkstock)

Manufactured in the United States of America

McFarland & Company, Inc., Publishers
　Box 611, Jefferson, North Carolina 28640
　　www.mcfarlandpub.com

Contents

Introduction   vii

Legislation

Reconstruction Finance Corporation Act (January 1932)   2
  and Amendments (June 1933)
Emergency Relief and Construction Act (July 1932)   16
Bank Holiday Proclamations (March 1933)   35
Emergency Banking Relief/Bank Conservation Act (March 1933)   39
  and Amendment (June 1933)
Credit Act (March 1933)   49
Unemployment Relief/Public Works Act (March 1933)   59
Agricultural Adjustment Act (May 1933)   61
Federal Emergency Relief Act (May 1933)   89
Tennessee Valley Authority Act (May 1933)   93
Securities Act (May 1933)   110
Uniform Value of Coins and Currencies, Joint   137
  Resolution (June 1933)
National Cooperative Employment Service Act (June 1933)   139
Home Owners' Loan Act (June 1933)   144
Banking Act (June 1933)   153
National Industrial Recovery Act (June 1933)   194
Emergency Railroad Transportation Act (June 1933)   214
Farm Credit Act (June 1933)   228

Tables

United States Population   250
International Migration   251

Vital Statistics   252
Social Welfare Expenditures Under Public Programs   253
Recreation   254
Education   255
Crime and Correction   256
Unemployed   257
Earnings in Current Dollars   258
Index of Employee Output   260
Wholesale Price Indexes   261
Wholesale Prices of Selected Commodities   262
Consumer Price Indexes   263
Retail Prices of Selected Foods in U.S. Cities   264
Apparent Civilian per Capita Consumption of Foods   266
Gross National Product   268
Agriculture — Farms   269
Farm Income and Expenses   270
Indexes of Prices Received and Paid by Farmers   271
Agriculture — Crops   272
Agriculture — Livestock, Poultry, and Eggs   273
Agriculture — Dairy Products   274
Forest Products   275
Minerals — Price   276
Construction — Value and Cost Indexes   277
Rail and Highway Transportation   278
Telephones   279
Average Annual Earnings per Full-Time Employee
    in Distribution and Selected Service Industries   280
Electric Production, and Residential Service   282
Value of Exports and Imports   283
Retail Store Sales by Kind of Store   284
Business   286
Indexes of National Productivity   287
Net Public and Private Debt   288
Currency Stock and Currency in Circulation   289
Interest Rates, Stocks Volume, Consumer Credit, and Banks   290
Life Insurance Companies and Sales   291
Federal Government Employment and Finances   292
Various Social and Economic Data for Selected Years
    Pre-, Post-, and During the Great Depression   293

Bibliography   313

Index   315

Introduction

This book is a compilation of laws and economic data that together should provide the reader or researcher with a clear picture of that period of time when the United States was immersed in the Great Depression.

The Depression, the decade or so from 1929/1930 to 1939/1940 during which many people were impoverished in the United States as well as worldwide, is in many ways still not fully understood. Not only are there numerous views of how it started, but there are various suppositions about how recovery was accomplished.

An economic depression is commonly associated with a rapid stock market decline of great magnitude, although such a decline in stock prices may occur without being followed by a depression. However, the real impact of economic strife is not the loss of value in stocks but the longer term associated impact on the value of goods and services, along with the accompanying unemployment and human suffering.

In this book, other than to some minor extent in this introduction, there is no attempt to draw conclusions or to make observations. The purpose of this effort is first, to bring together in a concise form the basic legislation of the Congress of the United States and the Franklin D. Roosevelt administration that was directed toward the seriously depressed economy of the United States in 1933 and to display the macroeconomic data that reflect what actually happened during that time.

In this book each act is preceded by a summary of its provisions. This should be helpful in focusing on the basic elements of the act prior to reading it in total.

The Great Depression years essentially encompassed the decade of the 1930's but statistically, in order to provide a frame of reference, data for pre-Depression and post-Depression years are presented. Post-Depression data are through 1946 to cover the impact of the Second World War.

New Deal legislation, as well as the statistics from 1926 through 1946, are meaningful in total rather than in part, although knowledge of the parts is necessary. That is, the Agricultural Adjustment Act (May 12, 1933) does not stand alone but must be viewed in conjunction with other acts of the New Deal. Similarly, the statistics for agriculture, for example, reflect the total impact of the New Deal and not that of any one act.

Depressions have been with us from the earliest days of the United States but few have been as disruptive, and none have lasted as long as the Great Depression. It has now been over 50 years since the end of that depression and many of the people who lived through it are no longer alive to provide first-hand experience. It is because of the inherent danger of losing touch with the past that a review of the legislation and statistics of the time is important. Although today we live in a significantly different world and some economic, financial, and social safeguards are in place, many of which are the direct result of the New Deal legislation, there is no assurance that another economic downturn equal to the Great Depression will not occur.

New Deal legislation dealt with virtually all basic economic activity of the nation, such as banking, employment, unemployment, housing, agriculture, transportation, salaries and wages, credit, insurance, and regional economic development. There were many adversaries to the New Deal and the constitutionality of some of the laws was subjected to the scrutiny of the United States Supreme Court. However, in 1933, in a social and economic situation which was bad and getting worse, action was called for, action that perhaps at another time would not have been acceptable. To what extent New Deal legislation hastened or slowed recovery will likely remain a question for continued discussion.

The data associated with basic economic activity of the time are interesting since for the most part the fall and rise of major economic indicators moved in concert with one another. Looking at employment, consumer prices, and construction we see: nonagricultural employment declining by 24.4 percent from 1929 to 1933 and increasing by 30.9 percent from 1933 to 1937; the price of food at home declining by 36.6 percent from 1929 to 1933 and increasing by 25.2 percent from 1933 to 1937; and the value of new private construction declining by 80.4 pecent from 1929 to 1933 and increasing by 154.4 percent from 1933 to 1937. While these three indexes, like most other economic indexes of the time, had not reached pre-Depression levels by 1937, the trend was clearly and substantially moving in that direction despite some ground lost in 1938.

The national debt changed in just the way that might be expected. The total gross debt increased from $16,931,088,000 in 1929 to $22,538,637,000 in 1933 or 23 percent. By 1937 the total gross debt had reached $36,424,614,000 which was 115 percent greater than in 1929.

The Great Depression began during the administration of President Herbert Hoover. During that time two significant laws, related to what was to be the New Deal, were passed. They were the Reconstruction Finance Act, passed January 22, 1932, which provided emergency financing of facilities for financial institutions, and aided in the financing of agriculture, commerce, and industry; and the Emergency Relief and Construction Act of 1932, passed July 21, 1932, which was to relieve destitution, broaden the lending powers of the Reconstruction Finance Corporation, and create employment by providing for, and expediting, a public-works program.

While these acts are not part of the New Deal laws they could be considered forerunners of those laws.

The New Deal laws themselves were forerunners of legislation that followed from 1934 to 1938, often extending or providing application of New Deal legislation.

Post-New Deal acts of particular significance were:

The *Banking Act* of 1935, which provided for major changes in the Federal Reserve System including enhanced coordination of the banking system, improved monetary management and credit control, and a greater role for the Federal Reserve Board in economic policy;

The *Public Utility Holding Company Act* of 1935, which gave the Federal Trade Commission and the Federal Power Commission the authority to regulate interstate shipments of natural gas and the interstate transmission of electric power, respectively;

The *Social Security Act* of 1935, which provided for a number of programs. There was old-age insurance, unemployment compensation, assistance to the destitute and the blind, and assistance for homeless, crippled, dependent, and delinquent children;

The *National Labor Relations Act* of 1935, under which labor's rights to organize, bargain collectively, and strike were protected;

The *Revenue Act* of 1935, which established a graduated income tax;

The *Emergency Relief Appropriations Act* of 1935, which provided a total of $4,800,000,000 for use in work relief programs. In conjunction with this act the Works Progress Administration (WPA) was created by executive order. The WPA built hospitals, schools, airports, highways, streets, parks, and other public facilities. It also supported programs of health, education, and social services in general. Under the Reorganization Act of 1939, the WPA was renamed the Works Projects Administration;

The *Rural Electrification Administration Act* of 1936, which followed the executive order by which President Roosevelt created the Rural Electrification Administration (REA) in 1935. The act was passed in May of 1936. The REA provided low-interest-rate, long-amortization loans to rural electric cooperatives for the construction of rural power systems;

The *Farm Tenant Act* of 1937, which created the Farm Security Administration (FSA). The FSA established camps for migrant farm workers, provided medical care for those workers and their families, and helped in finding jobs.

The *National Housing Act* of 1937, under which the U.S. Housing Authority was established, providing capital for the construction of public housing; and

The *Fair Labor Standards Act* of 1938, which legislated against the labor of children under age 16. It also set minimum wages and maximum hours for industrial workers.

Two principal source documents have been used in compiling this work. The laws are from the *United States Statutes at Large of the Congress of the United States,* while the economic data come from the *Historical Statistics of the United States, Colonial Times to 1970,* prepared by the United States Department of Commerce, Bureau of the Census.

Legislation

RECONSTRUCTION FINANCE CORPORATION ACT (1932) AND AMENDMENTS (1933)

Editor's comments: This Act created the Reconstruction Finance Corporation (RFC) to aid in the support of agriculture finance, and industry. To accomplish this the RFC was empowered to make loans to various types of financial institutions. Such loans were to be "fully and adequately secured." There was also provision for loans to be made to railroads engaged in interstate commerce upon approval by the Interstate Commerce Commission.

The RFC was authorized to issue various types of interest bearing obligations that were exempt from all taxation as to both principal and interest. In order for the RFC to carry out the provisions of the Act, such reports and records relating to an entity to which loans were to be issued would be made available by other government agencies.

The amendment of June 10, 1933, provided for the subscription of preferred stock and the purchase of capital notes of insurance companies by the RFC. The amendment of June 14, 1933, authorized the RFC to issue loans to closed building and loan associations.

An Act to Provide Emergency Financing Facilities for Financial Institutions, to Aid in Financing Agriculture, Commerce, and Industry, and for Other Purposes
January 22, 1932

Be it enacted by the Senate and House of Representatives of the United States of America in Congress assembled, That there be, and is hereby, created a body corporate with the name "Reconstruction Finance Corporation" (herein called the corporation). That the principal office of the corporation shall be located in the District of Columbia, but there may be established agencies or branch offices in any city or cities of the United States under rules and regulations prescribed by the board of directors. This Act may be cited as the "Reconstruction Finance Corporation Act."

Sec. 2. The Corporation shall have capital stock of $500,000,000, subscribed by the United States of America, payment for which shall be subject to call in whole or in part by the board of directors of the corporation.

There is hereby authorized to be appropriated, out of any money in the Treasury not otherwise appropriated, the sum of $500,000,000, for the purpose of making payments upon such subscription when called: *Provided*, That $50,000,000 of the amount so subscribed, and the expansion of same through the notes, debentures, bonds, or other obligations as set out in section 9 shall be allocated and made available to the Secretary of Agriculture, which sum, or so much thereof as may be necessary, shall be expended by the Secretary of Agriculture for the purpose of making loans or advances to farmers in the several States of the United States in cases where he finds that an emergency exists as a result of which farmers are unable to obtain loans for crop production during the year 1932: *Provided further,* That the Secretary of Agriculture shall give preference in making such loans or advances to farmers who suffered from crop failures in 1931. Such advances or loans shall be made upon such terms and conditions and subject to such regulations as the Secretary of Agriculture shall prescribe. A first lien on all crops growing, or to be planted and grown, shall, in the discretion of the Secretary of Agriculture, be deemed sufficient security for such loan or advance. All such loans or advances shall be made through such agencies as the Secretary of Agriculture may designate, and in such amounts as such agencies, with the approval of the Secretary of Agriculture, may determine. Any person who shall knowingly make any material false representation for the purpose of obtaining an advance or loan, or in assisting in obtaining such advance or loan under this section shall, upon conviction thereof, be punished by a fine of not exceeding $1,000 or by imprisonment not exceeding six months, or both.

Receipts for payments by the United States of America for or on account of such stock shall be issued by the corporation to the Secretary of the Treasury and shall be evidence of the stock ownership of the United States of America.

Sec. 3. The management of the corporation shall be vested in a board of directors consisting of the Secretary of the Treasury, or, in his absence, the Under Secretary of the Treasury, the governor of the Federal Reserve Board, and the Farm Loan Commissioner, who shall be members ex officio, and four other persons appointed by the President of the United States, by and with the advice and consent of the Senate. Of the seven members of the board of directors not more than four shall be members of any one political party and not more than one shall be appointed from any one Federal reserve district. Each director shall devote his time not otherwise required by the business of the United States principally to the business of the corporation. Before entering upon his duties each of the directors so appointed and each officer of the corporation shall take an oath faithfully to discharge the duties of his office. Nothing contained in this or in any other Act shall be construed to prevent the appointment and compensation as an employee of the corporation of any officer or employee of the United States in any board, commission, independent establishment, or executive department thereof. The terms of the directors appointed by the President of the United States shall be two years and run from the date of the enactment hereof and until their successors are appointed and qualified. Whenever a vacancy shall occur among the directors so appointed, the person appointed to fill such vacancy shall hold office for the unexpired portion of the term of the director whose place he is selected to fill. The directors of the corporation appointed as hereinbefore provided shall receive salaries at the rate of $10,000 per annum each. No director, officer, attorney, agent, or employee of the corporation shall in any manner, directly or indirectly, participate in the deliberation upon or the determination of any question affecting his personal interests, or the interests of any corporation, partnership, or association in which he is directly or indirectly interested.

Sec. 4. The corporation shall have succession for a period of ten years from the date of the enactment hereof, unless it is sooner dissolved by an Act of Congress. It shall have power to adopt, alter, and use a corporate seal; to make contracts; to lease such real estate as may be necessary for the transaction of its business; to sue and be sued, to complain and to defend, in any court of competent jurisdiction, State or Federal; to select, employ, and fix the compensation of such officers, employees, attorneys, and agents as shall be necessary for the transaction of the business of the corporation, without regard to the provisions of other laws applicable to the employment and compensation of officers or employees of the United States; to define their authority and duties, require bonds of them and fix the penalties thereof, and to dismiss at pleasure such officers, employees, attorneys, and agents; and to prescribe, amend, and repeal, by its board of directors, by-laws, rules, and regulations governing the manner in which its general business may be conducted and the powers granted to it by law may be exercised and enjoyed, including the selection of its chairman and vice chairman, together with provision for such committees and the functions thereof as the board of directors may deem necessary for facilitating its business under this Act. The board of directors of the corporation shall determine and prescribe the manner in which its obligations shall be incurred and its expenses allowed and paid. The corporation shall be entitled to the free use of the United States mails in the same manner as the executive departments of the Government. The corporation, with the consent of any board, commission, independent establishment, or executive department of the Government, including any field service thereof, may avail itself of the use of information, services, facilities, officers, and employees thereof in carrying out the provisions of this Act.

Sec. 5. To aid in financing agriculture, commerce, and industry, including facilitating the exportation of agricultural and other products the corporation is authorized and empowered to make loans, upon such terms and conditions not inconsistent with this Act as it may determine, to any bank, savings bank, trust company, building and loan association, insurance company, mortgage loan company, credit union, Federal land bank, joint-stock land bank, Federal intermediate credit bank, agricultural credit corporation, livestock credit corporation, organized under the laws of any State or of the United States, including loans secured by the assets of any bank that is closed, or in process of liquidation to aid in the reorganization or liquidation of such banks, upon application of the receiver or liquidating agent of such bank and any receiver of any national bank is hereby authorized to contract for such loans and to pledge any assets of the bank for securing the same: *Provided,* That not more than $200,000,000 shall be used for the relief of banks that are closed or in the process of liquidation.

All loans made under the foregoing provisions shall be fully and adequately secured. The corporation, under such conditions as it shall prescribe, may take over or provide for the administration and liquidation of any collateral accepted by it as security for such loans. Such loans may be made directly upon promissory notes or by way of discount or rediscount of obligations tendered for the purpose, or otherwise in such form and in such amount and at such interest or discount rates as the corporation may approve: *Provided*, That no loans or advances shall be made upon foreign securities or foreign acceptances as collateral or for the purpose of assisting in the carrying or liquidation of such foreign securities and foreign acceptances. In no case shall the aggregate amount of advances made under this section to any one corporation and its subsidiary or affiliated organizations exceed at any one time 5 per centum of (1) the authorized capital stock of the Reconstruction Finance Corporation plus (2) the aggregate amount of bonds of the corporation authorized to be outstanding when the capital stock is fully subscribed.

Each such loan may be made for a period not exceeding three years, and the corporation may from time to time extend the time of payment of any such loan, through renewal, substitution of new obligations, or otherwise, but the time for such payment shall not be extended beyond five years from the date upon which such loan was made originally. Except as provided in section 5a hereof, no loan or advancement shall be made by the corporation for the purpose of initiating, setting on foot, or financing any enterprise not initiated, set on foot, or undertaken prior to the adoption of this Act: *Provided*, That the foregoing limitation shall not apply to loans made to agricultural or livestock credit corporations, or Federal land banks, joint-stock land banks, or Federal intermediate credit banks, nor to loans made to banks for the purpose of financing agricultural operations. The corporation may make loans under this section at any time prior to the expiration of one year from the date of the enactment hereof; and the President may from time to time postpone such date of expiration for such additional period or periods as he may deem necessary, not to exceed two years from the date of the enactment hereof. Within the foregoing limitations of this section, the corporation may also, upon the approval of the Interstate Commerce Commission, make loans to aid in the temporary financing of railroads and railways engaged in interstate commerce, to railroads and railways in process of construction, and to receivers of such railroads and railways, when in the opinion of the board of directors of the corporation such railroads or railways are unable to obtain funds upon reasonable terms through banking channels or from the general public and the corporation will be adequately secured: *Provided*, That no fee or commission shall be paid by any applicant for a loan under the provisions hereof in connection with any such application or any loan made or to be made hereunder, and the agreement to pay or payment of any such fee or commission shall be unlawful. Any such railroad may obligate itself in such form as shall be prescribed and otherwise comply with the requirements of the Interstate Commerce Commission and the corporation with respect to the deposit or assignment of security hereunder, without the authorization or approval of any authority, State or Federal, and without compliance with any requirement, State or Federal, as to notification, other than such as may be imposed by the Interstate Commerce Commission and the corporation under the provisions of this section.

Sec. 5a. The corporation is authorized and empowered to accept drafts and bills of exchange drawn upon it which grow out of transactions involving the exportation of agricultural or other products actually sold or transported for sale subsequent to the enactment hereof and in process of shipment to buyers in foreign countries: *Provided,* That the corporation shall not make any such acceptances growing out of transactions involving the sale or shipment of armaments, munitions, or other war materials, or the sale or shipment into countries which are at war of any merchandise or commodities except food and supplies for the actual use of noncombatants. No bill of exchange or draft shall be eligible for acceptance if such bill shall have at time of acceptance a maturity of more than twelve months. All drafts and bills of exchange accepted under this section shall be in terms payable in the United States, in currency of the United States, and in addition to the draft or bill of exchange shall at all times be fully secured by American securities deposited as collateral or shall be guaranteed by a bank or trust company of undoubted solvency organized under the laws of the United States or any State, Territory, or insular possession thereof: *Provided,* That such securities shall not include goods stored or in process of shipment in foreign countries or the obligation of any foreign government, corporation, firm, or person.

Sec. 6. Section 5202 of the Revised Statutes of the United States, as amended, is hereby amended by striking out the words "War Finance Corporation Act" and inserting in lieu thereof the words "Reconstruction Finance Corporation Act."

Sec. 7. All moneys of the corporation not otherwise employed may be deposited with the Treasurer of the United States subject to check by authority of the corporation or in any Federal reserve bank, or may, by authorization of the board of directors of the corporation, be used in the purchase for redemption and retirement of any notes, debentures, bonds, or other obligations issued by the corporation, and the corporation may reimburse such Federal reserve bank for their services in the manner as may be agreed upon. The Federal reserve banks are authorized and directed to act as depositaries, custodians, and fiscal agents for the Reconstruction Finance Corporation in the general performance of its powers conferred by this Act.

Sec. 8. In order to enable the corporation to carry out the provisions of this Act, the Treasury Department, the Federal Farm Loan Board, the Comptroller of the Currency, the Federal Reserve Board, the Federal reserve banks, and the Interstate Commerce Commission are hereby authorized, under such conditions as they may prescribe, to make available to the corporation, in confidence, such reports, records, or other information as they may have available relating to the condition of financial institutions and railroads or railways with respect to which the corporation has had or contemplates having transactions under this Act, or relating to individuals, associations, partnerships, or corporations whose obligations are offered to or held by the corporation as security for loans to financial institutions or railroads or railways under this Act, and to make through their examiners or other employees for the confidential use of the corporation, examinations of such financial institutions or railroads and railways. Every applicant for a loan under this Act shall, as a condition precedent thereto, consent to such examinations as the corporation may require for the purposes of this Act and that reports of examinations by constituted authorities may be furnished by such authorities to the corporation upon request therefor.

Sec. 9. The corporation is authorized and empowered, with the approval of the Secretary of the Treasury, to issue, and to have outstanding at any one time in an amount aggregating not more than three times its subscribed capital, its notes, debentures, bonds, or other such obligations; such obligations to mature not more than five years from their respective dates of issue, to be redeemable at the option of the corporation before maturity in such manner as may be stipulated in such obligations, and to bear such rate or rates of interest as may be determined by the corporation: *Provided,* That the corporation, with the approval of the Secretary of the Treasury, may sell on a discount basis short-term obligations payable at maturity without interest. The notes, debentures, bonds, and other obligations of the corporation may be secured by assets of the corporation in such manner as shall be prescribed by its board of directors: *Provided,* That the aggregate of all obligations issued under this section shall not exceed three times the amount of the subscribed capital stock. Such obligations may be issued in payment of any loan authorized by this Act or may be offered for sale at such price or prices as the corporation may determine with the approval of the Secretary of the Treasury. The said obligations shall be fully and unconditionally guaranteed both as to interest and principal by the United States and such guaranty shall be expressed on the face thereof. In the event that the corporation shall be unable to pay upon demand, when due, the principal of or interest on notes, debentures, bonds, or other such obligations issued by it, the Secretary of the Treasury shall pay the amount thereof, which is hereby authorized to be appropriated, out of any moneys in the Treasury not otherwise appropriated, and thereupon to the extent of the amounts so paid the Secretary of the Treasury shall succeed to all the rights of the holders of such notes, debentures, bonds, or other obligations. The Secretary of the Treasury, in his discretion, is authorized to purchase any obligations of the corporation to be issued hereunder, and for such purpose the Secretary of the Treasury is authorized to use as a public-debt transaction the proceeds from the sale of any securities hereafter issued under the Second Liberty Bond Act, as amended, and the purposes for which securities may be issued under the Second Liberty Bond Act, as amended, are extended to include any purchases of the corporation's obligations hereunder. The Secretary of the Treasury may, at any time, sell any of the obligations of the corporation acquired by him under this section. All redemptions, purchases, and sales by the Secretary of the Treasury of the obligations of the corporation shall be treated as public-debt transactions of the United States. Such obligations shall not be eligible for discount or purchase by any Federal reserve bank.

Sec. 10. Any and all notes, debentures, bonds, or other such obligations issued by the corporation shall be exempt both as to principal and interest from all taxation (except surtaxes, estate, inheritance, and gift taxes) now or hereafter imposed by the United States, by any Territory, dependency, or possession thereof, or by any State, county, municipality, or local taxing authority. The corporation, including its franchise, its capital, reserves, and surplus, and its income shall be exempt from all taxation now or hereafter imposed by the United States, by any Territory, dependency, or possession thereof, or by any State, county, municipality, or local taxing authority; except that any real property of the coporation shall be subject to State, Territorial, county, municipal, or local taxation to the same extent according to its value as other real property is taxed.

Sec. 11. In order that the corporation may be supplied with such forms of notes, debentures, bonds, or other such obligations as it may need for issuance under this Act, the Secretary of the Treasury is authorized to prepare such forms as shall be suitable and approved by the corporation, to be held in the Treasury subject to delivery, upon order of the corporation. The engraved plates, dies, bed pieces, and so forth, executed in connection therewith shall remain in the custody of the Secretary of the Treasury. The corporation shall reimburse the Secretary of the Treasury for any expenses incurred in the preparation, custody and delivery of such notes, debentures, bonds, or other obligations.

Sec. 12. When designated for that purpose by the Secretary of the Treasury, the corporation shall be a depositary of public money, except receipts from customs, under such regulations as may be prescribed by said Secretary; and it may also be employed as a financial agent of the Government; and it shall perform all such reasonable duties, as depositary of public money and financial agent of the Government, as may be required of it. Obligations of the corporation shall be lawful investments, and may be accepted as security, for all fiduciary, trusts, and public funds the investment or deposit of which shall be under the authority or control of the United States or any officer or officers thereof.

Sec. 13. Upon the expiration of the period of one year within which the corporation may make loans, or of any extension thereof by the President under the authority of this Act, the board of directors of the corporation shall, except as otherwise herein specifically authorized, proceed to liquidate its assets and wind up its affairs. It may with the approval of the Secretary of the Treasury deposit with the Treasurer of the United States as a special fund any money belonging to the corporation or from time to time received by it in the course of liquidation or otherwise, for the payment of principal and interest of its outstanding obligations or for the purpose of redemption of such obligations in accordance with the terms thereof, which fund may be drawn upon or paid out for no other purpose. The corporation may also at any time pay to the Treasurer of the United States as miscellaneous receipts any money belonging to the corporation or from time to time received by it in the course of liquidation or otherwise in excess of reasonable amounts reserved to meet its requirements during liquidations. Upon such deposit being made, such amount of the capital stock of the corporation as may be specified by the corporation with the approval of the Secretary of the Treasury but not exceeding in par value the amount so paid in shall be canceled and retired. Any balance remaining after the liquidation of all the corporation's assets and after provision has been made for payment of all legal obligations of any kind and character shall be paid into the Treasury of the United States as miscellaneous receipts. Thereupon the corporation shall be dissolved and the residue, if any, of its capital stock shall be canceled and retired.

Sec. 14. If at the expiration of the ten years for which the corporation has succession hereunder its board of directors shall not have completed the liquidation of its assets and the winding up of its affairs, the duty of completing such liquidation and winding up of its affairs shall be transferred to the Secretary of the Treasury, who for such purpose shall succeed to all the powers and duties of the board of directors of the corporation under this Act. In such event he may assign to any officer or officers of the United States in the Treasury Department the exercise and performance, under his general supervision and direction, of any such powers and duties; and nothing herein shall be construed to affect any right or privilege accrued, any penalty or liability incurred, any criminal or civil proceeding commenced, or any authority conferred hereunder, except as herein provided in connection with the liquidation of the remaining assets and the winding up of the affairs of the corporation, until the Secretary of the Treasury shall find that such liquidation will no longer be advantageous to the United States and that all of its legal obligations have been provided for, whereupon he shall retire any capital stock then outstanding, pay into the Treasury as miscellaneous receipts the unused balance of the moneys belonging to the corporation, and make the final report of the corporation to the Congress. Thereupon the corporation shall be deemed to be dissolved.

Sec. 15. The corporation shall make and publish a report quarterly of its operations to the Congress stating the aggregate loans made to each of the classes of borrowers provided for and the number of borrowers by States in each class. The statement shall show the assets and liabilities of the corporation, and the first report shall be made on April 1, 1932, and quarterly thereafter. It shall also show the names and compensation of all persons employed by the corporation whose compensation exceeds $400 a month.

Sec. 16. (a) Whoever makes any statement knowing it to be false, or whoever willfully overvalues any security, for the purpose of obtaining for himself or for any applicant any loan, or extension thereof by renewal, deferment of action, or otherwise, or the acceptance, release, or substitution of security therefor, or for the purpose of influencing in any way the action of the corporation, or for the purpose of obtaining money, property, or anything of value, under this Act, shall be punished by a fine of not more than $5,000 or by imprisonment for not more than two years, or both.

(b) Whoever (1) falsely makes, forges, or counterfeits any note, debenture, bond, or other obligation, or coupon, in imitation of or purporting to be a note, debenture, bond, or other obligation, or coupon, issued by the corporation, or (2) passes, utters or publishes, or attempts to pass, utter or publish, any false, forged or counterfeited note, debenture, bond, or other obligation, or coupon, purporting to have been issued by the corporation, knowing the same to be false, forged or counterfeited, or (3) falsely alters any note, debenture, bond, or other obligation, or coupon, issued or purporting to have been issued by the corporation, or (4) passes, utters or publishes, or attempts to pass, utter or publish, as true any falsely altered or spurious note, debenture, bond, or other obligation, or coupon, issued or purporting to have been issued by the corporation, knowing the same to be falsely altered or spurious, or any person who willfully violates any other provision of this Act, shall be punished by a fine of not more than $10,000 or by imprisonment for not more than five years, or both.

(c) Whoever, being connected in any capacity with the corporation, (1) embezzles, abstracts, purloins, or willfully misapplies any moneys, funds, securities, or other things of value, whether belonging to it or pledged or otherwise entrusted to it, or (2) with intent to defraud the corporation or any other body politic or corporate, or any individual, or to deceive any officer, auditor, or examiner of the corporation, makes any false entry in any book, report, or statement of or to the corporation, or, without being duly authorized, draws any order or issues, puts forth or assigns any note, debenture, bond, or other obligation, or draft, bill of exchange, mortgage, judgment, or decree thereof, or (3) with intent to defraud participates, shares, receives directly or indirectly any money, profit, property or benefit through any transaction, loan, commission, contract, or any other act of the corporation, or (4) gives any unauthorized information concerning any future action or plan of the corporation which might affect the value of the securities, or, having such knowledge, invests or speculates, directly or indirectly, in the securities or property of any company, bank, or corporation receiving loans or other assistance from the corporation, shall be punished by a fine of not more than $10,000 or by imprisonment for not more than five years, or both.

(d) No individual, association, partnership, or corporation shall use the words "Reconstruction Finance Corporation" or a combination of these three words, as the name or a part thereof under which he or it shall do business. Every individual, partnership, association, or corporation violating this prohibition shall be guilty of a misdemeanor and shall be punished by a fine of not exceeding $1,000 or imprisonment not exceeding one year, or both.

(e) The provisions of sections 112, 113, 114, 115, 116, and 117 of the Criminal Code of the United States (U. S. C., title 18, ch. 5, secs. 202 to 207, inclusive) in so far as applicable, are extended to apply to contracts or agreements with the corporation under this Act, which for the purposes hereof shall be held to include loans, advances, discounts, and rediscounts; extensions and renewals thereof; and acceptances, releases, and substitutions of security therefor.

Sec. 17. The right to alter, amend, or repeal this Act is hereby expressly reserved. If any clause, sentence, paragraph, or part of this Act shall for any reason be adjudged by any court of competent jurisdiction to be invalid, such judgment shall not affect, impair, or invalidate the remainder of this Act, but shall be confined in its operation to the clause, sentence, paragraph, or part thereof directly involved in the controversy in which such judgment shall have been rendered.

Approved, January 22, 1932.

An Act to Authorize the Reconstruction Finance Corporation to Subscribe for Preferred Stock and Purchase the Capital Notes of Insurance Companies, and for Other Purposes
June 10, 1933

Be it enacted by the Senate and House of Representatives of the United States of America in Congress assembled, That during the continuance of the existing emergency heretofore recognized by Public No. 1 of the 73d Congress or until this Act shall be declared no longer operative by proclamation of the President, and notwithstanding any other provision of any other law, if, in the opinion of the Secretary of the Treasury, any insurance company of any State of the United States is in need of funds for capital purposes either in connection with the organization of such company or otherwise, he may, with the approval of the President, request the Reconstruction Finance Corporation to subscribe for preferred stock of any class, exempt from assessment or additional liability, in such insurance company, or to make loans secured by such stock as collateral, and the Reconstruction Finance Corporation may comply with such request. The Reconstruction Finance Corporation may, with the approval of the Secretary of the Treasury and under such rules and regulations as he may prescribe, sell in the open market the whole or any part of the preferred stock of any such insurance company acquired by the corporation pursuant to this section. The total face amount of loans outstanding, preferred stock subscribed for, and capital notes purchased and held by the Reconstruction Finance Corporation, under the provisions of this section and section 2, shall not exceed at any one time $50,000,000, and the amount of notes, bonds, debentures, and other such obligations which the Reconstruction Finance Corporation is authorized and empowered to issue and to have outstanding at any one time under existing law is hereby increased by an amount sufficient to carry out the provisions of this section and section 2.

Sec. 2. In the event that any such insurance company shall be incorporated under the laws of any State which does not permit it to issue preferred stock, exempt from assessment or additional liability, or if such laws permit such issue of preferred stock only by unanimous consent of stockholders, or upon notice of more than twenty days, the Reconstruction Finance Corporation is authorized for the purposes of this Act to purchase the legally issued capital notes of such insurance company or to make loans secured by such notes as collateral, which may be subordinated in whole or in part or to any degree to claims of other creditors.

Sec. 3. The Reconstruction Finance Corporation shall not subscribe for or purchase any preferred stock or capital notes of any applicant insurance company, (1) until the applicant shows to the satisfaction of the Corporation that it has unimpaired capital stock, or that it will furnish new capital which will be subordinate to the preferred stock or capital notes to be subscribed for or purchased by the Corporation, equal to the amount of said preferred stock or capital notes so subscribed for or purchased by the Corporation: *Provided,* That the Corporation may make loans upon said preferred stock or capital notes, if, in its opinion, such loans will be adequately secured by said stock or capital notes, and/or such other forms of security as the Corporation may require; (2) if at the time of such subscription, purchase, or loan any officer, director, or employee of the applicant is receiving total compensation in a sum in excess of $17,500 per annum from the applicant and/or any of its affiliates, and (3) unless at such time the applicant agrees to the satisfaction of the Corporation not to increase the compensation of any of its officers, directors, or employees, and not to retire any of its stock, notes, bonds, or debentures issued for capital purposes, while any part of the preferred stock, notes, bonds, or debentures of such company is held by the Corporation. For the purposes of this section, the term "compensation" includes any salary, fee, bonus, commission, or other payment, direct or indirect, in money or otherwise, for personal services.

Sec. 4. The Reconstruction Finance Corporation shall not make, renew, or extend any loan under the Reconstruction Finance Corporation Act, as amended, or under the Emergency Relief and Construction Act of 1932, (1) if at the time of making, renewing, or extending such loan any officer, director, or employee of the applicant is receiving compensation at a rate in excess of what appears reasonable to the Reconstruction Finance Corporation, and (2) unless at such time the applicant agrees to the satisfaction of the Corporation not to increase the compensation of any of its officers, directors, or employees to any amount in excess of what appears reasonable to the Reconstruction Finance Corporation while such loan is outstanding and unpaid. For the purposes of this section the term "compensation" includes any salary, fee, bonus, commission, or other payment, direct or indirect, in money or otherwise for personal services.

Sec. 5. That the second and third sentences of paragraph (6) of section 201 (a) of the Emergency Relief and Construction Act of 1932, as amended, are hereby amended to read as follows: "Obligations accepted hereunder shall be collateraled (a) in the case of loans for the repair or reconstruction of private property, by the obligations of the owner of such property secured by a paramount lien except as to taxes and special assessments on the property repaired or reconstructed, or on other property of the borrower, and (b) in the case of municipalities or political subdivisions of States or their public agencies, including public-school boards and public-school districts, by an obligation of such municipality, political subdivision, public agency, public-school board, or public-school district. The Corporation shall not deny an otherwise acceptable application for loans for repair or construction of the buildings of municipalities, political subdivisions, public agencies, public-school boards, or public- school districts because of constitutional or other legal inhibitions affecting the collateral."

Sec. 6. The fourth sentence of paragraph (6) of section 201 (a) of such Act, as amended, is hereby amended by striking out the period at the end of thereof and inserting in lieu thereof the following: "in case of loans made under clause (a) of this paragraph, and not exceeding twenty years in case of loans made under clause (b)."

Sec. 7. The fifth sentence of paragraph (6) of section 201 (a) of such Act, as amended, is hereby amended by striking out the period at the end thereof and inserting in lieu thereof a comma and the following: "and, in case of loans made under clause (b), shall be deemed to be so secured if, in the opinion of the Reconstruction Finance Corporation, such loans will be repaid from any source, including taxation, within a reasonable period, not exceeding twenty years."

Sec. 8. The seventh sentence of paragraph (6) of section 201 (a) of such Act, as amended, is hereby amended to read as follows: "The aggregate of loans made under clause (a) shall not exceed $5,000,000, and the aggregate of loans made under clause (b) shall not exceed $12,000,000."

Sec. 9. The first sentence in section 201 (a) of such Act, as amended, which follows paragraph (6) thereof is hereby amended by striking out the period at the end of such sentence and inserting in lieu thereof a comma and the following: "except that for the purpose of clause (b) of paragraph (6) of this subsection a project shall be deemed to be self-liquidating if the construction cost thereof will be returned by any means, including taxation, within a reasonable period, not exceeding twenty years."

Sec. 10. That an Act entitled "An Act to provide emergency financing facilities for financial institutions, to aid in financing agriculture, commerce, and industry, and for other purposes", approved January 22, 1932, and amended by an Act approved July 21, 1932, be further amended by adding at the end of section 5 thereof the following: "*Provided further,* That the Corporation may make said loans to trustees of railroads which proceed to reorganize under section 77 of the Bankruptcy Act of March 3, 1933."

Sec. 11. As used in this Act the term "insurance company" shall include any corporation engaged in the business of insurance or in the writing of annuity contracts, irrespective of the nature thereof, and operating under the supervision of a State superintendent or department of insurance in any of the States of the United States.

Sec. 12. Section 5 of the Reconstruction Finance Corporation Act, as amended, is amended by adding at the end thereof the following new paragraph:

"The Reconstruction Finance Corporation is further authorized and empowered to make loans if adequately secured to any State insurance fund established or created by the laws of any State for the purpose of paying or insuring payment of compensation to injured workmen and those disabled as a result of disease contracted in the course of their employment, or to their dependents. As used in this paragraph, the term 'State' includes the several States and Alaska, Hawaii, and Puerto Rico."

Sec. 13. Section 5 of the Reconstruction Finance Corporation Act, as amended, is amended by adding at the end thereof the following new paragraph:

"The Reconstruction Finance Corporation is further authorized and empowered to make loans if adequately secured to any fund created by any State for the purpose of insuring the repayment of deposits of public moneys of such State or any of its political subdivisions in banks or depositories qualified under the law of such State to receive such deposits. Such loans may be made at any time prior to January 23, 1934, and upon such terms and conditions as the corporation may prescribe; except that any fund which receives a loan under this paragraph shall be required to assign to the corporation, to the extent of such loan, all amounts which may be received by such fund as dividends or otherwise from the liquidation of any such bank or depository in which deposits of such public moneys were made. As used in this paragraph, the term 'State' includes the several States and Alaska, Hawaii, and Puerto Rico."

Sec. 14. The right to alter or amend or repeal this Act is hereby expressly reserved. If any provision of this Act, or the application thereof to any person, firm, association, or corporation, is held invalid, the remainder of the Act, and the application of such provision to any other person, firm, association, or corporation, shall not be affected thereby.

Approved, June 10, 1933.

An Act to Amend the Reconstruction Finance Corporation Act, as Amended, to Provide for Loans to Closed Building and Loan Associations
June 14, 1933

Be it enacted by the Senate and House of Representatives of the United States of America in Congress assembled, That the first paragraph of section 5 of the Reconstruction Finance Corporation Act, as amended, is amended to read as follows:

"Sec. 5. To aid in financing agriculture, commerce, and industry, including facilitating the exportation of agricultural and other products, the Corporation is authorized and empowered to make loans, upon such terms and conditions not inconsistent with this Act as it may determine, to any bank, savings bank, trust company, building and loan association, insurance company, mortgage-loan company, credit union, Federal land bank, joint-stock land bank, Federal intermediate credit bank, agricultural credit corporation, livestock credit corporation, organized under the laws of any State or of the United States, including loans secured by the assets of any bank, savings bank, or building and loan association that is closed, or in process of liquidation to aid in the reorganization or liquidation of such banks or building and loan associations, upon application of the receiver or liquidating agent of such bank or building and loan association, and any receiver of any national bank is hereby authorized to contract for such loans and to pledge any assets of the bank for securing the same."

Approved, June 14, 1933.

EMERGENCY RELIEF AND CONSTRUCTION ACT (1932)

Editor's comments: The Emergency Relief and Construction Act authorized the Reconstruction Finance Corporation (RFC) to make certain of its funds available to the States and Territories for relief of "needy and distressed people" resulting from the hardship of unemployment.

The RFC was authorized, among other things, to:

- *Finance the construction of public projects that were self-liquidating.*
- *Assist with providing housing for low income families and with the reconstruction of slum areas.*
- *Make loans to finance projects of private limited dividend corporations for the protection and development of forests.*
- *Make loans specifically for the building of bridges used for railroads, railways, or highways.*
- *Assist, through financing, the sales of agricultural products in foreign markets.*
- *Assist, through financing, the "orderly marketing of agricultural commodities and livestock produced in the United States."*

To assist in decreasing employment, the RFC was authorized to spend the sum of $322,224,000 for the "emergency construction of certain authorized public works."

An Act to Relieve Destitution, to Broaden the Lending Powers of the Reconstruction Finance Corporation, and to Create Employment by Providing for and Expediting a Public-Works Program

July 21, 1932

Be it enacted by the Senate and House of Representatives of the United States of America in Congress assembled, That this Act may be cited as the "Emergency Relief and Construction Act of 1932."

Title I — Relief of Destitution

Section 1. (a) The Reconstruction Finance Corporation is authorized and empowered to make available out of the funds of the corporation the sum of $300,000,000, under the terms and conditions hereinafter set forth, to the several States and Territories, to be used in furnishing relief and work relief to needy and distressed people and in relieving the hardship resulting from unemployment, but not more than 15 per centum of such sum shall be available to any one State or Territory. Such sum of $300,000,000 shall, until the expiration of two years after the date of enactment of this Act, be available for payment to the governors of the several States and Territories for the purposes of this section, upon application therefor by them in accordance with subsection (c), and upon approval of such applications by the corporation.

(b) All amounts paid under this section shall bear interest at the rate of 3 per centum per annum, and, except in the case of Puerto Rico and the Territory of Alaska, shall be reimbursed to the corporation, with interest thereon at the rate of 3 per centum per annum, by making annual deductions, beginning with the fiscal year 1935, from regular apportionments made from future Federal authorizations in aid of the States and Territories for the construction of highways and rural post roads, of an amount equal to one-fifth of the share which such State or Territory would be entitled to receive under such apportionment, except for the provisions of this section, or of an amount equal to one-fifth of the amounts so paid to the governor of such State or Territory pursuant to this section and all accrued interest thereon to the date of such deduction, whichever is the lesser, until the sum of such deductions equals the total amounts paid under this section and all accrued interest thereon. Whenever any such deduction is made, the Secretary of the Treasury shall immediately pay to the corporation an amount equal to the amount so deducted. If any State or Territory shall, within two years after the date of enactment of this Act, enter into an agreement with the corporation for the repayment to the corporation of the amounts paid under this section to the governor of such State or Territory, with interest thereon as herein provided, in such installments and upon such terms as may be agreed upon, then the deduction under this subsection shall not be made unless such State or Territory shall be in default in the performance of the terms of such agreement. In the case of a default by the State or Territory in any such agreement, the agreement shall thereupon be terminated and reimbursement of the unpaid balance of the amount covered by such agreement shall be made by making annual deductions in the manner above provided (beginning with the fiscal year next following such default) from regular apportionments made to such State or Territory from future Federal authorizations in aid of the States and Territories for the construction of highways and rural post roads. Before any amount is paid under this section to the Governor of Puerto Rico or of the Territory of Alaska, Puerto Rico or the Territory of Alaska shall enter into an agreement with the corporation for the repayment of such amount with interest thereon as herein provided, in such installments and upon such terms and conditions as may be agreed upon.

(c) The governor of any State or Territory may from time to time make application for funds under this section, and in each application so made shall certify the necessity for such funds and that the resources of the State or Territory, including moneys then available and which can be made available by the State or Territory, its political subdivisions, and private contributions, are inadequate to meet its relief needs. All amounts paid to the governor of a State or Territory under this section shall be administered by the governor, or under his direction, and upon his responsibility. The governor shall file with the corporation and with the auditor of the State or Territory (or, if there is no auditor, then with the official exercising comparable authority) a statement of the disbursements made by him under this section.

(d) Nothing in this section shall be construed to authorize the corporation to deny an otherwise acceptable application under this section because of constitutional or other legal inhibitions or because the State or Territory has borrowed to the full extent authorized by law. Whenever an application under this section is approved by the corporation in whole or in part, the amount approved shall be immediately paid to the governor of the State or Territory upon delivery by him to the corporation of a receipt therefor stating that the payment is accepted subject to the terms of this section.

(e) Any portion of the amount approved by the corporation for payment to the governor of a State or Territory shall, at his request, and with the approval of the corporation, be paid to any municipality or political subdivision of such State or Territory if (1) the governor makes as to such municipality or political subdivision a like certificate as provided in subsection (c) as to the State or Territory, and (2) such municipality or political subdivision enters into an agreement with the corporation for the repayment to the corporation of the amount so paid, with interest at the rate of 3 per centum per annum, at such times, and upon such other terms and conditions, as may be agreed upon between the corporation and such municipality or political subdivision. The amount paid to any municipality or political subdivision under this subsection shall not be included in any amounts reimbursable to the corporation under subsection (b) of this section.

(f) As used in this section the term "Territory" means Alaska, Hawaii, and Puerto Rico.

Title II — Loans by Reconstruction Finance Corporation

Sec. 201. (a) The Reconstruction Finance Corporation is authorized and empowered-

(1) to make loans to, or contracts with, States, municipalities, and political subdivisions of States, public agencies of States, of municipalities, and of political subdivisions of States, public corporations, boards and commissions, and public municipal instrumentalities of one or more States, to aid in financing projects authorized under Federal, State, or municipal law which are self-liquidating in character, such loans or contracts to be made through the purchase of their securities, or otherwise, and for such purpose the Reconstruction Finance Corporation is authorized to bid for such securities: *Provided,* That nothing herein contained shall be construed to prohibit the Reconstruction Finance Corporation, in carrying out the provisions of this paragraph, from purchasing securities having a maturity of more than ten years;

(2) to make loans to corporations formed wholly for the purpose of providing housing for families of low income, or for reconstruction of slum areas, which are regulated by State or municipal law as to rents, charges, capital structure, rate of return, and areas and methods of operation, to aid

in financing projects undertaken by such corporations which are self-liquidating in character;

(3) to make loans to private corporations to aid in carrying out the construction, replacement, or improvement of bridges, tunnels, docks, viaducts, waterworks, canals, and markets, devoted to public use and which are self-liquidating in character;

(4) to make loans to private limited dividend corporations to aid in financing projects for the protection and development of forests and other renewable natural resources, which are regulated by a State or political subdivision of a State and are self-liquidating in character; and

(5) to make loans to aid in financing the construction of any publicly owned bridge to be used for railroad, railway, and highway uses, the construction cost of which will be returned in part by means of tolls, fees, rents, or other charges, and the remainder by means of taxes imposed pursuant to State law enacted before the date of enactment of the Emergency Relief and Construction Act of 1932; and the Reconstruction Finance Corporation is further authorized and empowered to purchase bonds of any State, municipality, or other public body or agency issued for the purpose of financing the construction of any such bridge irrespective of the dates of maturity of such bonds.

For the purposes of this subsection a project shall be deemed to be self-liquidating if such project will be made self-supporting and financially solvent and if the construction cost thereof will be returned within a reasonable period by means of tolls, fees, rents, or other charges, or by such other means (other than by taxation) as may be prescribed by the statutes which provide for the project. All loans and contracts made by the Reconstruction Finance Corporation in respect of projects of the character specified in paragraphs (1) to (5) of this subsection shall be subject to the conditions that no convict labor shall be directly employed on any such project, and that (except in executive, administrative, and supervisory positions), so far as practicable, no individual directly employed on any such project shall be permitted to work more than thirty hours in any one week, and that in the employment of labor in connection with any such project preference shall be given, where they are qualified, to ex-service men with dependents.

The provisions of this subsection shall apply with respect to projects in Puerto Rico and the Territories to the same extent as in the case of projects in the several States, and as used in this subsection the term "States" includes Puerto Rico and the Territories.

(b) The Reconstruction Finance Corporation shall submit monthly to the President and to the Senate and the House of Representatives (or the Secretary of the Senate and the Clerk of the House of Representatives, if those bodies are not in session) a report of its activities and expenditures under this section and under the Reconstruction Finance Corporation Act, together with a statement showing the names of the borrowers to whom loans and advances were made, and the amount and rate of interest involved in each case.

(c) In order that the surpluses of agricultural products may not have a depressing effect upon current prices of such products, the corporation is authorized and directed to make loans, in such amounts as may in its judgment be necessary, for the purpose of financing sales of such surpluses in the markets of foreign countries in which such sales can not be financed in the normal course of commerce; but no such sales shall be financed by the corporation if, in its judgment, such sales will affect adversely the world markets for such products: *Provided, however,* That no such loan shall be made to finance the sale in the markets of foreign countries of cotton owned by the Federal Farm Board or the Cotton Stabilization Corporation.

(d) The Resonstruction Finance Corporation is authorized and empowered to make loans to bona fide institutions, organized under the laws of any State or of the United States and having resources adequate for their undertakings, for the purpose of enabling them to finance the carrying and orderly marketing of agricultural commodities and livestock produced in the United States.

(e) The Reconstruction Finance Corporation is further authorized to create in any of the twelve Federal land-bank districts where it may deem the same to be desirable a regional agricultural credit corporation with a paid-up capital of not less than $3,000,000, to be subscribed for by the Reconstruction Finance Corporation and paid for out of the unexpended balance of the amounts allocated and made available to the Secretary of Agriculture under section 2 of the Reconstruction Finance Corporation Act. Such corporations shall be managed by officers and agents to be appointed by the Reconstruction Finance Corporation under such rules and regulations as its board of directors may prescribe. Such corporations are hereby authorized and empowered to make loans or advances to farmers and stockmen, the proceeds of which are to be used for an agricultural purpose (including crop production), or for the raising, breeding, fattening, or marketing of livestock, to charge such rates of interest or discount thereon as in their judgment are fair and equitable, subject to the approval of the Reconstruction Finance Corporation, and to rediscount with the Reconstruction Finance Corporation and the various Federal reserve banks and Federal intermediate credit banks any paper that they acquire which is eligible for such purpose. All expenses incurred in connection with the operation of such corporations shall be supervised and paid by the Reconstruction Finance Corporation under such rules and regulations as its board of directors may prescribe.

(f) All loans made under this section, and all contracts of the character described in paragraph (1) of subsection (a), shall be fully and adequately secured. The corporation, under such conditions as it shall prescribe, may take over or provide for the administration and liquidation of any collateral accepted by it as security for such loans. Such loans shall be made on such terms and conditions, not inconsistent with this Act, as the corporation may prescribe, and may be made directly upon promissory notes or by way of discount or rediscount or obligations tendered for the purpose, or otherwise in such form and in such amount and at such interest or discount rates as the corporation may approve: *Provided,* That no loans or advances (except loans under subsection (c) shall be made upon foreign securities or foreign acceptances as collateral.

(g) Each such loan may be made for a period not exceeding three years, and the corporation may, from time to time, extend the time of payment of any such loan, through renewal, substitution of new obligations, or otherwise, but the time for such payment shall not be extended beyond five years from the date upon which such loan was made originally: *Provided,* That loans or contracts of the character described in subsection (a) may be made for a period not exceeding ten years: *Provided further,* That loans or contracts of the character described in paragraph (1) or (5) of subsection (a) may be made for a period exceeding ten years when it is the judgment of the board of directors of the corporation that it is necessary to purchase securities as provided in such paragraphs and that it is not practicable to require the reimbursement of the corporation, within ten years, through the repurchase or payment of such securities, or in any other manner.

(h) The corporation may make loans under this section at any time prior to January 23, 1934.

(i) No fee or commission shall be paid by any applicant for a loan under the provisions of this section in connection with any such application or any loan made or to be made under this section, and the agreement to pay or payment of any such fee or commission shall be unlawful.

(j) No loan under this section shall be made to a railroad or to a receiver of a railroad except on the approval of the Interstate Commerce Commission. Any railroad may obligate itself in such form as shall be prescribed and otherwise comply with the requirements of the Interstate Commerce Commission and the corporation with respect to the deposit or assignment of security hereunder, without the authorization or approval of any authority, State or Federal, and without compliance with any requirement, State or Federal, as to notification, other than such as may be imposed by the Interstate Commerce Commission and the corporation under the provisions of this section.

Sec. 202. The last sentence of the second paragraph of section 5 of the Reconstruction Finance Corporation Act is amended by striking out "5" and inserting "2 5/8" in lieu thereof.

Sec. 203. The second sentence of the third paragraph of section 5 of the Reconstruction Finance Corporation Act is hereby repealed.

Sec. 204. Section 8 of the Reconstruction Finance Corporation Act is amended to read as follows:

"Sec. 8. In order to enable the corporation to carry out the provisions of this Act and the Emergency Relief and Construction Act of 1932, the Treasury Department, the Federal Farm Loan Board, the Comptroller of the Currency, the Federal Reserve Board, the Federal reserve banks, and the Interstate Commerce Commission are hereby authorized, under such conditions as they may prescribe, to make available to the corporation, in confidence, such reports, records, or other information as they may have available relating to the condition of applicants with respect to whom the corporation has had or contemplates having transactions under either of such Acts, or relating to individuals, associations, partnerships, corporations, or other obligors whose obligations are offered to or held by the corporation as security for loans under either of such Acts, and to make, through their examiners or other employees for the confidential use of the corporation, examinations of applicants for loans. Every applicant for a loan under either of such Acts shall, as a condition precedent thereto, consent to such examination as the corporation may require for the purposes of either of such Acts and that reports of examinations by constituted authorities may be furnished by such authorities to the corporation upon request therefor."

Sec. 205. (a) The amount of notes, debentures, bonds, or other such obligations which the Reconstruction Finance Corporation is authorized and empowered under section 9 of the Reconstruction Finance Corporation Act to have outstanding at any one time is increased to an aggregate of six and three-fifths times its subscribed capital stock.

(b) The first proviso of section 2 of the Reconstruction Finance Corporation Act is amended by inserting after "as set out in section 9" the following: "(as in force prior to the enactment of the Emergency Relief and Construction Act of 1932)," but the Secretary of Agriculture is directed to continue making loans to farmers under the provisions of such section 2.

Sec. 206. The Reconstruction Finance Corporation is authorized and empowered to make loans under the Reconstruction Finance Corporation Act to financial institutions, corporations, railroads, and other classes of borrowers specified in section 5 of such Act, organized under the laws of the District of Columbia, Alaska, Hawaii, and Puerto Rico. As used in this title and in section 15 of the Reconstruction Finance Corporation Act the term "State" includes the District of Columbia, Alaska, Hawaii, and Puerto Rico.

Sec. 207. No loan or advance shall be approved under this section or under the Reconstruction Finance Corporation Act, directly or indirectly, to any financial institution any officer or director of which is a member of the board of directors of the Reconstruction Finance Corporation or has been such a member within the twelve months preceding the approval of the loan or advance.

Sec. 208. (a) The first sentence of section 3 of the Reconstruction Finance Corporation Act is amended, effective at the expiration of ten days after the date of enactment of this Act, to read as follows: "The management of the corporation shall be vested in a board of directors consisting of the Secretary of the Treasury (or, in his absence, the Under Secretary of the Treasury), who shall be a member ex officio, and six other persons appointed by the President of the United States by and with the advice and consent of the Senate."

(b) Nothing in this section shall be construed to affect in any manner the terms of office of the appointed members of the board of directors of the Reconstruction Finance Corporation, nor to require their reappointment.

Sec. 209. Section 9 of the Reconstruction Finance Corporation Act is hereby amended by adding at the end thereof the following:

"The Secretary of the Treasury, at the request of the Reconstruction Finance Corporation, is authorized to market for the corporation its notes, debentures, bonds, and other such obligations, using therefor all the facilities of the Treasury Department now authorized by law for the marketing of obligations of the United States. The proceeds of the obligations of the corporation so marketed shall be deposited in the same manner as proceeds derived from the sale of obligations of the United States, and the amount thereof shall be credited to the corporation on the books of the Treasury."

Sec. 210. Section 13 of the Federal Reserve Act, as amended, is further amended by adding after the second paragraph thereof the following new paragraph:

"In unusual and exigent circumstances, the Federal Reserve Board, by the affirmative vote of not less than five members, may authorize any Federal reserve bank, during such periods as the said board may determine, at rates established in accordance with the provisions of section 14, subdivision (d), of this Act, to discount for any individual, partnership, or corporation, notes, drafts, and bills of exchange of the kinds and maturities made eligible for discount for member banks under other provisions of this Act when such notes, drafts, and bills of exchange are indorsed and otherwise secured to the satisfaction of the Federal reserve bank: *Provided,* That before discounting any such note, draft, or bill of exchange for an individual or a partnership or corporation the Federal reserve bank shall obtain evidence that such individual, partnership, or corporation is unable to secure adequate credit accommodations from other banking institutions. All such discounts for individuals, partnerships, or corporations shall be subject to such limitations, restrictions, and regulations as the Federal Reserve Board may prescribe."

Sec. 211. The first paragraph of section 5 of the Reconstruction Finance Corporation Act is hereby amended to read as follows:

"Sec. 5. To aid in financing agriculture, commerce, and industry, including facilitating the exportation of agricultural and other products the corporation is authorized and empowered to make loans, upon such terms and conditions not inconsistent with this Act as it may determine, to any bank, savings bank, trust company, building and loan association, insurance company, mortgage loan company, credit union, Federal land bank, joint-stock land bank, Federal intermediate credit bank, agricultural credit corporation, livestock credit corporation, organized under the laws of any State or of the United States, including loans secured by the assets of any bank or savings bank that is closed, or in process of liquidation to aid in the reorganization or liquidation of such banks, upon application of the receiver or liquidating agent of such bank and any receiver of any national bank is hereby authorized to contract for such loans and to pledge any assets of the bank for securing the same: *Provided,* That not more than $200,000,000 shall be used for the relief of banks (including savings banks) that are closed or in the process of liquidation."

Title III — Public Works

Sec. 301. (a) For the purpose of providing for emergency construction of certain authorized public works with a view to increasing employment and carrying out the policy declared in the Employment Stabilization Act of 1931, there is hereby appropriated, out of any money in the Treasury not otherwise appropriated, the sum of $322,224,000, which shall be allocated as follows:

(1) For expenditure in emergency construction on the Federal-aid highway system, $120,000,000. Such sum shall be apportioned by the Secretary of Agriculture to the several States by the method provided in section 21 of the Federal Highway Act, as amended and supplemented (U.S.C., title 23, sec. 21). The amounts apportioned to the States shall be available as a temporary advance of funds to meet the provisions of such Act as to State funds. The amount apportioned to any State under this paragraph may be used to match the regular annual Federal-aid apportionments made to such State (including the one for the fiscal year ending June 30, 1933), and when so used such amount shall be available for expenditure in paying the share of such State in the cost of Federal-aid projects. No amounts apportioned under this paragraph shall be advanced except for work on the Federal-aid highway system performed before July 1, 1933: *Provided,* That the amounts so advanced shall be reimbursed to the Federal Government over a period of ten years, commencing with the fiscal year 1938, by making annual deductions from regular apportionments made from future authorizations for carrying out the provisions of such Act, as amended and supplemented: *Provided further,* That all contracts involving the expenditure of such amounts shall contain provisions establishing minimum rates of wages, to be predetermined by the State highway department, which contractors shall pay to skilled and unskilled labor, and such minimum rates shall be stated in the invitation for bids and shall be included in proposals or bids for the work: *And provided further,* That in the expenditure of such amounts, the limitations in the Federal

Highway Act, as amended and supplemented, upon highway construction, reconstruction, and bridges within municipalities and upon payments per mile which may be made from Federal funds, shall not apply. As used in this paragraph, the term "State" includes the Territory of Hawaii. The term "highway," as defined in the Federal Highway Act, approved November 9, 1921, as amended and supplemented, for the purposes of this paragraph only, shall be deemed to include such main State parkways as may be designated by the State and approved by the Secretary of Agriculture as part of the Federal-aid highway system.

(2) For expenditure in emergency construction during the fiscal year ending June 30, 1933, $16,000,000, as follows: (A) For the construction and improvement of national-forest highways, $5,000,000; (B) for the construction and maintenance of roads, trails, bridges, fire lanes, and so forth, including the same objects specified in the paragraph commencing with the words "Improvement of the national forests" under the heading "National Forest Administration" in the Agricultural Appropriation Act for the fiscal year ending June 30, 1932, approved February 23, 1931 (46 Stat. 1242), $5,000,000; (C) for the construction, reconstruction, and improvement of roads and trails, inclusive of necessary bridges, in the national parks and national monuments under the jurisdiction of the Department of the Interior, including areas to be established as national parks authorized under the Act of May 22, 1926 (U.S.C., Supp. V, title 16, secs. 403 to 403c), and under the Act of May 25, 1926 (U.S.C., Supp. V, title 16, secs. 404 to 404c), and national park and monument approach roads authorized by the Act of January 31, 1931 (46 Stat. 1053), as amended, or any one section of such roads of not less than eight miles, which crosses lands wholly or to the extent of 90 per centum owned by the Government of the United States, $3,000,000; (D) for construction and improvement of Indian reservation roads under the provisions of the Act approved May 26, 1928 (U.S.C., Supp. V, title 25, sec. 318a), $1,000,000; and (E) for the survey, construction, reconstruction, and maintenance of main roads through unappropriated or unreserved public lands, nontaxable Indian lands, or other Federal reservations other than the forest reservations, under the provisions of section 3 of the Federal Highway Act, as amended and supplemented (U.S.C., Supp. V, title 23, secs. 3 and 3a), $2,000,000. The Secretary of Agriculture and the Secretary of the Interior, respectively, are authorized to make rules and regulations for carrying out the foregoing provisions of this section with a view to providing the maximum employment of local labor consistent with reasonable economy of construction.

(3) For the prosecution of river and harbor projects heretofore authorized, $30,000,000.

(4) For the prosecution of flood-control projects heretofore authorized, $15,500,000.

(5) For the continuation of construction of the Hoover Dam and incidental works, as authorized by the Boulder Canyon Project Act, approved December 21, 1928 (U.S.C., Supp. V, title 43, ch. 12A), $10,000,000.

(6) For expenditure by the Department of Commerce for air-navigation facilities, including equipment, $500,000.

(7) For constructing or purchasing and equipping lighthouse tenders and light vessels for the Lighthouse Service as may be specifically approved by the Secretary of Commerce, $950,000, and for establishing and improving aids to navigation and other works as may be specifically approved by the Secretary of Commerce, $2,860,000.

(8) For the engineering work of the Coast and Geodetic Survey, Department of Commerce, heretofore authorized, $1,250,000.

(9) For the construction of projects included in the report of the Federal Employment Stabilization Board, laid before the Senate January 25, 1932, which have heretofore been authorized or which do not require specific authorization, under the Bureau of Yards and Docks, Navy Department, $10,000,000, of which not to exceed $300,000 shall be available for the employment of classified personal services in the Bureau of Yards and Docks and in the field service to be engaged upon such work and to be in addition to employees otherwise provided for.

(10) For emergency construction of public building projects outside the District of Columbia (including the acquisition, where necessary, by purchase, condemnation or otherwise, of sites and additional land for such buildings, the demolition of old buildings where necessary, and the construction, remodeling, or extension of buildings), such projects to be selected by the Secretary of the Treasury and the Postmaster General from the public building projects specified in House Document Numbered 788, Seventy-first Congress, third session, $100,000,000. Such projects shall be carried out within the limits of cost specified in such document (except as modified by law), and in selecting such projects preference shall be given to places where Government facilities are housed in rented buildings under leases which will expire on or before July 1, 1934, or which may be terminated on or prior to that date by the Government.

(11) For the construction and installation at military posts of such buildings and utilities and appurtenances thereto as may be necessary, $15,164,000, as follows:

Albrook Field, Canal Zone: Quartermaster maintenance building, $20,000; post exchange, theater, and gymnasium, completion of, $42,000.

Barksdale Field, Louisiana: Noncommissioned officers' quarters, $252,000; officers' quarters, $609,000; barracks, $474,000; hospital, completion of, $225,000; garage, completion of, $30,000; quartermaster warehouse, completion of, $15,000.

William Beaumont General Hospital, Texas: Noncommissioned officers' quarters, $7,000; warehouse, $15,000.

Fort Benning, Georgia: Barracks, $650,000.

Fort Bliss, Texas: Noncommissioned officers' quarters, $50,000; officers' quarters, $150,000.

Bolling Field, District of Columbia: Noncommissioned officers' quarters, $54,000; dispensary, completion of, $30,000; post exchange, theater, and gymnasium, completion of, $45,000; officers' mess, $50,000; enlargement of central heating plant to provide for quarters area, $95,000.

Fort Bragg, North Carolina: Barracks, completion of, $40,000; noncommissioned officers' quarters, $160,000.

Carlisle Barracks, Pennsylvania: Heating plant, $200,000.

Chanute Field, Illinois: Noncommissioned officers' quarters, $137,000; central heating plant for technical and quarters area, $200,000.

Camp Devens, Massachusetts: Roads and sidewalks, $75,000; service club, $30,000; post exchange and gymnasium, $50,000.

Fort Douglas, Utah: Noncommissioned officers' quarters, $15,000.

Dryden, Texas: Barracks, $20,000.

Duncan Field, Texas: Quartermaster warehouse, $40,000; quartermaster maintenance building, $20,000; garage, $40,000; fire and guard house, $25,000.

Fort Du Pont, Delaware: Noncommissioned officers' quarters, $60,000.

Edgewood Arsenal, Maryland: Noncommissioned officers' quarters, $70,000.

Fitzsimons General Hospital, Colorado: Gymnasium, recreation, and social hall, $150,000.

Hamilton Field, California: Officers' quarters, $215,000; noncommissioned officers' quarters, $120,000.

Fort Hamilton, New York: Noncommissioned officers' quarters, $100,000.

Fort Benjamin Harrison, Indiana: Noncommissioned officers' quarters, $120,000.

Hensley Field, Texas: Noncommissioned officers' quarters, $8,000; officers' quarters, $30,000; roads, utilities, and improvement of flying field, $25,000; replacement of pumping plant, $3,000; sewage-disposal plant, $3,000.

Holabird Quartermaster Depot, Maryland: Hospital, $120,000.

Fort Sam Houston, Texas: Noncommissioned officers' quarters, $150,000; officers' quarters, $350,000.

Fort Howard, Maryland: Hospital, $150,000.

Fort Holye, Maryland: Noncommissioned officers' quarters, $70,000.

Fort Humphreys, Virginia: Officers' quarters, $150,000.

Fort Huachuca, Arizona: Post exchange, gymnasium, and service club, $100,000.

Fort Jay, New York: Noncommissioned officers' quarters, $130,000;

barracks, completion of, $70,000; officers' quarters, $125,000; nurses' quarters, completion of, $35,000.

Jefferson Barracks, Missouri: Noncommissioned officers' quarters, $65,000; additions to kitchens and mess halls, $55,000.

Camp Knox, Kentucky: Hospital, $200,000.

Langley Field, Virginia: Central heating plant for quarters area, $60,000; quartermaster maintenance building, $20,000; fire house, $20,000; barracks, medical detachment, $30,000; garage, completion of, $15,000; magazine, completion of, $10,000.

Fort Lawton, Washington: Noncommissioned officers' quarters, $30,000.

Fort Leavenworth, Kansas: Nurses' quarters, $60,000.

Letterman General Hospital, California: Two wards, $150,000.

Fort Lewis, Washington: Barracks, completion of, $30,000; water main, $30,000; noncommissioned officers' quarters, $75,000; officers' quarters, $65,000.

Fort Logan, Colorado: Noncommissioned officers' quarters, $53,000.

Fort McClellan, Alabama: Headquarters, $50,000; recreation hall, $35,000; gymnasium, $45,000.

Fort McPherson, Georgia: Nurses' quarters, $70,000; contagious ward for hospital, $70,000.

Maxwell Field, Alabama: Officers' quarters, $940,000; officers' mess, $55,000.

March Field, California: Barracks for medical detachment, $25,000; contagious ward for hospital, $12,000; bakery, $15,000; laundry, $60,000; enlisted men's service club, $50,000; officers' mess, $50,000; theater, $40,000.

Fort Mason, California: Officers' quarters, $110,000.

Fort Meade, South Dakota: Riding hall, $25,000.

Fort George G. Meade, Maryland: Noncommissioned officers' quarters, $150,000; officers' quarters, $50,000.

Mitchel Field, New York: Noncommissioned officers' quarters, $118,000; bakery, $15,000; incinerator, $10,000; enlisted men's service club, $50,000; theater, $40,000; sewage-disposal plant, $40,000; fence, $31,000; quartermaster gasoline storage, $3,000; magazine, $15,000; officers' mess, $50,000; coal storage and handling system, $70,000; roads, walks, and surface-drainage system, $86,000.

Fort Monmouth, New Jersey: Addition to hospital, $75,000; noncommissioned officers' quarters, $170,000; band barracks, $35,000.

Fort Myer, Virginia: Barracks, $100,000.

Fort Oglethorpe, Georgia: Noncommissioned officers' quarters, $120,000.

Fort Ontario, New York: Noncommissioned officers' quarters, $50,000.

Plattsburg Barracks, New York: Additions to barracks, $25,000; barracks, $255,000.

Pope Field, North Carolina, for the Air Corps troops: Barracks, $140,000; noncommissioned officers' quarters, $84,000; officers' quarters, $140,000.

Post Field, Oklahoma, for Air Corps troops: Barracks, $140,000; noncommissioned officers' quarters, $84,000; officers' quarters, $140,000.

Presidio of San Francisco, California: Noncommissioned officers' quarters, $60,000; addition to headquarters, $50,000.

Randolph Field, Texas: Barracks, completion of, $56,000; gymnasium, completion of, $70,000; roads and utilities, $243,000; completion of chapel and school, $50,000.

Raritan Arsenal, New Jersey: Noncommissioned officers' quarters, $75,000.

Walter Reed General Hospital, District of Columbia: Noncommissioned officers' quarters, $120,000; addition to nurses' quarters, $300,000.

Rock Island Arsenal, Illinois: Noncommissioned officers' quarters, $15,000.

Rockwell Field, California: Noncommissioned officers' quarters, $234,000; officers' quarters, $266,000.

Fort Winfield Scott, California: Noncommissioned officers' quarters, $140,000.

Selfridge Field, Michigan: Gymnasium and theater, $80,000; garage, $40,000; quartermaster maintenance building, $20,000; post exchange, $45,000; officers' mess, $60,000; enlisted men's service club, $50,000; bakery, $15,000; roads and utilities, $75,000.

Fort Sill, Oklahoma: Barracks, $875,000; noncommissioned officers' quarters, $72,000; officers' quarters, $75,000; gun sheds, $48,000; stables, $30,000; vehicle shed, $10,000.

Fort Snelling, Minnesota: Quartermaster warehouse, $65,000; barracks, medical detachment, $40,000.

Fort Totten, New York: Noncommissioned officers' quarters, $30,000.

Fort Wadsworth, New York: Officers' quarters, $75,000.

Fort Francis E. Warren, Wyoming: Noncommissioned officers' quarters, $120,000.

West Point, New York: For addition to hospital, $250,000; barracks for service detachment, $250,000.

Fort George Wright, Washington: Noncommissioned officers' quarters, $60,000.

(b) No part of the sum appropriated by this section, except the amount for expenditure under paragraph (1) or (2) of subsection (a), shall be expended if the Secretary of the Treasury certifies to the President that the amount necessary for such expenditure is not available and can not be obtained upon reasonable terms.

Sec. 302. There is hereby authorized to be appropriated not to exceed $7,436,000, to be expended for the construction and installation at military posts, and at airports and landing fields, of such technical buildings and utilities and appurtenances thereto as may be necessary, as follows:

Albrook Field, Canal Zone: Technical buildings and installations, completion of, $293,000; gasoline-storage system, completion of, $25,000.

Barksdale Field, Louisiana: Hangers, $350,000; headquarters and operations buildings, completion of, $89,000; gasoline-storage system, completion of, $20,000; paved aprons, $100,000.

Fort Benning, Georgia: Hangar, combination, $88,000; gasoline-storage system, $10,000; improvement of landing field and building area, $25,000; heating plant, $20,000; paved aprons, $20,000.

Benton Field, Alameda, California: Completion of shops, including assembly and test hangars, dope storage, heating and engine test block, $605,500; depot warehouse $500,000; administration building, $80,000; railroad spur, $8,000; quartermaster warehouse, maintenance and salvage building, $35,000; garage, $48,000; fire and guard house, $30,000; pier, $125,000; paint, oil, and dope storage and oil reclamation, $35,000; gasoline-storage system, $20,000; paved aprons, $80,000.

Fort Bliss, Texas: Operations building, $10,000.

Bolling Field, District of Columbia: Paved aprons, completion of, $22,800; heating plant for technical area, completion of, $78,000; field shops, completion of, $6,000; improvement of landing field and building area, $615,000.

Chanute Field, Illinois: Hangars, $170,000; paved aprons, $30,000; improvement of landing field and technical area, $15,000; enlargement of central heating plant and steam lines, $185,000.

Dryden, Texas: Paved aprons and hangar floor, $15,000.

Duncan Field, Texas: Depot administration building, $60,000; gasoline-storage system, completion of, $15,000.

Hatbox Field, Muskogee, Oklahoma: Roofing and sidewalls for hangar, and paved aprons, $15,000.

Hamilton Field, California: Headquarters and operations building, to complete, $35,000; improvement of landing field and building area, $120,000.

Langley Field, Virginia: Remodeling two hangars into shops, and for ceilings in and additions to hangars, $91,000; gasoline-storage system, completion of, $21,000; bomb storage, $19,000; improvement of landing field and building area, $25,000; machine-gun range, $6,000.

Luke Field, Hawaiian Department: Air depot, plane overhaul and assembly, $200,000.

March Field, California: Gasoline-storage system, completion of, $10,000; aircraft-bomb storage, $5,000.

Maxwell Field, Alabama: Squadron officers' school and/or additions to school building, $150,000; gasoline-storage system, $10,200; improvement of landing field, $100,000; camera obscura, $4,000; bomb storage, $13,000; machine-gun and bombing range, $6,000.

Mitchel Field, New York: Improvement of landing field, $80,000; gasoline-storage system, completion of, $5,000; bomb storage, $13,000; machine-gun range, $2,000.

Panama Canal Zone: Improvement of emergency landing fields at Gamboa Reach and Camp Gaillard, $20,000.

Patterson Field, Ohio: Hangars, headquarters and operations, and heating plant, completion of, $251,300; improvement of landing field and building area, $5,000; gasoline-storage system, completion of, $10,000.

Pope Field, North Carolina: Hangar—ballon-dismantle, transfer, and reerection of, $110,000; paved aprons, $15,000; paint, oil, and dope storage, $5,000.

Post Field, Oklahoma: Hangar—ballon-dismantle, transfer, and reerection of, $110,000; paved aprons, $15,000.

Randolph Field, Texas: Engine-test stands and building, $40,000; oil storage, $15,000; gasoline-storage system, completion of, $10,000; aerial target range, $20,000.

Rockwell Field, California: Hangars, $576,000; Air Corps warehouse, $80,000; operations building, $20,000; remodeling a permanent building for radio, parachute, and armament building, $20,000; administration building, $80,000; photographic building, $36,000; paint, oil, and dope storage, $15,000; gasoline-storage system, $30,000; paved aprons, $95,000; central heating plants, $100,000; improvement of landing field and technical building area, $100,000; camera obscura, $5,000; bomb storage, $15,000.

Schoen Field, Indiana: Grading landing field, $5,000.

Scott Field, Illinois: Hangar, $90,000; headquarters and operations buildings, $80,000; barracks, $271,000; radio building, $10,000; photo building, $36,000; gas plant and chemical storage, $50,000; central heating plants, $145,000; gasoline-storage system, $10,000; paved aprons, $40,000; improvement of landing field and building area, $50,000; machine-gun butts, $3,000.

Selfridge Field, Michigan: Gasoline-storage system, completion of, $10,000.

Wheeler Field, Hawaiian Department: Gasoline-storage system, completion of, $31,000; paved aprons, $38,000.

Sec. 303. No money shall be available for expenditure under this title in connection with a project in the District of Columbia, except as provided in section 301 (a) (11) or 302.

Sec. 304. The last paragraph of section 6 of the Federal Highway Act, approved November 9, 1921, as amended and supplemented (U.S.C., title 23, sec. 6), is hereby amended to read as follows:

"Whenever provision has been made by any State for the completion and maintenance of 90 per centum of its system of primary or interstate and secondary or intercounty highways equal to 7 per centum of the total mileage of such State, as required by this Act, said State through its State highway department, by and with the approval of the Secretary of Agriculture, is hereby authorized to increase the mileage of the primary or interstate and secondary or intercounty systems by additional mileage equal to not more than 1 per centum of said total mileage of such State, and thereafter to make like increases in the mileage of said systems whenever provision has been made for the completion and maintenance of 90 per centum of the mileage of said systems previously authorized in accordance herewith."

Sec. 305. After the date of the enactment of this Act, in the acquisition of any land or site for the purposes of section 301 (a) (10):

(1) The period of solicitation of proposals by public advertisement shall be ten days in lieu of twenty days;

(2) In any case in which such site or land is to be acquired by condemnation, the provisions of section 355 of the Revised Statutes, as amended, shall not apply; and

(3) Notwithstanding the provisions of section 1 of the Act entitled "An Act to expedite the construction of public buildings and works outside of the District of Columbia by enabling possession and title of sites to be taken in advance of final judgment in proceedings for the acquisition thereof under the power of eminent domain," approved February 26, 1931 (U.S.C., Supp. V, title 40, sec. 258a), in any case in which any land or any interest therein is to be acquired by condemnation, the Secretary of the Treasury, through the Attorney General, may, prior to the institution of condemnation proceedings, file with the clerk of the district court of the district in which such land is located a declaration of taking, containing the matters required by such section to be included in a declaration of taking. The declaration of taking shall be accompanied by the deposit with such clerk, to the use of the parties who may be found to be entitled thereto, of the amount of the estimated compensation stated in the declaration. As soon as practicable after the filing of such declaration of taking, the Secretary of the Treasury shall cause to be posted in a prominent place upon the land a notice reciting (A) that the land or the interest therein is taken by the United States for public use, (B) that a declaration of taking in respect of such land or interest therein has been filed with the clerk of the court of the district, and (C) that there has been deposited with such clerk, to the use of the parties who may be found to be entitled thereto, the estimated just compensation for the land or interest therein taken. The Secretary of the Treasury shall give written notice similar to the posted notice, by personal service in the case of actual occupants of the premises or, if with reasonable diligence such personal service can not be made, he shall send such notice by registered mail directed to the premises,

and he shall send notice by registered mail directed to their last known address in the case of all parties who the Secretary ascertains have or may have an interest in such land, and he may give such additional notice by newspaper publication or otherwise as he deems necessary. Upon posting notice on the land, title to the land or interest therein shall vest in the United States, and the right to just compensation therefor shall vest in the parties entitled thereto. The Secretary of the Treasury shall cause notice to be personally served upon, or if with reasonable diligence such service can not be made, to be sent by registered mail to actual occupants of the premises, setting a time (not earlier than twenty days after the service or sending of such notice) at which such parties shall surrender possession, and at the end of such time the right to possession shall vest in the United States. The Secretary of the Treasury may designate any person to serve any notice under the preceding provisions of this subsection and such person shall have power to enter upon such land for the purpose of posting notice or to make personal service of notice. If any such party fails or refuses so to surrender possession, upon summary petition for an order to surrender possession filed in such district court by or on behalf of the Secretary of the Treasury, the court may, by writ of assistance or other process, order the surrender of possession. A petition in condemnation shall be filed in such district court as soon after the filing of the declaration of taking as practicable. In any such condemnation proceeding, no further declaration of taking shall be required, and the provisions of section 1 of such Act of February 26, 1931, authorizing the court to fix the time when parties in possession shall be required to surrender possession, shall not apply. If such petition for condemnation is not filed within a reasonable time after the filing of such declaration of taking, any person entitled to just compensation in respect of the property so taken shall be entitled to sue the United States in the court in which such declaration of taking was filed. The procedure in such suit shall be the same as in suits against the United States founded upon contract, except that such suit may be heard even if the amount of the claim is greater than $10,000 and except that the procedure for the ascertainment of the amount of just compensation shall be the same as such procedure in condemnation proceedings. If the petition for condemnation is filed prior to the time the commissioners in condemnation, jurors, or other persons charged with the duty of valuing the property are empaneled, such suit shall be dismissed, except that such suit and the condemnation proceedings may, in the discretion of the court, and under rules prescribed by it, be consolidated to such extent as the court may deem practicable. In any suit authorized to be brought under this subsection or in any condemnation proceeding involving land acquired in accordance with this subsection, the court shall enter judgment against the United States in favor of the parties entitled for the sum or sums awarded as just compensation, respectively, for the land or interest therein taken for the use of the United

States and such judgment shall be paid out of the sums deposited with the court and such additional sums as may be awarded shall be paid in the same manner as sums awarded in judgments in cases in which the United States has consented to be sued. The provisions of such Act of February 26, 1931, except as modified by this subsection, shall apply to all such suits or condemnation proceedings. The provisions of this subsection shall not be construed to be in substitution for, but shall be supplemental to, any method of acquiring land or interests therein provided in existing law.

Sec. 306. In the construction of post offices and of buildings for post offices and other offices provided for in section 301 (a) (10), the Secretary of the Treasury with the cooperation of the Postmaster General may use such standard plans (heretofore or hereafter prepared) as may be most adaptable to the particular building to be constructed.

Sec. 307. All contracts let for construction projects pursuant to this title shall be subject to the conditions that no convict labor shall be directly employed on any such project, and that (except in executive, administrative, and supervisory positions), so far as practicable, no individual directly employed on any such project shall be permitted to work more than thirty hours in any one week, and that in the employment of labor in connection with any such project, preference shall be given, where they are qualified, to ex-service men with dependents.

Sec. 308. For each fiscal year beginning with the fiscal year 1934, there is authorized to be appropriated, for the purposes of the sinking fund provided in section 6 of the Victory Liberty Loan Act, as amended, in addition to amounts otherwise appropriated, an amount equal to 2-1/2 per centum of the aggregate amount of the expenditures made, out of appropriations made or authorized in this title, on or after the date of the enactment of this Act and on or before the last day of the fiscal year for which the appropriation is made.

Approved, July 21, 1932.

BANK HOLIDAY PROCLAMATIONS

Editor's comments: *There were three bank holiday Proclamations issued by the President. The first was on March 6, 1933, which provided for the suspension of banking transactions from March 6 through 9, 1933, inclusive. By Proclamation on March 9, 1933, the President continued the bank holiday "until further proclamation." The bank holiday was ended by the Proclamation issued on March 10, 1933.*

A Proclamation by the President
of the United States of America
Bank Holiday, March 6-9, 1933, Inclusive
March 6, 1933

WHEREAS there have been heavy and unwarranted withdrawals of gold and currency from our banking institutions for the purpose of hoarding; and

WHEREAS continuous and increasingly extensive speculative activity abroad in foreign exchange has resulted in severe drains on the Nation's stocks of gold; and

WHEREAS these conditions have created a national emergency; and

WHEREAS it is in the best interests of all bank depositors that a period of respite be provided with a view to preventing further hoarding coin, bullion or currency or speculation in foreign exchange and permitting the application of appropriate measures to protect the interests of our people; and

WHEREAS it is provided in Section 5(b) of the Act of October 6, 1917, (40 Stat. L. 411) as amended, "That the President may investigate, regulate, or prohibit, under such rules and regulations as he may prescribe, by means of licenses or otherwise, any transactions in foreign exchange and the export, hoarding, melting, or earmarkings of gold or silver coin or bullion or currency..."; and

WHEREAS it is provided in Section 16 of the said Act "that whoever shall willfully violate any of the provisions of this Act or of any license, rule, or regulation issued thereunder, and whoever shall willfully violate, neglect, or refuse to comply with any order of the President issued in compliance with the provisions of this Act, shall, upon conviction, be fined not more than $10,000, or, if a natural person, imprisoned for not more than ten years, or both;...";

NOW, THEREFORE, I, Franklin D. Roosevelt, President of the United States of America, in view of such national emergency and by virtue of the authority vested in me by said Act and in order to prevent the export, hoarding, or earmarking of gold or silver coin or bullion or currency, do hereby proclaim, order, direct and declare that from Monday, the sixth day of March, to Thursday, the ninth day of March, Nineteen Hundred and Thirty Three, both dates inclusive, there shall be maintained and observed by all banking institutions and all branches thereof located in the United States of America, including the territories and insular possessions, a bank holiday, and that during said period all banking transactions shall be suspended. During such holiday, excepting as hereinafter provided, no such banking institution or branch shall pay out, export, earmark or permit the withdrawal or transfer in any manner or by any device whatsoever, of any gold or silver coin or bullion or currency or take any other action which might facilitate the hoarding thereof; nor shall any such banking institution or branch pay out deposits, make loans or discounts, deal in foreign exchange, transfer credits from the United States to any place abroad, or transact any other banking business whatsoever.

During such holiday, the Secretary of the Treasury, with the approval of the President and under such regulations as he may prescribe, is authorized and empowered (a) to permit any or all of such banking institutions to perform any or all of the usual banking functions, (b) to direct, require or permit the issuance of clearing house certificates or other evidences of claims against assets of banking institutions, and (c) to authorize and direct the creation in such banking institutions of special trust accounts for the receipt of new deposits which shall be subject to withdrawal on demand without any restriction or limitation and shall be kept separately in cash or on deposit in Federal Reserve Banks or invested in obligations of the United States.

As used in this order the term "banking institutions" shall include all Federal Reserve banks, national banking associations, banks, trust companies, saving banks, building and loan associations, credit unions, or other corporations, partnerships, associations or persons, engaged in the business of receiving deposits, making loans, discounting business paper, or transacting any other form of banking business.

IN WITNESS WHEREOF, I have hereunto set my hand and caused the seal of the United States to be affixed.

Done in the City of Washington this 6th day of March—1 A.M. in the year of our Lord One Thousand Nine Hundred and
[SEAL] Thirty- three, and of the Independence of the United States the One Hundred and Fifty-seventh.

FRANKLIN D. ROOSEVELT

By the President:
Cordell Hull
Secretary of State

A Proclamation by the President of the United States of America Continuing in Force the Bank Holiday Proclamation of March 6, 1933 *(March 9, 1933)*

WHEREAS, on March 6, 1933, I, FRANKLIN D. ROOSEVELT President of the United States of America, by Proclamation declared the existence of a national emergency and proclaimed a bank holiday extending from Monday the 6th day of March to Thursday the 9th day of March, 1933, both dates inclusive, in order to prevent the export, hoarding or earmarking of gold or silver coin, or bullion or currency, or speculation in foreign exchange; and

WHEREAS, under the Act of March 9, 1933, all Proclamations heretofore or hereafter issued by the President pursuant to the authority conferred by section 5(b) of the Act of October 6, 1917, as amended, are approved and confirmed; and

WHEREAS, said national emergency still continues and it is necessary to take further measures extending beyond March 9, 1933, in order to accomplish such purposes:

NOW, THEREFORE, I, Franklin D. Roosevelt, President of the United States of America, in view of such continuing national emergency and by the virtue of the authority vested in me by Section 5(b) of the Act of October 6, 1917 (40 Stat. L., 411) as amended by the Act of March 9, 1933, do hereby proclaim, order, direct and declare that all the terms and provisions of said Proclamation of March 6, 1933, and the regulations and orders issued thereunder are hereby continued in full force and effect until further proclamation by the President.

IN WITNESS WHEREOF I have hereunto set my hand and have caused the seal of the United States to be affixed.

Done in the District of Columbia, this 9th day of March, in the Year of our Lord One Thousand Nine Hundred and Thirty-
[SEAL] three, and of the Independence of the United States the One Hundredth and Fifty-seventh.

FRANKLIN D. ROOSEVELT

By the President:
Cordell Hull
Secretary of State.

A Proclamation by the President of the United States of America Reopening of Banks *(March 10, 1933)*

By virtue of the authority vested in me by Section 5(b) of the Act of October 6, 1917 (40 Stat. L., 411), as amended by the Act of March 9, 1933, and by virtue of all other authority vested in me, I hereby issue the following executive order.

The Secretary of the Treasury is authorized and empowered under such regulations as he may prescribe to permit any member bank of the Federal Reserve System and any other banking institution organized under the laws of the United States, to perform any or all of their usual banking functions, except as otherwise prohibited.

The appropriate authority having immediate supervision of banking institutions in each State or any place subject to the jurisdiction of the United States is authorized and empowered under such regulations as such authority may prescribe to permit any banking institution in such State or place, other than banking institutions covered by the foregoing paragraph, to perform any or all of their usual banking functions, except as otherwise prohibited.

All banks which are members of the Federal Reserve System, desiring to reopen for the performance of all usual and normal banking functions, except as otherwise prohibited, shall apply for a license therefor to the Secretary of the Treasury. Such application shall be filed immediately through the Federal Reserve Banks. The Federal Reserve Bank shall then transmit such applications to the Secretary of the Treasury. Licenses will be issued by the Federal Reserve Bank upon approval of the Secretary of the Treasury. The Federal Reserve Banks are hereby designated as agents of the Secretary of the Treasury for the receiving of application and the issuance of licenses in his behalf and upon his instructions.

Until further order, no individual, partnership, association, or corporation, including any banking institution, shall export or otherwise remove or permit to be withdrawn from the United States or any place subject to the jurisdiction thereof any gold coin, gold bullion, or gold certificates, except in accordance with regulations prescribed by or under license issued by the Secretary of the Treasury.

No permission to any banking institution to perform any banking functions shall authorize such institution to pay out any gold coin, gold bullion or gold certificates except as authorized by the Secretary of the Treasury, nor to allow withdrawal of any currency for hoarding, nor to engage in any transaction in foreign exchange except such as may be undertaken for legitimate and normal business requirements, for reasonable traveling and other personal requirements, and for the fulfillment of contracts entered into prior to March 6, 1933.

Every Federal Reserve Bank is authorized and instructed to keep itself currently informed as to transactions in foreign exchange entered into or consummated within its district and shall report to the Secretary of the Treasury all transactions in foreign exchange which are prohibited.

FRANKLIN D. ROOSEVELT

By the President:
Cordell Hull
Secretary of State.

EMERGENCY BANKING RELIEF/BANK CONSERVATION ACT AND AMENDMENT

Editor's Comments: *The five titles of this Act responded to the "serious emergency" in the banking system and provided "remedies of uniform national applications."*

Section 1 of Title I approved emergency actions taken by the President or the Secretary of the Treasury since March 4, 1933. Section 2 amended the emergency powers granted to the President by the act of October 6, 1917. Section 3 amended section 11 of the Federal Reserve Act and provided for action by the Secretary of the Treasury to "protect the currency system of the United States," specifically by the emergency impoundment of gold. Section 4 provided that the member banks of the Federal Reserve System were to undertake transactions as prescribed by the Secretary of the Treasury.

Title II, known as the Bank Conservation Act, dealt with the appointment of a conservator, if so required to protect a bank's assets and depositors, and the conduct of business by a conservator. Also, there was a provision for bank examinations and for returning a bank's control to its board of directors.

The issuance of preferred stock by a national banking association and the priority of dividend payment on common and preferred stock was the focus of Title III.

Several paragraphs of the Federal Reserve Act were amended under Title IV while Title V appropriated the money to carry out the Act.

The amendment of June 15, 1933, dealt with the issuance and provisions of preferred stock.

An Act to Provide Relief in the Existing National Emergency in Banking, and for Other Purposes
March 9, 1933

Be it enacted by the Senate and House of Representatives of the United States of America in Congress assembled, That the Congress hereby declares that a serious emergency exists and that it is imperatively necessary speedily to put into effect remedies of uniform national application.

Title I

Section 1. The actions, regulations, rules, licenses, orders and proclamations heretofore or hereafter taken, promulgated, made, or issued by the President of the United States or the Secretary of the Treasury since March 4, 1933, pursuant to the authority conferred by subdivision (b) of section 5 of the Act of October 6, 1917, as amended, are hereby approved and confirmed.

Sec. 2. Subdivision (b) of section 5 of the Act of October 6, 1917 (40 Stat. L. 411), as amended, is hereby amended to read as follows:

"(b) During time of war or during any other period of national emergency declared by the President, the President may, through any agency that he may designate, or otherwise, investigate, regulate, or prohibit, under such rules and regulations as he may prescribe, by means of licenses or otherwise, any transactions in foreign exchange, transfers of credit between or payments by banking institutions as defined by the President, and export, hoarding, melting, or earmarking of gold or silver coin or bullion or currency, by any person within the United States or any place subject to the jurisdiction thereof; and the President may require any person engaged in any transaction referred to in this subdivision to furnish under oath, complete information relative thereto, including the production of any books of account, contracts, letters or other papers, in connection therewith in the custody or control of such person, either before or after such transaction is completed. Whoever willfully violates any of the provisions of this subdivision or of any license, order, rule or regulation issued thereunder, shall, upon conviction, be fined not more than $10,000, or, if a natural person, may be imprisoned for not more than ten years, or both; and any officer, director, or agent of any corporation who knowingly participates in such violation may be punished by a like fine, imprisonment, or both. As used in this subdivision the term 'person' means an individual, partnership, association, or corporation."

Sec. 3. Section 11 of the Federal Reserve Act is amended by adding at the end thereof the following new subsection:

"(n) Whenever in the judgement of the Secretary of the Treasury such action is necessary to protect the currency system of the United States, the Secretary of the Treasury, in his discretion, may require any or all individuals, partnerships, associations and corporations to pay and deliver to the Treasurer of the United States any or all gold coin, gold bullion, and gold certificates owned by such individuals, partnerships, associations and corporations. Upon receipt of such gold coin, gold bullion or gold certificates, the Secretary of the Treasury shall pay therefor an equivalent amount of any other form of coin or currency coined or issued under the laws of the United States. The Secretary of the Treasury shall pay all costs of the transportation of such gold bullion, gold certificates, coin, or currency, including the cost of insurance, protection, and such other incidental costs as may be reasonably necessary. Any individual, partnership, association, or corporation failing to comply with any requirement of the Secretary of the Treasury made under this subsection shall be subject to a penalty equal to twice the value of the gold or gold certificates in respect of which such failure occurred, and such penalty may be collected by the Secretary of the Treasury by suit or otherwise."

Sec. 4. In order to provide for the safer and more effective operation of the National Banking System and the Federal Reserve System, to preserve for the people the full benefits of the currency provided for by the Congress through the National Banking System and the Federal Reserve System, and to relieve interestate commerce of the burdens and obstructions resulting from the receipt on an unsound or unsafe basis of deposits subject to withdrawal by check, during such emergency period as the President of the United States by proclamation may prescribe, no member bank of the Federal

Reserve System shall transact any banking business except to such extent and subject to such regulations, limitations and restrictions as may be prescribed by the Secretary of the Treasury, with the approval of the President. Any individual, partnership, corporation, or association, or any director, officer or employee thereof, violating any of the provisions of this section shall be deemed guilty of a misdemeanor and, upon conviction thereof, shall be fined not more than $10,000 or, if a natural person, may, in addition to such fine, be imprisoned for a term not exceeding ten years. Each day that any such violation continues shall be deemed a separate offense.

Title II

Sec. 201. This title may be cited as the "Bank Conservation Act."

Sec. 202. As used in this title, the term "bank" means (1) any national banking association, and (2) any bank or trust company located in the District of Columbia and operating under the supervision of the Comptroller of the Currency; and the term "State" means any State, Territory, or possession of the United States, and the Canal Zone.

Sec. 203. Whenever he shall deem it necessary in order to conserve the assets of any bank for the benefit of the depositors and other creditors thereof, the Comptroller of the Currency may appoint a conservator for such bank and require of him such bond and security as the Comptroller of the Currency deems proper. The conservator, under the direction of the Comptroller, shall take possession of the books, records, and assets of every description of such bank, and take such action as may be necessary to conserve the assets of such bank pending further disposition of its business as provided by law. Such conservator shall have all the rights, powers, and privileges now possessed by or hereafter given receivers of insolvent national banks and shall be subject to the obligations and penalties, not inconsistent with the provisions of this title, to which receivers are now or may hereafter become subject. During the time that such conservator remains in possession of such bank, the rights of all parties with respect thereto shall, subject to the other provisions of this title, be the same as if a receiver had been appointed therefor. All expenses of any such conservatorship shall be paid out of the assets of such bank and shall be a lien thereon which shall be prior to any other lien provided by this Act or otherwise. The conservator shall recieve as salary an amount no greater than that paid to employees of the Federal Government for similar services.

Sec. 204. The Comptroller of the Currency shall cause to be made such examinations of the affairs of such bank as shall be necessary to inform him as to the financial condition of such bank, and the examiner shall make a report thereon to the Comptroller of the Currency at the earliest practicable date.

Sec. 205. If the Comptroller of the Currency becomes satisfied that it may safely be done and that it would be in the public interest, he may, in his discretion, terminate the conservatorship and permit such bank to resume the transaction of its business subject to such terms, conditions, restrictions and limitations as he may prescribe.

Sec. 206. While such bank is in the hands of the conservator appointed by the Comptroller of the Currency, the Comptroller may require the conservator to set aside and make available for withdrawal by depositors and payment to other creditors, on a ratable basis, such amounts as in the opinion of the Comptroller may safely be used for this purpose; and the Comptroller may, in his discretion, permit the conservator to receive deposits, but deposits received while the bank is in the hands of the conservator shall not be subject to any limitation as to payment or withdrawal, and such deposits shall be segregated and shall not be used to liquidate any indebtedness of such bank existing at the time that a conservator was appointed for it, or any subsequent indebtedness incurred for the purpose of liquidating any indebtedness of such bank existing at the time such conservator was appointed. Such deposits received while the bank is in the hands of the conservator shall be kept on hand in cash, invested in the direct obligations of the United States, or deposited with a Federal reserve bank. The Federal reserve banks are hereby authorized to open and maintain separate deposit accounts for such purpose, or for the purpose of receiving deposits from State officials in charge of State banks under similar circumstances.

Sec. 207. In any reorganization of any national banking association under a plan of a kind which, under existing law, requires the consent, as the case may be, (a) of depositors and other creditors or (b) of stockholders or (c) of both depositors and other creditors and stockholders, such reorganization shall become effective only (1) when the Comptroller of the Currency shall be satisfied that the plan of reorganization is fair and equitable as to all depositors, other creditors and stockholders and is in the public interest and shall have approved the plan subject to such conditions, restrictions and limitations as he may prescribe and (2) when, after reasonable notice of such reorganization, as the case may require, (A) depositors and other creditors of such bank representing at least 75 per cent in amount of its total deposits and other liabilities as shown by the books of the national banking association or (B) stockholders owning at least two-thirds of its outstanding capital stock as shown by the books of the national banking association or (C) both depositors and other creditors representing at least 75 per cent in amount of the total deposits and other liabilities and stockholders owning at least two-thirds of its outstanding capital stock as shown by the books of the national banking association, shall have consented in writing to the plan of reorganization: *Provided, however,* That claims of depositors or other creditors which will be satisfied in full under the provisions of the plan of reorganization shall not be included among the total deposits and other liabilities of the national banking association in determining the 75 per cent thereof as above provided. When such reorganization becomes effective, all books, records, and assets of the national banking association shall be disposed of in accordance with the provisions of the plan and the affairs of the national banking association shall be conducted by its board of directors in the manner provided by the plan and under the conditions, restrictions and limitations which may have been prescribed by the Comptroller of the Currency. In any reorganization which shall have been approved and shall have become effective as provided herein, all depositors and other creditors and stockholders of such national banking association, whether or not they shall have consented to such plan of reogranization, shall be fully and in in all respects subject to and bound by its provisions, and claims of all depositors and other creditors shall be treated as if they had consented to such plan of reorganization.

Sec. 208. After fifteen days after the affairs of a bank shall have been turned back to its board of directors by the conservator, either with or without a reorganization as provided in section 207 hereof, the provisions of section 206 of this title with respect to the segregation of deposits received while it is in the hands of the conservator and with respect to the use of such deposits to liquidate the indebtedness of such bank shall no longer be effective: *Provided,* That before the conservator shall turn back the affairs of the bank to its board of directors he shall cause to be published in a newspaper published in the city, town or county in which such bank is located, and if no newspaper is published in such city, town or county, in a newspaper to be selected by the Comptroller of the Currency published in the State in which the bank is located, a notice in form approved by the Comptroller, stating the date on which the affairs of the bank will be returned to its board of directors and that the said provisions of section 206 will not be effective after fifteen days after such date; and on the date of the publication of such notice the conservator shall immediately send to every person who is a depositor in such bank under section 206 a copy of such notice by registered mail addressed to the last known address of such person as shown by the records of the bank, and the conservator shall send similar notice in like manner to every person making deposit in such bank under section 206 after the date of such newspaper publication and before the time when the affairs of the bank are returned to its directors.

Sec. 209. Conservators appointed pursuant to the provisions of this title shall be subject to the provisions of and to the penalties prescribed by section 5209 of the Revised Statutes (U.S.C., Title 12, sec. 592); and sections 112, 113, 114, 115, 116 and 117 of the Criminal Code of the United States (U.S.C., Title 18, secs. 202, 203, 204, 205, 206 and 207), in so far as applicable, are extended to apply to contracts, agreements, proceedings, dealings, claims and controversies by or with any such conservator or the Comptroller of the Currency under the provisions of this title.

Sec. 210. Nothing in this title shall be construed to impair in any manner any powers of the President, the Secretary of the Treasury, the Comptroller of the Currency, or the Federal Reserve Board.

Sec. 211. The Comptroller of the Currency is hereby authorized and empowered, with the approval of the Secretary of the Treasury, to prescribe such rules and regulations as he may deem necessary in order to carry out the provisions of this title. Whoever violates any rule or regulation made pursuant to this section shall be deemed guilty of a misdemeanor and, upon conviction thereof, shall be fined not more than $5,000, or imprisoned not more than one year, or both.

Title III

Sec. 301. Notwithstanding any other provision of law, any national banking association may, with the approval of the Comptroller of the Currency and by vote of shareholders owning a majority of the stock of such association, upon not less than five days' notice, given by registered mail pursuant to action taken by its board of directors, issue preferred stock in such amount and with such par value as shall be approved by said Comptroller, and make such amendments to its articles of association as may be necessary for this purpose; but, in the case of any newly organized national banking association which has not yet issued common stock, the requirement of notice to and vote of shareholders shall not apply. No issue of preferred stock shall be valid until the par value of all stock so issued shall be paid in.

Sec. 302. (a) The holders of such preferred stock shall be entitled to cumulative dividends at a rate not exceeding 6 per centum per annum, but shall not be held individually responsible as such holders for any debts, contracts, or engagements of such association and shall not be liable for assessments to restore impairments in the capital of such association as now provided by law with reference to holders of common stock. Notwithstanding any other provision of law, the holders of such preferred stock shall have such voting rights, and such stock shall be subject to retirement in such manner and on such terms and conditions, as may be provided in the articles of association with the approval of the Comptroller of the Currency.

(b) No dividends shall be declared or paid on common stock until the cumulative dividends on the preferred stock shall have been paid in full; and, if the association is placed in voluntary liquidation or a conservator or a receiver is appointed therefor, no payments shall be made to the holders of the common stock until the holders of the preferred stock shall have been paid in full the par value of such stock plus all accumulated dividends.

Sec. 303. The term "common stock" as used in this title means stock of national banking associations other than preferred stock issued under the provisions of this title. The term "capital" as used in provisions of law relating to the capital of national banking associations shall mean the amount of unimpaired common stock plus the amount of preferred stock outstanding and unimpaired; and the term "capital stock," as used in section 12 of the Act of March 14, 1900, shall mean only the amount of common stock outstanding.

Sec. 304. If in the opinion of the Secretary of the Treasury any national banking association or any State bank or trust company is in need of funds for capital purposes either in connection with the organization or reorganization of such association, State bank or trust company or otherwise, he may, with the approval of the President, request the Reconstruction Finance Corporation to subscribe for preferred stock in such association, State bank or trust company, or to make loans secured by such stock as collateral, and the Reconstruction Finance Corporation may comply with such request. The Reconstruction Finance Corporation may, with the approval of the Secretary of the Treasury, and under such rules and regulations as he may prescribe, sell in the open market or otherwise the whole or any part of the preferred stock of any national banking association, State bank or trust company acquired by the Corporation pursuant to this section. The amount of notes, bonds, debentures, and other such obligations which the Reconstruction Finance Corporation is authorized and empowered to issue and to have outstanding at any one time under existing law is hereby increased by an amount sufficient to carry out the provisions of this section.

Title IV

Sec. 401. The sixth paragraph of Section 18 of the Federal Reserve Act is amended to read as follows:

"Upon the deposit with the Treasurer of the United States, (a) of any direct obligations of the United States or (b) of any notes, drafts, bills of exchange, or bankers' acceptances acquired under the provisions of this Act, any Federal reserve bank making such deposit in the manner prescribed by the Secretary of the Treasury shall be entitled to receive from the Comptroller of the Currency circulating notes in blank, duly registered and countersigned. When such circulating notes are issued against the security of obligations of the United States, the amount of such circulating notes shall be equal to the face value of the direct obligations of the United States so deposited as security; and, when issued against the security of notes, drafts, bills of exchange and bankers' acceptances acquired under the provisions of this Act, the amount thereof shall be equal to not more than 90 per cent of the estimated value of such notes, drafts, bills of exchange and bankers' acceptances so deposited as security. Such notes shall be the obligations of the Federal reserve bank procuring the same, shall be in form prescribed by the Secretary of the Treasury, shall be receivable at par in all parts of the United States for the same purposes as are national bank notes, and shall be redeemable in lawful money of the United States on presentation at the United States Treasury or at the bank of issue. The Secretary of the Treasury is authorized and empowered to prescribe regulations governing the issuance, redemption, replacement, retirement and destruction of such circulating notes and the release and substitution of security therefor. Such circulating notes shall be subject to the same tax as is provided by law for the circulating notes of national banks secured by 2 per cent bonds of the United States. No such circulating notes shall be issued under this paragraph after the President has declared by proclamation that the emergency recognized by the President by proclamation of March 6, 1933, has terminated, unless such circulating notes are secured by deposits of bonds of the United States bearing the circulation privilege. When required to do so by the Secretary of the Treasury, each Federal reserve agent shall act as agent of the Treasurer of the United States or of the Comptroller of the Currency, or both, for the performance of any of the functions which the Treasurer or the Comptroller may be called upon to perform in carrying out the provisions of this paragraph. Appropriations available for distinctive paper and printing United States currency or national bank currency are hereby made available for the production of the circulating notes of Federal reserve banks herein provided; but the United States shall be reimbursed by the Federal reserve bank to which such notes are issued for all expenses necessarily incurred in connection with the procuring of such notes and all other expenses incidental to their issue, redemption, replacement, retirement and destruction."

Sec. 402. Section 10(b) of the Federal Reserve Act, as amended, is further amended to read as follows:

"Sec. 10(b). In exceptional and exigent circumstances, and when any member bank has no further eligible and acceptable assets available to enable it to obtain adequate credit accommodations through rediscounting at the Federal reserve bank or any other method provided by this Act other than that provided by section 10 (a), any Federal reserve bank, under rules and regulations prescribed by the Federal Reserve Board, may make advances to such member bank on its time or demand notes secured to the satisfaction of such Federal reserve bank. Each such note shall bear interest at a rate not less than 1 per centum per annum higher than the highest discount rate in effect at such Federal reserve bank on the date of such note. No advance shall be made under this section after March 3, 1934, or after the expiration of such additional period not exceeding one year as the President may prescribe."

Sec. 403. Section 13 of the Federal Reserve Act, as amended, is amended by adding at the end thereof the following new paragraph:

"Subject to such limitations, restrictions and regulations as the Federal Reserve Board may prescribe, any Federal reserve bank may make advances to any individual, partnership or corporation on the promissory notes of such individuals, partnership or corporation secured by direct obligations of the United States. Such advances shall be made for periods not exceeding 90 days and shall bear interest at rates fixed from time to time by the Federal reserve bank, subject to the review and determination of the Federal Reserve Board."

Title V

Sec. 501. There is hereby appropriated, out of the money in the Treasury not otherwise appropriated, the sum of $2,000,000, which shall be available for expenditure, under the direction of the President and in his discretion, for any purpose in connection with the carrying out of this Act.

Sec. 502. The right to alter, amend, or repeal this Act is hereby expressly reserved. If any provision of this Act, or the application thereof to any person or circumstances, is held invalid, the remainder of the Act, and the application of such provision to other persons or circumstances, shall not be affected thereby.

Approved, March 9, 1933, 8:30 p.m.

An Act to Amend the Act Entitled "An Act to Provide Relief in the Existing National Emergency in Banking, for Other Purposes," Approved March 9, 1933
June 15, 1933

Be it enacted by the Senate and House of Representatives of the United States of America in Congress assembled, That the Act entitled "An Act to provide relief in the existing national emergency in banking, and for other purposes," approved March 9, 1933, is amended by—

(a) striking out the whole section 301 of title III thereof and inserting in lieu thereof the following:

"Sec. 301. Notwithstanding any other provision of law, any national banking association may, with the approval of the Comptroller of the Currency and by vote of shareholders owning a majority of the stock of such association, upon not less than five days' notice, given by registered mail pursuant to action taken by its board of directors, issue preferred stock of one or more classes, in such amount and with such par value as shall be approved by said Comptroller, and make such amendments to its articles of association as may be necessary for this purpose; but, in the case of any newly organized national banking association which has not yet issued common stock, the requirement of notice to and vote of shareholders shall not apply. No issue of preferred stock shall be valid until the par value of all stock so issued shall be paid in."

(b) striking out the whole of subsection (a) of section 302 of the said title III and inserting in lieu thereof the following:

"Notwithstanding any other provisions of law, whether relating to restriction upon the payment of dividends upon capital stock or otherwise, the holders of such preferred stock shall be entitled to receive such cumulative dividends at a rate not exceeding 6 per centum per annum and shall have such voting and conversion rights and such control of management, and such stock shall be subject to retirement in such manner and upon such conditions, as may be provided in the articles of association with the approval of the Comptroller of the Currency. The holders of such preferred stock shall not be held individually responsible as such holders for any debts, contracts, or engagements of such association, and shall not be liable for assessments to restore impairments in the capital of such association as now provided by law with reference to holders of common stock."

Approved, June 15, 1933.

CREDIT ACT

Editor's comments: *This Act (three titles) identified those veterans and dependents of veterans who were entitled to a pension. Only veterans who had fought in wars subsequent to the Civil War, including the Boxer Rebellion and the Philippine Insurrection, were entitled to benefits under this Act.*

Management of veterans' pensions was to be done by the Administrator of Veterans Affairs which also was to provide veterans with domiciliary care.

Civilian officers and employees of the United States were defined as was the term "compensation" as used in Title II of the Act.

The method of determining officer and employee compensation, for part of fiscal year 1933 and all of fiscal year 1934, is set forth with the provision for a reduction in compensation. It also provided that "temporary reductions in compensation . . . shall not operate to reduce the rate of compensation upon which the retired pay or retirement benefits of any officer or employee would be based."

An Act to Maintain the Credit of the United States Government
March 20, 1933

Be it enacted by the Senate and House of Representatives of the United States of America in Congress assembled,

Title I

Veterans

Section 1. That subject to such requirements and limitations as shall be contained in regulations to be issued by the President, and within the limits of appropriations made by Congress, the following classes of persons may be paid a pension:

(a) Any person who served in the active military or naval service and who is disabled as a result of disease or injury or aggravation of a preexisting disease or injury incurred in line of duty in such service.

(b) Any person who served in the active military or naval service during the Spanish-American War, including the Boxer Rebellion and the Philippine Insurrection, or the World War, and who is permanently disabled as a result of injury or disease: *Provided,* That nothing contained in this title shall deny a pension to a Spanish-American War veteran past the age of sixty-two years entitled to a pension under existing law, but the President may reduce the rate of pension as he may deem proper.

(c) The widow, child, or children, dependent mother or father, of any person who dies as a result of disease or injury incurred or aggravated in line of duty in the active military or naval service.

(d) The widow and/or child of any deceased person who served in the active military or naval service during the Spanish-American War, including the Boxer Rebellion and the Philippine Insurrection.

(e) For the purpose of subparagraph (b) of this section, the World War shall be deemed to have ended November 11, 1918.

Sec. 2. The minimum and maximum monthly rate of pension which may be paid for disability or death shall be as follows: For disability, from $6 to $275; for death, from $12 to $75.

Sec. 3. For each class of persons specified in subparagraphs (a) and (b) of section 1 of this title the President is hereby authorized to prescribe by regulation the minimum degrees of disability and such higher degrees of disability, if any, as in his judgment should be recognized and prescribe the rate of pension payable for each such degree of disability. In fixing rates of pensions for disability or death the President shall prescribe by regulation such differentiation as he may deem just and equitable, in the rates to be paid to veterans of different wars and/or their dependents and to be paid for

(a) Disabilities and deaths resulting from disease or injury incurred or aggravated in line of duty in war-time service;

(b) Disabilities and deaths resulting from disease or injury incurred or aggravated in line of duty in peace-time service;

(c) Disabilities and deaths not incurred in service.

Sec. 4. The President shall prescribe by regulation (subject to the provisions of section 1 (e) of this title) the date of the beginning and of the termination of the period in each war subsequent to the Civil War, including the Boxer Rebellion and the Philippine Insurrection, service within which shall for the purposes of this Act be deemed war-time service. The President shall further prescribe by regulation the required number of days of war or peace time service for each class of veterans, the time limit on filing of claims for each class of veterans and their dependents, the nature and extent of proofs and presumptions for such different classes, and any other requirments as to entitlement as he shall deem equitable and just. The President in establishing conditions precedent may prescribe different requirements or conditions for the veterans of different wars and their dependents and may further subdivide the classes of persons as outlined in section 1 of this title and apply different requirements or conditions to such subdivisions.

Sec. 5. All decisions rendered by the Administrator of Veterans' Affairs under the provisions of this title, or the regulations issued pursuant thereto, shall be final and conclusive on all questions of law and fact, and no other official or court of the United States shall have jurisdiction to review by mandamus or otherwise any such decision.

Sec. 6. In addition to the pensions provided in this title, the Administrator of Veterans' Affairs is hereby authorized under such limitations as may be prescribed by the President, and within the limits of existing Veterans' Administration facilities, to furnish to veterans of any war, including the Boxer Rebellion and the Philippine Insurrection, domiciliary care where they are suffering with permanent disabilities, tuberculosis or neuropsychiatric ailments and medical and hospital treatment for diseases or injuries.

Sec. 7. The Administrator of Veterans' Affairs subject to the general direction of the President and in accordance with regulations to be issued by the President shall administer, execute, and enforce the provisions of this title and for such purpose shall have the same authority and powers as are provided in sections 425, 430, 431, 432, 433, 434, 440, 442, 443, 444, 447, 450, 451, 453, 455, 457, 458, 459, 459a, 459c, 459d, 459e, 459f, title 38, U.S.C., and such other sections of title 38, U.S.C., as relate to the administration of the laws granting pensions.

Sec. 8. The Administrator of Veterans' Affairs is hereby authorized in carrying out the provisions of Title 1 of this Act or any other pension Act to delegate authority to render decisions to such person or persons as he may find necessary. Within the limitations of such delegations, any decisions rendered by such person or persons shall have the same force and effect as though rendered by the Administrator of Veterans' Affairs. The President shall personally approve all regulations issued under the provisions of this title.

Sec. 9. Claims for benefits under this title shall be filed with the Veterans' Administration under such regulations, including provisions for hearing, determination, and administrative review, as the President may approve, and payments shall not be made for any period prior to date of application. When a claim shall be finally disallowed under this title and the regulations issued thereunder, it may not thereafter be reopened or allowed. No person who is entitled to any benefits under this title shall participate in any determination or decision with respect to any claim for benefits under this title.

Sec. 10. Notwithstanding the provisions of section 2 of this title, any person who served as an officer of the Army, Navy, or Marine Corps of the United States during the World War, other than as an officer of the Regular Army, Navy, or Marine Corps during the World War, who made valid application for retirement under the provisions of Public No. 506, Seventieth Congress, enacted May 24, 1928, sections 581 and 582, title 38, United States Code, and who prior to the passage of this Act has been granted retirement with pay, shall be entitled to continue to receive retirement pay at the monthly rate now being paid him if the disability for which he has been retired resulted from disease or injury or aggravation of a preexisting disease or injury incurred in line of duty during such service: *Provided,* That such person entered active service between April 6, 1917, and November 11, 1918: *Provided,* That the disease or injury or aggravation of the disease or injury directly resulted from the performance of military or naval duty, and that such person otherwise meets the requirements of the regulations which may be issued under the provisions of this Act.

Sec. 11. All offenses committed and all penalties or forfeiture incurred under the acts repealed by section 17 of this title may be prosecuted and punished in the same manner and with the same effect as if said repeal had not been made and any person who forfeited rights to benefits under any such acts shall not be entitled to any benefits under this title.

Sec. 12. That whoever in any claim for benefits under this title or by regulations issued pursuant to this title, makes any sworn statement of a material fact knowing it to be false, shall be guilty of perjury and shall be punished by a fine of not more than $5,000 or by imprisonment for not more than two years, or both.

Sec. 13. That if any person entitled to payment of pension under this title, whose right to such payment under this title or under any regulation issued under this title, ceases upon the happening of any contingency, thereafter fraudulently accepts any such payment, he shall be punished by a fine of not more than $2,000 or by imprisonment for not more than one year, or both.

Sec. 14. That whoever shall obtain or receive any money, check, or pension under this title, or regulations issued under this title, without being entitled to the same, and with intent to defraud the United States or any beneficiary of the United States, shall be punished by a fine of not more than $2,000, or by imprisonment for not more than one year, or both.

Sec. 15. Any person who shall knowingly make or cause to be made, or conspire, combine, aid, or assist in, agree to, arrange for, or in any wise procure the making or presentation of a false or fraudulent affidavit, declaration, certificate, statement, voucher, or paper, or writing purporting to be such, concerning any claim for benefits under this title, shall forfeit all rights, claims, and benefits under this title, and, in addition to any and all other penalties imposed by law, shall be guilty of a misdemeanor and upon conviction thereof shall be punished by a fine of not more than $1,000 or imprisonment for not more than one year, or both.

Sec. 16. Every guardian, curator, conservator, committee, or person legally vested with the responsibility or care of a claimant or his estate, having charge and custody in a fiduciary capacity of money paid, under the provisions of this title, for the benefit of any minor or incompetent claimant, who shall embezzle the same in violation of his trust, or convert the same to his own use, shall be punished by a fine not exceeding $2,000 or imprisonment at hard labor for a term not exceeding five years, or both.

Sec. 17. All public laws granting medical or hospital treatment, domiciliary care, compensation and other allowances, pension, disability allowance, or retirement pay to veterans and the dependents of veterans of the Spanish-American War, including the Boxer Rebellion and the Philippine Insurrection, and the World War, or to former members of the military or naval service for injury or disease incurred or aggravated in the line of duty in the military or naval service (except so far as they relate to persons who served prior to the Spanish-American War and to the dependents of such persons, and the retirement of officers and enlisted men of the Regular Army, Navy, Marine Corps, or Coast Guard) are hereby repealed, and all laws granting or pertaining to yearly renewable term insurance are hereby repealed, but payments in accordance with such laws shall continue to the last day of the third calendar month following the month during which this Act is enacted. The Administrator of Veterans' Affairs under the general direction of the President shall immediately cause to be reviewed all allowed claims under the above referred to laws and where a person is found entitled under this Act, authorize payment or allowance of benefits in accordance with the provisions of this Act commencing with the first day of the fourth calendar month following the month during which this Act is enacted and notwithstanding the provisions of section 9 of this Act, no further claim in such cases shall be required: *Provided,* That nothing contained in this section shall interfere with payments heretofore made or hereafter to be made under contracts of yearly renewable term insurance which have matured prior to the date of enactment of this Act and under which payments have been commenced, or on any judgment heretofore rendered in a court of competent jurisdiction in any suit on a contract of yearly renewable term insurance, or which may hereafter be rendered in any such suit now pending: *Provided further,* That, subject to such regulations as the President may prescribe, allowances may be grated for burial and funeral expenses and transportation of the bodies (including preparation of the bodies) of deceased veterans of any war to the places of burial thereof in a sum not to exceed $107 in any one case.

The provisions of this title shall not apply to compensation or pension (except as to rates, time of entry into active service and special statutory allowances), being paid to veterans disabled, or dependents of veterans who died, as the result of disease or injury directly connected with active military or naval service (without benefit of statutory or regulatory presumption of service connection) pursuant to the provisions of the laws in effect on the date of enactment of this Act. The term "compensation or pension" as used in this paragraph shall not be construed to include emergency officers' retired pay referred to in section 10 of this title.

Sec. 18. For the fiscal year ending June 30, 1934, any pension, and/or any other monetary gratuity, payable to former members of the military or naval service in wars prior to the Spanish-American War, and their dependents, for service, age, disease, or injury, except retired pay of officers and enlisted men of the Regular Army, Navy, Marine Corps, or Coast Guard, shall be reduced by 10 per centum of the amount payable.

Sec. 19. The regulations issued by the President under this title which are in effect at the expiration of two years after the date of enactment of this

Act shall continue in effect without further change or modification until the Congress by law shall otherwise provide.

Sec. 20. The President shall transmit to the Congress, as soon as practicable after the date of their issue, copies of all regulations issued pursuant to this title.

Title II

Officers and Employees

Sec. 1. When used in this title —

(a) The terms "officer" and "employee" mean any person rendering services in or under any branch or service of the United States Government or the government of the District of Columbia, but do not include (1) officers whose compensation may not, under the Constitution, be diminished during their continuance in office; (2) the Vice President, the Speaker of the House of Representatives, Senators, Representatives in Congress, Delegates, and Resident Commissioners; (3) officers and employees on the rolls of the Senate and House of Representatives; (4) any person in respect of any office, position, or employment the amount of compensation of which is expressly fixed by international agreement; and (5) any person in respect of any office, position, or employment the compensation of which is paid under the terms of any contract in effect on the date of the enactment of this title, if such compensation may not lawfully be reduced.

(b) The term "compensation" means any salary, pay, wage, allowance (except allowances for travel), or other emolument paid for services rendered in any civilian or noncivilian office, position, or employment; and includes the retired pay of judges (except judges whose compensation, prior to retirement or resignation, could not, under the Constitution, have been diminished), and the retired pay of all commissioned and other personnel of the Coast and Geodetic Survey, the Lighthouse Service, and the Public Health Service, and the retired pay of all commissioned and other personnel of the Army, Navy, Marine Corps, and Coast Guard; but does not include payments out of any retirement, disability, or relief fund made up wholly or in part of contributions of employees.

Sec. 2. For that portion of the fiscal year 1933 beginning with the first day of the calendar month following the month during which this Act is enacted, and for the fiscal year ending June 30, 1934, the compensation of every officer or employee shall be determined as follows:

(a) The compensation which such officer or employee would receive under the provisions of any existing law, schedule, regulation, Executive order, or departmental order shall first be determined as though this title (except section 4) had not been enacted.

(b) The compensation as determined under subparagraph (a) of this section shall be reduced by the percentage, if any, determined in accordance with section 3 of this title.

Sec. 3. (a) The President is authorized to investigate through established agencies of the Government the facts relating to the cost of living in the United States during the six months period ending June 30, 1928, to be known as the base period, and upon the basis of such facts and the application thereto of such principles as he may find proper, determine an index figure of the cost of living during such period. The President is further authorized to make a similar investigation and determination of an index figure of the cost of living during the six months period ending December 31, 1932, and each six months period thereafter.

(b) The President shall announce by Executive order the index figure for the base period and for each subsequent period determined by him under paragraph (a) of this section. The percentage, if any, by which the cost of living index for any six months' period, as provided in paragraph (a) of this section, is lower than such index for the base period, shall be the percentage of reduction applicable under section 2 (b) of this title in determining compensation to be paid during the following six months' period, or such portion thereof during which this title is in effect: *Provided,* That such percentage of reduction (including reductions made under any existing law, regulation, or Executive order, in the case of subsistence and rental allowances for the services mentioned in the Pay Act of June 10, 1922) shall not exceed 15 per centum.

Sec. 4. (a) Section 4 of An Act Making Appropriations for the Treasury and Post Office Departments for the fiscal year ending June 30, 1934, and for other purposes, approved March 3, 1933, is hereby amended to read as follows:

"Sec. 4. (a) The provisions of the following sections of Part II of the Legislative Appropriation Act, fiscal year 1933, are hereby continued in full force and effect during the fiscal year ending June 30, 1934, namely sections 105 (except subsections (d) and (e) thereof), 107 (except paragraph (5) of subsection (a) thereof and subsection (b) thereof), 201, 203, 206 (except subsection (a) thereof), 214, 216, 304, 315, 317, 318, and 323, and for the purpose of continuing such sections, in the application of such sections with respect to the fiscal year ending June 30, 1934, the figures '1933' shall be read as '1934'; the figures '1934' as '1935'; and the figures '1935' as '1936'; and in the case of section 203, the figures '1932' shall be read as '1933'; except that in the application of such sections with respect to the fiscal year ending June 30, 1934 (but not with respect to the fiscal year ending June 30, 1933), the following amendments shall apply:

"(1) Section 216 is amended by striking out the period at the end thereof and inserting in lieu thereof a colon and the following: '*Provided further,* That no employee under the classified civil service shall be furloughed under the provisions of this section for a total of more than 90 days during the fiscal year 1934, except after full and complete compliance with all the provisions of the civil-service laws and regulations relating to reductions in personnel.'

"(2) Section 317 is amended by striking out the period at the end thereof and inserting in lieu thereof a colon and the following: '*Provided further,* That no part of any appropriation for "public works", nor any part of any allotment or portion available for "public works" under any appropriation, shall be transferred pursuant to the authority of this section to any appropriation for expenditure for personnel unless such personnel is required upon or in connection with "public works." "Public works" as used in this section shall comprise all projects falling in the general classes enumerated in Budget Statement No. 9, pages A177 to A182, inclusive, of the Budget for the fiscal year 1934, and shall also include the procurement of new airplanes and the construction of vessels under appropriations for "Increase of the Navy." The interpretation by the Director of the Bureau of the Budget, or by the President in the cases of the War Department and the Navy Department, of "public works" as defined and designated herein shall be conclusive.'

"(b) All Acts or parts of Acts inconsistent or in conflict with the provisions of such sections as amended, are hereby suspended during the period in which such sections, as amended, are in effect.

"(c) No court of the United States shall have jurisdiction of any suit against the United States or (unless brought by the United States) against any officer, agency, or instrumentality of the United States arising out of the application as provided in this section, of such sections 105 or 107, as amended, unless such suit involves the Constitution of the United States.

"(d) The appropriations or portions of appropriations unexpended by reason of the operation of the amendments made in subsection (a) of this section shall not be used for any purpose, but shall be impounded and returned to the Treasury.

"(e) Each permanent specific annual appropriation available during the fiscal year ending June 30, 1934, is hereby reduced for that fiscal year by such estimated amount as the Director of the Bureau of the Budget may determine will be equivalent to the savings that will be effected in such appropriation by reason of the application of this section and section 7."

(b) Sections 5 and 6 of the Treasury and Post Office Appropriation Act, fiscal year 1934, are hereby repealed.

(c) Section 215 of the Legislative Appropriation Act, fiscal year 1933 (relating to the limitation on annual leave), is amended by striking out "*Provided further,* That nothing herein shall apply to civilian officers and employees of the Panama Canal located on the Isthmus and who are American citizens, or to officers and employees of the Foreign Services of the United States holding official station outside the continental United States" and inserting in lieu thereof "*Provided further,* That nothing herein shall apply to officers and employees of the Panama Canal and Panama Railroad Company on the Isthmus of Panama, or to officers and employees of the United States (including enlisted personnel) holding official station outside the continental United States or in Alaska."

(d) The following sections of Part II of the Legislative Appropriation Act, fiscal year 1933, are hereby repealed effective on the first day of the calendar month following the month in which this Act is enacted; namely, sections 101, 102, 103, 104, subsections (d) and (e) of section 105, 106, 107 (except paragraphs (1), (2), (3), and (4) of subsection (a) thereof), 108, 112, and 211.

(e) Subsection (a) of section 105 of the Legislative Appropriation Act, fiscal year 1933, is amended to read as follows, beginning with the first day of the calendar month following the month during which this Act is enacted:

"(a) The salaries of the Vice President and the Speaker of the House of Representatives are reduced by 15 per centum; and the salaries of Senators, Representatives in Congress, Delegates, and Resident Commissioners are reduced by 15 per centum."

(f) Subsection (b) of section 105 of the Legislative Appropriation Act, fiscal year 1933, is amended to read as follows, beginning with the first day of the calendar month following the month during which this Act is enacted:

"(b) The allowance for clerk hire of Representatives in Congress, Delegates, and Resident Commissioners is reduced by the percentage applicable by law to other employees on the roll of the House of Representatives, such reduced allowance to be apportioned by the Representative, Delegate, or Resident Commissioner among his clerks as he may determine, subject to the limitations of existing law, but the compensation of such clerks shall not be subject to reduction under subsection (c) of this section."

(g) Subsection (c) of section 105 of the Legislative Appropriation Act, fiscal year 1933, is amended to read as follows, beginning with the first day of the calendar month following the month during which this Act is enacted:

"(c) The rate of compensation of any person on the rolls of the Senate or of the House of Representatives (other than persons included within subsection (a), is reduced by the percentage applicable by law to employees of the Government generally."

Sec. 5. The provisions of this title providing for temporary reductions in compensation and suspension in automatic increases in compensation shall not operate to reduce the rate of compensation upon which the retired pay or retirement benefits of any officer or employee would be based but for the application of such provisions, but the amount of retired pay shall be reduced as provided in this title: *Provided,* That retirement deductions authorized by law to be made from the salary, pay, or compensation of officers or employees and transferred or deposited to the credit of a retirement fund, shall be based on the regular rate of salary, pay, or compensation instead of on the rate as temporarily reduced under the provisions of this title.

Sec. 6. In the case of a corporation the majority of the stock of which is owned by the United States, the holders of the stock on behalf of the United States, or such persons as represent the interest of the United States in such corporation, shall take such action as may be necessary to apply the provisions of this title to offices, positions, and employments under such corporation and to officers and employees thereof, with proper allowance for any reduction in compensation since December 31, 1931.

Sec. 7. In any case in which the application of the provisions of this title to any person would result in a diminution of compensation prohibited by the Constitution, the Secretary of the Treasury is authorized to accept from such person, and cover into the Treasury as miscellaneous receipts, remittance of such part of the compensation of such person as would not be paid to him if such diminution of compensation were not prohibited.

Sec. 8. The appropriations or portions of appropriations unexpended by reason of the operation of this Act shall not be used for any purpose, but shall be impounded and returned to the Treasury.

Sec. 9. No court of the United States shall have jurisdiction of any suit against the United States or (unless brought by the United States) against any officer, agency, or instrumentality of the United States arising out of the application of any provision of this title, unless such suit involves the Constitution of the United States.

Title III

Amendments to Legislative Appropriation Act, Fiscal Year, 1933

Section 1. Sections 407 and 409 of Title IV of Part II of the Legislative Appropriation Act, fiscal year 1933, as amended by section 17 of the Treasury and Post Office Appropriation Act, approved March 3, 1933, are amended to read as follows:

"Sec. 407. Whenever the President makes an Executive order under the provisions of this title, such Executive order shall be submitted to the Congress while in session and shall not become effective until after the expiration of sixty calendar days after such transmission, unless Congress shall by law provide for an earlier effective date of such Executive order or orders.

"Sec. 409. No Executive order issued by the President in pursuance of the provisions of section 403 of this title shall become effective unless transmitted to the Congress within two years from the date of the enactment of this Act."

Approved, March 20, 1933.

UNEMPLOYMENT RELIEF/ PUBLIC WORKS ACT

> Editor's comments: *To aid in relieving unemployment, this Act provided for the hiring, without discrimination on account of race, color, or creed, a force of civilians to undertake various useful public works projects. The President was authorized to furnish housing, subsistence, clothing, medical attendance and hospitalization for persons so employed. Further, persons given employment under this Act were given coverage under the act approved September 7, 1916, as amended, which provided compensation for employees of the United States suffering injuries while in the performance of their duties.*

An Act for the Relief of Unemployment
Through the Performance of Useful Public Work,
and for Other Purposes
March 31, 1933

Be it enacted by the Senate and House of Representatives of the United States of America in Congress assembled, That for the purpose of relieving the acute condition of widespread distress and unemployment now existing in the United States, and in order to provide for the restoration of the country's depleted natural resources and the advancement of an orderly program of useful public works, the President is authorized, under such rules and regulations as he may prescribe and by utilizing such existing departments or agencies as he may designate, to provide for employing citizens of the United States who are unemployed, in the construction, maintenance and carrying on of works of a public nature in connection with the forestation of lands belonging to the United States or to the several States which are suitable for timber production, the prevention of forest fires, floods and soil erosion, plant pest and disease control, the construction, maintenance or repair of paths, trails and fire-lanes in the national parks and national forests, and such other work on the public domain, national and State, and Government reservations incidental to or necessary in connection with any projects of the character enumerated, as the President may determine to be desirable: *Provided,* That the President may in his discretion extend the provisions of this Act to lands owned by counties and municipalities and lands in private ownership, but only for the purpose of doing thereon such kinds of cooperative work as are now provided for by Acts of Congress in preventing and controlling forest fires and the attacks of forest tree pests and diseases and such work as is necessary in the public interest to control floods. The President is further authorized, by regulation, to provide for housing the persons so employed and for furnishing them with such subsistence, clothing, medical attendance and hospitalization, and cash allowance, as may be necessary, during the period they are so employed, and, in his discretion, to provide for the transportation of such persons to and from the places of employment. That in employing citizens for the purposes of the Act no discrimination shall be made on account of race, color, or creed; and no person under conviction for crime and serving sentence therefor shall be employed under the provisions of this Act. The President is further authorized to allocate funds available for the purposes of this Act, for forest research, including forest products investigations by the Forest Products Laboratory.

Sec. 2. For the purpose of carrying out the provisions of this Act the President is authorized to enter into such contracts or agreements with States as may be necessary, including provisions for utilization of existing State administrative agencies, and the President, or the head of any department or agency authorized by him to construct any project or to carry on any such public works, shall be authorized to acquire real property by purchase, donation, condemnation, or otherwise, but the provisions of section 355 of the Revised Statutes shall not apply to any property so acquired.

Sec. 3. Insofar as applicable, the benefits of the Act entitled "An Act to provide compensation for employees of the United States suffering injuries while in the performance of their duties, and for other purposes," approved September 7, 1916, as amended, shall extend to persons given employment under the provisions of this Act.

Sec. 4. For the purpose of carrying out the provisions of this Act, there is hereby authorized to be expended, under the direction of the President, out of any unobligated moneys heretofore appropriated for public works (except for projects on which actual construction has been commenced or may be commenced within ninety days, and except maintenance funds for river and harbor improvements already allocated), such sums as may be necessary; and an amount equal to the amount so expended is hereby authorized to be appropriated for the same purposes for which such moneys were originally appropriated.

Sec. 5. That the unexpended and unallotted balance of the sum of $300,000,000 made available under the terms and conditions of the Act approved July 21, 1932, entitled "An Act to relieve destitution", and so forth, may be made available, or any portion thereof, to any State or Territory or States or Territories without regard to the limitation of 15 per centum or other limitations as to per centum.

Sec. 6. The authority of the President under this Act shall continue for the period of two years next after the date of the passage hereof and no longer.

Approved, March 31, 1933.

AGRICULTURAL ADJUSTMENT ACT

Editor's comments: *The purpose of this Act was to increase agricultural purchasing power as a means of relieving the national economic emergency. The disparity between prices of agriculture and other commodities was fully recognized and this recognition was expressed in section 1, Title I of the Act. Section 2, of Title I stated in part, "It is hereby declared to be the policy of Congress—(1) To establish and maintain such balance between the production and consumption of agricultural commodities, . . . as will reestablish prices to farmers at a level that will give agricultural commodities a purchasing power with respect to articles that farmers buy, . . ."*

The Secretary of Agriculture was authorized to buy cotton, and to provide for the reduction in acreage or reduction of production for market of any basic agricultural commodity. Licenses were required that permitted the handling of agriculture commodities, and processing taxes were levied to raise revenue to cover expenses resulting from the economic emergency.

The Federal Farm Loan Act was extensively amended by this Act and provision for credit to farmers was enhanced.

An Act to Relieve the Existing National Economic Emergency by Increasing Agricultural Purchasing Power, to Raise Revenue for Extraordinary Expenses Incurred by Reason of Such Emergency, to Provide Emergency Relief with Respect to Agricultural Indebtedness, to Provide for the Orderly Liquidation of Joint-Stock Land Banks, and for Other Purposes
May 12, 1933

Be it enacted by the Senate and House of Representatives of the United States of America in Congress Assembled,

Title I—Agricultural Adjustment

Declaration of Emergency

That the present acute economic emergency being in part the consequence of a severe and increasing disparity between the prices of agricultural and other commodities, which disparity has largely destroyed the purchasing power of farmers for industrial products, has broken down the orderly exchange of commodities, and has seriously impaired the agricultural assets supporting the national credit structure, it is hereby declared that these conditions in the basic industry of agriculture have affected transactions in agricultural commodities with a national public interest, have burdened and obstructed the normal currents of commerce in such commodities, and render imperative the immediate enactment of title I of this Act.

Sec. 2. It is hereby declared to be the policy of Congress—
(1) To establish and maintain such balance between the production and

consumption of agricultural commodities, and such marketing conditions therefor, as will reestablish prices to farmers at a level that will give agricultural commodities a purchasing power with respect to articles that farmers buy, equivalent to the purchasing power of agricultural commodities in the base period. The base period in the case of all agricultural commodities except tobacco shall be the prewar period, August 1909-July 1914. In the case of tobacco, the base period shall be the postwar period, August 1919-July 1929.

(2) To approach such equality of purchasing power by gradual correction of the present inequalities therein at as rapid a rate as is deemed feasible in view of the current consumptive demand in domestic and foreign markets.

(3) To protect the consumers' interest by readjusting farm production at such level as will not increase the percentage of the consumers' retail expenditures for agricultural commodities, or products derived therefrom, which is returned to the farmer, above the percentage which was returned to the farmer in the prewar period, August 1909-July 1914.

Part 1 — Cotton Option Contracts

Sec. 3. The Federal Farm Board and all departments and other agencies of the Government, not including the Federal intermediate credit banks, are hereby directed —

(a) To sell to the Secretary of Agriculture at such price as may be agreed upon, not in excess of the market price, all cotton now owned by them.

(b) To take such action and to make such settlements as are necessary in order to acquire full legal title to all cotton on which money has been loaned or advanced by any department or agency of the United States, including futures contracts for cotton or which is held as collateral for loans or advances and to make final settlement of such loans and advances as follows:

(1) In making such settlements with regard to cotton, including operations to which such cotton is related, such cotton shall be taken over by all such departments or agencies other than the Secretary of Agriculture at a price or sum equal to the amounts directly or indirectly loaned or advanced thereon and outstanding, including loans by the Government department or agency and any loans senior thereto, plus any sums required to adjust advances to growers to 90 per centum of the value of their cotton at the date of its delivery in the first instance as collateral to the department or agency involved, such sums to be computed by subtracting the total amount already advanced to growers on account of pools of which such cotton was a part, from 90 per centum of the value of the cotton to be taken over as of the time of such delivery as collateral, plus unpaid accrued carrying charges and operating costs on such cotton, less, however, any existing assets of the borrower derived from net income, earnings, or profits arising from such cotton,

and from operations to which such cotton is related; all as determined by the department or agency making the settlement.

(2) The Secretary of Agriculture shall make settlements with respect to cotton held as collateral for loans or advances made by him on such terms as in his judgment may be deemed advisable, and to carry out the provisions of this section, is authorized to indemnify or furnish bonds to warehousemen for lost warehouse receipts and to pay the premiums on such bonds.

When full legal title to the cotton referred to in (b) has been acquired, it shall be sold to the Secretary of Agriculture for the purposes of this section, in the same manner as provided in (a).

(c) The Secretary of Agriculture is hereby authorized to purchase the cotton specified in paragraphs (a) and (b).

Sec. 4. The Secretary of Agriculture shall have authority to borrow money upon all cotton in his possession or control and deposit as collateral for such loans the warehouse receipts for such cotton.

Sec. 5. The Reconstruction Finance Corporation is hereby authorized and directed to advance money and to make loans to the Secretary of Agriculture to acquire such cotton and to pay the classing, carrying, and merchandising costs thereon, in such amounts and upon such terms as may be agreed upon by the Secretary and the Reconstruction Finance Corporation, with such warehouse receipts as collateral security: *Provided, however,* That in any instance where is is impossible or impracticable for the Secretary to deliver such warehouse receipts as collateral security for the advances and loans herein provided to be made, the Reconstruction Finance Corporation may accept in lieu of all or any part thereof such other security as it may consider acceptable for the purposes aforesaid, including an assignment or assignments of the equity and interest of the Secretary in warehouse receipts pledged to secure other indebtedness. The amount of notes, bonds, debentures, and other such obligations which the Reconstruction Finance Corporation is authorized and empowered to issue and to have outstanding at any one time under existing law is hereby increased by an amount sufficient to carry out the provisions of this section.

Sec. 6. (a) The Secretary of Agriculture is hereby authorized to enter into option contracts with the producers of cotton to sell to any such producer an amount of cotton to be agreed upon not in excess of the amount of reduction in production of cotton by such producer below the amount produced by him in the preceding crop year, in all cases where such producer agrees in writing to reduce the amount of cotton produced by him in 1933, below his production in the previous year, by not less than 30 per centum, without increase in commercial fertilization per acre.

(b) To any such producer so agreeing to reduce production the Secretary of Agriculture shall deliver a nontransferable-option contract agreeing to sell to said producer an amount, equivalent to the amount of his agreed reduction, of the cotton in the possession and control of the Secretary.

(c) The producer is to have the option to buy said cotton at the average price paid by the Secretary for the cotton procured under section 3, and is to have the right at any time up to January 1, 1934, to exercise his option, upon proof that he has complied with his contract and with all the rules and regulations of the Secretary of Agriculture with respect thereto, by taking said cotton upon payment by him of his option price and all actual carrying charges on such cotton; or the Secretary may sell such cotton for the account of such producer, paying him the excess of the market price at the date of sale over the average price above referred to after deducting all actual and necessary carrying charges: *Provided,* That in no event shall the producer be held responsible or liable for financial loss incurred in the holding of such cotton or on account of the carrying charges therein: *Provided further,* That such agreement to curtail cotton production shall contain a further provision that such cotton producer shall not use the land taken out of cotton production for the production for sale, directly or indirectly, of any other nationally produced agricultural commodity or product.

(d) If any cotton held by the Secretary of Agriculture is not disposed of under subsection (c), the Secretary is authorized to enter into similar option contracts with respect to such cotton, conditioned upon a like reduction of production in 1934, and permitting the producer in each case to exercise his option at any time up to January 1, 1935.

Sec. 7. The Secretary shall sell the cotton held by him at his discretion, but subject to the foregoing provisions: *Provided,* That he shall dispose of all cotton held by him by March 1, 1936: *Provided further,* That the Secretary shall have authority to enter into additional option contracts for so much of such cotton as is not necessary to comply with the provisions of section 6, in combination with benefit payments as provided for in part 2 of this title.

Part 2 — Commodity Benefits

General Powers

Sec. 8. In order to effecuate[1] the declared policy, the Secretary of Agriculture shall have power —

(1) To provide for reduction in the acreage or reduction in the production for market, or both, of any basic agricultural commodity, through agreements with producers or by other voluntary methods, and to provide for rental or benefit payments in connection therewith or upon that part of the production of any basic agricultural commodity required for domestic consumption, in such amounts as the Secretary deems fair and reasonable, to be

---

[1] *So in original.*

paid out of any moneys available for such payments. Under regulations of the Secretary of Agriculture requiring adequate facilities for the storage of any non-perishable agricultural commodity on the farm, inspection and measurement of any such commodity so stored, and the locking and sealing thereof, and such other regulations as may be prescribed by the Secretary of Agriculture for the protection of such commodity and for the marketing thereof, a reasonable percentage of any benefit payment may be advanced on any such commodity so stored. In any such case, such deduction may be made from the amount of the benefit payment as the Secretary of Agriculture determines will reasonably compensate for the cost of inspection and sealing, but no deduction may be made for interest.

(2) To enter into marketing agreements with processors, associations of producers, and others engaged in the handling, in the current of interstate or foreign commerce of any agricultural commodity or product thereof, after due notice and opportunity for hearing to interested parties. The making of any such agreement shall not be held to be in violation of any of the antitrust laws of the United States, and any such agreement shall be deemed to be lawful: *Provided*, That no such agreement shall remain in force after the termination of this Act. For the purpose of carrying out any such agreement the parties thereto shall be eligible for loans from the Reconstruction Finance Corporation under section 5 of the Reconstruction Finance Corporation Act. Such loans shall not be in excess of such amounts as may be authorized by the agreements.

(3) To issue licenses permitting processors, associations of producers, and others to engage in the handling, in the current of interstate or foreign commerce, of any agricultural commodity or product thereof, or any competing commodity or product thereof. Such licenses shall be subject to such terms and conditions, not in conflict with existing Acts of Congress or regulations pursuant thereto, as may be necessary to eliminate unfair practices or charges that prevent or tend to prevent the effectuation of the declared policy and the restoration of normal economic conditions in the marketing of such commodities or products and the financing thereof. The Secretary of Agriculture may suspend or revoke any such license, after due notice and opportunity for hearing, for violations of the terms or conditions thereof. Any order of the Secretary suspending or revoking any such license shall be final if in accordance with law. Any such person engaged in such handling without a license as required by the Secretary under this section shall be subject to a fine of not more than $1,000 for each day during which the violation continues.

(4) To require any licensee under this section to furnish such reports as to quantities of agricultural commodities or products thereof bought and sold and the prices thereof, and as to trade practices and charges, and to keep such systems of accounts, as may be necessary for the purpose of part 2 of this title.

(5) No person engaged in the storage in a public warehouse of any basic agricultural commodity in the current of interestate or foreign commerce, shall deliver any such commodity upon which a warehouse receipt has been issued and is outstanding, without prior surrender and cancellation of such warehouse receipt. Any person violating any of the provisions of this subsection shall, upon conviction, be punished by a fine of not more than $5,000, or by imprisonment for not more than two years, or both. The Secretary of Agriculture may revoke any license issued under subsection (3) of this section, if he finds, after due notice and opportunity for hearing, that the licensee has violated the provisions of this subsection.

Processing Tax

Sec. 9. (a) To obtain revenue for extraordinary expenses incurred by reason of the national economic emergency, there shall be levied processing taxes as hereinafter provided. When the Secretary of Agriculture determines that rental or benefit payments are to be made with respect to any basic agricultural commodity, he shall proclaim such determination, and a processing tax shall be in effect with respect to such commodity from the beginning of the marketing year therefor next following the date of such proclamation. The processing tax shall be levied, assessed, and collected upon the first domestic processing of the commodity, whether of domestic production or imported, and shall be paid by the processor. The rate of tax shall conform to the requirements of subsection (b). Such rate shall be determined by the Secretary of Agriculture as of the date the tax first takes effect, and the rate so determined shall, at such intervals as the Secretary finds necessary to effectuate the declared policy, be adjusted by him to conform to such requirements. The processing tax shall terminate at the end of the marketing year current at the time the Secretary proclaims that rental or benefit payments are to be discontinued with respect to such commodity. The marketing year for each commodity shall be ascertained and prescribed by regulations of the Secretary of Agriculture: *Provided,* That upon any article upon which a manufacturers' sales tax is levied under the authority of the Revenue Act of 1932 and which manufacturers' sales tax is computed on the basis of weight, such manufacturers' sales tax shall be computed on the basis of the weight of said finished article less the weight of the processed cotton contained therein on which a processing tax has been paid.

(b) The processing tax shall be at such rate as equals the difference between the current average farm price for the commodity and the fair exchange value of the commodity; except that if the Secretary has reason to believe that the tax at such rate will cause such reduction in the quantity of the commodity or products thereof domestically consumed as to result in the accumulation of surplus stocks of the commodity or products thereof or in the depression of the farm price of the commodity, then he shall cause an appropriate investigation to be made and afford due notice and opportunity for hearing to interested parties. If thereupon the Secretary finds that such result will occur, then the processing tax shall be at such rate as will prevent such accumulation of surplus stocks and depression of the farm price of the commodity. In computing the current average farm price in the case of wheat, premiums paid producers for protein content shall not be taken into account.

(c) For the purposes of part 2 of this title, the fair exchange value of a commodity shall be the price therefor that will give the commodity the same purchasing power, with respect to articles farmers buy, as such commodity had during the base period specified in section 2; and the current average farm price and the fair exchange value shall be ascertained by the Secretary of Agriculture from available statistics of the Department of Agriculture.

(d) As used in part 2 of this title —

(1) In case of wheat, rice, and corn, the term "processing" means the milling or other processing (except cleaning and drying) of wheat, rice, or corn for market, including custom milling for toll as well as commercial milling, but shall not include the grinding or cracking thereof not in the form of flour for feed purposes only.

(2) In case of cotton, the term "processing" means the spinning, manufacturing, or other processing (except ginning) of cotton; and the term "cotton" shall not include cotton linters.

(3) In case of tobacco, the term "processing" means the manufacturing or other processing (except drying or converting into insecticides and fertilizers) of tobacco.

(4) In case of hogs, the term "processing" means the slaughter of hogs for market.

(5) In the case of any other commodity, the term "processing" means any manufacturing or other processing involving a change in the form of the commodity or its preparation for market, as defined by regulations of the Secretary of Agriculture; and in prescribing such regulations the Secretary shall give due weight to the customs of the industry.

(e) When any processing tax, or increase or decrease therein, takes effect in respect of a commodity the Secretary of Agriculture, in order to prevent pyramiding of the processing tax and profiteering in the sale of the products derived from the commodity, shall make public such information as he deems necessary regarding (1) the relationship between the processing tax and the price paid to producers of the commodity, (2) the effect of the processing tax upon prices to consumers of products of the commodity, (3) the relationship, in previous periods, between prices paid to the producers of the commodity and prices to consumers of the products thereof, and (4) the situation in foreign countries relating to prices paid to producers of the commodity and prices to consumers of the products thereof.

Miscellaneous

Sec. 10. (a) The Secretary of Agriculture may appoint such officers and employees, subject to the provisions of the Classification Act of 1923 and Acts amendatory thereof, and such experts as are necessary to execute the functions vested in him by this title; and the Secretary may make such appointments without regard to the civil service laws or regulations: *Provided,* That no salary in excess of $10,000 per annum shall be paid to any officer, employee, or expert of the Agricultural Adjustment Administration, which the Secretary shall establish in the Department of Agriculture for the administration of the functions vested in him by this title. Title II of the Act entitled "An Act to maintain the credit of the United States Government," approved March 20, 1933, to the extent that it provides for the impoundment of appropriations on account of reductions in compensation, shall not operate to require such impoundment under appropriations contained in this Act.

(b) The Secretary of Agriculture is authorized to establish, for the more effective administration of the functions vested in him by this title, State and local committees, or associations of producers, and to permit cooperative associations of producers, when in his judgment they are qualified to do so, to act as agents of their members and patrons in connection with the distribution of rental or benefit payments.

(c) The Secretary of Agriculture is authorized, with the approval of the President, to make such regulations with the force and effect of law as may be necessary to carry out the powers vested in him by this title, including regulations establishing conversion factors for any commodity and article processed therefrom to determine the amount of tax imposed or refunds to be made with respect thereto. Any violation of any regulation shall be subject to such penalty, not in excess of $100, as may be provided therein.

(d) The Secretary of the Treasury is authorized to make such regulations as may be necessary to carry out the powers vested in him by this title.

(e) The action of any officer, employee, or agent in determining the amount of and in making any rental or benefit payment shall not be subject to review by any officer of the Government other than the Secretary of Agriculture or Secretary of the Treasury.

(f) The provisions of this title shall be applicable to the United States and its possessions, except the Philippine Islands, the Virgin Islands, American Samoa, the Canal Zone, and the island of Guam.

(g) No person shall, while acting in any official capacity in the administration of this title, speculate, directly or indirectly, in any agricultural commodity or product thereof, to which this title applies, or in contracts relating thereto, or in the stock or membership interests of any association or corporation engaged in handling, processing, or disposing of any such commodity or product. Any person violating this subsection shall upon conviction thereof be fined not more than $10,000 or imprisoned not more than two years, or both.

(h) For the efficient administration of the provisions of part 2 of this title, the provisions, including penalties, of sections 8, 9, and 10 of the Federal Trade Commission Act, approved September 26, 1914, are made applicable to the jurisdiction, powers, and duties of the Secretary in administering the provisions of this title and to any person subject to the provisions of this title, whether or not a corporation. Hearings authorized or required under this title shall be conducted by the Secretary of Agriculture or such officer or employee of the Department as he may designate for the purpose. The Secretary may report any violation of any agreement entered into under part 2 of this title to the Attorney General of the United States, who shall cause appropriate proceedings to enforce such agreement to be commenced and prosecuted in the proper courts of the United States without delay.

Commodities

Sec. 11. As used in this title, the term "basic agricultural commodity" means wheat, cotton, field corn, hogs, rice, tobacco, and milk and its products, and any regional or market classification, type, or grade thereof; but the Secretary of Agriculture shall exclude from the operation of the provisions of this title, during any period, any such commodity or classification, type, or grade thereof if he finds, upon investigation at any time and after due notice and opportunity for hearing to interested parties, that the conditions of production, marketing, and consumption are such that during such period this title can not be effectively administered to the end of effectuating the declared policy with respect to such commodity or classification, type, or grade thereof.

Appropriation

Sec. 12. (a) There is hereby appropriated, out of any money in the Treasury not otherwise appropriated, the sum of $100,000,000 to be available to the Secretary of Agriculture for administrative expenses under this title and for rental and benefit payments made with respect to reduction in acreage or reduction in production for market under part 2 of this title. Such sum shall remain available until expended.

(b) In addition to the foregoing, the proceeds derived from all taxes imposed under this title are hereby appropriated to be available to the Secretary of Agriculture for expansion of markets and removal of surplus agricultural products and the following purposes under part 2 of this title: Administrative expenses, rental and benefit payments, and refunds on taxes. The Secretary of Agriculture and the Secretary of the Treasury shall jointly estimate from time to time the amounts, in addition to any money available under subsection (a), currently required for such purposes; and the Secretary of the

Treasury shall, out of any money in the Treasury not otherwise appropriated, advance to the Secretary of Agriculture the amounts so estimated. The amount of any such advance shall be deducted from such tax proceeds as shall subsequently become available under this subsection.

(c) The administrative expenses provided for under this section shall include, among others, expenditures for personal services and rent in the District of Columbia and elsewhere, for law books and books of reference, for contract stenographic reporting services, and for printing and paper in addition to allotments under the existing law. The Secretary of Agriculture shall transfer to the Treasury Department, and is authorized to transfer to other agencies, out of funds available for administrative expenses under this title, such sums as are required to pay administrative expenses incurred and refunds made by such department or agencies in the administration of this title.

Termination of Act

Sec. 13. This title shall cease to be in effect whenever the President finds and proclaims that the national economic emergency in relation to agriculture has been ended; and pending such time the President shall by proclamation terminate with respect to any basic agricultural commodity such provisions of this title as he finds are not requisite to carrying out the declared policy with respect to such commodity. The Secretary of Agriculture shall make such investigations and reports thereon to the President as may be necessary to aid him in executing this section.

Separability of Provisions

Sec. 14. If any provision of this title is declared unconstitutional, or the applicability thereof to any person, circumstance, or commodity is held invalid the validity of the remainder of this title and the applicability thereof to other persons, circumstances, or commodities shall not be affected thereby.

Supplementary Revenue Provisions, Exemptions and Compensating Taxes

Sec. 15. (a) If the Secretary of Agriculture finds, upon investigation at any time and after due notice and opportunity for hearing to interested parties, that any class of products of any commodity is of such low value compared with the quantity of the commodity used for their manufacture that the imposition of the processing tax would prevent in whole or in large part the use of the commodity in the manufacture of such products and thereby substantially reduce consumption and increase the surplus of the commodity, then the Secretary of Agriculture shall so certify to the Secretary of the Treasury, and the Secretary of the Treasury shall abate or refund any processing tax assessed or paid after the date of such certification with respect to such amount of the commodity as is used in the manufacture of such products.

(b) No tax shall be required to be paid on the processing of any commodity by or for the producer thereof for consumption by his own family, employees, or household; and the Secretary of Agriculture is authorized, by regulations, to exempt from the payment of the processing tax the processing of commodities by or for the producer thereof for sale by him where, in the judgment of the Secretary, the imposition of a processing tax with respect thereto is unnecessary to effectuate the declared policy.

(c) Any person delivering any product to any organization for charitable distribution or use shall, if such product or the commodity from which processed, is under this title subject to tax, be entitled to a refund of the amount of any tax paid under this title with respect to such product so delivered.

(d) The Secretary of Agriculture shall ascertain from time to time whether the payment of the processing tax upon any basic agricultural commodity is causing or will cause to the processors thereof disadvantages in competition from competing commodities by reason of excessive shifts in consumption between such commodities or products thereof. If the Secretary of Agriculture finds, after investigation and due notice and opportunity for hearing to interested parties, that such disadvantages in competition exist, or will exist, he shall proclaim such finding. The Secretary shall specify in this proclamation the competing commodity and the compensating rate of tax on the processing thereof necessary to prevent such disadvantages in competition. Thereafter there shall be levied, assessed, and collected upon the first domestic processing of such competing commodity a tax, to be paid by the processor, at the rate specified, until such rate is altered pursuant to a further finding under this section, or the tax or rate thereof on the basic agricultural commodity is altered or terminated. In no case shall the tax imposed upon such competing commodity exceed that imposed per equivalent unit, as determined by the Secretary, upon the basic agricultural commodity.

(e) During any period for which a processing tax is in effect with respect to any commodity there shall be levied, assessed, collected, and paid upon any article processed or manufactured wholly or in chief value from such commodity and imported into the United States or any possession thereof to which this title applies, from any foreign country or from any possession of the United States to which this title does not apply, a compensating tax equal to the amount of the processing tax in effect with respect to domestic processing at the time of importation: *Provided,* That all taxes collected under this subsection upon articles coming from the possessions of the United States to which this title does not apply shall not be covered into the general fund of the Treasury of the United States but shall be held as a separate fund and paid into the Treasury of the said possessions, respectively, to be used and expended by the governments thereof for the benefit of agriculture. Such tax shall be paid prior to the release of the article from customs custody or control.

Floor Stocks

Sec. 16. (a) Upon the sale or other disposition of any article processed wholly or in chief value from any commodity with respect to which a processing tax is to be levied, that on the date the tax first takes effect or wholly terminates with respect to the commodity, is held for sale or other disposition (including articles in transit) by any person, there shall be made a tax adjustment as follows:

(1) Whenever the processing tax first takes effect, there shall be levied, assessed, and collected a tax to be paid by such person equivalent to the amount of the processing tax which would be payable with respect to the commodity from which processed if the processing had occurred on such date.

(2) Whenever the processing tax is wholly terminated, there shall be refunded to such person a sum (or if it has not been paid, the tax shall be abated) in an amount equivalent to the processing tax with respect to the commodity from which processed.

(b) The tax imposed by subsection (a) shall not apply to the retail stocks of persons engaged in retail trade, held at the date the processing tax first takes effect; but such retail stocks shall not be deemed to include stocks held in a warehouse on such date, or such portion of other stocks held on such date as are not sold or otherwise disposed of within thirty days thereafter. The tax refund or abatement provided in subsection (a) shall not apply to the retail stocks of persons engaged in retail trade, held on the date the processing tax is wholly terminated.

Exportations

Sec. 17. (a) Upon the exportation to any foreign country (including the Philippine Islands, the Virgin Islands, American Samoa, and the island of Guam) of any product with respect to which a tax has been paid under this title, or of any product processed wholly or in chief value from a commodity with respect to which a tax has been paid under this title the exporter thereof shall be entitled at the time of exportation to a refund of the amount of such tax.

(b) Upon the giving of bond satisfactory to the Secretary of the Treasury for the faithful observance of the provisions of this title requiring the payment of taxes, any person shall be entitled, without payment of the tax, to process for such exportation any commodity with respect to which a tax is imposed by this title, or to hold for such exportation any article processed wholly or in chief value therefrom.

Existing Contracts

Sec. 18. (a) If (1) any processor, jobber, or wholesaler has, prior to the date a tax with respect to any commodity is first imposed under this title, made a bona fide contract of sale for delivery on or after such date, of any article processed wholly or in chief value from such commodity, and if (2) such contract does not permit the addition to the amount to be paid thereunder of the whole of such tax, then (unless the contract prohibits such addition) the vendee shall pay so much of the tax as is not permitted to be added to the contract price.

(b) Taxes payable by the vendee shall be paid to the vendor at the time the sale is consummated and shall be collected and paid to the United States by the vendor in the same manner as other taxes under this title. In case of failure or refusal by the vendee to pay such taxes to the vendor, the vendor shall report the facts to the Commissioner of Internal Revenue who shall cause collections of such taxes to be made from the vendee.

Collection of Taxes

Sec. 19. (a) The taxes provided in this title shall be collected by the Bureau of Internal Revenue under the direction of the Secretary of the Treasury. Such taxes shall be paid into the Treasury of the United States.

(b) All provisions of law, including penalties, applicable with respect to the taxes imposed by section 600 of the Revenue Act of 1926, and the provisions of section 626 of the Revenue Act of 1932, shall, in so far as applicable and not inconsistent with the provisions of this title, be applicable in respect of taxes imposed by this title: *Provided,* That the Secretary of the Treasury is authorized to permit postponement, for a period not exceeding ninety days, of the payment of taxes covered by any return under this title.

(c) In order that the payment of taxes under this title may not impose any immediate undue financial burden upon processors or distributors, any processor or distributor subject to such taxes shall be eligible for loans from the Reconstruction Finance Corporation under section 5 of the Reconstruction Finance Corporation Act.

Title II — Agricultural Credits

Part 1 — Amendments to Federal Farm Loan Act
Issuance of Bonds by Land Banks

Section 21. Section 32 of the Federal Farm Loan Act, as amended (U.S.C., title 12, sec. 991), is amended by adding at the end thereof the following new paragraph:

"Until such time as the Farm Loan Commissioner determines that Federal farm-loan bonds (other than those issued under this paragraph) are readily salable in the open market at a yield not in excess of 4 per centum per annum, but in no case more than two years after this paragraph takes effect, Federal land banks may issue farm-loan bonds as authorized under this Act, for the purpose of making new loans, or for purchasing mortgages or exchanging bonds for mortgages as provided in paragraph 'Second' of section 13 of this Act. The aggregate amount of the bonds issued under this paragraph shall not exceed $2,000,000,000, and such bonds shall be issued in such demoninations as the Farm Loan Commissioner shall prescribe, shall bear interest at a rate not in excess of 4 per centum per annum, and shall be fully and unconditionally guaranteed as to interest by the United States, and such guaranty shall be expressed on the face thereof. In the event that it shall appear to the Farm Loan Commissioner that the issuing bank or banks will be unable to pay upon demand, when due, the interest on any such bonds, the Secretary of the Treasury shall, upon the request of the Commissioner, pay the amount thereof, which is hereby authorized to be appropriated out of any money in the Treasury not otherwise appropriated. Upon the payment of such interest by the Secretary of the Treasury the amount so paid shall become an obligation to the United States of the issuing bank or banks and shall bear interest at the same rate as that borne by the bonds upon which the interest has been so paid. After the expiration of one year from the date this paragraph takes effect, if in the opinion of the Farm Loan Commissioner any part of the proceeds of the bonds authorized to be issued under this paragraph is not required for the purpose of making new loans or for purchasing mortgages or exchanging bonds for mortgages as herein provided, such bonds may be issued within the maximum limit herein specified for the purpose of refinancing any outstanding issues of Federal farm-loan bonds; but no such bonds shall be issued after two years from the date this paragraph takes effect for the purpose of such refinancing. Any borrower who obtains a loan from a Federal land bank after the date this paragraph takes effect may, at any time after the expiration of five years from the date such loan was made, tender to such bank on any regular installment date, bonds issued under this paragraph in an amount not to exceed the unpaid principal of his loan, and the bonds so tendered shall be accepted by the bank at par in payment of any part of such unpaid principal."

Purchase, Reduction, and Refinancing of Farm Mortgages

Sec. 22. Paragraph "Second" of section 13 of the Federal Farm Loan Act, as amended, is amended by adding at the end thereof the following new sentence:

"In order to reduce and/or refinance farm mortgages, to invest such funds as may be in its possession in the purchase of first mortgages on farm lands situated within the Federal land-bank district within which it is organized or for which it is acting, or to exchange farm-loan bonds for any duly recorded first mortgages on farm lands executed prior to the date this paragraph, as amended, takes effect, at a price which shall not exceed in each individual case the amount of the unpaid principal of the mortgage on the date of such purchase or exchange, or 50 per centum of the normal value of the land mortgaged and 20 per centum of the value of the permanent insured improvements thereon as determined upon an appraisal made pursuant to this Act, whichever is the smaller: *Provided,* That any mortgagor whose mortgage is acquired by a Federal land bank under this paragraph shall be entitled to have his farm-mortgage indebtedness refinanced in accordance with the provisions of sections 7 and 8 of this Act on the basis of the amount paid by the bank for his mortgage."

Extension of Loans

Sec. 23. Paragraph "Tenth" of section 13 of the Federal Farm Loan Act, as amended (U.S.C., title 12, sec. 781), is amended by adding at the end thereof the following: "The terms of any such extension shall be such as will not defer the collection of any obligation due by any borrower which, after investigation by the bank of the situation of such borrower, is shown to be within his capacity to meet. In the case of any such extension made prior to the expiration of five years from the date this paragraph as amended takes effect, or in the case of any deferment of principal as provided in paragraph 'Twelfth' of section 12 of this Act, it shall be the duty of the Secretary of the Treasury, on behalf of the United States, upon the request of the Federal land bank making the extension, and with the approval of the Farm Loan Commissioner, to subscribe at such periods as the Commissioner shall determine, to the paid-in surplus of such bank an amount equal to the amount of all such extensions and deferments made by the bank during the preceding period. Such subscriptions shall be subject to call, in whole or in part, by the bank with the approval of the Commissioner upon thirty days' notice. To enable the Secretary of the Treasury to make such subscriptions to the paid-in surplus of the Federal land banks, there is hereby authorized to be appropriated the sum of $50,000,000, to be immediately available and remain available until expended. Upon payment to any Federal land bank of the amount of any such subscription, such bank shall execute and deliver a receipt therefor to the Secretary of the Treasury in form to be prescribed by the Farm Loan Commissioner. The amount of any subscriptions to the paid-in surplus of any such bank may be repaid in whole or in part at any time in the discretion of the bank and with the approval of the Farm Loan Commissioner, and the Commissioner may at any time require such subscriptions to be repaid in whole or in part if in his opinion the bank has resources available therefor."

Reduction of Interest on Loans and Deferment of Principal

Sec. 24. Section 12 of the Federal Farm Loan Act, as amended (U.S.C., title 12, secs. 771-772), is amended by adding at the end thereof the following new paragraph:

"Twelfth. Notwithstanding the provisions of paragraph 'Second', the rate of interest on any loans on mortgage made through national farm-loan associations or through agents as provided in section 15, or purchased from joint-stock land banks, by any Federal land bank, outstanding on the date this paragraph takes effect or made through national farm-loan associations within two years after such date, shall not exceed 4½ per centum per annum for all interest payable on installment dates occurring within a period of five years commencing sixty days after the date this paragraph takes effect; and no payment of the principal portion of any installment of any such loan shall be required during such five-year period if the borrower shall not be in default with respect to any other condition or covenant of his mortgage. The foregoing provisions shall apply to loans made by Federal land banks through branches, except that the rate of interest on such loans for such five-year period shall be 5 per centum in lieu of 4½ per centum. The Secretary of the Treasury shall pay each Federal land bank, as soon as practicable after October 1, 1933, and after the end of each quarter thereafter, such amount as the Farm Loan Commissioner certifies to the Secretary of the Treasury is equal to the amount by which interest payments on mortgages held by such bank have been reduced, during the preceding quarter, by reason of this paragraph; but in any case in which the Farm Loan Commissioner finds that the amount of interest payable by such bank during any quarter has been reduced by reason of the refinancing of bonds under section 32 of this Act, the amount of the reduction so found shall be deducted from the amount payable to such bank under this paragraph. No payments shall be made to a bank with respect to any period after June 30, 1938. There is authorized to be appropriated, out of any money in the Treasury not otherwise appropriated, the sum of $15,000,000 for the purpose of enabling the Secretary of the Treasury to make payments to Federal land banks which accrue during the fiscal year ending June 30, 1934, and such additional amounts as may be necessary to make payments accruing during subsequent fiscal years."

Increase of Amount of Loans to Borrowers

Sec. 25. Paragraph "Seventh" of section 12 of the Federal Farm Loan Act, as amended (U.S.C., title 12, sec. 771) (relating to the limitations as to amount of loans), is amended by striking out "$25,000" and inserting "$50,000, but loans to any one borrower shall not exceed $25,000 unless approved by the Farm Loan Commissioner."

Direct Loans

Sec. 26. Section 7 of the Federal Farm Loan Act, as amended, is amended by striking out the last paragraph and inserting in lieu thereof the following new paragraphs:

"Whenever it shall appear to the Farm Loan Commissioner that national farm-loan associations have not been formed in any locality in the continental United States, or that the farmers residing in the territory covered by the charter of a national farm-loan association are unable to apply to the Federal land bank of the district for loans on account of the inability of the bank to accept applications from such association, the Farm Loan Commissioner shall authorize said bank to make direct loans to borrowers secured by first mortgages on farm lands situated within any such locality or territory. Except as herein otherwise specifically provided, all provisions of this Act applicable with respect to loans made through national farm-loan associations shall, insofar as practicable, apply with respect to such direct loans, and the Farm Loan Commissioner is authorized to make such rules and regulations as he may deem necessary with respect to such direct loans.

"The rate of interest on such direct loans made at any time by any Federal land bank shall be one-half of 1 per centum per annum in excess of the rate of interest charged to borrowers on mortgage loans made at such time by the bank through national farm-loan associations.

"Each borrower who obtains a direct loan from a Federal land bank shall subscribe and pay for stock in such bank in the sum of $5 for each $100 or fraction thereof borrowed. Such stock shall be held by such Federal land bank as collateral security for the loan of the borrower and shall participate in all dividends. Upon full payment of the loan such stock shall, if still outstanding, be canceled at par, or, in the event that such stock shall have become impaired, at the estimated value thereof as approved by the Farm Loan Commissioner, and the proceeds thereof shall be paid to the borrower.

"Each such borrower may covenant in his mortgage that, whenever there are ten or more borrowers who have obtained from a Federal land bank direct loans under the provisions of this section aggregating not less than $20,000, and who reside in a locality which may, in the opinion of the Farm Loan Commissioner, be conveniently covered by the charter of and served by a national farm-loan association, he will unite with such other borrowers to form a national farm-loan association. Such borrowers shall organize the association subject to the requirements and the conditions specified in this section, so far as the same may be applicable, and in accordance with rules and regulations of the Farm Loan Commissioner. As soon as the organization of the association has been approved by the Farm Loan Commissioner, the stock in the Federal land banks held by each of the members of such association shall be canceled at par, and in lieu thereof the bank shall issue in the name of the association an equal amount of stock in said bank, which stock shall be held by said bank as collateral security as provided in this section with respect to other loans through national farm-loan associations. Thereupon there shall be issued to each such member an amount of capital stock in the association equal to the amount which he previously held in said bank, which stock shall be held by said association as collateral security as provided in section 8 of this Act. The board of directors of said association shall adopt a resolution authorizing and directing its secretary-treasurer on behalf of said association to endorse, and thereby become liable for the payment of, the mortgages taken from its charter members by the Federal land bank. When it shall appear to the satisfaction of the Farm Loan Commissioner that all the foregoing conditions have been complied with, and upon the granting of the charter by the Farm Loan Commissioner, the interest rate paid by each charter member of such association whose loan is in good standing shall, beginning with his next regular installment date, be reduced to the rate of interest paid by borrowers on new loans made through national farm-loan associations in the same Federal land-bank district at the time the said loan was made to such charter member.

"Charges to be paid by applicants for direct loans from a Federal land bank shall not exceed amounts to be fixed by the Farm Loan Commissioner and shall in no case exceed the charges which may be made to applicants for loans and borrowers through national farm-loan associations under the provisions of sections 11 and 13 of this Act."

Loans to Receivers

Sec. 27. Any receiver appointed by the Federal Farm Loan Board pursuant to section 29 of the Federal Farm Loan Act, as amended, or any receiver appointed by a district court of the United States, is authorized, for the purpose of paying taxes on farm real estate owned by the bank or securing the mortgages held by it, with the approval of the Farm Loan Commissioner, to borrow from the Reconstruction Finance Corporation and to issue receiver's certificates against the assets of such bank as security for any loan received from the Corporation under this section, and such certificates shall constitute a prior lien on such assets. The Reconstruction Finance Corporation is authorized to make loans to such receivers for the purposes of this section.

Federal Farm-Loan Bonds as Security for Advances by Federal Reserve Banks

Sec. 28. The eighth paragraph of section 13 of the Federal Reserve Act, as amended, is amended by inserting before the period at the end thereof a comma and the following: "or by the deposit or pledge of bonds issued pursuant to the paragraph added to section 32 of the Federal Farm Loan Act, as amended by section 21 of the Emergency Farm Mortgage Act of 1933."

Part 2 — Joint-Stock Land Banks

Limitations on Issue of Bonds and Lending

Sec. 29. After the date of enactment of this Act, no joint-stock land bank shall issue any tax-exempt bonds or make any farm loans except such as are necessary and incidental to the refinancing of existing loans or bond issues or to the sale of any real estate now owned or hereafter acquired by such bank.

Loans to Joint-Stock Land Banks to Provide for Orderly Liquidation

Sec. 30. (a) The Reconstruction Finance Corporation is authorized and directed to make available to the Farm Loan Commissioner, out of the funds of the Corporation, the sum of $100,000,000, to be used, for a period not exceeding two years from the date of enactment of this Act, for the purpose of making loans to the joint-stock land banks organized and doing business under the Federal Farm Loan Act, as amended, at a rate of interest not to exceed 4 per centum per annum, payable annually. Such loans shall be made upon application therefor by such banks and upon compliance with the requirements of this section. The amount which may be loaned hereunder to any such bank shall not exceed an amount having the same proportion to the said $100,000,000 as the unpaid principal of the mortgages held by such bank on the date of enactment of this Act bears to the total amount of the unpaid principal of the mortgages held by all the joint-stock land banks on such date.

(b) Any joint-stock land bank applying for a loan under this section shall deliver to the Farm Loan Commissioner as collateral security therefor first mortgages or purchase-money mortgages on farm lands, first mortgages on farm real estate owned by the bank in fee simple, or such other collateral as may be available to said bank, including sales contracts and sheriff's certificates on farm lands. The real estate upon which such collateral is based shall be appraised by appraisers appointed under the Federal Farm Loan Act, as amended, and the borrowing bank shall be entitled to borrow not to exceed 60 per centum of the normal value of such real estate as determined by such appraisal. Fees for such appraisals shall be paid by the applicant banks in such amounts as may be fixed by the Farm Loan Commissioner. No such loan shall be made until the applicant bank, under regulations to be prescribed by the Farm Loan Commissioner, (1) shall have agreed to grant to each borrower then indebted to the bank under the terms of a first mortgage a reduction to 5 per centum per annum in the rate of interest specified in such mortgage, beginning at his next regular installment date occurring more than sixty days after the date of enactment of this Act, and (2) shall have agreed to the satisfaction of the Commissioner that during a period of two years from the date of enactment of this Act the bank will not proceed against the mortgagor on account of default in the payment of interest or principal due under the terms of its mortgage and will not foreclose its mortgage unless the property covered by such mortgage is abandoned by the mortgagor or unless, in the opinion of the Commissioner, such foreclosure is necessary for other reasons. Such loans shall be made to aid the orderly liquidation of any such bank in accordance with such plan as may be approved by the Farm Loan Commissioner. Before any such plan is approved by the Commissioner he shall be satisfied that the plan carries out the purposes of this section and that such part of the proceeds of the loan as is devoted to settlements with bondholders will be used only to effect an equitable settlement with all bondholders. After the plan has been approved by the Commissioner he shall require the bank to mail a copy thereof to all its known bondholders and to publish a notice setting forth its provisions in at least three newspapers having general circulation.

Loans by the Farm Loan Commissioner to Joint-Stock Land Banks for Emergency Purposes

Sec. 31. (a) Out of the funds made available to him under section 30, the Farm Loan Commissioner is authorized to make loans, in an aggregate amount not exceeding $25,000,000, at a rate of interest not to exceed 4 percentum per annum, to any joint-stock land bank for the purpose of securing the postponement for two years from the date of the enactment of this Act of the foreclosure of first mortgages held by such banks on account of (1) default in the payment of interest and principal due under the terms of the mortgage, and (2) unpaid delinquent taxes, excluding interest and penalties, which may be secured by the lien of said mortgage: *Provided,* That during the period of postponement of foreclosure such bank shall charge the mortgagor interest at a rate not exceeding 4 per centum per annum on the aggregate amount of such delinquent taxes and defaulted interest and principal with respect to which loans are made pursuant to this section. The amount loaned to any joint-stock land bank under this section shall be made without reappraisal: *Provided,* That the amount loaned with respect to any mortgage on account of unpaid principal shall not exceed 5 per centum of the total unpaid principal of such mortgage, and the total amount loaned to any such land bank with respect to any mortgage shall not exceed 25 per centum of the total unpaid principal of such mortgage.

(b) No such loan shall be made with respect to any mortgage unless the Farm Loan Commissioner is satisfied that the mortgagor, after exercising ordinary diligence to pay his accrued delinquent taxes, and meet accrued interest and principal payments, has defaulted thereon; and unless the bank shall have agreed to the satisfaction of the Farm Loan Commissioner that during such two-year period the bank will not foreclose such mortgage unless the property covered thereby is abandoned by the mortgagor or unless in the opinion of the Farm Loan Commissioner such foreclosure is necessary for other reasons.

(c) Each such loan shall be secured by an assignment to the Farm Loan Commissioner of the lien of the taxes and/or of the bank's mortgage with respect to which the loan is made: *Provided,* That the part of each such lien so assigned representing the interest and principal due and unpaid in any such mortgage which has been assigned to the farm loan registrar shall be subordinate to the existing lien of the bank for the balance of the indebtedness then or thereafter to become due under the terms of such mortgage; but the Farm Loan Commissioner may require the bank to furnish additional collateral as security for such loan, if such collateral is available to the bank.

(d) The Farm Loan Commissioner is authorized to make such rules and regulations as may be necessary to carry out the purposes of this section and to make the relief contemplated immediately available.

Part 3 — Loans to Farmers by Farm Loan Commissioner

Reduction of Debts and Redemption of Foreclosed Farms

Sec. 32. The Reconstruction Finance Corporation is authorized and directed to allocate and make available to the Farm Loan Commissioner the sum of $200,000,000, or so much thereof as may be necessary, to be used for the purpose of making loans as hereinafter provided to any farmer, secured by a first or second mortgage upon the whole or any part of the farm property, real or personal, including crops, of the farmer. The amount of the mortgage given by any farmer, together with all prior mortgages or other evidences of indebtedness secured by such farm property of the farmer, shall not exceed 75 per centum of the normal value thereof, as determined upon an appraisal made pursuant to the Federal Farm Loan Act, as amended; nor shall a loan in excess of $5,000, be made to any one farmer. Every mortgage made under this section shall contain an agreement providing for the repayment of the loan on an amortization plan by means of a fixed number of annual or semiannual installments, sufficient to cover (1) interest on unpaid principal at a rate not to exceed 5 per centum per annum and (2) such payments equal in amount to be applied on principal as will extinguish the debt within an agreed period of not more than ten years or, in the case of a first or second mortgage secured wholly by real property and made for the purpose of reducing and refinancing an existing mortgage within an agreed period no greater than that for which loans may be made under the Federal Farm Loan Act, as amended, from the date the first payment on principal is due: *Provided,* That during the first three years the loan is in effect payments of interest only may be required if the borrower shall not be in default with respect to any other condition or covenant of his mortgage. No loan shall be made under this section unless the holder of any prior mortgage or instrument of indebtedness secured by such farm property arranges to the satisfaction of the Farm Loan Commissioner to limit his right to proceed against the farmer and such farm property for default in payment of principal. Loans under this section shall be made for the following purposes only: (1) Refinancing, either in connection with proceedings under chapter VIII of the Bankruptcy Act of July 1, 1898, as amended (relating to agricultural compositions and extensions), or otherwise, any indebtedness, secured or unsecured, of the farmer, (2) providing working capital for his farm operations, and (3) enabling any farmer to redeem and/or repurchase farm property owned by him prior to foreclosure which has been foreclosed at any time between July 1, 1931, and the date of the enactment of this Act, or which is foreclosed after the enactment of this Act. The provisions of paragraph "Ninth" of section 13 of the Federal Farm Loan Act, as amended (relating to charges to applicants for loans and borrowers from the Federal land banks), shall, so far as practicable, apply to loans made under this section. As used in this section, the term "farmer" means any individual who is bona fide engaged in farming operations, either personally or through an agent or tenant, or the principal part of whose income is derived from farming operations, and includes a personal representative of a deceased farmer.

Regulations

Sec. 33. The Farm Loan Commissioner is authorized to make such rules and regulations, and to appoint, employ, and fix the composition of such officers, employees, attorneys, and agents as may be necessary to carry out the purposes of this title and to make the relief contemplated by this title immediately available, without regard to the provisions of other laws applicable to the employment and compensation of officers and employees of the United States: *Provided,* That no salary or compensation in excess of $10,000 shall be paid to any person employed under the terms of the foregoing section.

Facilities of Federal Land Banks and National Farm Loan Associations Made Available

Sec. 34. The Federal land banks and national farm loan associations are authorized, upon request of the Farm Loan Commissioner, to make available to him their services and facilities to aid in administering the provisions of this title.

Penalties

Sec. 35. Any person who shall knowingly make any material false representation for the purpose of obtaining any loan under part 3 of this title, or in assisting in obtaining any such loan, shall, upon conviction thereof, be fined not more than $1,000, or imprisoned not more than six months, or both.

Part 4 — Refinancing of Agricultural Improvement District

Indebtedness for the Benefit of Farmers Loans by Reconstruction Finance Corporation

Sec. 36. The Reconstruction Finance Corporation is authorized and empowered to make loans as hereinafter provided, in an aggregate amount not exceeding $50,000,000; to drainage districts, levee districts, levee and drainage districts, irrigation districts, and similar districts, duly organized under the laws of any State, and to political subdivisions of States, which prior to the date of enactment of this Act, have completed projects devoted chiefly to the improvement of lands for agricultural purposes. Such loans shall be made for the purpose of enabling any such district or political subdivision (hereafter referred to as the "borrower") to reduce and refinance its outstanding indebtedness incurred in connection with any such project, and shall be subject to the same terms and conditions as loans made under section 5 of the Reconstruction Finance Corporation Act, as amended; except that (1) the term of any such loan shall not exceed forty years; (2) each such loan shall be secured by refunding bonds issued to the Corporation by the borrower which are a lien on the real property within the project or on the amount of the assessments levied on such property by the borrower pursuant to State law, or by such other collateral as may be acceptable to the Corporation; (3) the borrower shall agree not to issue during the term of the loan any bonds so secured except with the consent of the Corporation; (4) the borrower shall pay to the Corporation, until all bonds of the borrower held by the Corporation are retired, an amount equal to the amount by which the assessments against the real property within the project collected by the borrower exceed the costs of operation and maintenance of the project and interest on its outstanding obligations; and (5) the borrower shall agree, to the satisfaction of the Corporation, to reduce the outstanding indebtedness to the borrower of the landowners within such project by an amount corresponding to that by which the indebtedness of the borrower is reduced by reason of the operation of this section, to distribute the amount of such reduction among such landowners on a pro rata basis, to cancel and retire its outstanding bonds in an aggregate amount equal to the amount of the reduction so distributed, and to permit the Corporation, in the case of the payment of the bonds of the borrower or the liquidation of such project, to participate in such payment or in the proceeds of such liquidation on the basis of the face amount of the bonds so retired plus the face amount of the bonds held by the Corporation as security for the loan. No loan shall be made under this section until the Reconstruction Finance Corporation (A) has caused an appraisal to be made of the property securing and/or underlying the outstanding bonds of the applicant, (B) has determined that the project of the applicant is economically sound, and (C) has been satisfied that an agreement has been entered into between the applicant and the holders of its outstanding bonds under which the applicant will be able to purchase or refund such bonds at a price determined by the Corporation to be reasonable after taking into consideration the average market price of such bonds over the six months' period ending March 1, 1933, and under which a substantial reduction will be brought about in the amount of the outstanding indebtedness of the applicant.

Sec. 37. The Reconstruction Finance Corporation, upon request of the Secretary of the Interior, is authorized and empowered to advance from funds made available by section 2 of the Act of January 22, 1932 (47 Stat.L. 5), to the reclamation fund created by the Act of June 17, 1902 (32 Stat.L. 388), such sum or sums as the Secretary of the Interior may deem necessary, not exceeding $5,000,000, for the completion of projects or divisions of projects now under construction, or projects approved and authorized. Funds so advanced shall be repaid out of any receipts and accretions accruing to the reclamation fund within such time as may be fixed by the Reconstruction Finance Corporation, not exceeding five years from the date of advance, with interest at the rate of 4 per centum per annum. Sums so advanced may be expended in the same way as other moneys in the reclamation fund.

Part 5 — Increase of Lending Power of Reconstruction Finance Corporation

Sec. 38. In order to provide funds to carry out the purposes of this title, the amount of notes, debentures, bonds, or other such obligations which the Reconstruction Finance Corporation is authorized and empowered under section 9 of the Reconstruction Finance Corporation Act, as amended, to have outstanding at any one time, is hereby increased by $300,000,000.

Part 6 — Functions of Farm Loan Commissioner Under Executive Orders

Sec. 39. If and when any executive order heretofore transmitted to the Congress pursuant to title IV of part II of the Legislative Appropriation Act of 1933, as amended, shall become effective, all functions, powers, authority, and duties conferred upon or vested in the Farm Loan Commissioner by this title shall be held and exercised by him subject to all the terms and conditions in any such Executive order the same as if such functions, powers, authority, and duties were specifically named in such Executive order or orders.

Part 7 — Miscellaneous

Perfecting Organization Farm Credit Administration

Sec. 40. The Governor of the Farm Credit Administration is authorized, in carrying out the powers and duties now or hereafter vested in him or the Farm Credit Administration by law or under any Executive order made under title IV of part II of the Legislative Appropriation Act of 1933, as amended, to establish, and to fix the powers and duties of, such divisions, agencies, corporations, and instrumentalities as he may deem necessary to the efficient functioning of the Farm Credit Administration and the successful execution of the powers and duties so vested in the Governor and the Farm Credit Administration. This section shall not be construed to restrict the authority of the President under title IV of such Act, as amended: *Provided,* That no salary or compensation shall be paid to any officer, agent, or other person employed under this section in excess of $10,000 per annum.

Loans to Fruit Growers

Sec. 41. That in making loans to owners of groves and orchards, including citrus-fruit groves and other fruit groves and orchards, the Federal land banks, the farm land banks, and all Government agencies making loans upon such character of property may, in appraising the property offered as security, give a reasonable and fair valuation to the fruit trees located and growing upon said property and constituting a substantial part of its value.

Part 8 — Short Title

Sec. 42. This title may be cited as the "Emergency Farm Mortgage Act of 1933."

Title III — Financing and Exercising Power Conferred by Section 8 of Article I of the Constitution:

To Coin Money and to Regulate the Value Thereof

Sec. 43. Whenever the President finds, upon investigation, that (1) the foreign commerce of the United States is adversely affected by reason of the depreciation in the value of the currency of any other government or governments in relation to the present standard value of gold, or (2) action under this section is necessary in order to regulate and maintain the parity of currency issues of the United States, or (3) an economic emergency requires an expansion of credit, or (4) an expansion of credit is necessary to secure by international agreement a stabilization at proper levels of the currencies of various governments, the President is authorized, in his discretion —

(a) To direct the Secretary of the Treasury to enter into agreements with the several Federal Reserve banks and with the Federal Reserve Board whereby the Federal Reserve Board will, and it is hereby authorized to, notwithstanding any provisions of law or rules and regulations to the contrary, permit such reserve banks to agree that they will, (1) conduct, pursuant to existing law, throughout specified periods, open market operations in obligations of the United States Government or corporations in which the United States is the majority stockholder, and (2) purchase directly and hold in portfolio for an agreed period or periods of time Treasury bills or other obligations of the United States Government in an aggregate sum of $3,000,000,000 in addition to those they may then hold, unless prior to the termination of such period or periods the Secretary shall consent to their sale. No suspension of reserve requirements of the Federal Reserve banks, under the terms of section 11(c) of the Federal Reserve Act, necessitated by reason of operations under this section, shall require the imposition of the graduated tax upon any deficiency in reserves as provided in said section 11(c). Nor shall it require any automatic increase in the rates of interest or discount charged by any Federal Reserve bank, as otherwise specified in that section. The Federal Reserve Board, with the approval of the Secretary of the Treasury, may require the Federal Reserve banks to take such action as may be necessary, in the judgment of the Board and of the Secretary of the Treasury, to prevent undue credit expansion.

(b) If the Secretary, when directed by the President, is unable to secure the assent of the several Federal Reserve banks and the Federal Reserve Board to the agreements authorized in this section, or if operations under the above provisions prove to be inadequate to meet the purposes of this section, or if for any other reason additional measures are required in the judgment of the President to meet such purposes, then the President is authorized—

(1) To direct the Secretary of the Treasury to cause to be issued in such amount or amounts as he may from time to time order, United States notes, as provided in the Act entitled "An Act to authorize the issue of United States notes and for the redemption of funding thereof and for funding the floating debt of the United States," approved February 25, 1862, and Acts supplementary thereto and amendatory thereof, in the same size and of similar color to the Federal Reserve notes heretofore issued and in denominations of $1, $5, $10, $20, $50, $100, $500, $1,000, and $10,000; but notes issued under this subsection shall be issued only for the purpose of meeting maturing Federal obligations to repay sums borrowed by the United States and for purchasing United States bonds and other interest-bearing obligations of the United States: *Provided,* That when any such notes are used for such purpose the bond or other obligation so acquired or taken up shall be retired and canceled. Such notes shall be issued at such times and in such amounts as the President may approve but the aggregate amount of such notes outstanding at any time shall not exceed $3,000,000,000. There is hereby appropriated, out of any money

in the Treasury not otherwise appropriated, an amount sufficient to enable the Secretary of the Treasury to retire and cancel 4 per centum annually of such outstanding notes, and the Secretary of the Treasury is hereby directed to retire and cancel annually 4 per centum of such outstanding notes. Such notes and all other coins and currencies heretofore or hereafter coined or issued by or under the authority of the United States shall be legal tender for all debts public and private.

(2) By proclamation to fix the weight of the gold dollar in grains nine tenths fine and also to fix the weight of the silver dollar in grains nine tenths fine at a definite fixed ration in relation to the gold dollar at such amounts as he finds necessary from his investigation to stabilize domestic prices or to protect the foreign commerce against the adverse effect of depreciated foreign currencies, and to provide for the unlimited coinage of such gold and silver at the ratio so fixed, or in case the Government of the United States enters into an agreement with any government or governments under the terms of which the ratio between the value of gold and other currency issued by the United States and by any such government or governments is established, the President may fix the weight of the gold dollar in accordance with the ratio so agreed upon, and such gold dollar, the weight of which is so fixed, shall be the standard unit of value, and all forms of money issued or coined by the United States shall be maintained at a parity with this standard and it shall be the duty of the Secretary of the Treasury to maintain such parity, but in no event shall the weight of the gold dollar be fixed so as to reduce its present weight by more than 50 per centum.

Sec. 44. The Secretary of the Treasury, with the approval of the President, is hereby authorized to make and promulgate rules and regulations covering any action taken or to be taken by the President under subsection (a) or (b) of section 43.

Sec. 45. (a) The President is authorized, for a period of six months from the date of the passage of this Act, to accept silver in payment of the whole or any part of the principal or interest now due, or to become due within six months after such date, from any foreign government or governments on account of any indebtedness to the United States, such silver to be accepted at not to exceed the price of 50 cents an ounce in United States currency. The aggregate value of the silver accepted under this section shall not exceed $200,000,000.

(b) The silver bullion accepted and received under the provisions of this section shall be subject to the requirements of existing law and the regulations of the mint service governing the methods of determining the amount of pure silver contained, and the amount of the charges or deductions, if any, to be made; but such silver bullion shall not be counted as part of the silver bullion authorized or required to be purchased and coined under the provisions of existing law.

(c) The silver accepted and received under the provisions of this section shall be deposited in the Treasury of the United States, to be held, used, and disposed of as in this section provided.

(d) The Secretary of the Treasury shall cause silver certificates to be issued in such denominations as he deems advisable to the total number of dollars for which such silver was accepted in payment of debts. Such silver certificates shall be used by the Treasurer of the United States in payment of any obligations of the United States.

(e) The silver so accepted and received under this section shall be coined into standard silver dollars and subsidiary coins sufficient, in the opinion of the Secretary of the Treasury, to meet any demands for redemption of such silver certificates issued under the provisions of this section, and such coins shall be retained in the Treasury for the payment of such certificates on demand. The silver so accepted and received under this section, except so much thereof as is coined under the provisions of this section, shall be held in the Treasury for the sole purpose of aiding in maintaining the parity of such certificates as provided in existing law. Any such certificates or reissued certificates, when presented at the Treasury, shall be redeemed in standard silver dollars, or in subsidiary silver coin, at the option of the holder of the certificates: *Provided,* That, in the redemption of such silver certificates issued under this section, not to exceed one third of the coin required for such redemption may in the judgment of the Secretary of the Treasury be made in subsidiary coins, the balance to be made in standard silver dollars.

(f) When any silver certificates issued under the provisions of this section are redeemed or received into the Treasury from any source whatsoever, and belong to the United States, they shall not be retired, canceled, or destroyed, but shall be reissued and paid out again and kept in circulation; but nothing herein shall prevent the cancellation and destruction of mutilated certificates and the issue of other certificates of like denomination in their stead, as provided by law.

(g) The Secretary of the Treasury is authorized to make rules and regulations for carrying out the provisions of this section.

Sec. 46. Section 19 of the Federal Reserve Act, as amended, is amended by inserting immediately after paragraph (c) thereof the following new paragraph:

"Notwithstanding the foregoing provisions of this section, the Federal Reserve Board, upon the affirmative vote of not less than five of its members and with the approval of the President, may declare than an emergency exists by reason of credit expansion, and may by regulation during such emergency increase or decrease from time to time, in its discretion, the reserve balance required to be maintained against either demand or time deposits."

Approved, May 12, 1933.

FEDERAL EMERGENCY RELIEF ACT

> Editor's comments: *This Act created the Federal Emergency Relief Administration (FERA) under the direction of an administrator appointed by the President. Funding of FERA was to be provided by the Reconstruction Finance Corporation in an amount up to $500,000,000.*
>
> *The administrator of FERA was authorized to make grants to the States for providing relief to persons in need resulting from the "present emergency, . . . whether resident, transient, or homeless."*
>
> *To obtain FERA funds a State, through its Governor, would make application showing that certain standards could and would be met.*

An Act to Provide for Cooperation by the Federal Government with the Several States and Territories and the District of Columbia in Relieving the Hardship and Suffering Caused by Unemployment, and for Other Purposes
May 12, 1933

Be it enacted by the Senate and House of Representatives of the United States of America in Congress assembled, That the Congress hereby declares that the present economic depression has created a serious emergency, due to widespread unemployment and increasing inadequacy of State and local relief funds, resulting in the existing or threatened deprivation of a considerable number of families and individuals of the necessities of life, and making it imperative that the Federal Government cooperate more effectively with the several States and Territories and the District of Columbia in furnishing relief to their needy and distressed people.

Sec. 2. (a) The Reconstruction Finance Corporation is authorized and directed to make available out of the funds of the Corporation not to exceed $500,000,000, in addition to the funds authorized under title I of the Emergency Relief and Construction Act of 1932, for expenditure under the provisions of this Act upon certification by the Federal Emergency Relief Administrator provided for in section 3.

(b) The amount of notes, debentures, bonds, or other such obligations which the Reconstruction Finance Corporation is authorized and empowered under section 9 of the Reconstruction Finance Corporation Act, as amended, to have outstanding at any one time is increased by $500,000,000: *Provided,* That no such additional notes, debentures, bonds, or other such obligations authorized by this subsection shall be issued except at such times and in such amounts as the President shall approve.

(c) After the expiration of ten days after the date upon which the Federal Emergency Relief Administration has qualified and has taken office, no application shall be approved by the Reconstruction Finance Corporation under the provisions of title I of the Emergency Relief and Construction Act of 1932, and the Federal Emergency Relief Administrator shall have access to all files and records of the Reconstruction Finance Corporation relating to the administration of funds under title I of such Act. At the expiration of such ten-day period, the unexpended and unobligated balance of the funds authorized under title I of such Act shall be available for the purposes of this Act.

Sec. 3. (a) There is hereby created a Federal Emergency Relief Administration, all the powers of which shall be exercised by a Federal Emergency Relief Administrator (referred to in this Act as the "Administrator") to be appointed by the President, by and with the advice and consent of the Senate. The Administrator shall receive a salary to be fixed by the President at not to exceed $10,000, and necessary traveling and subsistence expenses within the limitations prescribed by law for civilian employees in the executive branch of the Government. The Federal Emergency Relief Administration and the office of Federal Emergency Relief Administrator shall cease to exist upon the expiration of two years after the date of enactment of this Act, and the unexpended balance on such date of any funds made available under the provisions of this Act shall be disposed of as the Congress may by law provide.

(b) The Administrator may appoint and fix the compensation of such experts and their appointment may be made and compensation fixed without regard to the civil service laws, or the Classification Act of 1923, as amended, and the Administrator may, in the same manner, appoint and fix the compensation of such other officers and employees as are necessary to carry out the provisions of this Act, but such compensation shall not exceed in any case the sum of $8,000; and may make such expenditures (including expenditures for personal services and rent at the seat of government and elsewhere and for printing and binding), not to exceed $350,000, as are necessary to carry out the provisions of this Act, to be paid by the Reconstruction Finance Corporation out of funds made available by this Act upon presentation of vouchers approved by the Administrator or by an officer of the Administration designated by him for that purpose. The Administrator may, under rules and regulations prescribed by the President, assume control of the administration in any State or States where, in his judgment, more effective and efficient cooperation between the State and Federal authorities may thereby be secured in carrying out the purposes of this Act.

(c) In executing any of the provisions of this Act, the Administrator, and any person duly authorized or designated by him, may conduct any investigation pertinent or material to the furtherance of the purposes of this Act and, at the request of the President, shall make such further investigations and studies as the President may deem necessary in dealing with problems of unemployment relief.

(d) The Administrator shall print monthly, and shall submit to the

President and to the Senate and the House of Representatives (or to the Secretary of the Senate and the Clerk of the House of Representatives, if those bodies are not in session), a report of his activities and expenditures under this Act. Such reports shall, when submitted, be printed as public documents.

Sec. 4. (a) Out of the funds of the Reconstruction Finance Corporation made available by this Act, the Administrator is authorized to make grants to the several States to aid in meeting the costs of furnishing relief and work relief and in relieving the hardship and suffering caused by unemployment in the form of money, service, materials, and/or commodities to provide the necessities of life to persons in need as a result of the present emergency, and/or to their dependents, whether resident, transient, or homeless.

(b) Of the amounts made available by this Act not to exceed $250,000,000 shall be granted to the several States applying therefor, in the following manner: Each state shall be entitled to receive grants equal to one third of the amount expended by such State, including the civil subdivisions thereof, out of public moneys from all sources for the purposes set forth in subsection (a) of this section; and such grants shall be made quarterly, beginning with the second quarter in the calendar year 1933, and shall be made during any quarter upon the basis of such expenditures certified by the States to have been made during the preceding quarter.

(c) The balance of the amounts made available by this Act, except the amount required for administrative expenditures under section 3, shall be used for grants to be made whenever, from an application presented by a State, the Administrator finds that the combined moneys which can be made available within the State from all sources, supplemented by any moneys, available under subsection (b) of this section, will fall below the estimated needs within the State for the purposes specified in subsection (a) of this section: *Provided,* That the Administrator may certify out of the funds made available by this subsection additional grants to States applying therefor to aid needy persons who have no legal setlement in any one State or community, and to aid in assisting cooperative and self-help associations for the barter of goods and services.

(d) After October 1, 1933, notwithstanding the provisions of subsection (b), the unexpended balance of the amounts available for the purposes of subsection (b) may, in the discretion of the Administrator and with the approval of the President, be available for grants under subsection (c).

(e) The decision of the Administrator as to the purpose of any expenditure shall be final.

(f) The amount available to any one State under subsections (b) and (c) of this section shall not exceed 15 per centum of the total amount made available by such subsections.

Sec. 5. Any State desiring to obtain funds under this Act shall through its Governor make application therefor from time to time to the Administrator. Each application so made shall present in the manner requested by the Administrator information showing (1) the amounts necessary to meet relief needs in the State during the period covered by such application and the amounts available from public or private sources within the State, its political subdivisions, and private agencies, to meet the relief needs of the State, (2) the provision made to assure adequate administrative supervision, (3) the provision made for suitable standards of relief, and (4) the purposes for which the funds requested will be used.

Sec. 6. The Administrator upon approving a grant to any State shall so certify to the Reconstruction Finance Corporation which shall, except upon revocation of a certificate by the Administrator, make payments without delay to the State in such amounts and at such times as may be prescribed in the certificate. The Governor of each State receiving grants under this Act shall file monthly with the Administrator, and in the form required by him, a report of the disbursements made under such grants.

Sec. 7. As used in the foregoing provisions of this Act, the term "State" shall include the District of Columbia, Alaska, Hawaii, the Virgin Islands, and Puerto Rico; and the term "Governor" shall include the Commissioners of the District of Columbia.

Sec. 8. This Act may be cited as the "Federal Emergency Relief Act of 1933."

Approved, May 12, 1933.

TENNESSEE VALLEY AUTHORITY ACT

> Editor's comments: *The Tennessee Valley Authority (TVA), a corporate body, was created in the interest of national defense, economic development, and Tennessee River navigation and flood control.*
>
> *The board of directors, appointed by the President, was authorized to build dams, reservoirs, hydroelectric generation, steam power plants, and transmission lines; to make and sell fixed nitrogen and fertilizer; to sell power surplus to its operations; and to undertake various other activities to develop the area within the drainage basin of the Tennessee River.*
>
> *To fund the construction of dams, reservoirs, generation and transmission facilities, the TVA was empowered to issue and sell, on the credit of the United States, serial bonds.*

An Act to Improve the Navigability and to Provide for the Flood Control of the Tennessee River: To Provide for Reforestation and the Proper Use of Marginal Lands in the Tennessee Valley; to Provide for the Agricultural and Industrial Development of Said Valley; to Provide for the National Defense by the Creation of a Corporation for the Operation of Government Properties at and Near Muscle Shoals in the State of Alabama, and for Other Purposes
May 18, 1933

Be it enacted by the Senate and House of Representatives of the United States of America in Congress assembled, That for the purpose of maintaining and operating the properties now owned by the United States in the vicinity of Muscle Shoals, Alabama, in the interest of the national defense and for agriculture and industrial development, and to improve navigation in the Tennessee River and to control the destructive flood waters in the Tennessee River and Mississippi River Basins, there is hereby created a body corporate by the name of the "Tennessee Valley Authority" (hereinafter referred to as the "Corporation"). The board of directors first appointed shall be deemed the incorporators, and the incorporation shall be held to have been effected from the date of the first meeting of the board. This Act may be cited as the "Tennessee Valley Authority Act of 1933."

Sec. 2. (a) The board of directors of the Corporation (hereinafter referred to as the "board") shall be composed of three members, to be appointed by the President, by and with the advice and consent of the Senate. In appointing the members of the board, the President shall designate the chairman. All other officials, agents, and employees shall be designated and selected by the board.

(b) The terms of office of the members first taking office after the approval of this Act shall expire as designated by the President at the time of nomination, one at the end of the third year, one at the end of the sixth year, and one at the end of the ninth year, after the date of approval of this Act. A successor to a member of the board shall be appointed in the same manner as the original members and shall have a term of office expiring nine years from the date of the expiration of the term for which his predecessor was appointed.

(c) Any member appointed to fill a vacancy in the board occurring prior to the expiration of the term for which his predecessor was appointed shall be appointed for the remainder of such term.

(d) Vacancies in the board so long as there shall be two members in office shall not impair the powers of the board to execute the functions of the Corporation, and two of the members in office shall consitute a quorum for the transaction of the business of the board.

(e) Each of the members of the board shall be a citizen of the United States, and shall receive a salary at the rate of $10,000 a year, to be paid by the Corporation as current expenses. Each member of the board, in addition to his salary, shall be permitted to occupy as his residence one of the dwelling houses owned by the Government in the vicinity of Muscle Shoals, Alabama, the same to be designated by the President of the United States. Members of the board shall be reimbursed by the Corporation for actual expenses (including traveling and subsistence expenses) incurred by them in the performance of the duties vested in the board by this Act. No member of said board shall, during his continuance in office, be engaged in other business, but each member shall devote himself to the work of the Corporation.

(f) No director shall have financial interest in any public-utility corporation engaged in the business of distributing and selling power to the public nor in any corporation engaged in the manufacture, selling, or distribution of fixed nitrogen or fertilizer, or any ingredients thereof, nor shall any member have any interest in any business that may be adversely affected by the success of the Corporation as a producer of concentrated fertilizers or as a producer of electric power.

(g) The board shall direct the exercise of all the powers of the Corporation.

(h) All members of the board shall be persons who profess a belief in the feasibility and wisdom of this Act.

Sec. 3. The Board shall without regard to the provisions of Civil Service laws applicable to officers and employees of the United States, appoint such managers, assistant managers, officers, employees, attorneys, and agents, as are necessary for the transaction of its business, fix their compensation, define their duties, require bonds of such of them as the board may designate, and provide a system of organization to fix responsibility and promote efficiency. Any appointee of the board may be removed in the discretion of the board.

No regular officer or employee of the Corporation shall receive a salary in excess of that received by the members of the board.

All contracts to which the Corporation is a party and which require the employment of laborers and mechanics in the construction, alteration, maintenance, or repair of buildings, dams, locks, or other projects shall contain a provision that not less than the prevailing rate of wages for work of a similar nature prevailing in the vicinity shall be paid to such laborers or mechanics.

In the event any dispute arises as to what are the prevailing rates of wages, the question shall be referred to the Secretary of Labor for determination, and his decision shall be final. In the determination of such prevailing rate or rates, due regard shall be given to those rates which have been secured through collective agreement by representatives of employers and employees.

Where such work as is described in the two preceding paragraphs is done directly by the Corporation the prevailing rate of wages shall be paid in the same manner as though such work had been let by contract.

Insofar as applicable, the benefits of the Act entitled "An Act to provide compensation for employees of the United States suffering injuries while in the performance of their duties, and for other purposes," approved September 7, 1916, as amended, shall extend to persons given employment under the provisions of this Act.

Sec. 4. Except as otherwise specifically provided in this Act, the Corporation—

(a) Shall have succession in its corporate name.

(b) May sue and be sued in its corporate name.

(c) May adopt and use a corporate seal, which shall be judicially noticed.

(d) May make contracts, as herein authorized.

(e) May adopt, amend, and repeal bylaws.

(f) May purchase or lease and hold such real and personal property as it deems necessary or convenient in the transaction of its business, and may dispose of any such personal property held by it.

The board shall select a treasurer and as many assistant treasurers as it deems proper, which treasurer and assistant treasurers shall give such bonds for the safe-keeping of the securities and moneys of the said Corporation as the board may require: *Provided,* That any member of said board may be removed from office at any time by a concurrent resolution of the Senate and the House of Representatives.

(g) Shall have such powers as may be necessary or appropriate for the exercise of the powers herein specifically conferred upon the Corporation.

(h) Shall have power in the name of the United States of America to exercise the right of eminent domain, and in the purchase of any real estate or the acquisition of real estate by condemnation proceedings, the title to such real estate shall be taken in the name of the United States of America, and thereupon all such real estate shall be entrusted to the Corporation as the agent of the United States to accomplish the purposes of this Act.

(i) Shall have power to acquire real estate for the construction of dams, reservoirs, transmission lines, power houses, and other structures, and navigation projects at any point along the Tennessee River, or any of its tributaries, and in the event that the owner or owners of such property shall fail and refuse to sell to the Corporation at a price deemed fair and reasonable by the board, then the Corporation may proceed to exercise the right of eminent domain, and to condemn all property that it deems necessary for carrying out the purposes of this Act, and all such condemnation proceedings shall be had pursuant to the provisons and requirements hereinafter specified, with reference to any and all condemnation proceedings.

(j) Shall have power to construct dams, reservoirs, power houses, power structures, transmission lines, navigation projects, and incidental works in the Tennessee River and its tributaries, and to unite the various power installations into one or more systems by transmission lines.

Sec. 5. The board is hereby authorized—

(a) To contract with commercial producers for the production of such fertilizers or fertilizer materials as may be needed in the Government's program of development and introduction in excess of that produced by Government plants. Such contracts may provide either for outright purchase of materials by the board or only for the payment of carrying charges on special materials manufactured at the board's request for its program.

(b) To arrange with farmers and farm organizations for largescale practical use of the new forms of fertilizers under conditions permitting an accurate measure of the economic return they produce.

(c) To cooperate with National, State, district, or county experimental stations or demonstration farms, for the use of new forms of fertilizer or fertilizer practices during the initial or experimental period of their introduction.

(d) The board in order to improve and cheapen the production of fertilizer is authorized to manufacture and sell fixed nitrogen, fertilizer, and fertilizer ingredients at Muscle Shoals by the employment of existing facilities, by modernizing existing plants, or by any other process or processes that in its judgment shall appear wise and profitable for the fixation of atmospheric nitrogen or the cheapening of the production of fertilizer.

(e) Under the authority of this Act the board may make donations or sales of the product of the plant or plants operated by it to be fairly and equitably distributed through the agency of county demonstration agents, agricultural colleges, or otherwise as the board may direct, for experimentation, education, and introduction of the use of such products in cooperation with practical farmers so as to obtain information as to the value, effect, and best methods of their use.

(f) The board is authorized to make alterations, modifications, or improvements in existing plants and facilities, and to construct new plants.

(g) In the event it is not used for the fixation of nitrogen for agricultural purposes or leased, then the board shall maintain in stand-by condition nitrate plant numbered 2, or its equivalent, for the fixation of atmospheric nitrogen, for the production of explosives in the event of war or a national emergency, until the Congress shall by joint resolution release the board from this obligation, and if any part thereof be used by the board for the manufacture or phosphoric acid or potash, the balance of nitrate plant numbered 2 shall be kept in stand-by condition.

(h) To establish, maintain, and operate laboratories and experimental plants, and to undertake experiments for the purpose of enabling the Corporation to furnish nitrogen products for military purposes, and nitrogen and other fertilizer products for agricultural purposes in the most economical manner and at the highest standard of efficiency.

(i) To request the assistance and advice of any officer, agent, or employee of any executive department or of any independent office of the United States, to enable the Corporation the better to carry out its powers successfully, and as far as practicable shall utilize the services of such officers, agents, and employees, and the President shall, if in his opinion, the public interest, service, or economy so require, direct that such assistance, advice, and service be rendered to the Corporation, and any individual that may be by the President directed to render such assistance, advice, and service shall be thereafter subject to the orders, rules, and regulations of the board: *Provided,* That any invention or discovery made by virtue of and incidental to such service by an employee of the Government of the United States serving under this section, or by any employee of the Corporation, together with any patents which may be granted thereon, shall be the sole and exclusive property of the Corporation, which is hereby authorized to grant licenses thereunder as shall be authorized by the board: *Provided further,* That the board may pay to such inventor such sum from the income from sale of licenses as it may deem proper.

(j) Upon the requisition of the Secretary of War or the Secretary of the Navy to manufacture for and sell at cost to the United States explosives or their nitrogenous content.

(k) Upon the requisition of the Secretary of War the Corporation shall allot and deliver without charge to the War Department so much power as shall be necessary in the judgment of said Department for use in operation of all locks, lifts, or other facilities in aid of navigation.

(l) To produce, distribute, and sell electric power, as herein particularly specified.

(m) No products of the Corporation shall be sold for use outside of the United States, its Territories and possessions, except to the United States Government for the use of its Army and Navy, or to its allies in case of war.

(n) The President is authorized, within twelve months after the passage of this Act, to lease to any responsible farm organization or to any corporation organized by it nitrate plant number 2 and Waco Quarry, together with the railroad connecting said quarry with nitrate plant number 2, for a term not exceeding fifty years at a rental of not less than $1 per year, but such authority shall be subject to the express condition that the lessee shall use said property during the term of said lease exclusively for the manufacture of fertilizer and fertilizer ingredients to be used only in the manufacture of fertilizer by said lessee and sold for use as fertilizer. The said lessee shall convenant to keep said property in first-class condition, but the lessee shall be authorized to modernize said plant numbered 2 by the installation of such machinery as may be necessary, and is authorized to amortize the cost of said machinery and improvements over the term of said lease or any part thereof. Said lease shall also provide that the board shall sell to the lessee power for the operation of said plant at the same schedule of prices that it charges all other customers for power of the same class and quantity. Said lease shall also provide that, if the said lessee does not desire to buy power of the publicly owned plant, it shall have the right to purchase power for the operation of said plant of the Alabama Power Company or any other publicly or privately owned corporation engaged in the generation and sale of electrical power, and in such case the lease shall provide further that the said lessee shall have a free right of way to build a transmission line over Government property to said plant paying the actual expenses and damages, if any, incurred by the Corporation on account of such line. Said lease shall also provide that the said lessee shall covenant that during the term of said lease the said lessee shall not enter into any illegal monopoly, combination, or trust with any privately owned corporation engaged in the manufacture, production, and sale of fertilizer with the object or effect of increasing the price of fertilizer to the farmer.

Sec. 6. In the appointment of officials and the selection of employees for said Corporation, and in the promotion of any such employees or officials, no political test or qualification shall be permitted or given consideration, but all such appointments and promotions shall be given and made on the basis of merit and efficiency. Any member of said board who is found by the President of the United States to be guilty of a violation of this section shall be removed from office by the President of the United States, and any appointee of said board who is found by the board to be guilty of a violation of this section shall be removed from office by said board.

Sec. 7. In order to enable the Corporation to exercise the powers and duties vested in it by this Act—

(a) The exclusive use, possession, and control of the United States nitrate plants numbered 1 and 2, including steam plants, located, respectively, at Sheffield, Alabama, and Muscle Shoals, Alabama, together with all real estate and buildings connected therewith, all tools and machinery, equipment, accessories, and materials belonging thereto, and all laboratories and plants used as auxiliaries thereto; the fixed-nitrogen research laboratory, the Waco limestone quarry, in Alabama, and Dam Numbered 2, located at Muscle Shoals, its power house, and all hydroelectric and operating appurtenances (except the locks), and all machinery, lands, and buildings in connection therewith, and all appurtenances thereof, and all other property to be acquired by the Corporation in its own name or in the name of the United States of America, are hereby intrusted to the Corporation for the purposes of the Act.

(b) The President of the United States is authorized to provide for the transfer to the Corporation of the use, possession, and control of such other real or personal property of the United States as he may from time to time deem necessary and proper for the purposes of the Corporation as herein stated.

Sec. 8. (a) The Corporation shall maintain its principal office in the immediate vicinity of Muscle Shaols, Alabama. The Corporation shall be held to be an inhabitant and resident of the northern judicial district of Alabama within the meaning of the laws of the United States relating to the venue of civil suits.

(b) The Corporation shall at all times maintain complete and accurate books of accounts.

(c) Each member of the board, before entering upon the duties of his office, shall subscribe to an oath (or affirmation) to support the Constitution of the United States and to faithfully and impartially perform the duties imposed upon him by this Act.

Sec. 9. (a) The board shall file with the President and with the Congress, in December of each year, a financial statement and a complete report as to the business of the Corporation covering the preceding governmental fiscal year. This report shall include an itemized statement of the cost of power at each power station, the total number of employees and the names, salaries, and duties of those receiving compensation at the rate of more than $1,500 a year.

(b) The Comptroller General of the United States shall audit the transactions of the Corporation at such times as he shall determine, but not less frequently than once each governmental fiscal year, with personnel of his selection. In such connection he and his representatives shall have free and open access to all papers, books, records, files, accounts, plants, warehouses, offices, and all other things, property and places belonging to or under the control of or used or employed by the Corporation, and shall be afforded full facilities for counting all cash and verifying transactions with and balances in depositaries. He shall make report of each such audit in quadruplicate, one copy for the President of the United States, one for the chairman of the board, one for public inspection at the principal office of the Corporation, and the other to be retained by him for the uses of the Congress. The expenses for each such audit may be paid from moneys advanced therefor by the Corporation, or from any appropriation or appropriations for the General Accounting Office, and appropriations so used shall be reimbursed promptly by the Corporation as billed by the Comptroller General. All such audit expenses shall be charged to operating expenses of the Corporation. The Comptroller General shall make special report to the President of the United States and to the Congress of any transaction or condition found by him to be in conflict with the powers or duties intrusted to the Corporation by law.

Sec. 10. The board is hereby empowered and authorized to sell the surplus power not used in its operations, and for operation of locks and other works generated by it, to States, counties, municipalities, corporations, partnerships, or individuals, according to the policies hereinafter set forth; and to carry out said authority, the board is authorized to enter into contracts for such sale for a term not exceeding twenty years, and in the sale of such current by the board it shall give preference to States, counties, municipalities, and cooperative organizations of citizens or farmers, not organized or doing business for profit, but primarily for the purpose of supplying electricity to its own citizens or members: *Provided,* That all contracts made with private companies or individuals for the sale of power, which is to be resold for a profit, shall contain a provision authorizing the board to cancel said contract upon five years' notice in writing, if the board needs said power to supply the demands of States, counties, or municipalities. In order to promote and encourage the fullest possible use of electric light and power on farms within reasonable distance of any of its transmission lines the board in its discretion shall have power to construct transmission lines to farms and small villages that are not otherwise supplied with electricity at reasonable rates, and to make such rules and regulations governing such sale and distribution of such electric power as in its judgment may be just and equitable: *Provided further,* That the board is hereby authorized and directed to make studies, experiments, and determinations to promote the wider and better use of electric power for agricultural and domestic use, or for small or local industries, and it may cooperate with State governments, or their subdivisions or agencies, with educational or research institutions, and with cooperatives or other organizations, in the application of electric power to the fuller and better balanced development of the resources of the region.

Sec. 11. It is hereby declared to be the policy of the Government so far as practical to distribute and sell the surplus power generated at Muscle Shoals equitably among the States, counties, and municipalities within transmission distance. This policy is further declared to be that the projects herein provided for shall be considered primarily as for the benefit of the people of the section as a whole and particularly the domestic and rural consumers to whom the power can economically be made available, and accordingly that sale to and use by industry shall be a secondary purpose, to be utilized principally to secure a sufficiently high load factor and revenue returns which will permit domestic and rural use at the lowest possible rates and in such manner as to encourage increased domestic and rural use of electricity. It is further hereby declared to be the policy of the Government to utilize the Muscle Shoals properties so far as may be necessary to improve, increase, and cheapen the production of fertilizer and fertilizer ingredients by carrying out the provisions of this Act.

Sec. 12. In order to place the board upon a fair basis for making such contracts and for receiving bids for the sale of such power, it is hereby expressly authorized, either from appropriations made by Congress or from funds secured from the sale of such power, or from funds secured by the sale of bonds hereafter provided for, to construct, lease, purchase, or authorize the construction of transmission lines within transmission distance from the place where generated, and to interconnect with other systems. The board is also authorized to lease to any person, persons, or corporation the use of any transmission line owned by the Government and operated by the board, but no such lease shall be made that in any way interferes with the use of such transmission line by the board: *Provided,* That if any State, county, municipality, or other public or cooperative organization of citizens or farmers, not organized or doing business for profit, but primarily for the purpose of supplying electricity to its own citizens or members, or any two or more of such municipalities or organizations, shall construct or agree to construct and maintain a properly designed and built transmission line to the Government reservation upon which is located a Government generating plant, or to a main transmission line owned by the Government or leased by the board and under the control of the board, the board is hereby authorized and directed to contract with such State, county, municipality, or other organization, or two or more of them, for the sale of electricity for a term not exceeding thirty years; and in such case the board shall give to such State, county, municipality, or other organization ample time to fully comply with any local law now in existence or hereafter enacted providing for the necessary legal authority for such State, county, municipality, or other organization to contract with the board for such power: *Provided further,* That all contracts entered into between the Corporation and any municipality or other political subdivision or cooperative organization shall provide that the electric power shall be sold and distributed to the ultimate consumer without discrimination as between consumers of the same class, and such contract shall be voidable at the election of the board if a discriminatory rate, rebate, or other special concession is made or given to any consumer or user by the municipality or other political subdivision or cooperative organization: *And provided further,* That as to any surplus power not so sold as above provided to States, counties, municipalities, or other said organizations, before the board shall sell the same to any person or corporation engaged in the distribution and resale of electricity for profit, it shall require said person or corporation to agree that any resale of such electric power by said person or corporation shall be made to the ultimate consumer of such electric power at prices that shall not exceed a schedule fixed by the board from time to time as reasonable, just, and fair; and in case of any such sale, if an amount is charged the ultimate consumer which is in excess of the price so deemed to be just, reasonable, and fair by the board, the contract for such sale between the board and such distributor of electricity shall be voidable at the election of the board: *And provided further,* That the board is hereby authorized to enter into contracts with other power systems for the mutual exchange of unused excess power upon suitable terms, for the conservation of stored water, and as an emergency or break-down relief.

Sec. 13. Five per centum of the gross proceeds received by the board for the sale of power generated at Dam Numbered 2, or from any other hydropower plant hereafter constructed in the State of Alabama, shall be paid to the State of Alabama; and 5 per centum of the gross proceeds from the sale of power generated at Cove Creek Dam, hereinafter provided for, or any other dam located in the State of Tennessee, shall be paid to the State of Tennessee. Upon the completion of said Cove Creek Dam the board shall ascertain how much additional power is thereby generated at Dam Numbered 2 and at any other dam hereafter constructed by the Government of the United States on the Tennessee River, in the State of Alabama, or in the State of Tennessee, and from the gross proceeds of the sale of such additional power 2½ per centum shall be paid to the State of Alabama and 2½ per centum to the State of Tennessee. These percentages shall apply to any other dam that may hereafter be constructed and controlled and operated by the board on the Tennessee River or any of its tributaries, the main purpose of which is to control flood waters and where the development of electric power is incidental to the operation of such flood-control dam. In ascertaining the gross proceeds from the sale of such power upon which a percentage is paid to the States of Alabama and Tennessee, the board shall not take into consideration the proceeds of any power sold or delivered to the Government of the United States, or any department or agency of the Government of the United States, used in the operation of any locks on the Tennessee River or for any experimental purpose, or for the manufacture of fertilizer or any of the ingredients thereof, or for any other governmental purpose: *Provided,* That the percentages to be paid to the States of Alabama and Tennessee, as provided in this section, shall be subject to revision and change by the board, and any new percentages established by the board, when approved by the President, shall remain in effect until and unless again changed by the board with the approval of the President. No change of said percentages shall be made more often than once in five years, and no change shall be made without giving to the States of Alabama and Tennessee an opportunity to be heard.

Sec. 14. The board shall make a thorough investigation as to the present value of Dam Numbered 2, and the steam plants at nitrate plant numbered 1, and nitrate plant numbered 2, and as to the cost of Cove Creek Dam, for the purpose of ascertaining how much of the value or the cost of said properties shall be allocated and charged up to (1) flood control, (2) navigation, (3) fertilizer, (4) national defense, and (5) the development of power. The findings thus made by the board, when approved by the President of the United States, shall be final, and such findings shall thereafter be used in all allocation of value for the purpose of keeping the book value of said properties. In like manner, the cost and book value of any dams, steam plants, or other similar improvements hereafter constructed and turned over to said board for the purpose of control and management shall be ascertained and allocated.

Sec. 15. In the construction of any future dam, steam plant, or other facility, to be used in whole or in part for the generation or transmission of electric power the board is hereby authorized and empowered to issue on the credit of the United States and to sell serial bonds not exceeding $50,000,000 in amount, having a maturity not more than fifty years from the date of issue thereof, and bearing interest not exceeding 3-1/2 per centum per annum. Said bonds shall be issued and sold in amounts and prices approved by the Secretary of the Treasury, but all such bonds as may be so issued and sold shall have equal rank. None of said bonds shall be sold below par, and no fee, commission, or compensation whatever shall be paid to any person, firm, or corporation for handling, negotiating the sale, or selling the said bonds. All of such bonds so issued and sold shall have all the rights and privileges accorded by law to Panama Canal bonds, authorized by section 8 of the Act of June 28, 1902, chapter 1302, as amended by the Act of December 21, 1905 (ch. 3, sec. 1, 34 Stat. 5), as now compiled in section 743 of title 31 of the United States Code. All funds derived from the sale of such bonds shall be paid over to the Corporation.

Sec. 16. The board, whenever the President deems it advisable, is hereby empowered and directed to complete Dam Numbered 2 at Muscle Shoals, Alabama, and the steam plant at nitrate plant numbered 2, in the vicinity of Muscle Shoals, by installing in Dam Numbered 2 the additional power units according to the plans and specifications of said dam, and the additional power unit in the steam plant at nitrate plant numbered 2.

Sec. 17. The Secretary of War, or the Secretary of the Interior, is hereby authorized to construct, either directly or by contract to the lowest responsible bidder, after due advertisement, a dam in and across Clinch River in the State of Tennessee, which has by long custom become known and designated as the Cove Creek Dam, together with a transmission line from Muscle Shoals, according to the latest and most approved designs, including power house and hydroelectric installations and equipment for the generation of power, in order that the waters of the said Clinch River may be impounded and stored above said dam for the purpose of increasing and regulating the flow of the Clinch River and the Tennessee River below, so that the maximum amount of primary power may be developed at Dam Numbered 2 and at any and all other dams below the said Cove Creek Dam: *Provided, however,* That the President is hereby authorized by appropriate order to direct the employment by the Secretary of War, or by the Secretary of the Interior, of such engineer or engineers as he may designate, to perform such duties and obligations as he may deem proper, either in the drawing of plans and specifications for said dam, or to perform any other work in the building or construction of the same. The President may, by such order, place the control of the construction of said dam in the hands of such engineer or engineers taken from private life as he may deisre: *And provided further,* That the President is hereby expressly authorized, without regard to the restriction or limitation of any other statute, to select attorneys and assistants for the purpose of making any investigation he may deem proper to ascertain whether, in the control and management of Dam Numbered 2, or any other dam or property owned by the Government in the Tennessee River Basin, or in the authorization of any improvement therein, there has been any undue or unfair advantage given to private persons, partnerships, or coprorations, by any officials or employees of the Government, or whether in any such matters the Government has been injured or unjustly deprived of any of its rights.

Sec. 18. In order to enable and empower the Secretary of War, the Secretary of the Interior, or the board to carry out the authority hereby conferred, in the most economical and efficient manner, he or it is hereby authorized and empowered in the exercise of the powers of national defense in aid of navigation, and in the control of the flood waters of the Tennessee and Mississippi Rivers, constituting channels of interstate commerce, to exercise the right of eminent domain for all purposes of this Act, and to condemn all lands, easements, rights of way, and other area necessary in order to obtain a site for said Cove Creek Dam, and the flowage rights for the reservoir of water above said dam, and to negotiate and conclude contracts with States, counties, municipalities, and all State agencies and with railroads, railroad corporations, common carriers, and all public utility commissions and any other person, firm or corporation, for the relocation of railroad tracks, highways, highway bridges, mills, ferries, electric-light plants, and any and all other properties, enterprises, and projects whose removal may be necessary in order to carry out the provisions of this Act. When said Cove Creek Dam, transmission line, and power house shall have been completed, the possession, use, and control thereof shall be intrusted to the Corporation for use and operation in connection with the general Tennessee Valley project, and to promote flood control and navigation in the Tennessee River.

Sec. 19. The Corporation, as an instrumentality and agency of the Government of the United States for the purpose of executing its constitutional powers, shall have access to the Patent Office of the United States for the purpose of studying, ascertaining, and copying all methods, formulae, and scientific information (not including access to pending applications for patents) necessary to enable the Corporation to use and employ the most efficacious and economical process for the production of fixed nitrogen, or any essential ingredient of fertilizer, or any method of improving and cheapening the production of hydroelectric power, and any owner of a patent whose patent rights may have been thus in any way copied, used, infringed, or employed by the exercise of this authority by the Corporation shall have as the exclusive remedy a cause of action against the Corporation to be instituted and prosecuted on the equity side of the appropriate district court of the United States, for the recovery of reasonable compensation for such infringement. The Commissioner of Patents shall furnish to the Corporation, at its request and without payment of fees, copies of documents on file in his office: *Provided,* That the benefits of this section shall not apply to any art, machine, method of manufacture, or composition of matter, discovered or invented by such employee during the time of his employment or services with the Corporation or with the Government of the United States.

Sec. 20. The Government of the United States hereby reserves the right, in case of war or national emergency declared by Congress, to take possession of all or any part of the property described or referred to in this Act for the purpose of manufacturing explosives or for other war purposes; but, if this right is exercised by the Government, it shall pay the reasonable and fair damages that may be suffered by any party whose contract for the purchase of electric power or fixed nitrogen or fertilizer ingredients is hereby violated, after the amount of the damages has been fixed by the United States Court of Claims in proceedings instituted and conducted for that purpose under rules prescribed by the court.

Sec. 21. (a) All general penal statutes relating to the larceny, embezzlement, conversion, or to the improper handling, retention, use, or disposal of public moneys or property of the United States, shall apply to the moneys and property of the Corporation and to moneys and properties of the United States intrusted to the Corporation.

(b) Any person who, with intent to defraud the Corporation, or to deceive any director, officer, or employee of the Corporation or any officer or employee of the United States (1) makes any false entry in any book of the Corporation, or (2) makes any false report or statement for the Corporation, shall, upon conviction thereof, be fined not more than $10,000 or imprisoned not more than five years, or both.

(c) Any person who shall receive any compensation, rebate, or reward, or shall enter into any conspiracy, collusion, or agreement, express or implied, with intent to defraud the Corporation or wrongfully and unlawfully to defeat its purposes, shall, on conviction thereof, be fined not more than $5,000 or imprisoned not more than five years, or both.

Sec. 22. To aid further the proper use, conservation, and development of the natural resources of the Tennessee River drainage basin and of such adjoining territory as may be related to or materially affected by the development consequent to this Act, and to provide for the general welfare of the citizens of said areas, the President is hereby authorized, by such means or methods as he may deem proper within the limits of appropriations made therefor by Congress, to make such surveys of and general plans for said Tennessee basin and adjoining territory as may be useful to the Congress and to the several States in guiding and controlling the extent, sequence, and nature of development that may be equitably and economically advanced through the expenditure of public funds, or through the guidance or control of public authority, all for the general purpose of fostering an orderly and proper physical, economic, and social development of said areas; and the President is further authorized in making said surveys and plans to cooperate with the States affected thereby, or subdivisions or agencies of such States, or with cooperative or other organizations, and to make such studies, experiments, or demonstrations as may be necessary and suitable to that end.

Sec. 23. The President shall, from time to time, as the work provided for in the preceding section progresses, recommend to Congress such legislation as he deems proper to carry out the general purposes stated in said section, and for the especial purpose of bringing about in said Tennessee drainage basin and adjoining territory in conformity with said general purposes (1) the maximum amount of flood control; (2) the maximum development of said Tennessee River for navigation purposes; (3) the maximum generation of electric power consistent with flood control and navigation; (4) the proper use of marginal lands; (5) the proper method of reforestation of all lands in said drainage basin suitable for reforestation; and (6) the economic and social well-being of the people living in said river basin.

Sec. 24. For the purpose of securing any rights of flowage, or obtaining title to or possession of any property, real or personal, that may be necessary or may become necessary, in the carrying out of any of the provisions of this Act, the President of the United States for a period of three years from the date of the enactment of this Act, is hereby authorized to acquire title in the name of the United States to such rights or such property, and to provide for the payment for same by directing the board to contract to deliver power generated at any of the plants now owned or hereafter owned or constructed by the Government or by said Corporation, such future delivery of power to continue for a period not exceeding thirty years. Likewise, for one year after the enactment of this Act, the President is further authorized to sell or lease any parcel or part of any vacant real estate now owned by the Government in said Tennessee River Basin, to persons, firms, or corporations who shall contract to erect thereon factories or manufacturing establishments, and who shall contract to purchase of said Corporation electric power for the operation of any such factory or manufacturing establishment. No contract shall be made by the President for the sale of any of such real estate as may be necessary for present or future use on the part of the Government for any of the purposes of this Act. Any such contract made by the President of the United States shall be carried out by the board: *Provided,* That no such contract shall be made that will in any way abridge or take away the preference right to purchase power given in this Act to States, counties, municipalities, or farm organizations: *Provided further,* That no lease shall be for a term to exceed fifty years: *Provided further,* That any sale shall be on condition that said land shall be used for industrial purposes only.

Sec. 25. The Corporation may cause proceedings to be instituted for the acquisition by condemnation of any lands, easements, or rights of way which, in the opinion of the Corporation, are necessary to carry out the provisions of this Act. The proceedings shall be instituted in the United States district court for the district in which the land, easement, right of way, or other interest, or any part thereof, is located, and such court shall have full jurisdiction to divest the complete title to the property sought to be acquired out of all persons or claimants and vest the same in the United States in fee simple, and to enter a decree quieting the title thereto in the United States of America.

Upon the filing of a petition for condemnation and for the purpose of ascertaining the value of the property to be acquired, and assessing the compensation to be paid, the court shall appoint three commissioners who shall be disinterested persons and who shall take and subscribe an oath that they do not own any lands, or interest or easement in any lands, which it may be desirable for the United States to acquire in the furtherance of said project and such commissioners shall not be selected from the locality wherein the land sought to be condemned lies. Such commissioners shall receive a per diem of not to exceed $15 for their services, together with an additional amount of $5 per day for subsistence for time actually spent in performing their duties as commissioners.

It shall be the duty of such commissioners to examine into the value of the lands sought to be condemned, to conduct hearings and receive evidence, and generally to take such appropriate steps as may be proper for the determination of the value of the said lands sought to be condemned, and for such purpose the commissioners are authorized to administer oaths and subpoena witnesses, which said witnesses shall receive the same fees as are provided for witnesses in the Federal courts. The said commissioners shall thereupon file a report setting forth their conclusions as to the value of the said property sought to be condemned, making a separate award and valuation in the premises with respect to each separate parcel involved. Upon the filing of such award in court the clerk of said court shall give notice of the filing of such award to the parties to said proceeding, in manner and form as directed by the judge of said court.

Either or both parties may file exceptions to the award of said commissioners within twenty days from the date of the filing of said award in court. Exceptions filed to such award shall be heard before three Federal district judges unless the parties, in writing, in person, or by their attorneys, stipulate that the exceptions may be heard before a lesser number of judges. On such hearing such judges shall pass de novo upon the proceedings had before the commissioners, may view the property, and may take additional evidence. Upon such hearings the said judges shall file their own award, fixing therein the value of the property sought to be condemned, regardless of the award previously made by the said commissioners.

At any time within thirty days from the filing of the decision of the district judges upon the hearing on exceptions to the award made by the commissioners, either party may appeal from such decision of the said judges to the circuit court of appeals, and the said circuit court of appeals shall upon the hearing on said appeal dispose of the same upon the record, without regard to the awards or findings theretofore made by the commissioners or the district judges, and such circuit court of appeals shall thereupon fix the value of the said property sought to be condemned.

Upon acceptance of an award by the owner of any property herein provided to be appropriated, and the payment of the money awarded or upon the failure of either party to file exceptions to the award of the commissioners within the time specified, or upon the award of the commissioners, and the payment of the money by the United States pursuant thereto, or the payment of the money awarded into the registry of the court by the Corporation, the title to said property and the right to the possession thereof shall pass to the United States, and the United States shall be entitled to a writ in the same proceeding to dispossess the former owner of said property, and all lessees, agents, and attorneys of such former owner, and to put the United States, by its corporate creature and agent, the Corporation, into possession of said property.

In the event of any property owned in whole or in part by minors, or insane persons, or incompetent persons, or estates of deceased persons, then the legal representatives of such minors, insane persons, incompetent persons, or estates shall have power, by and with the consent and approval of the trial judge in whose court said matter is for determination, to consent to or reject the awards of the commissioners herein provided for, and in the event that there be no legal representatives, or that the legal representatives for such minors, insale persons, or incompetent persons shall fail or decline to act, then such trial judge may, upon motion, appoint a guardian ad litem to act for such minors, insane persons, or incompetent persons, and such guardian ad litem shall act to the full extent and to the same purpose and effect as his ward could act, if competent, and such guardian ad litem shall be deemed to have full power and authority to respond, to conduct, or to maintain any proceeding herein provided for affecting his said ward.

Sec. 26. The net proceeds derived by the board from the sale of power and any of the products manufactured by the Corporation, after deducting the cost of operation, maintenance, depreciation, amortization, and an amount deemed by the board as necessary to withhold as operating capital, or devoted by the board to new construction, shall be paid into the Treasury of the United States at the end of each calendar year.

Sec. 27. All appropriations necessary to carry out the provisions of this Act are hereby authorized.

Sec. 28. That all Acts or parts of Acts in conflict herewith are hereby repealed, so far as they affect the operations contemplated by this Act.

Sec. 29. The right to alter, amend, or repeal this Act is hereby expressly declared and reserved, but no such amendment or repeal shall operate to impair the obligation of any contract made by said Corporation under any power conferred by this Act.

Sec. 30. The sections of this Act are hereby declared to be separable, and in the event any one or more sections of this Act be held to be unconstitutional, the same shall not affect the validity of other sections of this Act.

Approved, May 18, 1933.

SECURITIES ACT

Editor's comments: *The Securities Act of 1933 was to prevent the fraudulent sale of securities as well as to provide full disclosure of the character of securities. To achieve this goal, some of the provisions relating to the sale of securities were:*
- *Identified and defined relevant terms.*
- *Identified transactions exempt from coverage by the Act.*
- *Provided certain activities relating to interstate commerce and the mails.*
- *Provided for registration and information required in registration statements.*
- *Listed information to be included in a prospectus.*
- *Provided for civil penalties for dispensing false information.*
- *Gave certain investigative powers to the Federal Trade Commission (FTC).*
- *Provided for FTC decisions to be subject to review in the Circuit Court of Appeals.*
- *Provided that all FTC hearings would be public.*
- *Set certain requirements related to the sale of foreign securities.*

An Act to Provide Full and Fair Disclosure of the Character of Securities Sold in Interstate and Foreign Commerce and Through the Mails, and to Prevent Frauds in the Sale Thereof, and for Other Purposes
May 27, 1933

Be it enacted by the Senate and House of Representatives of the United States of America in Congress assembled,

Title I

Short Title

Sec. 1. This title may be cited as the "Securities Act of 1933."

Definitions

Sec. 2 When used in this title, unelss the context otherwise requires—

(1) The term "security" means any note, stock, treasury stock, bond, debenture, evidence of indebtedness, certificate of interest or participation in any profit-sharing agreement, collateral-trust certificate, preorganization certificate or subscription, transferable share, investment contract, voting-trust certificate, certificate of interest in property, tangible or intangible, or, in general, any instrument commonly known as a security, or any certificate of interest or participation in, temporary or interim certificate for, receipt for, or warrant or right to subscribe to or purchase, any of the foregoing.

(2) The term "person" means an individual, a corporation, a partnership, an association, a joint-stock company, a trust, any unincorporated

organization, or a government or political subdivision thereof. As used in this paragraph the term "trust" shall include only a trust where the interest or interests of the beneficiary or beneficiaries are evidenced by a security.

(3) The term "sale", "sell", "offer to sell," or "offer for sale" shall include every contract of sale or disposition of, attempt or offer to dispose of, or solicitation of an offer to buy, a security or interest in a security, for value; except that such terms shall not include preliminary negotiations or agreements between an issuer and any underwriter. Any security given or delivered with, or as a bonus on account of, any purchase of securities or any other thing, shall be conclusively presumed to constitute a part of the subject of such purchase and to have been sold for value. The issue or transfer of a right or privilege, when originally issued or transferred with a security, giving the holder of such security the right to convert such security into another security of the same issuer or of another person, or giving a right to subscribe to another security of the same issuer or of another person, which right cannot be exercised until some future date, shall not be deemed to be a sale of such other security; but the issue or transfer of such other security upon the exercise of such right of conversion or subscription shall be deemed a sale of such other security.

(4) The term "issuer" means every person who issues or proposes to issue any security or who guarantees a security either as to principal or income; except that with respect to certificates of deposit, voting-trust certificates, or collateral-trust certificates, or with respect to certificates or interest or shares in an unincorporated investment trust not having a board of directors (or persons performing similar functions) or of the fixed, restricted management, or unit type, the term "issuer" means the person or persons performing the acts and assuming the duties of depositor or manager pursuant to the provisions of the trust or other agreement or instrument under which such securities are issued; and except that with respect to equipment-trust certificates or like securities, the term "issuer" means the person by whom the equipment or property is or is to be used.

(5) The term "Commission" means the Federal Trade Commission.

(6) The term "Territory" means Alaska, Hawaii, Puerto Rico, the Philippine Islands, Canal Zone, the Virgin Islands, and the insular possessions of the United States.

(7) The term "interstate commerce" means trade or commerce in securities or any transportation or communication relating thereto among the several States or between the District of Columbia or any Territory of the United States and any State or other Territory, or between any foreign country and any State, Territory, or the District of Columbia, or within the District of Columbia.

(8) The term "registration statement" means the statement provided for in section 6, and includes any amendment thereto and any report, document,

or memorandum accompanying such statement or incorporated therein by reference.

(9) The term "write" or "written" shall include printed, lithographed, or in any means of graphic communication.

(10) The term "prospectus" means any prospectus, notice, circular, advertisement, letter, or communication, written or by radio, which offers any security for sale; except that (a) a communication shall not be deemed a prospectus if it is proved that prior to such communication a written prospectus meeting the requirements of section 10 was received, by the person to whom the communication was made, from the person making such communication or his principal, and (b) a notice, circular, advertisement, letter, or communication in respect of a security shall not be deemed to be a prospectus if it states from whom a written prospectus meeting the requirements of section 10 may be obtained and, in addition, does no more than identify the security, state the price thereof, and state by whom orders will be executed.

(11) The term "underwriter" means any person who has purchased from an issuer with a view to, or sells for an issuer in connection with, the distribution of any security, or participates or has a direct or indirect participation in such undertaking, or participates or has a participation in the direct or indirect underwriting of any such undertaking; but such term shall not include a person whose interest is limited to a commission from an underwriter or dealer not in excess of the usual and customary distributors' or sellers' commission. As used in this paragraph the term "issuer" shall include, in addition to an issuer, any person directly or indirectly controlling or controlled by the issuer, or any person under direct or indirect common control with the issuer.

(12) The term "dealer" means any person who engages either for all or part of his time, directly or indirectly, as agent, broker, or principal, in the business of offering, buying, selling, or otherwise dealing or trading in securities issued by another person.

Exempted Securities

Sec. 3. (a) Except as hereinafter expressly provided, the provisions of this title shall not apply to any of the following classes of securities:

(1) Any security which, prior to or within sixty days after the enactment of this title, has been sold or disposed of by the issuer or bona fide offered to the public, but this exemption shall not apply to any new offering of any such security by an issuer or underwriter subsequent to such sixty days;

(2) Any security issued or guaranteed by the United States or any Territory thereof, or by the District of Columbia, or by any State of the United States, or by any political subdivision of a State or Territory, or by any public instrumentality of one or more States or Territories exercising an essential governmental function, or by any corporation created and controlled or

supervised by and acting as an instrumentality of the Government of the United States pursuant to authority granted by the Congress of the United States, or by any national bank, or by any banking institution organized under the laws of any State or Territory, the business of which is substantially confined to banking and is supervised by the State or territorial banking commission or similar official; or any security issued by or representing an interest in or a direct obligation of a Federal reserve bank;

(3) Any note, draft, bill of exchange, or banker's acceptance which arises out of a current transaction or the proceeds of which have been or are to be used for current transactions, and which has a maturity at the time of issuance of not exceeding nine months, exclusive of days of grace, or any renewal thereof the maturity of which is likewise limited;

(4) Any security issued by a corporation organized and operated exclusively for religious, educational, benevolent, fraternal, charitable, or reformatory purposes and not for pecuniary profit, and no part of the net earnings of which inures to the benefit of any person, private stockholder, or individual;

(5) Any security issued by a building and loan association, homestead association, savings and loan association, or similar institution, substantially all the business of which is confined to the making of loans to members (but the foregoing exemption shall not apply with respect to any such security where the issuer takes from the total amount paid or deposited by the purchaser, by way of any fee, cash value or other device whatsoever, either upon termination of the investment at maturity or before maturity, an aggregate amount in excess of 3 per centum of the face value of such security), or any security issued by a farmers' cooperative association as defined in paragraphs (12), (13), and (14) of section 103 of the Revenue Act of 1932;

(6) Any security issued by a common carrier which is subject to the provisions of section 20a of the Interstate Commerce Act, as amended;

(7) Certificates issued by a receiver or by a trustee in bankruptcy, with the approval of the court;

(8) Any insurance or endowment policy or annuity contract or optional annuity contract, issued by a corporation subject to the supervision of the insurance commissioner, bank commissioner, or any agency or officer performing like functions, of any State or Territory of the United States or the District of Columbia.

(b) The Commission may from time to time by its rules and regulations, and subject to such terms and conditions as may be prescribed therein, add any class of securities to the securities exempted as provided in this section, if it finds that the enforcement of this title with respect to such securities is not necessary in the public interest and for the protection of investors by reason of the small amount involved or the limited character of the public offering; but no issue of securities shall be exempted under this subsection where the aggregate amount at which such issue is offered to the public exceeds $100,000.

Exempted Transactions

Sec. 4. The provisions of section 5 shall not apply to any of the following transactions:

(1) Transactions by any person other than an issuer, underwriter, or dealer; transactions by an issuer not with or through an underwriter and not involving any public offering; or transactions by a dealer (including an underwriter no longer acting as an underwriter in respect of the security involved in such transaction), except transactions within one year after the last date upon which the security was bona fide offered to the public by the issuer or by or through an underwriter (excluding in the computation of such year any time during which a stop order issued under section 8 is in effect as to the security), and except transactions as to securities constituting the whole or a part of an unsold allotment to or subscription by such dealer as a participant in the distribution of such securities by the issuer or by or through an underwriter.

(2) Brokers' transactions, executed upon customers' orders on any exchange or in the open or counter market, but not the solicitation of such orders.

(3) The issuance of a security of a person exchanged by it with its existing security holders exclusively, where no commission or other remuneration is paid or given directly or indirectly in connection with such exchange; or the issuance of securities to the existing security holders or other existing creditors of a corporation in the process of a bona fide reorganization of such corporation under the supervision of any court, either in exchange for the securities of such security holders or claims of such creditors or partly for cash and partly in exchange for the securities or claims of such security holders or creditors.

Prohibitions Relating to Interstate Commerce and the Mails

Sec. 5. (a) Unless a registration statement is in effect as to a security, it shall be unlawful for any person, directly or indirectly—

(1) to make use of any means or instruments of transportation or communication in interstate commerce or of the mails to sell or offer to buy such security through the use or medium of any prospectus or otherwise; or

(2) to carry or cause to be carried through the mails or in interstate commerce, by any means or instruments of transportation, any such security for the purpose of sale or for delivery after sale.

(b) It shall be unlawful for any person, directly or indirectly—

(1) to make use of any means or instruments of transportation or communication in interstate commerce or of the mails to carry or transmit any

prospectus relating to any security registered under this title, unless such prospectus meets the requirements of section 10; or

(2) to carry or to cause to be carried through the mails or in interstate commerce any such security for the purpose of sale or for delivery after sale, unless accompanied or preceded by a prospectus that meets the requirements of section 10.

(c) The provisions of this section relating to the use of the mails shall not apply to the sale of any security where the issue of which it is a part is sold only to persons resident within a single State or Territory, where the issuer of such securities is a person resident and doing business within, or, if a corporation, incorporated by and doing business within, such State or Territory.

Registration of Securities and Signing of Registration Statement

Sec. 6. (a) Any security may be registered with the Commission under the terms and conditions hereinafter provided, by filing a registration statement in triplicate, at least one of which shall be signed by each issuer, its principal executive officer or officers, its principal financial officer, its comptroller or principal accounting officer, and the majority of its board of directors or persons performing similar functions (or, if there is no board of directors or persons performing similar functions, by the majority of the persons or board having the power of management of the issuer), and in case the issuer is a foreign or Territorial person by its duly authorized representative in the United States; except that when such registration statement relates to a security issued by a foreign government, or political subdivision thereof, it need be signed only by the underwriter of such security. Signatures of all such persons when written on the said registration statements shall be presumed to have been so written by authority of the person whose signature is so affixed and the burden of proof, in the event such authority shall be denied, shall be upon the party denying the same. The affixing of any signature without the authority of the purported signer shall constitute a violation of this title. A registration statement shall be deemed effective only as to the securities specified therein as proposed to be offered.

(b) At the time of filing a registration statement the applicant shall pay to the Commission a fee of one one-hundredth of 1 per centum of the maximum aggregate price at which such securities are proposed to be offered, but in no case shall such fee be less than $25.

(c) The filing with the Commission of a registration statement, or of an amendment to a registration statement, shall be deemed to have taken place upon the receipt thereof, but the filing of a registration statement shall not be deemed to have taken place unless it is accompanied by a United States postal money order or a certified bank check or cash for the amount of the fee required under subsection (b).

(d) The information contained in or filed with any registration statement shall be made available to the public under such regulations as the Commission may prescribe, and copies thereof, photostatic or otherwise, shall be furnished to every applicant at such reasonable charge as the Commission may prescribe.

(e) No registration statement may be filed within the first forty days following the enactment of this Act.

Information Required in Registration Statement

Sec. 7. The registration statement, when relating to a security other than a security issued by a foreign government, or political subdivision thereof, shall contain the information, and be accompanied by the documents, specified in Schedule A, and when relating to a security issued by a foreign government, or political subdivision thereof, shall contain the information, and be accompanied by the documents, specified in Schedule B; except that the Commission may by rules or regulations provide that any such information or document need not be included in respect of any class of issuers or securities if it finds tha the requirement of such information or document is inapplicable to such class and that disclosure fully adequate for the protection of investors is otherwise required to be included within the registration statement. If any accountant, engineer, or appraiser, or any person whose profession gives authority to a statement made by him, is named as having prepared or certified any part of the registration statement, or is named as having prepared or certified a report or valuation for use in connection with the registration statement, the written consent of such person shall be filed with the registration statement. If any such person is named as having prepared or certified a report or valuation (other than a public official document or statement) which is used in connection with the registration statement, but is not named as having prepared or certified such report or valuation for use in connection with the registration statement, the written consent of such person shall be filed with the registration statement unless the Commission dispenses with such filing as impracticable or as involving undue hardship on the person filing the registration statement. Any such registration statement shall contain such other information, and be accompanied by such other documents, as the Commission may by rules or regulations require as being necessary or appropriate in the public interest or for the protection of investors.

Taking Effect of Registration Statements and Amendments Thereto

Sec. 8. (a) The effective date of a registration statement shall be the twentieth day after the filing thereof, except as hereinafter provided, and except that in case of securities of any foreign public authority, which has continued the full service of its obligations in the United States, the proceeds of which are to be devoted to the refunding of obligations payable in the United States, the registration statement shall become effective seven days after the filing thereof. If any amendment to any such statement is filed prior to the effective date of such statement, the registration statement shall be deemed to have been filed when such amendment was filed; except that an amendment filed with the consent of the Commission, prior to the effective date of the registration statement, or filed pursuant to an order of the Commission, shall be treated as a part of the registration statement.

(b) If it appears to the Commission that a registration statement is on its face incomplete or inaccurate in any material respect, the Commission may, after notice by personal service or the sending of confirmed telegraphic notice not later than ten days after the filing of the registration statement, and opportunity for hearing (at a time fixed by the Commission) within ten days after such notice by personal service or the sending of such telegraphic notice, issue an order prior to the effective date of registration refusing to permit such statement to become effective until it has been amended in accordance with such order. When such statement has been amended in accordance with such order the Commission shall so declare and the registration shall become effective at the time provided in subsection (a) or upon the date of such declaration, whichever date is later.

(c) An amendment filed after the effective date of the registration statement, if such amendment, upon its face, appears to the Commission not to be incomplete or inaccurate in any material respect, shall become effective on such date as the Commission may determine, having due regard to the public interest and the protection of investors.

(d) If it appears to the Commission at any time that the registration statement includes any untrue statement of a material fact or omits to state any material fact required to be stated therein or necessary to make the statements therein not misleading, the Commission may, after notice by personal service or the sending of confirmed telegraphic notice, and after opportunity for hearing (at a time fixed by the Commission) within fifteen days after such notice by personal service or the sending of such telegraphic notice, issue a stop order suspending the effectiveness of the registration statement. When such statement has been amended in accordance with such stop order the Commission shall so declare and thereupon the stop order shall cease to be effective.

(e) The Commission is hereby empowered to make an examination in any case in order to determine whether a stop order should issue under subsection (d). In making such examination the Commission or any officer or officers designated by it shall have access to and may demand the production of any books and papers of, and may administer oaths and affirmations to and examine, the issuer, underwriter, or any other person, in respect of any matter relevant to the examination, and may, in its discretion, require the production of a balance sheet exhibiting the assets and liabilities of the issuer, or its income statement, or both, to be certified to by a public or certified accountant approved by the Commission. If the issuer or underwriter shall fail to cooperate, or shall obstruct or refuse to permit the making of an examination, such conduct shall be proper ground for the issuance of a stop order.

(f) Any notice required under this section shall be sent to or served on the issuer, or, in case of a foreign government or political subdivision thereof, to or on the underwriter, or, in the case of a foreign or Territorial person, to or on its duly authorized representative in the United States named in the registration statement, properly directed in each case of telegraphic notice to the address given in such statement.

Court Review of Orders

Sec. 9. (a) Any person aggrieved by an order of the Commission may obtain a review of such order in the Circuit Court of Appeals of the United States, within any circuit wherein such person resides or has his principal place of business, or in the Court of Appeals of the District of Columbia, by filing in such court, within sixty days after the entry of such order, a written petition praying that the order of the Commission be modified or be set aside in whole or in part. A copy of such petition shall be forthwith served upon the Commission, and thereupon the Commission shall certify and file in the court a transcript of the record upon which the order complained of was entered. No objection to the order of the Commission shall be considered by the court unless such objection shall have been urged before the Commission. The finding of the Commission as to the facts, if supported by evidence, shall be conclusive. If either party shall apply to the court for leave to adduce additional evidence, and shall show to the satisfaction of the court that such additional evidence is material and that there were reasonable grounds for failure to adduce such evidence in the hearing before the Commission, the court may order such additional evidence to be taken before the Commission and to be adduced upon the hearing of such manner and upon such terms and conditions as to the court may seem proper. The Commission may modify its findings as to the facts, by reason of the additional evidence so taken, and it shall file such modified or new findings, which, if supported by evidence, shall be conclusive, and its recommendation, if any, for the modification or setting aside of the original order. The jurisdiction of the court shall be exclusive and its judgment and decree, affirming, modifying, or setting aside, in whole or in part, any order of the Commission, shall be final, subject to review by the Supreme Court of the United States upon certiorari or certification as provided in sections 239 and 240 of the Judicial Code, as amended (U.S.C., title 28, secs. 346 and 347).

(b) The commencement of proceedings under subsection (a) shall not, unless specifically ordered by the court, operate as a stay of the Commission's order.

Information Required in Prospectus

Sec. 10. (a) A prospectus —

(1) when relating to a security other than a security issued by a foreign government or political subdivision thereof, shall contain the same statements made in the registration statement, but it need not include the documents referred to in paragraphs (28) to (32), inclusive, of Schedule A;

(2) when relating to a security issued by a foreign government or political subdivision thereof shall contain the same statements made in the registration statement, but it need not include the documents referred to in paragraphs (13) and (14) of Schedule B.

(b) Notwithstanding the provisions of subsection (a) —

(1) when a prospectus is used more than thirteen months after the effective date of the registration statement, the information in the statements contained therein shall be as of a date not more than twelve months prior to such use.

(2) there may be omitted from any prospectus any of the statements required under such subsection (a) which the Commission may by rules or regulations designate as not being necessary or appropriate in the public interest or for the protection of investors.

(3) any prospectus shall contain such other information as the Commission may by rules or regulations require as being necessary or appropriate in the public interest or for the protection of investors.

(4) in the exercise of its powers under paragraphs (2) and (3) of this subsection, the Commission shall have authority to classify prospectuses according to the nature and circumstances of their use, and, by rules and regulations and subject to such terms and conditions as it shall specify therein, to prescribe as to each class the form and contents which it may find appropriate to such use and consistent with the public interest and the protection of investors.

(c) The statements of information required to be included in a prospectus by or under authority of subsection (a) or (b), when written, shall be placed in a conspicuous part of the prospectus in type as large as that used generally in the body of the prospectus.

(d) In any case where a prospectus consists of a radio broadcast, copies thereof shall be filed with the Commission under such rules and regulations as it shall prescribe. The Commission may by rules and regulations require the filing with it of forms of prospectuses used in connection with the sale of securities registered under this title.

Civil Liabilities on Account of False Registration Statement

Sec. 11. (a) In case any part of the registration statement, when such part became effective, contained an untrue statement of a material fact or omitted to state a material fact required to be stated therein or necessary to make the statements therein not misleading, any person acquiring such security (unless it is proved that at the time of such acquisition he knew of such untruth or omission) may, either at law or in equity, in any court of competent jurisdiction, sue —

(1) every person who signed the registration statement;

(2) every person who was a director of (or person performing similar functions) or partner in, the issuer at the time of the filing of the part of the registration statement with respect to which his liability is asserted;

(3) every person who, with his consent, is named in the registration statement as being or about to become a director, person performing similar functions, or partner;

(4) every accountant, engineer, or appraiser, or any person whose profession gives authority to a statement made by him, who has with his consent been named as having prepared or certified any part of the registration statement, or as having prepared or certified any report or valuation which is used in connection with the registration statement, with respect to the statement in such registration statement, report, or valuation, which purports to have been prepared or certified by him;

(5) every underwriter with respect to such security.

(b) Notwithstanding the provisions of subsection (a) no person, other than the issuer, shall be liable as provided therein who shall sustain the burden of proof—

(1) that before the effective date of the part of the registration statement with respect to which his liability is asserted (A) he had resigned from or had taken such steps as are permitted by law to resign from, or ceased or refused to act in, every office, capacity, or relationship in which he was described in the registration statement as acting or agreeing to act, and (B) he had advised the Commission and the issuer in writing that he had taken such action and that he would not be responsible for such part of the registration statement; or

(2) that if such part of the registration statement became effective without his knowledge, upon becoming aware of such fact he forthwith acted and advised the Commission, in accordance with paragraph (1), and, in addition, gave reasonable public notice that such part of the registration statement had become effective without his knowledge; or

(3) that (A) as regards any part of the registration statement not purporting to be made on the authority of an expert, and not purporting to be a copy of or extract from a report or valuation of an expert, and not purporting to be made on the authority of a public official document or statement, he had, after reasonable investigation, reasonable ground to believe and did believe, at the time such part of the registration statement became effective, that the statements therein were true and that there was no omission to state a material fact required to be stated therein or necessary to make the statements therein not misleading; and (B) as regards any part of the

registration statement purporting to be made upon his authority as an expert or purporting to be a copy of or extract from a report or valuation of himself as an expert, (i) he had, after reasonable investigation, reasonable ground to believe and did believe, at the time such part of the registration statement became effective, that the statements therein were true and that there was no omission to state a material fact required to be stated therein or necessary to make the statements therein not misleading, or (ii) such part of the registration statement did not fairly represent his statement as an expert or was not a fair copy of or extract from his report or valuation as an expert; and (C) as regards any part of the registration statement purporting to be made on the authority of an expert (other than himself) or purporting to be a copy of or extract from a report or valuation of an expert (other than himself), he had reasonable ground to believe and did believe, at the time such part of the registration statement became effective, that the statements therein were true and that there was no omission to state a material fact required to be stated therein or necessary to make the statements therein not misleading, and that such part of the registration statement fairly represented the statement of the expert or was a fair copy of or extract from the report or valuation of the expert; and (D) as regards any part of the registration statement purporting to be a statement made by an official person or purporting to be a copy of or extract from a public official document, he had reasonable ground to believe and did believe, at the time such part of the registration statement became effective, that the statements therein were true, and that there was no omission to state a material fact required to be stated therein or necessary to make the statements therein not misleading, and that such part of the registration statement fairly represented the statement made by the official person or was a fair copy of or extract from the public official document.

(c) In determining, for the purpose of paragraph (3) of subsection (b) of this section, what constitutes reasonable investigation and reasonable ground for belief, the standard of reasonableness shall be that required of a person occupying a fiduciary relationship.

(d) If any person becomes an underwriter with respect to the security after the part of the registration statement with respect to which his liability is asserted has become effective, then for the purposes of paragraph (3) of subsection (b) of this section such part of the registration statement shall be considered as having become effective with respect to such person as of the time when he became an underwriter.

(e) The suit authorized under subsection (a) may be either (1) to recover the consideration paid for such security with interest thereon, less the amount of any income received thereon, upon the tender of such security, or (2) for damages if the person suing no longer owns the security.

(f) All or any one or more of the persons specified in subsection (a) shall be jointly and severally liable, and every person who becomes liable to make any payment under this section may recover contribution as in cases of contract from any person who, if sued separately, would have been liable to make the same payment, unless the person who has become liable was, and the other was not, guilty of fraudulent misrepresentation.

(g) In no case shall the amount recoverable under this section exceed the price at which the security was offered to the public.

Civil Liabilities Arising in Connection with Prospectuses and Communications

Sec. 12. Any person who—

(1) sells a security in violation of section 5, or

(2) sells a security (whether or not exempted by the provisions of section 3, other than paragraph (2) of subsection (a) thereof), by the use of any means or instruments of transportation or communication in interstate commerce or of the mails, by means of a prospectus or oral communication, which includes an untrue statement of a material fact or omits to state a material fact necessary in order to make the statements, in the light of the circumstances under which they were made, not misleading (the purchaser not knowing of such untruth or omission), and who shall not sustain the burden of proof that he did not know, and in the exercise of reasonable care could not have known, of such untruth or omission, shall be liable to the person purchasing such security from him, who may sue either at law or in equity in any court of competent jurisdiction, to recover the consideration paid for such security with interest thereon, less the amount of any income received thereon, upon the tender of such security, or for damages if he no longer owns the security.

Limitation of Actions

Sec. 13. No action shall be maintained to enforce any liability created under section 11 or section 12 (2) unless brought within two years after the discovery of the untrue statement or the omission, or after such discovery should have been made by the exercise of reasonable diligence, or, if the action is to enforce a liability created under section 12 (1), unless brought within two years after the violation upon which it is based. In no event shall any such action be brought to enforce a liability created under section 11 or section 12 (1) more than ten years after the security was bona fide offered to the public.

Contrary Stipulations Void

Sec. 14. Any condition, stipulation, or provision binding any person acquiring any security to waive compliance with any provision of this title or of the rules and regulations of the Commission shall be void.

Liability of Controlling Persons

Sec. 15. Every person who, by or through stock ownership, agency, or otherwise, or who, pursuant to or in connection with an agreement or understanding with one or more other persons by or through stock ownership, agency, or otherwise, controls any person liable under section 11 or 12, shall also be liable jointly and severally with and to the same extent as such controlled person to any person to whom such controlled person is liable.

Additional Remedies

Sec. 16. The rights and remedies provided by this title shall be in addition to any and all other rights and remedies that may exist at law or in equity.

Fraudulent Interstate Transactions

Sec. 17. (a) It shall be unlawful for any person in the sale of any securities by the use of any means or instruments of transportation or communication in interstate commerce or by the use of the mails, directly or indirectly—

(1) to employ any device, scheme, or artifice to defraud, or

(2) to obtain money or property by means of any untrue statement of a material fact or any omission to state a material fact necessary in order to make the statements made, in the light of the circumstances under which they were made, not misleading, or

(3) to engage in any transaction, practice, or course of business which operates or would operate as a fraud or deceit upon the purchaser.

(b) It shall be unlawful for any person, by the use of any means or instruments of transportation or communication in interstate commerce or by the use of the mails, to publish, give publicity to, or circulate any notice, circular, advertisement, newspaper, article, letter, investment service, or communication which, though not purporting to offer a security for sale, describes such security for a consideration received or to be received, directly or indirectly, from an issuer, underwriter, or dealer, without fully disclosing the receipt, whether past or prospective, of such consideration and the amount thereof.

(c) The exemptions provided in section 3 shall not apply to the provisions of this section.

State Control of Securities

Sec. 18. Nothing in this title shall affect the jurisdiction of the securities commission (or any agency or office performing like functions) of any State or Territory of the United States, or the District of Columbia, over any security or any person.

Special Powers of Commission

Sec. 19. (a) The Commission shall have authority from time to time to make, amend, and rescind such rules and regulations as may be necessary to carry out the provisions of this title, including rules and regulations governing registration statements and prospectuses for various classes of securities and issuers, and defining accounting and trade terms used in this title. Among other things, the Commission shall have authority, for the purposes of this title, to prescribe the form or forms in which required information shall be set forth, the items or details to be shown in the balance sheet and earning statement, and the methods to be followed in the preparation of accounts, in the appraisal or valuation of assets and liabilities, in the determination of depreciation and depletion, in the differentiation of recurring and nonrecurring income, in the differentiation of investment and operating income, and in the preparation, where the Commission deems it necessary or desirable, of consolidated balance sheets or income accounts of any person directly or indirectly controlling or controlled by the issuer, or any person under direct or indirect common control with the issuer; but insofar as they relate to any common carrier subject to the provisions of section 20 of the Interstate Commerce Act, as amended, the rules and regulations of the Commission with respect to accounts shall not be inconsistent with the requirements imposed by the Interstate Commerce Commission under authority of such section 20. The rules and regulations of the Commission shall be effective upon publication in the manner which the Commission shall prescribe.

(b) For the purpose of all investigations which, in the opinion of the Commission, are necessary and proper for the enforcement of this title, any member of the Commission or any officer or officers designated by it are empowered to administer oaths and affirmations, subpena witnesses, take evidence, and require the production of any books, papers, or other documents which the Commission deems relevant or material to the inquiry. Such attendance of witnesses and the production of such documentary evidence may be required from any place in the United States or any Territory at any designated place of hearing.

Injunctions and Prosecution of Offenses

Sec. 20. (a) Whenever it shall appear to the Commission, either upon complaint or otherwise, that the provisions of this title, or of any rule or regulation prescribed under authority thereof, have been or are about to be violated, it may, in its discretion, either require or permit such person to file with it a statement in writing, under oath, or otherwise, as to all the facts and circumstances concerning the subject matter which it believes to be in the public interest to investigate, and may investigate such facts.

(b) Whenever it shall appear to the Commission that any person is engaged or about to engage in any acts or practices which constitute or will constitute a violation of the provisions of this title, or of any rule or regulation prescribed under authority thereof, it may in its discretion, bring an action in any district court of the United States, United States court of any

Territory, or the Supreme Court of the District of Columbia to enjoin such acts or practices, and upon a proper showing a permanent or temporary injunction or restraining order shall be granted without bond. The Commission may transmit such evidence as may be available concerning such acts or practices to the Attorney General who may, in his discretion, institute the necessary criminal proceedings under this title. Any such criminal proceeding may be brought either in the district wherein the transmittal of the prospectus or security complained of begins, or in the district wherein such prospectus or security is received.

(c) Upon application of the Commission the district courts of the United States, the United States courts of any Territory, and the Supreme Court of the District of Columbia, shall also have jurisdiction to issue writs of mandamus commanding any person to comply with the provisions of this title or any order of the Commission made in pursuance thereof.

Hearings by Commission

Sec. 21. All hearings shall be public and may be held before the Commission or an officer or officers of the Commission designated by it, and appropriate records thereof shall be kept.

Jurisdiction of Offenses and Suits

Sec. 22. (a) The district courts of the United States, the United States courts of any Territory, and the Supreme Court of the District of Columbia shall have jurisdiction of offenses and violations under this title and under the rules and regulations promulgated by the Commission in respect thereto, and, concurrent with State and Territorial courts, of all suits in equity and actions at law brought to enforce any liability or duty created by this title. Any such suit or action may be brought in the district wherein the defendant is found or is an inhabitant or transacts business, or in the district where the sale took place, if the defendant participated therein, and process in such cases may be served in any other district of which the defendant is an inhabitant or wherever the defendant may be found. Judgments and decrees so rendered shall be subject to review as provided in sections 128 and 240 of the Judicial Code, as amended (U.S.C., title 28, secs. 225 and 347). No case arising under this title and brought in any State court or competent jurisdiction shall be removed to any court of the United States. No costs shall be assessed for or against the Commission in any proceeding under this title brought by or against it in the Supreme Court or such other courts.

(b) In case of contumacy or refusal to obey a subpena issued to any person, any of the said United States courts, within the jurisdiction of which said person guilty of contumacy or refusal to obey is found or resides, upon application by the Commission may issue to such person an order requiring such person to appear before the Commission, or one of its examiners designated by it, there to produce documentary evidence if so ordered, or there to give evidence touching the matter in question; and any failure to obey such order of the court may be punished by said court as a contempt thereof.

(c) No person shall be excused from attending and testifying or from producing books, papers, contracts, agreements, and other documents before the Commission, or in obedience to the subpena of the Commission or any member thereof or any officer designated by it, or in any cause or proceeding instituted by the Commission, on the ground that the testimony or evidence, documentary or otherwise, required of him, may tend to incriminate him or subject him to a penalty or forfeiture; but no individual shall be prosecuted or subjected to any penalty or forfeiture for or on account of any transaction, matter, or thing concerning which he is compelled, after having claimed his privilege against self-incrimination, to testify or produce evidence, documentary or otherwise, except that such individual so testifying shall not be exempt from prosecution and punishment for perjury committed in so testifying.

Unlawful Representations

Sec. 23. Neither the fact that the registration statement for a security has been filed or is in effect nor the fact that a stop order is not in effect with respect thereto shall be deemed a finding by the Commission that the registration statement is true and accurate on its face or that it does not contain an untrue statement of fact or omit to state a material fact, or be held to mean that the Commission has in any way passed upon the merits of, or given approval to, such security. It shall be unlawful to make, or cause to be made, to any prospective purchaser any representation contrary to the foregoing provisions of this section.

Penalties

Sec. 24. Any person who willfully violates any of the provisions of this title, or the rules and regulations promulgated by the Commission under authority thereof, or any person who willfully, in a registration statement filed under this title, makes any untrue statement of a material fact or omits to state any material fact required to be stated therein or necessary to make the statements therein not misleading, shall upon conviction be fined not more than $5,000 or imprisoned not more than five years, or both.

Jurisdiction of Other Government Agencies Over Securities

Sec. 25. Nothing in this title shall relieve any person from submitting to the respective supervisory units of the Government of the United States information, reports, or other documents that are now or may hereafter be required by any provision of law.

Separability of Provisions

Sec. 26. If any provision of this Act, or the application of such provision to any person or circumstance, shall be held invalid, the remainder of this Act, or the application of such provision to persons or circumstances other than those as to which it is held invalid, shall not be affected thereby.

Schedule A

(1) The name under which the issuer is doing or intends to do business;

(2) the name of the State or other sovereign power under which the issuer is organized;

(3) the location of the issuer's principal business office, and if the issuer is a foreign or territorial person, the name and address of its agent in the United States authorized to receive notice;

(4) the names and addresses of the directors or persons performing similar functions, and the chief executive, financial and accounting officers, chosen or to be chosen if the issuer be a corporation, association, trust, or other entity; of all partners, if the issuer be a partnership; and of the issuer, if the issuer be an individual; and of the promoters in the case of a business to be formed, or formed within two years prior to the filing of the registration statement;

(5) the names and addresses of the underwriters;

(6) the names and addresses of all persons, if any, owning of record or beneficially, if known, more than 10 per centum of any class of stock of the issuer, or more than 10 per centum in the aggregate of the outstanding stock of the issuer as of a date within twenty days prior to the filing of the registration statement;

(7) the amount of securities of the issuer held by any person specified in paragraphs (4), (5), and (6) of this schedule, as of a date within twenty days prior to the filing of the registration statement, and, if possible, as of one year prior thereto, and the amount of the securities, for which the registration statement is filed, to which such persons have indicated their intention to subscribe;

(8) the general character of the business actually transacted or to be transacted by the issuer;

(9) a statement of the capitalization of the issuer, including the authorized and outstanding amounts of its capital stock and the proportion thereof paid up, the number and classes of shares in which such capital stock is divided, par value thereof, or if it has no par value, the stated or assigned value thereof, a description of the respective voting rights, preferences, conversion and exchange rights, rights to dividends, profits, or capital of each class, with respect to each other class, including the retirement and liquidation rights or values thereof;

(10) a statement of the securities, if any, covered by options outstanding or to be created in connection with the security to be offered, together with the names and addresses of all persons, if any, to be allotted more than 10 per centum in the aggregate of such options;

(11) the amount of capital stock of each class issued or included in the shares of stock to be offered;

(12) the amount of the funded debt outstanding and to be created by the security to be offered, with a brief description of the date, maturity, and character of such debt, rate of interest, character of amortization provisions, and the security, if any, therefor. If substitution of any security is permissible, a summarized statement of the conditions under which such substitution is permitted. If substitution is permissible without notice, a specific statement to that effect;

(13) the specific purposes in detail and the approximate amounts to be devoted to such purposes, so far as determinable, for which the security to be offered is to supply funds, and if the funds are to be raised in part from other sources, the amounts thereof and the sources thereof, shall be stated;

(14) the remuneration, paid or estimated to be paid, by the issuer or its predecessor, directly or indirectly, during the past year and ensuing year to (a) the directors or persons performing similar functions, and (b) its officers and other persons, naming them wherever such remuneration exceeded $25,000 during any such year;

(15) the estimated net proceeds to be derived from the security to be offered;

(16) the price at which it is proposed that the security shall be offered to the public or the method by which such price is computed and any variation therefrom at which any portion of such security is proposed to be offered to any persons or classes of persons, other than the underwriters, naming them or specifying the class. A variation in price may be proposed prior to the date of the public offering of the security, but the Commission shall immediately be notified of such variation;

(17) all commissions or discounts paid or to be paid, directly or indirectly, by the issuer to the underwriters in respect of the sale of the security to be offered. Commissions shall include all cash, securities, contracts, or anything else of value, paid, to be set aside, disposed of, or understandings with or for the benefit of any other persons in which any underwriter is interested, made, in connection with the sale of such security. A commission paid or to be paid in connection with the sale of such security by a person in which the issuer has an interest or which is controlled or directed by, or under common control with, the issuer shall be deemed to have been paid by the issuer. Where any such commission is paid the amount of such commission paid to each underwriter shall be stated;

(18) the amount or estimated amounts, itemized in reasonable detail, of

expenses, other than commissions specified in paragraph (17) of this schedule, incurred or borne by or for the account of the issuer in connection with the sale of the security to be offered or properly chargeable thereto, including legal, engineering, certification, authentication, and other charges;

(19) the net proceeds derived from any security sold by the issuer during the two years preceding the filing of the registration statement, the price at which such security was offered to the public, and the names of the principal underwriters of such security;

(20) any amount paid within two years preceding the filing of the registration statement or intended to be paid to any promoter and the consideration for any such payment;

(21) the names and addresses of the vendors and the purchase price of any property, or good will, acquire or to be acquired, not in the ordinary course of business, which is to be defrayed in whole or in part from the proceeds of the security to be offered, the amount of any commission payable to any person in connection with such acquisition, and the name or names of such person or persons, together with any expense incurred or to be incurred in connection with such acquisition, including the cost of borrowing money to finance such acquisition;

(22) full particulars of the nature and extent of the interest, if any, of every director, principal executive officer, and of every stockholder holding more than 10 per centum of any class of stock or more than 10 per centum in the aggregate of the stock of the issuer, in any property acquired, not in the ordinary course of business of the issuer, within two years preceding the filing of the registration statement or proposed to be acquired at such date;

(23) the names and addresses of counsel who have passed on the legality of the issue;

(24) dates of and parties to, and the general effect concisely stated of every material contract made, not in the ordinary course of business, which contract is to be executed in whole or in part at or after the filing of the registraton statement or which contract has been made not more than two years before such filing. Any management contract or contract providing for special bonuses or profit-sharing arrangments, and every material patent or contract for a material patent right, and every contract by or with a public utility company or an affiliate thereof, providing for the giving or receiving of technical or financial advice or service (if such contract may involve a charge to any party thereto at a rate in excess of $2,500 per year in cash or securities or anything else of value), shall be deemed a material contract;

(25) a balance sheet as of a date not more than ninety days prior to the date of the filing of the registration statement showing all of the assets of the issuer, the nature and cost thereof, whenever determinable, in such detail and in such form as the Commission shall prescribe (with intangible items segregated), including any loan in excess of $20,000 to any officer, director,

stockholder or person directly or indirectly controlling or controlled by the issuer, or person under direct or indirect common control with the issuer. All the liabilities of the issuer in such detail and such form as the Commission shall prescribe, including surplus of the issuer showing how and from what sources such surplus was created, all as of a date not more than ninety days prior to the filing of the registration statement. If such statement be not certified by an independent public or certified accountant, in addition to the balance sheet required to be submitted under this schedule, a similar detailed balance sheet of the assets and liabilities of the issuer, certified by an independent public or certified accountant, of a date not more than one year prior to the filing of the registration statement, shall be submitted;

(26) a profit and loss statement of the issuer showing earnings and income, the nature and source thereof, and the expenses and fixed charges in such detail and such form as the Commission shall prescribe for the latest fiscal year for which such statement is available and for the two preceding fiscal years, year by year, or, if such issuer has been in actual business for less than three years, then for such time as the issuer has been in actual business, year by year. If the date of the filing of the registration statement is more than six months after the close of the last fiscal year, a statement from such closing date to the latest practicable date. Such statement shall show what the practice of the issuer has been during the three years or lesser period as to the character of the charges, dividends or other distributions made against its various surplus accounts, and as to depreciation, depletion, and maintenance charges, in such detail and form as the Commission shall prescribe, and if stock dividends or avails from the sale of rights have been credited to income, they shall be shown separately with a statement of the basis upon which the credit is computed. Such statement shall also differentiate between any recurring and nonrecurring income and between any investment and operating income. Such statement shall be certified by an independent public or certified accountant;

(27) if the proceeds, or any part of the proceeds, of the security to be issued is to be applied directly or indirectly to the purchase of any business, a profit and loss statement of such business certified by an independent public or certified accountant, meeting the requirements of paragraph (26) of this schedule, for the three preceding fiscal years, together with a balance sheet, similarly certified, of such business, meeting the requirements of paragraph (25) of this schedule of a date not more than ninety days prior to the filing of the registration statement or at the date such business was acquired by the issuer if the business was acquired by the issuer more than ninety days prior to the filing of the registration statement;

(28) a copy of any agreement or agreements (or, if identic agreements are used, the forms thereof) made with any underwriter, including

all contracts and agreements referred to in paragraph (17) of this schedule;

(29) a copy of the opinion or opinions of counsel in respect to the legality of the issue, with a translation of such opinion, when necessary, into the English language;

(30) a copy of all material contracts referred to in paragraph (24) of this schedule, but no disclosure shall be required of any portion of any such contract if the Commission determines that disclosure of such portion would impair the value of the contract and would not be necessary for the protection of the investors;

(31) unless previously filed and registered under the provisions of this title, and brought up to date, (a) a copy of its articles of incorporation, with all amendments thereof and of its existing bylaws or instruments corresponding thereto, whatever the name, if the issuer be a corporation; (b) copy of all instruments by which the trust is created or declared, if the issuer is a trust; (c) a copy of its articles of partnership or association and all other papers pertaining to its organization, if the issuer is a partnership, unincorporated association, joint-stock company, or any other form of organization; and

(32) a copy of the underlying agreements or indentures affecting any stock, bonds, or debentures offered or to be offered.

In case of certificates of deposit, voting trust certificates, collateral trust certificates, certificates of interest or shares in unincorporated investment trusts, equipment trust certificates, interim or other receipts for certificates, and like securities, the Commission shall establish rules and regulations requiring the submission of information of a like character applicable to such cases, together with such other information as it may deem appropriate and necessary regarding the character, financial or otherwise, of the actual issuer of the securities and/or the person performing the acts and assuming the duties of depositor or manager.

Schedule B

(1) Name of borrowing government or subdivision thereof;

(2) specific purposes in detail and the approximate amounts to be devoted to such purposes, so far as determinable, for which the security to be offered is to supply funds, and if the funds are to be raised in part from other sources, the amounts thereof and the sources thereof, shall be stated;

(3) the amount of the funded debt and the estimated amount of the floating debt outstanding and to be created by the security to be offered, excluding intergovernmental debt, and a brief description of the date, maturity, character of such debt, rate of interest, character of amortization provisions, and the security, if any, therefor. If substitution of any security

is permissible, a statement of the conditions under which such substitution is permitted. If substitution is permissible without notice, a specific statement to that effect;

(4) whether or not the issuer or its predecessor has, within a period of twenty years prior to the filing of the registration statement, defaulted on the principal or interest of any external security, excluding intergovernmental debt, and, if so, the date, amount, and circumstances of such default, and the terms of the succeeding arrangement, if any;

(5) the receipts, classified by source, and the expenditures, classified by purpose, in such detail and form as the Commission shall prescribe for the latest fiscal year for which such information is available and the two preceding fiscal years, year by year;

(6) the names and addresses of the underwriters;

(7) the name and address of its authorized agent, if any, in the United States;

(8) the estimated net proceeds to be derived from the sale in the United States of the security to be offered;

(9) the price at which it is proposed that the security shall be offered in the United States to the public or the method by which such price is computed. A variation in price may be proposed prior to the date of the public offering of the security, but the Commission shall immediately be notified of such variation;

(10) all commissions paid or to be paid, directly or indirectly, by the issuer to the underwriters in respect of the sale of the security to be offered. Commissions shall include all cash, securities, contracts, or anything else of value, paid, to be set aside, disposed of, or understandings with or for the benefit of any other persons in which the underwriter is interested, made, in connection with the sale of such security. Where any such commission is paid, the amount of such commission paid to each underwriter shall be stated;

(11) the amount or estimated amounts, itemized in reasonable detail, of expenses, other than the commissions specified in paragraph (10) of this schedule, incurred or borne by or for the account of the issuer in connection with the sale of the security to be offered or properly chargeable thereto, including legal, engineering, certification, and other charges;

(12) the names and addresses of counsel who have passed upon the legality of the issue;

(13) a copy of any agreement or agreements made with any underwriter governing the sale of the security within the United States; and

(14) an agreement of the issuer to furnish a copy of the opinion or opinions of counsel in respect to the legality of the issue, with a translation, where necessary, into the English language. Such opinion shall set out in full all laws, decrees, ordinances, or other acts of Government under which the issue of such security has been authorized.

Title II

Section 201. For the purpose of protecting, conserving, and advancing the interest of the holders of foreign securities in default, there is hereby created a body corporate with the name "Corporation of Foreign Security Holders" (herein called the "Corporation"). The principal office of the Corporation shall be located in the District of Columbia, but there may be established agencies or branch offices in any city or cities of the United States under rules and regulations prescribed by the board of directors.

Sec. 202. The control and management of the Corporation shall be vested in a board of six directors, who shall be appointed and hold office in the following manner: As soon as practicable after the date this Act takes effect the Federal Trade Commission (hereinafter in this title called "Commission") shall appoint six directors, and shall designate a chairman and a vice chairman from among their number. After the directors designated as chairman and vice chairman cease to be directors, their successors as chairman and vice chairman shall be elected by the board of directors itself. Of the directors first appointed, two shall continue in office for a term of two years, two for a term of four years, and two for a term of six years, from the date this Act takes effect, the term of each to be designated by the Commission at the time of appointment. Their successors shall be appointed by the Commission, each for a term of six years from the date of the expiration of the term for which his predecessor was appointed, except that any person appointed to fill a vacancy occurring prior to the expiration of the term for which his predecessor was appointed shall be appointed only for the unexpired term of such predecessor. No person shall be eligible to serve as a director who within the five years preceding has had any interest, direct or indirect, in any corporation, company, partnership, bank or association which has sold, or offered for sale any foreign securities. The office of a director shall be vacated if the board of directors shall at a meeting specially convened for that purpose by resolution passed by a majority of at least two thirds of the board of directors, remove such member from office, provided that the member whom it is proposed to remove shall have seven days' notice sent to him of such meeting and that he may be heard.

Sec. 203. The Corporation shall have power to adopt, alter, and use a corporate seal; to make contracts; to lease such real estate as may be necessary for the transaction of its business; to sue and be sued, to complain and to defend, in any court of competent jurisdiction, State or Federal; to require from trustees, financial agents, or dealers in foreign securities information relative to the original or present holders of foreign securities and such other information as may be required and to issue subpenas therefor; to take over the functions of any fiscal and paying agents of any foreign securities in default; to borrow money for the purposes of this title, and to pledge as collateral for such loans any securities deposited with the Corporation pursuant to this title; by and with the consent and approval of the Commission to select, employ, and fix the compensation of officers, directors, members of committees, employees, attorneys, and agents of the Corporation, without regard to the provisions of other laws applicable to the employment and compensation of officers or employees of the United States; to define their authority and duties, require bonds of them and fix the penalties thereof, and to dismiss at pleasure such officers, employees, attorneys, and agents; and to prescribe, amend, and repeal, by its board of directors, bylaws, rules, and regulations governing the manner in which its general business may be conducted and the powers granted to it by law may be exercised and enjoyed, together with provisions for such committees and the functions thereof as the board of directors may deem necessary for facilitating its business under this title. The board of directors of the Corporation shall determine and prescribe the manner in which its obligations shall be incurred and its expenses allowed and paid.

Sec. 204. The board of directors may—

(1) Convene meetings of holders of foreign securities.

(2) Invite the deposit and undertake the custody of foreign securities which have defaulted in the payment either of principal or interest, and issue receipts or certificates in the place of securities so deposited.

(3) Appoint committees from the directors of the Corporation and/or all other persons to represent holders of any class or classes of foreign securities which have defaulted in the payment either of principal or interest and determine and regulate the functions of such committees. The chairman and vice chairman of the board of directors shall be ex officio chairman and vice chairman of each committee.

(4) Negotiate and carry out, or assist in negotiating and carrying out, arrangements for the resumption of payments due or in arrears in respect of any foreign securities in default or for rearranging the terms on which such securities may in future be held or for converting and exchanging the same for new securities or for any other object in relation thereto; and under this paragraph any plan or agreement made with respect to such securities shall be binding upon depositors, providing that the consent of holders resident in the United States of 60 per centum of the securities deposited with the Corporation shall be obtained.

(5) Undertake, superintend, or take part in the collection and application of funds derived from foreign securities which come into the possession of or under the control or management of the Corporation.

(6) Collect, preserve, publish, circulate, and render available in readily accessible form, when deemed essential or necessary, documents, statistics, reports, and information of all kinds in respect of foreign securities, including particularly records of foreign external securities in default and records of the progress made toward the payment of past-due obligations.

(7) Take such steps as it may deem expedient with the view of securing the adoption of clear and simple forms of foreign securities and just and sound principles in the conditions and terms thereof.

(8) Generally, act in the name and on behalf of the holders of foreign securities the care or representation of whose interests may be entrusted to the Corporation; conserve and protect the rights and interests of holders of foreign securities issued, sold, or owned in the United States; adopt measures for the protection, vindication, and preservation or reservation of the rights and interests of holders of foreign securities either on any default in or on breach or contemplated breach of the conditions on which such foreign securities may have been issued, or otherwise; obtain for such holders such legal and other assistance and advice as the board of directors may deem expedient; and do all such other things as are incident or conducive to the attainment of the above objects.

Sec. 205. The board of directors shall cause accounts to be kept of all matters relating to or connected with the transactions and business of the Corporation, and cause a general account and balance sheet of the Corporation to be made out in each year, and cause all accounts to be audited by one or more auditors who shall examine the same and report thereon to the board of directors.

Sec. 206. The Corporation shall make, print, and make public an annual report of its operations during each year, send a copy thereof, together with a copy of the account and balance sheet and auditor's report, to the Commission and to both Houses of Congress, and provide one copy of such report but not more than one on the application of any person and on receipt of a sum not exceeding $1: *Provided,* That the board of directors in its discretion may distribute copies gratuitously.

Sec. 207. The Corporation may in its discretion levy charges, assessed on a pro rata basis, on the holders of foreign securities deposited with it: *Provided,* That any charge levied at the time of depositing securities with the Corporation shall not exceed one fifth of 1 per centum of the face value of such securities: *Provided further,* That any additional charges shall bear a close relationship to the cost of operations and negotiations including those enumerated in sections 203 and 204 and shall not exceed 1 per centum of the face value of such securities.

Sec. 208. The Corporation may receive subscriptions from any person, foundation with a public purpose, or agency of the United States Government, and such subscriptions may, in the discretion of the board of directors, be treated as loans repayable when and as the board of directors shall determine.

Sec. 209. The Reconstruction Finance Corporation is hereby authorized to loan out of its funds not to exceed $75,000 for the use of the Corporation.

Sec. 210. Notwithstanding the foregoing provisions of this title, it shall be unlawful for, and nothing in this title shall be taken or construed as permitting or authorizing, the Corporation in this title created, or any committee of said Corporation, or any person or persons acting for or representing or purporting to represent it —

(a) to claim or assert or pretend to be acting for or to represent the Department of State or the United States Government;

(b) to make any statements or representations of any kind to any foreign government or its officials or the officials of any political subdivision of any foreign government that said Corporation or any committee thereof or any individual or individuals connected therewith were speaking or acting for the said Department of State or the United States Government; or

(c) to do any act directly or indirectly which would interfere with or obstruct or hinder or which might be calculated to obstruct, hinder or interfere with the policy or policies of the said Department of State or the Government of the United States or any pending or contemplated diplomatic negotiations, arrangements, business or exchanges between the Government of the United States or said Department of State and any foreign government or any political subdivision thereof.

Sec. 211. This title shall not take effect until the President finds that its taking effect is in the public interest and by proclamation so declares.

Sec. 212. This title may be cited as the "Corporation of Foreign Bondholders Act, 1933."

Approved, May 27, 1933.

UNIFORM VALUE OF COINS AND CURRENCIES, JOINT RESOLUTION

Editor's comments: *Clauses in obligations requiring payment in gold were declared contrary to public policy, effectively taking the United States monetary system off of the gold standard.*

Joint Resolution to Assure Uniform Value
to the Coins and Currencies of the United States
June 5, 1933

Whereas the holding of or dealing in gold affect the public interest, and are therefore subject to proper regulation and restriction; and Whereas the existing emergency has disclosed that provisions of obligations which purport to give the obligee a right to require payment in gold or a particular kind of coin or currency of the United States, or in an amount in money of the United States measured thereby, obstruct the power of the Congress to regulate the value of the money of the United States, and are inconsistent with the declared policy of the Congress to maintain at all times the equal power of every dollar, coined or issued by the United States, in the markets and in the payment of debts. Now, therefore, be it

Resolved by the Senate and House of Representatives of the United States of America in Congress assembled, That (a) every provision contained in or made with respect to any obligation which purports to give the obligee a right to require payment in gold or a particular kind of coin or currency, or in an amount in money of the United States measured thereby, is declared to be against public policy; and no such provision shall be contained in or made with respect to any obligation hereafter incurred. Every obligation, heretofore or hereafter incurred, whether or not any such provision is contained therein or made with respect thereto, shall be discharged upon payment, dollar for dollar, in any coin or currency which at the time of payment is legal tender for public and private debts. Any such provision contained in any law authorizing obligations to be issued by or under authority of the United States, is hereby repealed, but the repeal of any such provision shall not invalidate any other provision or authority contained in such law.

(b) As used in this resolution, the term "obligation" means an obligation (including every obligation of and to the United States, excepting currency) payable in money of the United States; and the term "coin or currency" means coin or currency of the United States, including Federal Reserve notes and circulating notes of Federal Reserve banks and national banking associations.

Sec. 2. The last sentence of paragraph (1) of subsection (b) of section 43 of the Act entitled "An Act to relieve the existing national economic emergency by increasing agricultural purchasing power, to raise revenue for extraordinary expenses incurred by reason of such emergency, to provide emergency relief with respect to agricultural indebtedness, to provide for the orderly liquidation of joint-stock land banks, and for other purposes", approved May 12, 1933, is amended to read as follows:

"All coins and currencies of the United States (including Federal Reserve notes and circulating notes of Federal Reserve banks and national banking associations) heretofore or hereafter coined or issued, shall be legal tender for all debts, public and private, public charges, taxes, duties, and dues, except that gold coins, when below the standard weight and limit of tolerance provided by law for the single piece, shall be legal tender only at valuation in proportion to their actual weight."

Approved, June 5, 1933, 4:40 p.m.

NATIONAL COOPERATIVE EMPLOYMENT SERVICE ACT

Editor's comments: *This Act created a bureau within the United States Department of Labor, known as the United States Employment Service (ES), to promote and develop a national system of employment offices. The ES was to maintain a veterans' service, a farm placement service, a public employment service for the District of Columbia, and was to provide assistance for establishing public employment offices in several States.*

An Act to Provide for the Establishment
of a National Employment System and for Cooperation
with the States in the Promotion of Such System,
and for Other Purposes
June 6, 1933

Be it enacted by the Senate and House of Representatives of the United States of America in Congress assembled, That (a) in order to promote the establishment and maintenance of a national system of public employment offices there is hereby created in the Department of Labor a bureau to be known as the United States Employment Service, at the head of which shall be a director. The director shall be appointed by the President, by and with the advice and consent of the Senate, and shall receive a salary at the rate of $8,500 per annum.

(b) Upon the expiration of three months after the enactment of this Act the employment service now existing in the Department of Labor shall be abolished; and all records, files, and property (including office equipment) of the existing employment service shall thereupon be transferred to the United States Employment Service; and all the officers and employees of such service shall thereupon be transferred to the United States Employment Service created by this Act without change in classification or compensation.

Sec. 2. The Secretary of Labor is authorized, without regard to the civil service laws, to appoint and, without regard to the Classification Act of 1923, as amended, to fix the compensation of one or more assistant directors and such other officers, employees, and assistants, and to make such expenditures (including expenditures for personal services and rent at the seat of government and elsewhere and for law books, books of reference, and periodicals) as may be necessary to carry out the provisions of this Act. In case of appointments for service in the veterans' employment service provided for in section 3 of this Act, the Secretary shall appoint only veterans of wars of the United States.

Sec. 3. (a) It shall be the province and duty of the bureau to promote and develop a national system of employment offices for men, women, and juniors who are legally qualified to engage in gainful occupations, to maintain a veterans' service to be devoted to securing employment for veterans, to maintain a farm placement service, to maintain a public employment service for the District of Columbia and, in the manner hereinafter provided, to assist in establishing and maintaining systems of public employment offices in the several States and the political subdivisions thereof in which there shall be located a veterans' employment service. The bureau shall also assist in coordinating the public employment offices throughout the country and in increasing their usefulness by developing and prescribing minimum standards of efficiency, assisting them in meeting problems peculiar to their localities, promoting uniformity in their administrative and statistical procedure, furnishing and publishing information as to opportunities for employment and other information of value in the operation of the system, and maintaining a system for clearing labor between the several States.

(b) Whenever in this Act the word "State" or "States" is used it shall be understood to include the Territories of Hawaii and Alaska.

Sec. 4. In order to obtain the benefits of appropriations apportioned under section 5, a State shall, through its legislature, accept the provisions of this Act and designate or authorize the creation of a State agency vested with all powers necessary to cooperate with the United States Employment Service under this Act.

Sec. 5. (a) For the purpose of carrying out the provisions of this Act there is hereby authorized to be appropriated (1) the sum of $1,500,000 for the fiscal year ending June 30, 1934, (2) $4,000,000 for each fiscal year thereafter up to and including the fiscal year ending June 30, 1938, (3) and thereafter such sums annually as the Congress may deem necessary. Seventy-five per centum of the amounts appropriated under this Act shall be apportioned by the director among the several States in the proportion which their population bears to the total population of the States of the United States according to the next preceding United States census, to be available for the purpose of establishing and maintaining systems of public employment offices in the several States and the political subdivisions thereof in accordance with the provisions of this Act. No payment shall be made in any year out of the amount of such appropriations apportioned to any State until an equal sum has been appropriated or otherwise made available for that year by the State, or by any agency thereof, including appropriations made by local subdivisions, for the purpose of maintaining public employment offices as a part of a State-controlled system of public employment offices; except that the amounts so appropriated by the State shall not be less than 25 per centum of the apportionment according to population made by the director for such State for the current year, and in no event less than $5,000. The balance of the amounts appropriated under this Act shall be available for all the purposes of this Act other than for apportionment among the several States as herein provided.

(b) The amounts apportioned to any State for any fiscal year shall be available for payment to and expenditure by such State, for the purposes of this Act, until the close of the next succeeding fiscal year; except that amounts apportioned to any State for any fiscal year preceding the fiscal year during which is commenced the first regular session of the legislature of such State held after the enactment of this Act shall remain available for payment to and expenditure by such State until the close of the fiscal year next succeeding that in which such session is commenced. Subject to the foregoing limitations, any amount so apportioned unexpended at the end of the period during which it is available for expenditure under this Act shall, within sixty days thereafter, be reapportioned for the current fiscal year among all the States in the same manner and on the same basis, and certified to the Secretary of the Treasury and treasures of the States in the same manner, as if it were being apportioned under this Act for the first time.

Sec. 6. Within sixty days after any appropriation has been made under authority of this Act the director shall make the apportionment thereof as provided in section 5 and shall certify to the Secretary of the Treasury and to the treasurers of the several States the amount apportioned to each State for the fiscal year for which the appropriation has been made.

Sec. 7. Within sixty days after any appropriation has been made under the authority of this Act, and as often thereafter while such appropriation remains available as he deems advisable, the director shall ascertain as to each of the several States (1) whether the State has, through its legislature or its governor, as the case may be, accepted the provisions of this Act and designated or authorized the creation of an agency to cooperate with the United States Employment Service in the administration of this Act in compliance with the provisions of section 4 of this Act; and (2) the amounts, if any, which have been appropriated or otherwise made available by such State and by any agency thereof, including appropriations made by local subdivisions, in compliance with the provisions of section 5 of this Act. If the director finds that a State has complied with the requirements of such sections, and if plans have been submitted and approved in compliance with the provisions of section 8 of this Act, the director shall determine the amount of the payments, if any, to which the State is entitled under the provisions of section 5, and certify such amount to the Secretary of the Treasury. Such certificate shall be sufficient authority to the Secretary of the Treasury to make payments to the State in accordance therewith.

Sec. 8. Any State desiring to receive the benefits of this Act shall, by the agency designated to cooperate with the United States Employment Service, submit to the director detailed plans for carrying out the provisions of this Act within such State. In those States where a State board, department, or agency exists which is charged with the administration of State laws for vocational rehabilitation of physically handicapped persons, such plans shall include provision for cooperation between such board, department, or agency and the agency designated to cooperate with the United States Employment Service under this Act. If such plans are in conformity with the provisions of this Act and reasonably appropriate and adequate to carry out its purposes, they shall be approved by the director and due notice of such approval shall be given to the State agency.

Sec. 9. Each State agency cooperating with the United States Employment Service under this Act shall make such reports concerning its operations and expenditures as shall be prescribed by the director. It shall be the duty of the director to ascertain whether the system of public employment offices maintained in each State is conducted in accordance with the rules and regulations and the standards of efficiency prescribed by the director in accordance with the provisions of this Act. The director may revoke any existing certificates or withhold any further certificate provided for in section 7, whenever he shall determine, as to any State, that the cooperating State agency has not properly expended the moneys paid to it or the moneys herein required to be appropriated by such State, in accordance with plans approved under this Act. Before any such certificate shall be revoked or withheld from any State, the director shall give notice in writing to the State agency stating specifically wherein the State has failed to comply with such plans. The State agency may appeal to the Secretary of Labor from the action of the director in any such case, and the Secretary of Labor may either affirm or reverse the action of the director with such directions as he shall consider proper.

Sec. 10. During the current fiscal year and the two succeeding fiscal years the Director is authorized to expend in any State so much of the sum apportioned to such State according to population, and so much of the unapportioned balance of the appropriation made under the provisions of section 5 as he may deem necessary, as follows:

(a) In States where there is no State system of public employment offices, in establishing and maintaining a system of public employment offices under the control of the Director.

(b) In States where there is a State system of public employment offices, but where the State has not complied with the provisions of section 4, in establishing a cooperative Federal and State system of public employment offices to be maintained by such officer or board and in such manner as may be agreed upon by and between the Governor of the State and the Director.

The authority contained in this section shall terminate at the expiration of the period specified in the first paragraph of this section, and thereafter no assistance shall be rendered such States until the legislatures thereof provide for cooperation with the United States Employment Service as provided in section 4 of this Act.

Sec. 11. (a) The director shall establish a Federal Advisory Council composed of men and women representing employers and employees in equal numbers and the public for the purpose of formulating policies and discussing problems relating to employment and insuring impartiality, neutrality, and freedom from political influence in the solution of such problems. Members of such council shall be selected from time to time in such manner as the director shall prescribe and shall serve without compensation, but when attending meetings of the council they shall be allowed necessary traveling and subsistence expenses, or per diem allowance in lieu thereof, within the limitations prescribed by law for civilian employees in the executive branch of the Government. The council shall have access to all files and records of the United States Employment Service. The director shall also require the organization of similar State advisory councils composed of men and women representing employers and employees in equal numbers and the public.

(b) In carrying out the provisions of this Act the director is authorized and directed to provide for the giving of notice of strikes or lockouts to applicants before they are referred to employment.

Sec. 12. The director, with the approval of the Secretary of Labor, is hereby authorized to make such rules and regulations as may be necessary to carry out the provisions of this Act.

Sec. 13. The Postmaster General is hereby authorized and directed to extend to the United States Employment Service and to the system of employment offices operated by it in conformity with the provisions of this Act, and to all State employment systems which receive funds appropriated under authority of this Act, the privilege of free transmission of official mail matter.

Approved, June 6, 1933.

HOME OWNERS' LOAN ACT

Editor's comments: The Home Owners' Loan Act of 1933 repealed the direct loan provision of the Federal Home Loan Bank Act.

The Act also created two organizations, the Home Owners' Loan Corporation (HOLC) and the Federal Savings and Loan Associations (FSLA).

Section 4 of the Act authorized the Federal Home Loan Bank Board to creat the HOLC. Capital stock for the HOLC was authorized but was not to exceed an aggregate of $200,000,000; bonds could be issued to an aggregate of $2,000,000,000. Both principal and interest of the bonds were exempt from all taxation.

The HOLC was authorized to acquire home mortgages and other obligations in exchange for its bonds. In such exchange, transactions, taxes, assessments, maintenance, repairs, and incidental expenses could be paid for in cash.

Under section 5, the Board was authorized to provide for FSLAs "in order to provide local mutual thrift institutions in which people may invest their funds in order to provide for the financing of homes..."

An Act to Provide Emergency Relief with Respect to Home Mortgage Indebtedness, to Refinance Home Mortgages, to Extend Relief to the Owners of Homes Occupied by Them and Who Are Unable to Amortize Their Debt Elsewhere, to Amend the Federal Home Loan Bank Act, to Increase the Market for Obligations of the United States and for Other Purposes
June 13, 1933

Be it enacted by the Senate and House of Representatives of the United States of America in Congress assembled, That this Act may be cited as the "Home Owners' Loan Act of 1933."

Definitions

Sec. 2. As used in this Act—

(a) The term "Board" means the Federal Home Loan Bank Board created under the Federal Home Loan Bank Act.

(b) The term "Corporation" means the Home Owners' Loan Corporation created under section 4 of this Act.

(c) The term "home mortgage" means a first mortgage on real estate in fee simple or on a leasehold under a renewable lease for not less than ninety-nine years, upon which there is located a dwelling for not more than four families, used by the owner as a home or held by him as his homestead, and having a value not exceeding $20,000; and the term "first mortgage" includes such classes of first liens as are commonly given to secure advances on real estate under the laws of the State in which the real estate is located, together with the credit instruments, if any, secured thereby.

(d) The term "association" means a Federal Savings and Loan Association chartered by the Board as provided in section 5 of this Act.

Repeal of Direct Loan Provision of Federal Home Loan Bank Act

Sec. 3. Subsection (d) of section 4 of the Federal Home Loan Bank Act (providing for direct loans to home owners) is hereby repealed.

Creation of Home Owners' Loan Corporation

Sec. 4. (a) The Board is hereby authorized and directed to create a corporation to be known as the Home Owners' Loan Corporation, which shall be an instrumentality of the United States, which shall have authority to sue and to be sued in any court of competent jurisdiction, Federal or State, and which shall be under the direction of the Board and operated by it under such bylaws, rules, and regulations as it may prescribe for the accomplishment of the purposes and intent of this section. The members of the Board shall constitute the board of directors of the Corporation and shall serve as such directors without additional compensation.

(b) The Board shall determine the minimum amount of capital stock of the Corporation and is authorized to increase such capital stock from time to time in such amounts as may be necessary, but not to exceed in the aggregate $200,000,000. Such stock shall be subscribed for by the Secretary of the Treasury on behalf of the United States, and payments for such subscriptions shall be subject to call in whole or in part by the Board and shall be made at such time or times as the Secretary of the Treasury deems advisable. The Corporation shall issue to the Secretary of the Treasury receipts for payments by him for or on account of such stock, and such receipts shall be evidence of the stock ownership of the United States. In order to enable the Secretary of the Treasury to make such payments when called, the Reconstruction Finance Corporation is authorized and directed to allocate and make available to the Secretary of the Treasury the sum of $200,000,000, or so much thereof as may be necessary, and for such purpose the amount of the notes, bonds, debentures, or other such obligations which the Reconstruction Finance Corporation is authorized and empowered under section 9 of the Reconstruction Finance Corporation Act, as amended, to have outstanding at any one time, is hereby increased by such amounts as may be necessary.

(c) The Corporation is authorized to issue bonds in an aggregate amount not to exceed $2,000,000,000, which may be sold by the Corporation to obtain funds for carrying out the purposes of this section, or exchanged as hereinafter provided. Such bonds shall be issued in such denominations as the Board shall prescribe, shall mature within a period of not more than eighteen years from the date of their issue, shall bear interest at a rate not to exceed 4 per centum per annum, and shall be fully and unconditionally guaranteed as to interest only by the United States, and such guaranty shall be expressed on the face thereof. In the event that the Corporation shall be unable to pay upon demand, when due, the interest on any such bonds, the Secretary of the Treasury shall pay to the Corporation the amount of such interest, which is hereby authorized to be appropriated out of any money in the Treasury not otherwise appropriated, and the Corporation shall pay the amount of such interest to the holders of the bonds. Upon the payment of such interest by the Secretary of the Treasury the amount so paid shall become an obligation to the United States of the Corporation and shall bear interest at the same rate as that borne by the bonds upon which the interest has been so paid. The bonds issued by the Corporation under this subsection shall be exempt, both as to principal and interest, from all taxation (except surtaxes, estate, inheritance, and gift taxes) now or hereafter imposed by the United States or any District, Territory, dependency, or possession thereof, or by any State, county, municipality, or local taxing authority. The Corporation, including its franchise, its capital, reserves and surplus, and its loans and income, shall likewise be exempt from such taxation; except that any real property of the Corporation shall be subject to taxation to the same extent, according to its value, as other real property is taxed.

(d) The Corporation is authorized, for a period of three years after the date of enactment of this Act, (1) to acquire in exchange for bonds issued by it, home mortgages and other obligations and liens secured by real estate (including the interest of a vendor under a purchase-money mortgage or contract) recorded or filed in the proper office or executed prior to the date of the enactment of this Act, and (2) in connection with any such exchange, to make advances in cash to pay the taxes and assessments on the real estate, to provide for necessary maintenance and make necessary repairs, to meet the incidental expenses of the transaction, and to pay such amounts, not exceeding $50, to the holder of the mortgage, obligation, or lien acquired as may be the difference between the face value of the bonds exchanged plus accrued interest thereon and the purchase price of the mortgage, obligation, or lien. The face value of the bonds so exchanged plus accrued interest thereon and the cash so advanced shall not exceed in any case $14,000, or 80 per centum of the value of the real estate as determined by an appraisal made by the Corporation, whichever is the smaller. In any case in which the amount of the face value of the bonds exchanged plus accrued interest thereon and the cash advanced is less than the amount the home owner owes with respect to the home mortgage or other obligation or lien so acquired by the Corporation, the Corporation shall credit the difference between such amounts to the home owner and shall reduce the amount owed by the home owner to the Corporation to that extent. Each home mortgage or other obligation or lien so acquired shall be carried as a first lien or refinanced as a home mortgage by the Corporation on the basis of the price paid therefor by the Corporation, and shall be amortized by means of monthly payments sufficient to retire the interest and principal within a period of not to exceed fifteen years; but the amortization payments of any home owner may be made quarterly, semiannually, or annually, if in the judgment of the Corporation the situation of the home owner requires it. Interest on the unpaid balance of the obligation of the home owner to the Corporation shall be at a rate not exceeding 5 per centum per annum. The Corporation may at any time grant an extension of time to any home owner for the payment of any installment or principal or interest owned by him to the Corporation if, in the judgment of the Corporation, the circumstances of the home owner and the condition of the security justify such extension, and no payment of any installment of principal shall be required during the period of three years from the date this Act takes effect if the home owner shall not be in default with respect to any other condition or covenant of his mortgage. As used in this subsection, the term "real estate" includes only real estate held in fee simple or on a leasehold under a lease renewable for not less than ninety-nine years, upon which there is located a dwelling for not more than four families used by the owner as a home or held by him as a homestead and having a value not exceeding $20,000. No discrimination shall be made under this Act against any home mortgage by reason of the fact that the real estate securing such mortgage is located in a municipality, county, or taxing district which is in default upon any of its obligations.

(e) The Corporation is further authorized, for a period of three years from the date of enactment of this Act, to make loans in cash subject to the same limitations and for the same purposes for which cash advances may be made under subsection (d) of this section, in cases where the property is not otherwise encumbered; but no such loan shall exceed 50 per centum of the value of the property securing the same as determined upon an appraisal made by the Corporation. Each such loan shall be secured by a duly recorded home mortgage, and shall bear interest at the same rate and shall be subject to the same provisions with respect to amortization and extensions as are applicable in the case of obligations refinanced under subsection (d) of this section.

(f) The Corporation is further authorized, for a period of three years from the date of encactment of this Act, in any case in which the holder of a home mortgage or other obligation or lien eligible for exchange under subsection (d) of this section does not accept the bonds of the Corporation in exchange as provided in such subsection and in which the Corporation finds that the home owner cannot obtain a loan from ordinary lending agencies, to make cash advances to such home owner in an amount not to exceed 40 per centum of the value of the property for the purposes specified in such subsection (d). Each such loan shall be secured by a duly recorded home mortgage and shall bear interest at a rate of interest which shall be uniform throughout the United States, but which in no event shall exceed a rate of 6 per centum per annum, and shall be subject to the same provisions with respect to amortization and extensions as are applicable in cases of obligations refinanced under subsection (d) of this section.

(g) The Corporation is further authorized, for a period of three years from the date of the enactment of this Act, to exchange bonds and to advance cash, subject to the limitations provided in subsection (d) of this section, to redeem or recover homes lost by the owners by foreclosure or forced sale by a trustee under a deed of trust or under power of attorney, or by voluntary surrender to the mortgagee within two years prior to such exchange or advance.

(h) The Board shall make rules for the appraisal of the property on which loans are made under this section so as to accomplish the purposes of this Act.

(i) Any person indebted to the Corporation may make payment to it in part or in full by delivery to it of its bonds which shall be accepted for such purpose at face value.

(j) The Corporation shall have power to select, employ, and fix the compensation of such officers, employees, attorneys, or agents as shall be necessary for the performance of its duties under this Act, without regard to the provisions of other laws applicable to the employment or compensation of officers, employees, attorneys, or agents of the United States. No such officer, employee, attorney, or agent shall be paid compensation at a rate in excess of the rate provided by law in the case of the members of the Board. The Corporation shall be entitled to the free use of the United States mails for its official business in the same manner as the executive departments of the Government, and shall determine its necessary expenditures under this Act and the manner in which they shall be incurred, allowed, and paid, without regard to the provisions of any other law governing the expenditure of public funds. The Corporation shall pay such proportion of the salary and expenses of the members of the Board and of its officers and employees as the Board may determine to be equitable, and may use the facilities of Federal Home Loan Banks, upon making reasonable compensation therefor as determined by the Board.

(k) The Board is authorized to make such bylaws, rules and regulations, not inconsistent with the provisions of this section, as may be necessary for the proper conduct of the affairs of the Corporation. The Corporation is further authorized and directed to retire and cancel the bonds and stock of the Corporation as rapidly as the resources of the Corporation will permit. Upon the retirement of such stock, the reasonable value thereof as determined by the Board shall be paid into the Treasury of the United States and the receipts issued therefor shall be canceled. The Board shall proceed to liquidate the Corporation when its purposes have been accomplished, and shall pay any surplus or accumulated funds into the Treasury of the United States. The Corporation may declare and pay such dividends to the United States as may be earned and as in the judgment of the Board it is proper for the Corporation to pay.

Federal Savings and Loan Association

Sec. 5. (a) In order to provide local mutual thrift institutions in which people may invest their funds and in order to provide for the financing of homes, the Board is authorized, under such rules and regulations as it may prescribe, to provide for the organization, incorporation, examination, operation, and regulation of associations to be known as "Federal Savings and Loan Associations", and to issue charters therefor, giving primary consideration to the best practices of local mutual thrift and home-financing institutions in the United States.

(b) Such associations shall raise their capital only in the form of payments on such shares as are authorized in their charter, which shares may be retired as is therein provided. No deposits shall be accepted and no certificates of indebtedness shall be issued except for such borrowed money as may be authorized by regulations of the Board.

(c) Such associations shall lend their funds only on the security of their shares or on the security of first liens upon homes or combination of homes and business property within fifty miles of their home office: *Provided,* That not more than $20,000 shall be loaned on the security of a first lien upon any one such property; except that not exceeding 15 per centum of the assets of such association may be loaned on other improved real estate without regard to said $20,000 limitation, and without regard to said fifty-mile limit, but secured by first lien thereon: *And provided further,* That any portion of the assets of such associations may be invested in obligations of the United States or the stock or bonds of a Federal Home Loan Bank.

(d) The Board shall have full power to provide in the rules and regulations herein authorized for the reorganization, consolidation, merger, or liquidation of such associations, including the power to appoint a conservator or a receiver to take charge of the affairs of any such association, and to require an equitable readjustment of the capital structure of the same; and to release any such association from such control and permit its further operation.

(e) No charter shall be granted except to persons of good character and responsibility, nor unless in the judgment of the Board a necessity exists for such an institution in the community to be served, nor unless there is a reasonable probability of its usefulness and success, nor unless the same can be established without undue injury to properly conducted existing local thrift and home-financing institutions.

(f) Each such association, upon its incorporation, shall become automatically a member of the Federal Home Loan Bank of the district in which it is located, or if convenience shall require and the Board approve, shall become a member of a Federal Home Loan Bank of an adjoining district. Such associations shall qualify for such membership in the manner provided in the Federal Home Loan Bank Act with respect to other members.

(g) The Secretary of the Treasury is authorized on behalf of the United States to subscribe for preferred shares in such associations which shall be preferred as to the assets of the association and which shall be entitled to a dividend, if earned, after payment of expenses and provision for reasonable reserves, to the same extent as other shareholders. It shall be the duty of the Secretary of the Treasury to subscribe for such preferred shares upon the request of the Board; but the subscription by him to the shares of any one association shall not exceed $100,000, and no such subscription shall be called for unless in the judgment of the Board the funds are necessary for the encouragement of local home financing in the community to be served and for the reasonable financing of homes in such community. Payment on such shares may be called from time to time by the association, subject to the approval of the Board and the Secretary of the Treasury; but the amount paid in by the Secretary of the Treasury shall at no time exceed the amount paid in by all other shareholders, and the aggregate amount of shares held by the Secretary of the Treasury shall not exceed at any time the aggregate amount of shares held by all other shareholders. To enable the Secretary of the Treasury to make such subscriptions when called there is hereby authorized to be appropriated, out of any money in the Treasury not otherwise appropriated, the sum of $100,000,000, to be immediately available and to remain available until expended. Each such association shall issue receipts for such payments by the Secretary of the Treasury in such form as may be approved by the Board, and such receipts shall be evidence of the interest of the United States in such preferred shares to the extent of the amount so paid. Each such association shall make provision for the retirement of its preferred shares held by the Secretary of the Treasury, and beginning at the expiration of five years from the time of the investment in such shares, the association shall set aside one third of the receipts from its investing and borrowing shareholders to be used for the purpose of such retirement. In case of the liquidation of any such association the shares held by the Secretary of the Treasury shall be retired at par before any payments are made to other shareholders.

(h) Such associations, including their franchises, capital, reserves, and surplus, and their loans and income, shall be exempt from all taxation now or hereafter imposed by the United States, and all shares of such associations shall be exempt both as to their value and the income therefrom from all taxation (except surtaxes, estate, inheritance, and gift taxes) now or hereafter imposed by the United States; and no State, Territorial, county, municipal, or local taxing authority shall impose any tax on such associations or their franchise, capital, reserves, surplus, loans, or income greater than that imposed by such authority on other similar local mutual or cooperative thrift and home financing institutions.

(i) Any member of a Federal Home Loan Bank may convert itself into a Federal Savings and Loan Association under this Act upon a vote of its stockholders as provided by the law under which it operates; but such conversion shall be subject to such rules and regulations as the Board may prescribe, and thereafter the converted association shall be entitled to all the benefits of this section and shall be subject to examination and regulation to the same extent as other associations incorporated pursuant to this Act.

Encouragement of Saving and Home Financing

Sec. 6. To enable the Board to encourage local thrift and local home financing and to promote, organize, and develop the associations herein provided for or similar associations organized under local laws, there is hereby authorized to be appropriated, out of any money in the Treasury not otherwise appropriated, the sum of $150,000, to be immediately available and remain available until expended, subject to the call of the Board, which sum, or so much thereof as may be necessary, the Board is authorized to use in its discretion for the accomplishment of the purposes of this section without regard to the provisions of any other law governing the expenditure of public funds.

Sec. 7. The provisions of this Act shall apply to the continental United States, to the Territories of Alaska and Hawaii, and to Puerto Rico and the Virgin Islands.

Penalties

Sec. 8. (a) Whoever makes any statement, knowing it to be false, or whoever willfully overvalues any security, for the purpose of influencing in any way the action of the Home Owners' Loan Corporation or the Board or an association upon any application, advance, discount, purchase, or repurchase agreement, or loan, under this Act, or any extension thereof by renewal deferment, or action or otherwise, or the acceptance, release, or substitution of security therefor, shall be punished by a fine of not more than $5,000, or by imprisonment for not more than two years, or both.

(b) Whoever (1) falsely makes, forges, or counterfeits any note, debenture, bond, or other obligation or coupon, in imitation of or purporting to be a note, debenture, bond, or other obligation, or coupon, issued by the Home Owners' Loan Corporation or an association; or (2) passes, utters, or publishes, or attempts to pass, utter, or publish, any false, forged, or counterfeited note, debenture, bond, or other obligation, or coupon, purporting to have been issued by the Home Owners' Loan Corporation or an association, knowing the same to be false, forged, or counterfeited; or (3) falsely alters any note, debenture, bond or other obligation, or coupon, issued or purporting to have been issued by the Home Owners' Loan Corporation or an association; or (4) passes, utters, or publishes, or attempts to pass, utter, or publish, as true any falsely altered or spurious note, debenture, bond, or other obligation, or coupon, issued or purporting to have been issued by the Home Owners' Loan Corporation or an association, knowing the same to be falsely altered or spurious, shall be punished by a fine of not more than $10,000, or by imprisonment for not more than five years, or both.

(c) Whoever, being connected in any capacity with the Board or the Home Owners' Loan Corporation or an association (1) embezzles, abstracts, purloins, or willfully misapplies any moneys, funds, securities, or other things of value, whether belonging to it or pledged or otherwise intrusted to it; or (2) with intent to defraud the Board or the Home Owners' Loan Corporation or an association, or any other body politic or corporate, or any individual, or to deceive any officer, auditor, or examiners of the Board or the Home Owners' Loan Corporation or an association, makes any false entry in any book, report, or statement of or to the Board or the Home Owners' Loan Corporation or an association, or, without being duly authorized, draws any order or issues, puts forth, or assigns any note, debenture, bond, or other obligation, or draft, mortgage, judgment, or decree thereof, shall be punished by a fine of not more than $10,000, or by imprisonment for not more than five years, or both.

(d) The provisions of sections 112, 113, 114, 115, 116, and 117 of the Criminal Code of the United States (U.S.C., title 18, secs. 202 to 207, inclusive), insofar as applicable, are extended to apply to contracts or agreements of the Home Owners' Loan Corporation and an association under this Act, which, for the purposes hereof, shall be held to include advances, loans, discounts, and purchase and repurchase agreements; extensions and renewals thereof; and acceptances, releases, and substitutions of security therefor.

(e) No person, partnership, association, or corporation shall make any charge in connection with a loan by the Corporation or an exchange of bonds or cash advance under this Act except ordinary charges authorized and required by the Corporation for services actually rendered for examination and perfecting of title, appraisal, and like necessary services. Any person, partnership, association, or corporation violating the provisions of this subsection shall, upon conviction thereof, be fined not more than $10,000, or imprisoned not more than five years, or both.

Separability Provision

Sec. 9. If any provision of this Act, or the application thereof to any person or circumstances, is held invalid, the remainder of the Act, and the application of such provision to other persons or circumstances, shall not be affected thereby.

Approved, June 13, 1933.

BANKING ACT

Editor's comments: *Primarily, the Banking Act extensively amended various sections of the Federal Reserve Act by:*

- *Requiring that each Federal reserve bank keep itself informed about the loans of its member banks and the amounts of such loans.*
- *Requiring what affiliates of member banks furnish the member bank with reports which were to be filed with the appropriate Federal reserve bank.*
- *Providing for the examination of State member banks.*
- *Fixing the percentage of a member bank's capital and surplus represented by loans.*
- *Creating the Federal Deposit Insurance Corporation to insure bank deposits.*

An Act to Provide for the Safer and More Effective Use of the Assets of Banks, to Regulate Interbank Control, to Prevent the Undue Diversion of Funds into Speculative Operations, and for Other Purposes
June 16, 1933

Be it enacted by the Senate and House of Representatives of the United States of America in Congress assembled, That the short title of this Act shall be the "Banking Act of 1933."

Sec. 2. As used in this Act and in any provision of law amended by this Act—

(a) The terms "banks", "national bank", "national banking association", "member bank", "board", "district", and "reserve bank" shall have the meanings assigned to them in section 1 of the Federal Reserve Act, as amended.

(b) Except where otherwise specifically provided, the term "affiliate" shall include any corporation, business trust, association, or other similar organization—

(1) Of which a member bank, directly or indirectly, owns or controls either a majority of the voting shares or more than 50 per centum of the number of shares voted for the election of its directors, trustees, or other persons exercising similar functions at the preceding election, or controls in any manner the election of a majority of its directors, trustees, or other persons exercising similar functions; or

(2) Of which control is held, directly or indirectly, through stock ownership or in any other manner, by the shareholders of a member bank who own or control either a majority of the shares of such bank or more than 50 per centum of the number of shares voted for the election of directors of such bank at the preceding election, or by trustees for the benefit of the shareholders of any such bank; or

(3) Of which a majority of its directors, trustees, or other persons exercising similar functions are directors of any one member bank.

(c) The term "holding company affiliate" shall include any corporation, business trust, association, or other similar organization —

(1) Which owns or controls, directly or indirectly, either a majority of the shares of capital stock of a member bank or more than 50 per centum of the number of shares voted for the election of directors of any one bank at the preceding election, or controls in any manner the election of a majority of the directors of any one bank; or

(2) For the benefit of whose shareholders or members all or substantially all the capital stock of a member bank is held by trustees.

Sec. 3. (a) The fourth paragraph after paragraph "Eighth" of section 4 of the Federal Reserve Act, as amended (U.S.C., title 12, sec. 301), is amended to read as follows:

"Said board of directors shall administer the affairs of said bank fairly and impartially and without discrimination in favor of or against any member bank or banks and may, subject to the provisions of law and the orders of the Federal Reserve Board, extend to each member bank such discounts, advancements, and accommodations as may be safely and reasonably made with due regard for the claims and demands of other member banks, the maintenance of sound credit conditions, and the accommodation of commerce, industry, and agriculture. The Federal Reserve Board may prescribe regulations further defining within the limitations of this Act the conditions under which discounts, advancements, and the accommodations may be extended to member banks. Each Federal reserve bank shall keep itself informed of the general character and amount of the loans and investments of its member banks with a view to ascertaining whether undue use is being made of bank credit for the speculative carrying of or trading in securities, real estate, or commodities, or for any other purpose inconsistent with the maintenance of sound credit conditions; and, in determining whether to grant or refuse advances, rediscounts or other credit accommodations, the Federal reserve bank shall give consideration to such information. The chairman of the Federal reserve bank shall report to the Federal Reserve Board any such undue use of bank credit by any member bank, together with his recommendation. Whenever, in the judgment of the Federal Reserve Board, any member bank is making such undue use of bank credit, the Board may, in its discretion, after reasonable notice and an opportunity for a hearing, suspend such bank from the use of the credit facilities of the Federal Reserve System and may terminate such suspension or may renew it from time to time."

(b) The paragraph of section 4 of the Federal Reserve Act, as amended (U.S.C., title 12, sec. 304), which commences with the words "The Federal Reserve Board shall classify" is amended by inserting before the period at the end thereof a colon and the following: "*Provided,* That whenever any two or more member banks within the same Federal reserve district are affiliated with the same holding company affiliate, participation by such member banks in any such nomination or election shall be confined to one of such banks, which may be designated for the purpose by such holding company affiliate."

Sec. 4. The first paragraph of section 7 of the Federal Reserve Act, as amended (U.S.C., title 12, sec. 289), is amended, effective July 1, 1932, to read as follows:

"After all necessary expenses of a Federal reserve bank shall have been paid or provided for, the stockholders shall be entitled to receive an annual dividend of 6 per centum of the paid-in capital stock, which dividend shall be cumulative. After the aforesaid dividend claims have been fully met, the net earnings shall be paid into the surplus fund of the Federal reserve bank."

Sec. 5. (a) The first paragraph of section 9 of the Federal Reserve Act, as amended (U.S.C., title 12, sec. 321; Supp. VI, title 12, sec. 321), is amended by inserting immediately after the words "United States" a comma and the following: "including Morris Plan banks and other incorporated banking institutions engaged in similar business."

(b) The second paragraph of section 9 of the Federal Reserve Act, as amended, is amended by adding at the end thereof the following: "*Provided, however,* That nothing herein contained shall prevent any State member bank from establishing and operating branches in the United States or any dependency or insular possession thereof or in any foreign country, on the same terms and conditions and subject to the same limitations and restrictions as are applicable to the establishment of branches by national banks."

(c) Section 9 of the Federal Reserve Act, as amended (U.S.C., title 12, secs. 321-331; Supp. VI, title 12, secs. 321-332), is further amended by adding at the end thereof the following new paragraphs:

"Any mutual savings bank having no capital stock (including any other banking institution the capital of which consists of weekly or other time deposits which are segregated from all other deposits and are regarded as capital stock for the purposes of taxation and the declaration of dividends), but having surplus and undivided profits not less than the amount of capital required for the organization of a national bank in the same place, may apply for and be admitted to membership in the Federal Reserve System in the same manner and subject to the same provisions of law as State banks and trust companies, except that any such savings bank shall subscribe for capital stock of the Federal reserve bank in an amount equal to six-tenths of 1 per centum of its total deposit liabilities as shown by the most recent report of examination of such savings bank preceding its admission to membership. Thereafter such subscription shall be adjusted semiannually on the same percentage basis in accordance with rules and regulations prescribed by the Federal Reserve Board. If any such mutual savings bank applying for membership is not permitted by the laws under which it was organized to purchase stock in a Federal reserve bank, it shall, upon admission to the system, deposit with the Federal reserve bank an amount equal to the amount which it would have been required to pay in on account of a subscription to capital stock. Thereafter such deposit shall be adjusted semiannually in the same manner as subscriptions for stock. Such deposits shall be subject to the same conditions with respect to repayment as amounts paid upon subscriptions to capital stock by other member banks and the Federal reserve bank shall pay interest thereon at the same rate as dividends are actually paid on outstanding shares of stock of such Federal reserve bank. If the laws under which any such savings bank was organized be amended so as to authorize mutual savings banks to subscribe for Federal reserve bank stock, such savings bank shall thereupon subscribe for the appropriate amount of stock in the Federal reserve bank, and the deposit hereinbefore provided for in lieu of payment upon capital stock shall be applied upon such subscription. If the laws under which any such savings bank was organized be not amended at the next session of the legislature following the admission of such savings bank to membership so as to authorize mutual savings banks to purchase Federal reserve bank stock, or if such laws be so amended and such bank fail within six months thereafter to purchase such stock, all of its rights and privileges as a member bank shall be forfeited and its membership in the Federal Reserve System shall be terminated in the manner prescribed elsewhere in this section with respect to State member banks and trust companies. Each such mutual savings bank shall comply with all the provisions of law applicable to State member banks and trust companies, with the regulations of the Federal Reserve Board and with the conditions of membership prescribed for such savings bank at the time of admission to membership, except as otherwise hereinbefore provided with respect to capital stock.

"Each bank admitted to membership under this section shall obtain from each of its affiliates other than member banks and furnish to the Federal reserve bank of its district and to the Federal Reserve Board not less than three reports during each year. Such reports shall be in such form as the Federal Reserve Board may prescribe, shall be verified by the oath or affirmation of the president or such other officer as may be designated by the board of directors of such affiliate to verify such reports, and shall disclose the information hereinafter provided for as of dates identical with those fixed by the Federal Reserve Board for reports of the condition of the affiliated member bank. Each such report of an affiliate shall be transmitted as herein provided at the same time as the corresponding report of the affiliated member bank, except that the Federal Reserve Board may, in its discretion, extend such time for good cause shown. Each such report shall contain such information as in the judgment of the Federal Reserve Board shall be necessary to disclose fully the relations between such affiliate and such bank and to enable the Board to inform itself as to the effect of such relations upon the affiars of such bank. The reports of such affiliates shall be published by the bank under the same conditions as govern its own condition reports.

"Any such affiliated member bank may be required to obtain from any such affiliate such additional reports as in the opinion of its Federal reserve bank or the Federal Reserve Board may be necessary in order to obtain a full and complete knowledge of the condition of the affiliated member bank. Such additional reports shall be transmitted to the Federal reserve bank and the Federal Reserve Board and shall be in such form as the Federal Reserve Board may prescribe.

"Any such affiliated member bank which fails to obtain from any of its affiliates and furnish any report provided for by the two preceding paragraphs of this section shall be subject to a penalty of $100 for each day during which such failure continues, which, by direction of the Federal Reserve Board, may be collected, by suit or otherwise, by the Federal reserve bank of the district in which such member bank is located. For the purposes of this paragraph and the two preceding paragraphs of this section, the term "affiliate" shall include holding company affiliates as well as other affiliates.

"State member banks shall be subject to the same limitations and conditions with respect to the purchasing, selling, underwriting, and holding of investment securities and stock as are applicable in the case of national banks under paragraph "Seventh" of section 5136 of the Revised Statutes, as amended.

"After one year from the date of the enactment of the Banking Act of 1933, no certificate representing the stock of any State member bank shall represent the stock of any other corporation, except a member bank or a corporation existing on the date this paragraph takes effect engaged solely in holding the bank premises of such State member bank, nor shall the ownership, sale, or transfer of any certificate representing the stock of any such bank be conditioned in any manner whatsoever upon the ownership, sale, or transfer of a certificate representing the stock of any other corporation, except a member bank.

"Each State member bank affiliated with a holding company affiliate shall obtain from such holding company affiliate, within such time as the Federal Reserve Board shall prescribe, an agreement that such holding company affiliate shall be subject to the same conditions and limitations as are applicable under section 5144 of the Revised Statutes, as amended, in the case of holding company affiliates of national banks. A copy of each such agreement shall be filed with the Federal Reserve Board. Upon the failure of a State member bank affiliated with a holding company affiliate to obtain such an agreement within the time so prescribed, the Federal Reserve Board shall require such bank to surrender its stock in the Federal reserve bank and to forfeit all rights and privileges of membership in the Federal Reserve System as provided in this section. Whenever the Federal Reserve Board shall have revoked the voting permit of any such holding company affiliate, the Federal Reserve Board may, in its discretion, require any or all State member banks affiliated with such holding company affiliate to surrender their stock in the Federal reserve bank and to forfeit all rights and privileges of membership in the Federal Reserve System as provided in this section.

"In connection with examinations of State member banks, examiners selected or approved by the Federal Reserve Board shall make such examinations of the affairs of all affiliates of such banks as shall be necessary to disclose fully the relations between such banks and their affiliates and the effect of such relations upon the affairs of such banks. The expense of examination of affiliates of any State member bank may, in the discretion of the Federal Reserve Board, be assessed against such bank and, when so assessed, shall be paid by such bank. In the event of the refusal to give any information requested in the course of the examination of any such affiliate, or in the event of the refusal to permit such examination, or in the event of the refusal to pay any expense so assessed, the Federal Reserve Board may, in its discretion, require any or all State member banks affiliated with such affiliate to surrender their stock in the Federal reserve bank and to forfeit all rights and privileges of membership in the Federal Reserve System, as provided in this section."

Sec. 6. (a) The second paragraph of section 10 of the Federal Reserve Act, as amended (U.S.C., title 12, sec. 242), is amended to read as follows:

"The Secretary of the Treasury and the Comptroller of the Currency shall be ineligible during the time they are in office and for two years thereafter to hold any office, position, or employment in any member bank. The appointive members of the Federal Reserve Board shall be ineligible during the time they are in office and for two years thereafter to hold any office, position, or employment in any member bank, except that this restriction shall not apply to a member who has served the full term for which he was appointed. Upon the expiration of the term of any appointive member of the Federal Reserve Board in office when this paragraph as amended takes effect, the President shall fix the term of the successor to such member at not to exceed twelve years, as designated by the President at the time of nomination, but in such manner as to provide for the expiration of the term of not more than one appointive member in any two-year period, and thereafter each appointive member shall hold office for a term of twelve years from the expiration of the term of his predecessor. Of the six persons thus appointed, one shall be designated by the President as governor and one as vice governor of the Federal Reserve Board. The governor of the Federal Reserve Board, subject to its supervision, shall be its active executive officer. Each member of the Federal Reserve Board shall within fifteen days after notice of appointment make and subscribe to the oath of office."

(b) The fourth paragraph of section 10 of the Federal Reserve Act, as amended (U.S.C., title 12, sec. 244), is amended to read as follows:

"The principal offices of the Board shall be in the District of Columbia. At meetings of the Board the Secretary of the Treasury shall preside as chairman, and, in his absence, the governor shall preside. In the absence of both the Secretary of the Treasury and the governor the vice governor shall preside. In the absence of the Secretary of the Treasury, the governor, and the vice governor the Board shall elect a member to act as chairman pro tempore. The Board shall determine and prescribe the manner in which its obligations shall be incurred and its disbursements and expenses allowed and paid, and may leave on deposit in the Federal Reserve banks the proceeds of assessments levied upon them to defray its estimated expenses and the salaries of its members and employees, whose employment, compensation, leave, and expenses shall be governed solely by the provisions of this Act, specific amendments thereof, and rules and regulations of the Board not inconsistent therewith; and funds derived from such assessments shall not be construed to be Government funds or appropriated moneys. No member of the Federal Reserve Board shall be an officer or director of any bank, banking institution, trust company, or Federal reserve bank or hold stock in any bank, banking institution, or trust company; and before entering upon his duties as a member of the Federal Reserve Board he shall certify under oath that he has complied with this requirement, and such certification shall be filed with the secretary of the Board. Whenever a vacancy shall occur, other than by expiration of term, among the six members of the Federal Reserve Board appointed by the President as above provided, a successor shall be appointed by the President, by and with the advice and consent of the Senate, to fill such vacancy, and when appointed he shall hold office for the unexpired term of his predecessor."

Sec. 7. Paragraph (m) of section 11 of the Federal Reserve Act, as amended (U.S.C., title 12, sec. 248), is amended to read as follows:

"(m) Upon the affirmative vote of not less than six of its members the Federal Reserve Board shall have power to fix from time to time for each Federal reserve district the percentage of individual bank capital and surplus which may be represented by loans secured by stock or bond collateral made by member banks within such district, but no such loan shall be made by any such bank to any person in an amount in excess of 10 per centum of the unimpaired capital and surplus of such bank. Any percentage so fixed by the Federal Reserve Board shall be subject to change from time to time upon ten days' notice, and it shall be the duty of the Board to establish such percentages with a view to preventing the undue use of bank loans for the speculative carrying of securities. The Federal Reserve Board shall have power to direct any member bank to refrain from further increase of its loans secured by stock or bond collateral for any period up to one year under penalty of suspension of all rediscount privileges at Federal reserve banks."

Sec. 8. The Federal Reserve Act, as amended, is amended by inserting between sections 12 and 13 (U.S.C., title 12, secs. 261, 262, and 342), thereof the following new sections:

"Sec. 12A. (a) There is hereby created a Federal Open Market Committee (hereinafter referred to as the 'committee'), which shall consist of as many members as there are Federal reserve districts. Each Federal reserve bank by its board of directors shall annually select one member of said committee. The meetings of said committee shall be held at Washington, District of Columbia, at least four times each year, upon the call of the governor of the Federal Reserve Board or at the request of any three members of the committee, and, in the discretion of the Board, may be attended by the members of the Board.

"(b) No Federal reserve bank shall engage in open-market operations under section 14 of this Act except in accordance with regulations adopted by the Federal Reserve Board. The Board shall consider, adopt, and transmit to the committee and to the several Federal reserve banks regulations relating to the open-market transactions of such banks and the relations of the Federal Reserve System with foreign central or other foreign banks.

"(c) The time, character, and volume of all purchases and sales of paper described in section 14 of this Act as eligible for open-market operations shall be governed with a view to accommodating commerce and business and with regard to their bearing upon the general credit situation of the country.

"(d) If any Federal reserve bank shall decide not to participate in open-market operations recommended and approved as provided in paragraph (b) hereof, it shall file with the chairman of the committee within thirty days a notice of its decision, and transmit a copy thereof to the Federal Reserve Board.

"Sec. 12B. (a) There is hereby created a Federal Deposit Insurance Corporation (hereinafter referred to as the "Corporation"), whose duty it shall be to purchase, hold, and liquidate, as hereinafter provided, the assets of national banks which have been closed by action of the Comptroller of the Currency, or by vote of their directors, and the assets of State member banks which have been closed by action of the appropriate State authorities, or by vote of their directors; and to insure, as hereinafter provided, the deposits of all banks which are entitled to the benefits of insurance under this section.

"(b) The management of the Corporation shall be vested in a board of directors consisting of three members, one of whom shall be the Comptroller of the Currency, and two of whom shall be citizens of the United States to be appointed by the President, by and with the advice and consent of the Senate. One of the appointive members shall be the chairman of the board of directors of the Corporation and not more than two of the members of such board of directors shall be members of the same political party. Each such appointive member shall hold office for a term of six years and shall receive compensation at the rate of $10,000 per annum, payable monthly out of the funds of the Corporation, but the Comptroller of the Currency shall not receive additional compensation for his services as such member.

"(c) There is hereby authorized to be appropriated, out of any money in the Treasury not otherwise appropriated, the sum of $150,000,000, which shall be available for payment by the Secretary of the Treasury for capital stock of the Corporation in an equal amount, which shall be subscribed for by him on behalf of the United States. Payments upon such subscription shall be subject to call in whole or in part by the board of directors of the Corporation. Such stock shall be in addition to the amount of capital stock required to be subscribed for by Federal reserve banks and member and nonmember banks as hereinafter provided, and the United States shall be entitled to the payment of dividends on such stock to the same extent as member and nonmember banks are entitled to such payment on the class A stock of the Corporation held by them. Receipts for payments by the United States for or on account of such stock shall be issued by the Corporation to the Secretary of the Treasury and shall be evidence of the stock ownership of the United States.

"(d) The capital stock of the Corporation shall be divided into shares of $100 each. Certificates of stock of the Corporation shall be of two classes— class A and class B. Class A stock shall be held by member and nonmember banks as hereinafter provided and they shall be entitled to payment of dividends out of net earnings at the rate of 6 per centum per annum on the capital stock paid in by them, which dividends shall be cumulative, or to the extent of 30 per centum of such net earnings in any one year, whichever amount shall be the greater, but such stock shall have no vote at meetings of stockholders. Class B stock shall be held by Federal reserve banks only and shall not be entitled to the payment of dividends. Every Federal reserve bank shall subscribe to shares of class B stock in the Corporation to an amount equal to one half of the surplus of such bank on January 1, 1933, and its subscriptions shall be accompanied by a certified check payable to the Corporation in an amount equal to one half of such subscription. The remainder of such subscription shall be subject to call from time to time by the board upon ninety days' notice.

"(e) Every bank which is or which becomes a member of the Federal Reserve System on or before July 1, 1934, shall take all steps necessary to enable it to become a class A stockholder of the Corporation on or before July 1, 1934; and thereafter no State bank or trust company or mutual savings bank shall be admitted to membership in the Federal Reserve System until it becomes a class A stockholder of the Corporation, no national bank in the continental United States shall be granted a certificate by the Comptroller of the Currency authorizing it to commence the business of banking until it becomes a member of the Federal Reserve System and a class A stockholder of the Corporation, and no national bank in the continental United States for which a receiver or conservator has been appointed shall be permitted to resume the transaction of its banking business until it becomes a class A stockholder of the Corporation. Every member bank shall apply to the Corporation for class A stock of the Corporation in an amount equal to one half of 1 per centum of its total deposit liabilities as computed in accordance with regulations prescribed by the Federal Reserve Board; except that in the case of a member bank organized after the date this section takes effect, the amount of such class A stock applied for by such member bank during the first twelve months after its organization shall equal 5 per centum of its paid-up capital and surplus, and beginning after the expiration of such twelve months' period the amount of such class A stock of such member bank shall be adjusted annually in the same manner as in the case of other member banks. Upon receipt of such application the Corporation shall request the Federal Reserve Board, in the case of a State member bank, or the Comptroller of the Currency, in the case of a national bank, to certify upon the basis of a thorough examination of such bank whether or not the assets of the applying bank are adequate to enable it to meet all of its liabilities to depositors and other creditors as shown by the books of the bank; and the Federal Reserve Board or the Comptroller of the Currency shall make such certification as soon as practicable. If such certification be in the affirmative, the Corporation shall grant such application and the applying bank shall pay one half of its subscription in full and shall thereupon become a class A stockholder of the Corporation: *Provided,* That no member bank shall be required to make such payment or become a class A stockholder of the Corporation before July 1, 1934. The remainder of such subscription shall be subject to call from time to time by the board of directors of the Corporation. If such certification be in the negative, the Corporation shall deny such application. If any national bank shall have not become a class A stockholder of the Corporation on or before July 1, 1934, the Comptroller of the Currency shall appoint a receiver or conservator therefor in accordance with the provisions of existing law. Except as provided in subsection (g) of this section, if any State member bank shall not have become a class A stockholder of the Corporation on or before July 1, 1934, the Federal Reserve Board shall terminate its membership in the Federal Reserve System in accordance with the provisions of section 9 of this Act.

"(f) Any State bank or trust company or mutual savings bank which applies for membership in the Federal Reserve System or for conversion into a national banking association on or after July 1, 1936, may, with the consent of the Corporation, obtain the benefits of this section, pending action on such application, by subscribing and paying for the same amount of stock of the Corporation as it would be required to subscribe and pay for upon becoming a member bank. Thereupon the provisions of this section applicable to member banks shall be applicable to such State bank or trust company or mutual savings bank to the same extent as if it were already a member bank: *Provided,* That if the application of such State bank or trust company or mutual savings bank for membership in the Federal Reserve System or for conversion into a national banking association be approved and it shall not complete its membership in the Federal Reserve System or its conversion into a national banking association within a reasonable time, or if such application shall be disapproved, then the amount paid by such State bank or trust company or mutual savings bank on account of its subscription to the capital stock of the Corporation shall be repaid to it and it shall no longer be subject to the provisions or entitled to the privileges of this section.

"(g) If any State bank or trust company, or mutual savings bank (referred to in this subsection as 'State bank') which is or which becomes a member of the Federal Reserve System is not permitted by the laws under which it was organized to purchase stock in the corporation, it shall apply to the Corporation for admission to the benefits of this section and, if such application be granted after appropriate certification in accordance with this section, it shall deposit with the Corporation an amount equal to the amount which it would have been required to pay in on account of a subscription to capital stock of the Corporation. Thereafter such deposit shall be adjusted in the same manner as subscriptions for stock by class A stockholders. Such deposit shall be subject to the same conditions with respect to repayment as amounts paid on subscriptions to class A stock by other member banks and the Corporation shall pay interest thereon at the same rate as dividends are actually paid on outstanding shares of class A stock. As long as such deposit is maintained with the Corporation, such State bank shall, for the purposes of this section, be deemed to be a class A stockholder of the Corporation. If the laws under which such State bank was organized be amended so as to authorize State banks to subscribe for class A stock of the Corporation, such State bank shall within six months thereafter subscribe for an appropriate amount of such class A stock and the deposit hereinafter provided for in lieu of payment upon class A stock shall be applied upon such subscription. If the law under which such State bank was organized be not amended at the next session of the State legislature following the admission of such State bank to the benefits of this section so as to authorize State banks to purchase such class A stock, or, if the law be so amended and such State bank shall fail within six months thereafter to purchase such class A stock, the deposit previously made with the Corporation shall be returned to such State bank and it shall no longer be entitled to the benefits of this section, unless it shall have been closed in the meantime on account of inability to meet the demands of its depositors.

"(h) The amount of the outstanding class A stock of the Corporation held by member banks shall be annually adjusted as hereinafter provided as of the last preceding call date as member banks increase their time and demand deposits or as additional banks become members or subscribe to the stock of the Corporation, and such stock may be decreased in amount as member banks reduce their time and demand deposits or cease to be members. Shares of the capital stock of the Corporation owned by member banks shall not be transferred or hypothecated. When a member bank increases its time and demand deposits it shall, at the beginning of each calendar year, subscribe for an additional amount of capital stock of the Corporation equal to one half of 1 per centum of such increase in deposits. One half of the amount of such additional stock shall be paid for at the time of the subscriptions therefor, and the balance shall be subject to call by the board of directors of the Corporation. A bank organized on or before the date this section takes effect and admitted to membership in the Federal Reserve System at any time after the organization of the Corporation shall be required to subscribe for an amount of class A capital stock equal to one half of 1 per centum of the time and demand deposits of the applicant bank as of the date of such admission, paying therefor its par value plus one half of 1 per centum a month from the period of the last dividend on the class A stock of the Corporation. When a member bank reduces its time and demand deposits it shall surrender, not later than the 1st day of January thereafter, a proportionate amount of its holdings in the capital stock of the Corporation, and when a member bank voluntarily liquidates it shall surrender all its holdings of the capital stock of the Corporation and be released from its stock subscription not previously called. The shares so surrendered shall be canceled and the member bank shall receive in payment therefor, under regulations to be prescribed by the Corporation, a sum equal to its cash-paid subscriptions on the shares surrendered and its proportionate share of dividends not to exceed one half of 1 per centum a month, from the period of the last dividend on such stock, less any liability of such member bank to the Corporation.

"(i) If any member or nonmember bank shall be declared insolvent, or shall cease to be a member bank (or in the case of a nonmember bank, shall cease to be entitled to the benefits of insurance under this section), the stock held by it in the Corporation shall be cancelled, without impairment of the liability of such bank, and all cash-paid subscriptions on such stock, with its proportionate share of dividends not to exceed one half of 1 per centum per month from the period of last dividend on such stock shall be first applied to all debts of the insolvent bank or the receiver thereof to the Corporation, and the balance, if any, shall be paid to the receiver of the insolvent bank.

"(j) Upon the date of enactment of the Banking Act of 1933, the Corporation shall become a body corporate and as such shall have power—

"First. To adopt and use a corporate seal.

"Second. To have succession until dissolved by an Act of Congress.

"Third. To make contracts.

"Fourth. To sue and be sued, complain and defend, in any court of law or equity, State or Federal.

"Fifth. To appoint by its board of directors such officers and employees as are not otherwise provided for in this section, to define their duties, fix their compensation, require bonds of them and fix the penalty thereof, and to dismiss at pleasure such officers or employees. Nothing in this or any other Act shall be construed to prevent the appointment and compensation as an officer or employee of the Corporation of any officer or employee of the United States in any board, commission, independent establishment, or executive department thereof.

"Sixth. To prescribe by its board of directors, bylaws not inconsistent with law, regulating the manner in which its general business may be conducted, and the privileges granted to it by law may be exercised and enjoyed.

"Seventh. To exercise by its board of directors, or duly authorized officers or agents, all powers specifically granted by the provisions of this section and such incidental powers as shall be necessary to carry out the powers so granted.

"(k) The board of directors shall administer the affairs of the Corporation fairly and impartially and without discrimination. The board of directors of the Corporation shall determine and prescribe the manner in which its obligations shall be incurred and its expenses allowed and paid. The Corporation shall be entitled to the free use of the United States mails in the same manner as the executive departments of the Government. The Corporation with the consent of any Federal reserve bank or of any board, commission, independent establishment, or executive department of the Government, including any field service thereof, may avail itself of the use of information, services, and facilities thereof in carrying out the provisions of this section.

"(l) Effective on and after July 1, 1934 (thus affording ample time for examination and preparation), unless the President shall by proclamation fix an earlier date, the Corporation shall insure as hereinafter provided the deposits of all member banks, and on and after such date and until July 1, 1936, of all nonmember banks, which are class A stockholders of the Corporation. Notwithstanding any other provision of law, whenever any national bank which is a class A stockholder of the Corporation shall have been closed by action of its board of directors or by the Comptroller of the Currency, as the case may be, on account of inability to meet the demands of its depositors, the Comptroller of the Currency shall appoint the Corporation receiver for such bank. As soon as possible thereafter the Corporation shall organize a new national bank to assume the insured deposit liabilities of such closed bank, to receive new deposits and otherwise to perform temporarily the functions provided for it in this paragraph. For the purposes of this subsection, the term 'insured deposit liability' shall mean with respect to the owner of any claim arising out of a deposit liability of such closed bank the following percentages of the next amount due to such owner by such closed bank on account of deposit liabilities: 100 per centum of such net amount not exceeding $10,000; and 75 per centum of the amount, if any, by which such net amount exceeds $10,000 but does not exceed $50,000; and 50 per centum of the amount, if any, by which such net amount exceeds $50,000: *Provided,* That, in determining the amount due to such owner for the purpose of fixing such percentage, there shall be added together all net amounts due to such owner in the same capacity or the same right, on account of deposits, regardless of whether such deposits be maintained in his name or in the names of others for his benefit. For the purposes of this subsection, the term 'insured deposit liabilities' shall mean the aggregate amount of all such insured deposit liabilities of such closed bank. The Corporation shall determine as expeditiously as possible the net amounts due to depositors of the closed bank and shall make available to the new bank an amount equal to the insured deposit liabilities of such closed bank, whereupon such new bank shall assume the insured deposit liability of such closed bank to each of its depositors, and the Corporation shall be subrogated to all rights against the closed bank of the owners of such deposits and shall be entitled to receive the same dividends from the proceeds of the assets of such closed bank as would have been payable to each such depositor until such dividends shall equal the insured deposit liability to such depositor assumed by the new bank, whereupon all further dividends shall be payable to such depositor. Of the amount thus made available by the Corporation to the new bank, such portion shall be paid to it in cash as may be necessary to enable it to meet immediate cash demands and the remainder shall be credited to it on the books of the Corporation subject to withdrawal on demand and shall bear interest at the rate of 3 per centum per annum until withdrawn. The new bank may, with the approval of the Corporation, accept new deposits, which together with all amounts made available to the new bank by the Corporation, shall be kept on hand in cash, invested in direct obligations of the United States, or deposited with the Corporation or with a Federal reserve bank. Such new bank shall maintain on deposit with the Federal reserve bank of its district the reserves required by law of member banks but shall not be required to subscribe for stock of the Federal reserve bank until its own capital stock has been subscribed and paid for in the manner hereinafter provided. The articles of association and organization certificate of such new bank may be executed by such representatives of the Corporation as it may designate; the new bank shall not be required to have any directors at the time of its organization, but shall be managed by an executive officer to be designated by the Corporation; and no capital stock need be paid in by the Corporation; but in other respects such bank shall be organized in accordance with the existing provisions of law relating to the organization of national banks; and, until the requisite amount of capital stock for such bank has been subscribed and paid for in the manner hereinafter provided, such bank shall transact no business except that authorized by this subsection and such business as may be incidental to its organization. When in the judgment of the Corporation it is desirable to do so, the Corporation shall offer capital stock of the new bank for sale on such terms and conditions as the Corporation shall deem advisable, in an amount sufficient in the opinion of the Corporation to make possible the conduct of the business of the new bank on a sound basis, but in no event less that that required by section 5138 of the Revised Statutes, as amended (U.S.C., title 12, sec. 51), for the organization of a national bank in the place where such new bank is located, giving the stockholders of the closed bank the first opportunity to purchase such stock. Upon proof that an adequate amount of capital stock of the new bank has been subscribed and paid for in cash by subscribers satisfactory to the Comptroller of the Currency, he shall issue to such bank a certificate of authority to commence business and thereafter it shall be managed by directors elected by its own shareholders and may exercise all of the powers granted by law to national banking associations. If an adequate amount of capital for such new bank is not subscribed and paid in, the Corporation may offer to transfer its business to any other banking institution in the same place which will take over its assets, assume its liabilities, and pay to the Corporation for such business such amount as the Corporation may deem adequate. Unless the capital stock of the new bank is sold or its assets acquired and its liabilities assumed by another banking institution, in the manner herein prescribed, within two years from the date of its organization, the Corporation shall place the new bank in voluntary liquidation and wind up its affairs. The Corporation shall open on its books a deposit insurance account and, as soon as possible after taking possession of any closed national bank, the Corporation shall make an estimate of the amount which will be available from all sources for application in satisfaction of the portion of the claims of depositors to which it has been subrogated and shall debit to such deposit insurance account the excess, if any, of the amount made available by the Corporation to the new bank for depositors over and above the amount of such estimate. It shall be the duty of the Corporation to realize upon the assets of such closed bank, having due regard to the condition of credit in the district in which such closed bank is located; to enforce the individual liability of the stockholders and directors thereof; and to wind up the affairs of such closed bank in conformity with the provisions of law relating to the liquidation of closed national banks, except as herein otherwise provided, retaining for its own account such portion of the amount realized from such liquidation as it shall be entitled to receive on account of its subrogation to the claims of depositors and paying to depositors and other creditors the amount available for distribution to them, after deducting therefrom their share of the costs of the liquidation of the closed bank. If the total amount realized by the Corporation on account of its subrogration to the claims of depositors be less than the amount of the estimate hereinabove provided for, the deposit insurance account shall be charged with the deficiency and, if the total amount so realized shall exceed the amount of such estimate, such account shall be credited with such excess. With respect to such closed national banks, the Corporation shall have all the rights, powers, and privileges now possessed by or hereafter given receivers of insolvent national banks and shall be subject to the obligations and penalties not inconsistent with the provisions of this paragraph to which such receivers are now or may hereafter become subject.

"Whenever any State member bank which is a class A stockholder of the Corporaiton shall have been closed by action of its board of directors or by the appropriate State authority, as the case may be, on account of inability to meet the demands of its depositors, the Corporation shall accept appointment as receiver thereof, if such appointment be tendered by the appropriate State authority and be authorized or permitted by State law. Thereupon the Corporation shall organize a new national bank, in accordance with the provisions of this subsection, to assume the insured deposit liabilities of such closed State member bank, to receive new deposits and otherwise to perform temporarily the functions provided for in this subsection. Upon satisfactory recognition of the right of the Corporation to receive dividends on the same basis as in the case of a closed national bank under this subsection, such recognition being accorded by State law, by allowance of claims by the appropriate State authority, by assignment of claims by depositors, or by any other effective method, the Corporation shall make available to such new national bank, in the manner prescribed by this subsection, an amount equal to the insured deposit liabilities of such closed State member bank; and the Corporation and such new national bank shall perform all of the functions and duties and shall have all the rights and privileges with respect to such State member bank and the depositors thereof which are prescribed by this subsection with respect to closed national banks holding class A stock in the Corporation: *Provided,* That the rights of depositors and other creditors of such State member bank shall be determined in accordance with the applicable provisions of State law: *And provided further,* That, with respect to such State member bank, the Corporation shall possess the powers and privileges provided by State law with respect to a receiver of such State member bank, except in so far as the same are in conflict with the provisions of this subsection.

"Whenever any State member bank which is a class A stockholder of the Corporation shall have been closed by action of its board of directors or by the appropriate State authority, as the case may be, on account of inability to meet the demands of its depositors, and the applicable State law does not permit the appointment of the Corporation as receiver of such bank, the Corporation shall organize a new national bank, in accordance with the provisions of this subsection, to assume the insured deposit liabilities of such closed State member bank, to receive new deposits, and otherwise to perform temporarily the functions provided for in this subsection. Upon satisfactory recognition of the right of the Corporation to receive dividends on the same basis as in the case of a closed national bank under this subsection, such recognition being accorded by State law, by allowance of claims by the appropriate State authority, by assignment of claims by depositors, or by any other effective method, the Corporation shall make available to such new bank, in accordance with the provisions of this subsection, the amount of insured deposit liabilities as to which such recognition has been accorded; and such new bank shall assume such insured deposit liabilities and shall in other respects comply with the provisions of this subsection respecting new banks organized to assume insured deposit liabilities of closed national banks. In so far as possible in view of the applicable provisions of State law, the Corporation shall proceed with respect to the receiver of such closed bank and with respect to the new bank organized to assume its insured deposit liabilities in the manner prescribed by this subsection with respect to closed national banks and new banks organized to assume their insured deposit liabilities; except that the Corporation shall have none of the powers, duties, or responsibilities of a receiver with respect to the winding up of the affairs of such closed State member bank. The Corporation, in its discretion, however, may purchase and liquidate any or all of the assets of such bank.

"Whenever the net debit balance of the deposit insurance account of the Corporation shall equal or exceed one fourth of 1 per centum of the total deposit liabilities of all class A stockholders as of the date of the last preceding call report, the Corporation shall levy upon such stockholders an assessment equal to one fourth of 1 per centum of their total deposit liabilities and shall credit the amount collected from such assessment to such deposit insurance account. No bank which is a holder of class A stock shall pay any dividends until all assessments levied upon it by the Corporation shall have been paid in full; and any director or officer of any such bank who participates in the declaration or payment of any such dividend may, upon conviction, be fined not more than $1,000, or imprisoned for not more than one year, or both.

"The term, 'receiver' as used in this section shall mean a receiver, liquidating agent, or conservator of a national bank, and a receiver, liquidating agent, conservator, commission, person, or other agency charged by State law with the responsibility and the duty of winding up the affairs of an insolvent State member bank.

"For the purposes of this section only, the term 'national bank' shall include all national banking associations and all banks, banking associations, trust companies, savings banks, and other banking institutions located in the District of Columbia which are members of the Federal Reserve System; and the term 'State member bank' shall include all State banks, banking associations, trust companies, savings banks, and other banking institutions organized under the laws of any State, which are members of the Federal Reserve System.

"In any determination of the insured deposit liabilities of any closed bank or of the total deposit liabilities of any bank which is a holder of class A stock of the Corporation, or a member of the Fund provided for in subsection (y), for the purposes of this section, there shall be excluded the amounts of all deposits of such bank which are payable only at an office thereof located in a foreign country.

"The Corporation may make such rules, regulations, and contracts as it may deem necessary in order to carry out the provisions of this section.

"Money of the Corporation not otherwise employed shall be invested in securities of the Government of the United States, except that for temporary periods, in the discretion of the board of directors, funds of the Corporation may be deposited in any Federal reserve bank or with the Treasurer of the United States. When designated for that purpose by the Secretary of the Treasury, the Corporation shall be a depositary of public moneys, except receipts from customs, under such regulations as may be prescribed by the said Secretary, and may also be employed as a financial agent of the Government. It shall perform all such reasonable duties as depositary of public moneys and financial agent of the Government as may be required of it.

"(m) Nothing herein contained shall be construed to prevent the Corporation from making loans to national banks closed by action of the Comptroller of the Currency, or by vote of their directors, or to State member banks closed by action of the appropriate State authorities, or by vote of their directors, or from entering into negotiations to secure the reopening of such banks.

"(n) Receivers or liquidators of member banks which are now or may hereafter become insolvent or suspended shall be entitled to offer the assets of such banks for sale to the Corporation or as security for loans from the Corporation, upon receiving permission from the appropriate State authority in accordance with express provisions of State law in the case of State member banks, or from the Comptroller of the Currency in the case of national banks. The proceeds of every such sale or loan shall be utilized for the same purposes and in the same manner as other funds realized from the liquidation of the assets of such banks. The Comptroller of the Currency may, in his discretion, pay dividends on proved claims at any time after the expiration of the period of advertisement made pursuant to section 5235 of the Revised Statutes (U.S.C., title 12, sec. 193), and no liability shall attach to the Comptroller of the Currency or to the receiver of any national bank by reason of any such payment for failure to pay dividends to a claimant whose claim is not proved at the time of any such payment.

"(o) The Corporation is authorized and empowered to issue and to have outstanding at any one time in an amount aggregating not more than three times the amount of its capital, its notes, debentures, bonds, or other such obligations, to be redeemable at the option of the Corporation before maturity in such manner as may be stipulated in such obligations, and to bear such rate or rates of interest, and to mature at such time or times as may be determined by the Corporation: *Provided,* That the Corporation may sell on a discount basis short-term obligations payable at maturity without interest. The notes, debentures, bonds, and other such obligations of the Corporation may be secured by assets of the Corporation in such manner as shall be prescribed by its board of directors. Such obligations may be offered for sale at such price or prices as the Corporation may determine.

"(p) All notes, debentures, bonds, or other such obligations issued by the Corporation shall be exempt, both as to principal and interest, from all taxation (except estate and inheritance taxes) now or hereafter imposed by the United States, by any Territory, dependency, or possession thereof, or by any State, county, municipality, or local taxing authority. The Corporation, including its franchise, its capital, reserves, and surplus, and its income, shall be exempt from all taxation now or hereafter imposed by the United States, by any Territory, dependency, or possession thereof, or by any State, county, municipality, or local taxing authority, except that any real property of the Corporation shall be subject to State, Territorial, county, municipal or local taxation to the same extent according to its value as other real property is taxed.

"(q) In order that the Corporation may be supplied with such forms of notes, debentures, bonds, or other such obligations as it may need for issuance under this Act, the Secretary of the Treasury is authorized to prepare such forms as shall be suitable and approved by the Corporation, to be held in the Treasury subject to delivery, upon order of the Corporation. The engraved plates, dies, bed pieces, and other material executed in connection therewith shall remain in the custody of the Secretary of the Treasury. The Corporation shall reimburse the Secretary of the Treasury for any expenses incurred in the preparation, custody, and delivery of such notes, debentures, bonds, or other such obligations.

"(r) The Corporation shall annually make a report of its operations to the Congress as soon as practicable after the 1st day of January in each year.

"(s) Whoever, for the purpose of obtaining any loan from the Corporation, or any extension or renewal thereof, or the acceptance, release, or substitution of security therefor, or for the purpose of inducing the Corporation to purchase any assets, or for the purpose of influencing in any way the action of the Corporation under this section, makes any statement, knowing it to be false, or willfully overvalues any security, shall be punished by a fine of not more than $5,000, or by imprisonment for not more than two years, or both.

"(t) Whoever (1) falsely makes, forges, or counterfeits any obligation or coupon, in imitation of or purporting to be an obligation or coupon issued by the Corporation, or (2) passes, utters, or publishes, or attempts to pass, utter, or publish, any false, forged, or counterfeited obligation or coupon purporting to have been issued by the Corporation, knowing the same to be false, forged, or counterfeited, or (3) falsely alters any obligation or coupon issued or purporting to have been issued by the Corporation, or (4) passes, utters, or publishes, or attempts to pass, utter, or publish, as true, any falsely altered or spurious obligation or coupon, issued or purporting to have been issued by the Corporation, knowing the same to be falsely altered or spurious, shall be punished by a fine of not more than $10,000, or by imprisonment for not more than five years, or both.

"(u) Whoever, being connected in any capacity with the Corporation (1) embezzles, abstracts, purloins, or willfully misapplies any moneys, funds, securities, or other things of value, whether belonging to it or pledged, or otherwise intrusted to it, or (2) with intent to defraud the Corporation or any other body, politic or corporate, or any individual, or to deceive any officer, auditor, or examiner of the Corporation, makes any false entry in any book, report, or statement of or to the Corporation, or without being duly authorized draws any order or issues, puts forth, or assigns any note, debenture, bond, or other such obligation, or draft, bill of exchange, mortgage, judgment, or decree thereof, shall be punished by a fine of not more than $10,000, or by imprisonment for not more than five years, or both.

"(v) No individual, association, partnership, or corporation shall use the words 'Federal Deposit Insurance Corporation', or a combination or any three of these four words, as the name or a part thereof under which he or it shall do business. No individual, association, partnership, or corporation shall advertise or otherwise represent falsely by any device whatsoever that his or its deposit liabilities are insured or in anywise quaranteed by the Federal Deposit Insurance Corporation, or by the Government of the United States, or by any instrumentality thereof; and no class A stockholder of the Federal Deposit Insurance Corporation shall advertise or otherwise represent falsely by any device whatsoever the extent to which or the manner in which its deposit liabilities are insured by the Federal Deposit Insurance Corporation. Every individual, partnership, association, or corporation violating this subsection shall be punished by a fine of not exceeding $1,000, or by imprisonment not exceeding one year, or both.

"(w) The provisions of sections 112, 113, 114, 115, 116, and 117 of the Criminal Code of the United States (U.S.C., title 18, ch. 5, secs. 202 to 207, inclusive), in so far as applicable, are extended to apply to contracts or agreements with the Corporation under this section, which for the purposes hereof shall be held to include loans, advances, extensions, and renewals thereof, and acceptances, releases, and substitutions of security therefor, purchases or sales of assets, and all contracts and agreements pertaining to the same.

"(x) The Secret Service Division of the Treasury Department is authorized to detect, arrest, and deliver into the custody of the United States marshal having jurisdiction any person committing any of the offenses punishable under this section.

"(y) The Corporation shall open on its books a Temporary Federal Deposit Insurance Fund (hereinafter referred to as the 'Fund'), which shall become operative on January 1, 1934, unless the President shall by proclamation fix an earlier date, and it shall be the duty of the Corporation to insure deposits as hereinafter provided until July 1, 1934.

"Each member bank licensed before January 1, 1934, by the Secretary of the Treasury pursuant to the authority vested in him by the Executive order of the President issued March 10, 1933, shall, on or before January 1, 1934, become a member of the Fund; each member bank so licensed after such date, and each State bank trust company or mutual savings bank (referred to in this subsection as 'State bank', which term shall also include all banking institutions located in the District of Columbia) which becomes a member of the Federal Reserve System on or after such date, shall, upon being so licensed or so admitted to membership, become a member of the Fund; and any State bank which is not a member of the Federal Reserve System, with the approval of the authority having supervision of such State bank and certification to the Corporation by such authority that such State bank is in solvent condition, shall, after examination by, and with the approval of, the Corporation, be entitled to become a member of the Fund and to the privileges of this subsection upon agreeing to comply with the requirements thereof and upon paying to the Corporation an amount equal to the amount that would be required of it under this subsection if it were a member bank. The Corporation is authorized to prescribe rules and regulations for the further examination of such State bank, and to fix the compensation of examiners employed to make examinations of State banks.

"Each member of the Fund shall file with the Corporation on or before the date of its admission a certified statement under oath showing, as of the fifteenth day of the month preceding the month in which it was so admitted, the number of its depositors and the total amount of its deposits which are eligible for insurance under this subsection, and shall pay to the Corporation an amount equal to one-half of 1 per centum of the total amount of the deposits so certified. One-half of such payment shall be paid in full at the time of the admission of such member to the Fund, and the remainder of such payment shall be subject to call from time to time by the board of directors of the Corporation. Within a reasonable time fixed by the Corporation each such member shall file a similar statement showing, as of June 15, 1934, the number of its depositors and the total amount of its deposits which are eligible for such insurance and shall pay to the Corporation in the same manner an amount equal to one-half of 1 per centum of the increase, if any, in the total amount of such deposits since the date covered by the statement filed upon its admission to membership in the fund.

"If at any time prior to July 1, 1934, the Corporation requires additional funds with which to meet its obligations under this subsection, each member of the Fund shall be subject to one additional assessment only in an amount not exceeding the total amount theretofore paid to the Corporation by such member.

"If any member of the Fund shall be closed on or before June 30, 1934, on account of inability to meet its deposit liabilities, the Corporation shall proceed in accordance with the provisions of subsection (1) of this section to pay the insured deposit liabilities of such member; except that the Corporation shall pay not more than $2,500 on account of the net approved claim of the owner of any deposit. The provisions of such subsection (1) relating to State member banks shall be extended for the purposes of this subsection to members of the Fund which are not members of the Federal Reserve System; and the provisions of this subsection shall apply only to deposits of members of the Fund which have been made available since March 10, 1933, for withdrawal in the usual course of the banking business.

"Before July 1, 1934, the Corporation shall make an estimate of the balance, if any, which will remain in the Fund after providing for all liabilities of the Fund, including expenses of operation thereof under this subsection and allowing for anticipated recoveries. The Corporation shall refund such estimated balance, on such basis as the Corporation shall find to be equitable, to the members of the Fund other than those which have been closed prior to July 1, 1934.

"Each State bank which is a member of the Fund, in order to obtain the benefits of this section after July 1, 1934, shall, on or before such date, subscribe and pay for the same amount of class A stock of the Corporation as it would be required to subscribe and pay for upon becoming a member bank, or if such State bank is not permitted by the laws under which it was organized to purchase such stock, it shall deposit with the Corporation an amount equal to the amount it would have been required to pay in on account of a subscription to such stock; and thereafter such State bank shall be entitled to such benefits until July 1, 1936.

"It is not the purpose of this section to discriminate, in any manner, against State nonmember, and in favor of, national or member banks; but the purpose is to provide all banks with the same opportunity to obtain and enjoy the benefits of this section. No bank shall be discriminated against because its capital stock is less than the amount required for eligibility for admission into the Federal Reserve System."

Sec. 9. The eighth paragraph of section 13 of the Federal Reserve Act, as amended (U.S.C., title 12, sec. 347; Supp. VI, title 12, sec. 347), is amended to read as follows:

"Any Federal reserve bank may make advances for periods not exceeding fifteen days to its member banks on their promissory notes secured by the deposit or pledge of bonds, notes, certificates of indebtedness, or Treasury bills of the United States, or by the deposit or pledge of debentures or other such obligations of Federal intermediate credit banks which are eligible for purchase by Federal reserve banks under section 13 (a) of this Act; and any Federal reserve bank may make advances for periods not exceeding ninety days to its member banks on their promissory notes secured by such notes, drafts, bills of exchange, or bankers' acceptances as are eligible for rediscount or for purchase by Federal reserve banks under the provisions of this Act. All such advances shall be made at rates to be established by such Federal reserve banks, such rates to be subject to the review and determination of the Federal Reserve Board. If any member bank to which any such advance has been made shall, during the life or continuance of such advance, and despite an official warning of the reserve bank of the district or of the Federal Reserve Board to the contrary, increase its outstanding loans secured by collateral in the form of stocks, bonds, debentures, or other such obligations, or loans made to members of any organized stock exchange, investment house, or dealer in securities, upon any obligation, note, or bill, secured or unsecured, for the purpose of purchasing and/or carrying stocks, bonds, or other investment securities (except obligations of the United States) such advance shall be deemed immediately due and payable, and such member bank shall be ineligible as a borrower at the reserve bank of the district under the provisions of this paragraph for such period as the Federal Reserve Board shall determine: *Provided*, That no temporary carrying or clearance loans made solely for the purpose of facilitating the purchase or delivery of securities offered for public subscription shall be included in the loans referred to in this paragraph."

Sec. 10. Section 14 of the Federal Reserve Act, as amended (U.S.C., title 12, secs. 353-358), is amended by adding at the end thereof the following new paragraph:

"(g) The Federal Reserve Board shall exercise special supervision over all relationships and transactions of any kind entered into by any Federal reserve bank with any foreign bank or banker, or with any group of foreign banks or bankers, and all such relationships and transactions shall be subject to such regulations, conditions, and limitations as the Board may prescribe. No officer or other representative of any Federal reserve bank shall conduct negotiations of any kind with the officers or representatives of any foreign bank or banker without first obtaining the permission of the Federal Reserve Board. The Federal Reserve Board shall have the right, in its discretion, to be represented in any conference or negotiations by such representative or representatives as the Board may designate. A full report of all conferences or negotiations, and all understandings or agreements arrived at or transactions agreed upon, and all other material facts appertaining to such conferences or negotiations, shall be filed with the Federal Reserve Board in writing by a duly authorized officer of each Federal reserve bank which shall have participated in such conferences or negotiations."

Sec. 11. (a) Section 19 of the Federal Reserve Act, as amended (U.S.C., title 12, secs. 142, 374, 461–466; Supp. VI, title 12, sec. 462a), is amended by inserting after the sixth paragraph thereof the following new paragraph:

"No member bank shall act as the medium or agent of any nonbanking corporation, partnership, association, business trust, or individual in making loans on the security of stocks, bonds, and other investment securities to brokers or dealers in stocks, bonds, and other investment securities. Every violation of this provision by any member bank shall be punishable by a fine of not more than $100 per day during the continuance of such violation; and such fine may be collected, by suit or otherwise, by the Federal reserve bank of the district in which such member bank is located."

(b) Such section 19 of the Federal Reserve Act, as amended, is further amended by adding at the end thereof the following new paragraphs:

"No member bank shall, directly or indirectly by any device whatsoever, pay any interest on any deposit which is payable on demand: *Provided*, That nothing herein contained shall be construed as prohibiting the payment of interest in accordance with the terms of any certificate of deposit or other contract heretofore entered into in good faith which is in force on the date of the enactment of this paragraph; but no such certificate of deposit or other contract shall be renewed or extended unless it shall be modified to conform to this paragraph, and every member bank shall take such action as may be necessary to conform to this paragraph as soon as possible consistently with its contractual obligations: *Provided, however,* That this paragraph shall not apply to any deposit of such bank which is payable only at an office thereof located in a foreign country, and shall not apply to any deposit made by a mutual savings bank, nor to any deposit of public funds made by or on behalf of any State, county, school district, or other subdivision or municipality, with respect to which payment of interest is required under State law.

"The Federal Reserve Board shall from time to time limit by regulation the rate of interest which may be paid by member banks on time deposits, and may prescribe different rates for such payment on time and savings deposits having different maturities or subject to different conditions respecting withdrawal or repayment or subject to different conditions by reason of different locations. No member bank shall pay any time deposit before its maturity, or waive any requirement of notice before payment of any savings deposit except as to all savings deposits having the same requirement."

(c) Section 8 of the Act entitled "An Act to establish postal savings depositories for depositing savings at interest with the security of the Government for repayment thereof, and for other purposes," approved June 25, 1910, as amended (U.S.C., title 39, sec. 758), is amended by striking out the first sentence thereof and inserting in lieu thereof the following: "Any depositor may withdraw the whole or any part of the funds deposited to his or her credit with the accrued interest only on notice given sixty days in advance and under such regulations as the Postmaster General may prescribe; but withdrawal of any part of such funds may be made upon demand, but no interest shall be paid on any funds so withdrawn except interest accrued to the date of enactment of the Banking Act of 1933: *Provided,* That Postal Savings depositories may deposit funds in member banks on time under regulations to be prescribed by the Postmaster General."

(d) The second sentence of section 9 of the Act entitled "An Act to establish postal savings depositories for depositing savings at interest with the security of the Government for repayment thereof, and for other purposes", approved June 25, 1910, as amended (U.S.C., title 39, sec. 759), is amended by striking out the period at the end thereof and inserting in lieu thereof a colon and the following: "*Provided,* That no such security shall be required in case of such part of the deposits as are insured under section 12B of the Federal Reserve Act, as amended."

Sec. 12. Section 22 of the Federal Reserve Act, as amended (U.S.C., title 12, secs. 375, 376, 503, 593-595; Supp. VI, title 12, sec. 593), is further amended by adding at the end thereof the following new paragraph:

"(g) No executive officer of any member bank shall borrow from or otherwise become indebted to any member bank of which he is an executive officer, and no member bank shall make any loan or extend credit in any other manner to any of its own executive officers: *Provided,* That loans heretofore made to any such officer may be renewed or extended not more than two years from the date this paragraph takes effect, if in accord with sound banking practice. If any executive officer of any member bank borrow from or if he be or become indebted to any bank other than a member bank of which he is an executive officer, he shall make a written report to the chairman of the board of directors of the member bank of which he is an executive officer, stating the date and amount of such loan or indebtedness, the security therefor, and the purpose for which the proceeds have been or are to be used. Any executive officer of any member bank violating the provisions of this paragraph shall be deemed guilty of a misdemeanor and shall be imprisoned not exceeding one year, or fined not more than $5,000, or both; and any member bank violating the provisions of this paragraph shall be fined not more than $10,000, and may be fined a further sum equal to the amount so loaned or credit so extended."

Sec. 13. The Federal Reserve Act, as amended, is amended by inserting between sections 23 and 24 thereof (U.S.C., title 12, secs. 64 and 371; Supp. VI, title 12, sec. 371) the following new section:

"Sec. 23A. No member bank shall (1) make any loan or any extension of credit to, or purchase securities under repurchase agreement from, any of its affiliates, or (2) invest any of its funds in the capital stock, bonds, debentures, or other such obligations of any such affiliate, or (3) accept the capital stock, bonds, debentures, or other such obligations of any such affiliate as collateral security for advances made to any person, partnership, association, or corporation, if, in the case of any such affiliate, the aggregate amount of such loans, extensions of credit, repurchase agreements, investments, and advances against such collateral security will exceed 10 per centum of the capital stock and surplus of such member bank, or if, in the case of all such affiliates, the aggregate amount of such loans, extensions of credits, repurchase agreements, investments, and advances against such collateral security will exceed 20 per centum of the capital stock and surplus of such member bank.

"Within the foregoing limitations, each loan or extension of credit of any kind or character to an affiliate shall be secured by collateral in the form of stocks, bonds, debentures, or other such obligations having a market value at the time of making the loan or extension of credit of at least 20 per centum more than the amount of the loan or extension of credit, or of at least 10 per centum more than the amount of the loan or extension of credit if it is secured by obligations of any State, or of any political subdivision or agency thereof: *Provided,* That the provisions of this paragraph shall not apply to loans or extensions of credit secured by obligations of the United States Government, the Federal intermediate credit banks, the Federal land banks, the Federal Home Loan Banks, or the Home Owners' Loan Corporation, or by such notes, drafts, bills of exchange, or bankers' acceptances as are eligible for rediscount or for purchase by Federal reserve banks. A loan or extension of credit to a director, officer, clerk, or other employee or any representative of any such affiliate shall be deemed a loan to the affiliate to the extent that the proceeds of such loan are used for the benefit of, or transferred to, the affiliate.

"For the purposes of this section the term 'affiliate' shall include holding company affiliates as well as other affiliates, and the provisions of this section shall not apply to any affiliate (1) engaged solely in holding the bank premises of the member bank with which is is affiliated, (2) engaged solely in conducting a safe-deposit business or the business of an agricultural credit corporation or livestock loan company, (3) in the capital stock of which a national banking association is authorized to invest pursuant to section 25 of the Federal Reserve Act, as amended, (4) organized under section 25 (a) of the Federal Reserve Act, as amended, or (5) engaged solely in holding obligations of the United States Government, the Federal intermediate credit banks, the Federal land banks, the Federal Home Loan Banks, or the Home Owners' Loan Corporation; but as to any such affiliate, member banks shall continue to be subject to other provisions of law applicable to loans by such banks and investments by such banks in stocks, bonds, debentures, or other such obligations."

Sec. 14. The Federal Reserve Act, as amended, is amended by inserting between section 24 and section 25 thereof (U.S.C., title 12, secs. 371 and 601-605; Supp. VI, title 12, sec. 371) the following new section:

"Sec. 24A. Hereafter no national bank, without the approval of the Comptroller of the Currency, and no State member bank, without the approval of the Federal Reserve Board, shall (1) invest in bank premises, or in the stock, bonds, debentures, or other such obligations of any corporation holding the premises of such bank or (2) make loans to or upon the security of the stock of any such corporation, if the aggregate of all such investments and loans will exceed the amount of the capital stock of such bank."

Sec. 15. The Federal Reserve Act, as amended, is further amended by inserting after section 25 (a) thereof (U.S.C., title 12, sec. 611-631) the following new section:

"Sec. 25. (b) Notwithstanding any other provision of law all suits of a civil nature at common law or in equity to which any corporation organized under the laws of the United States shall be a party, arising out of transactions involving international or foreign banking, or banking in a dependency or insular possession of the United States, or out of other international or foreign financial operations, either directly or through the agency, ownership, or control of branches or local institutions in dependencies or insular possessions of the United States or in foreign countries, shall be deemed to arise under the laws of the United States, and the district courts of the United States shall have original jurisdiction of all such suits; and any defendant in any such suit may, at any time before the trial thereof, remove such suits from a State court into the district court of the United States for the proper district by following the procedure for the removal of causes otherwise provided by law. Such removal shall not cause undue delay in the trial of such case and a case so removed shall have a place on the calendar of the United States court to which it is removed relative to that which it held on the State court from which it was removed.

"Notwithstanding any other provision of law, all suits of a civil nature at common law or in equity to which any Federal Reserve bank shall be a party shall be deemed to arise under the laws of the United States, and the district courts of the United States shall have original jurisdiction of all such suits; and any Federal Reserve bank which is a defendant in any such suit may, at any time before the trial thereof, remove such suit from a State court into the district court of the United States for the proper district by following the procedure for the removal of causes otherwise provided by law. No attachment or execution shall be issued against any Federal Reserve bank or its property before final judgment in any suit, action, or proceeding in any State, county, municipal, or United States court."

Sec. 16. Paragraph "Seventh" of section 5136 of the Revised Statutes, as amended (U.S.C., title 12, sec. 24; Supp. VI, title 12, sec. 24), is amended to read as follows:

"Seventh. To exercise by its board of directors or duly authorized officers or agents, subject to law, all such incidental powers as shall be necessary to carry on the business of banking; by discounting and negotiating promissory notes, drafts, bills of exchange, and other evidences of debt; by receiving deposits; by buying and selling exchange, coin, and bullion; by loaning money on personal security; and by obtaining, issuing, and circulating notes according to the provisions of this title. The business of dealing in investment securities by the association shall be limited to purchasing and selling such securities without recourse, solely upon the order, and for the account of, customers, and in no case for its own account, and the association shall not underwrite any issue of securities: *Provided,* That the association may purchase for its own account investment securities under such limitations and restrictions as the Comptroller of the Currency may by regulation prescribe, but in no event (1) shall the total amount of any issue of investment securities of any one obligor or maker purchased after this section as amended takes effect and held by the association for its own account exceed at any time 10 per centum of the total amount of such issue outstanding, but this limitation shall not apply to any such issue the total amount of which does not exceed $100,000 and does not exceed 50 per centum of the capital of the association, nor (2) shall the total amount of the investment securities of any one obligor or maker purchased after this section as amended takes effect and held by the association for its own account exceed at any time 15 per centum of the amount of the capital stock of the association actually paid in and unimpaired and 25 per centum of its unimpaired surplus fund. As used in this section the term 'investment securities' shall mean marketable obligations evidencing indebtedness of any person, copartnership, association, or corporation in the form of bonds, notes and/ or debentures commonly known as investment securities under such further definition by the term 'investment securities' as may by regulation be prescribed by the Comptroller of the Currency. Except as hereinafter provided or otherwise permitted by law, nothing herein contained shall authorize the purchase by the association of any shares of stock of any corporation. The limitations and restrictions herein contained as to dealing in, underwriting and purchasing for its own account, investment securities shall not apply to obligations of the United States, or general obligations of any State or of any political subdivision thereof, or obligations issued under authority of the Federal Farm Loan Act, as amended, or issued by the Federal Home Loan Banks or the Home Owners' Loan Corporation: *Provided,* That in carrying on the business commonly known as the safe-deposit business the association shall not invest in the capital stock of a corporation organized under the law of any State to conduct a safe-deposit business in an amount in excess of 15 per centum of the capital stock of the association actually paid in and unimpaired and 15 per centum of its unimpaired surplus."

The restrictions of this section as to dealing in investment securities shall take effect one year after the date of the approval of this Act.

Sec. 17. (a) Section 5138 of the Revised Statutes, as amended (U.S.C., title 12, sec. 51; Supp. VI, title 12, sec. 51), is amended to read as follows:

"Sec. 5138. After this section as amended takes effect, no national banking association shall be organized with a less capital than $100,000, except that such associations with a capital of not less than $50,000 may be organized in any place the population of which does not exceed six thousand inhabitants. No such association shall be organized in a city the population of which exceeds fifty thousand persons with a capital of less than $200,000, except that in the outlying districts of such a city where the State laws permit the organization of State banks with a capital of $100,000 or less, national banking associations now organized or hereafter organized may, with the approval of the Comptroller of the Currency, have a capital of not less than $100,000."

(b) The tenth paragraph of section 9 of the Federal Reserve Act, as amended (U.S.C., title 12, sec. 329), is amended to read as follows:

"No applying bank shall be admitted to membership in a Federal reserve bank unless it possesses a paid-up unimpaired capital sufficient to entitle it to become a national banking association in the place where it is situated under the provisions of the National Bank Act, as amended: *Provided,* That this paragraph shall not apply to State banks and trust companies organized prior to the date this paragraph as amended takes effect and situated in a place the population of which does not exceed three thousand inhabitants and having a capital of not less than $25,000, nor to any State bank or trust company which is so situated and which, while it is entitled to the benefits of insurance under section 12B of this Act, increases its capital to not less than $25,000."

Sec. 18. Section 5139 of the Revised Statutes, as amended (U.S.C., title

12, sec. 52; Supp. VI, title 12, sec. 52), is amended by adding at the end thereof the following new paragraph:

"After one year from the date of the enactment of the Banking Act of 1933, no certificate representing the stock of any such association shall represent the stock of any other corporation, except a member bank or a corporation existing on the date this paragraph takes effect engaged solely in holding the bank premises of such association, nor shall the ownership, sale, or transfer of any certificate representing the stock of any such association be conditioned in any manner whatsoever upon the ownership, sale, or transfer of a certificate representing the stock of any other corporation, except a member bank."

Sec. 19. Section 5144 of the Revised Statutes, as amended (U.S.C., title 12, sec. 61), is amended to read as follows:

"Sec. 5144. In all elections of directors, each shareholder shall have the right to vote the number of shares owned by him for as many persons as there are directors to be elected, or to cumulate such shares and give one candidate as many votes as the number of directors multiplied by the number of his shares shall equal, or to distribute them on the same principle among as many candidates as he shall think fit; and in deciding all other questions at meetings of shareholders, each shareholder shall be entitled to one vote on each share of stock held by him; except (1) that shares of its own stock held by a national bank as sole trustee shall not be voted, and shares of its own stock held by a national bank and one or more persons as trustees may be voted by such other person or persons, as trustees, in the same manner as if he or they were the sole trustee, and (2) shares controlled by any holding company affiliate of a national bank shall not be voted unless such holding company affiliate shall have first obtained a voting permit as hereinafter provided, which permit is in force at the time such shares are voted. Shareholders may vote by proxies duly authorized in writing; but no officer, clerk, teller, or bookkeeper of such bank shall act as proxy; and no shareholder whose liability is past due and unpaid shall be allowed to vote.

"For the purposes of this section shares shall be deemed to be controlled by a holding company affiliate if they are owned or controlled directly or indirectly by such holding company affiliate, or held by any trustee for the benefit of the shareholders or members thereof.

"Any such holding company affiliate may make application to the Federal Reserve Board for a voting permit entitling it to cast one vote at all elections of directors and in deciding all questions at meetings of shareholders of such bank on each share of stock controlled by it or authorizing the trustee or trustees holding the stock for its benefit or for the benefit of its shareholders so to vote the same. The Federal Reserve Board may, in its discretion, grant or withhold such permit as the public interest may require. In acting upon such application, the Board shall consider the financial condition of the applicant, the general character of its management, and the probable effect of the granting of such permit upon the affairs of such bank, but no such permit shall be granted except upon the following conditions:

"(a) Every such holding company affiliate shall, in making the application for such permit, agree (1) to receive, on dates identical with those fixed for the examination of banks with which it is affiliated, examiners duly authorized to examine such banks, who shall make such examinations of such holding company affiliate as shall be necessary to disclose fully the relations between such banks and such holding company affiliate and the effect of such relations upon the affairs of such banks, such examinations to be at the expense of the holding company affiliate so examined; (2) that the reports of such examiners shall contain such information as shall be necessary to disclose fully the relations between such affiliate and such banks and the effect of such relations upon the affairs of such banks; (3) that such examiners may examine each bank owned or controlled by the holding company affiliate, both individually and in conjunction with other banks owned or controlled by such holding company affiliate; and (4) that publication of individual or consolidated statements of condition of such banks may be required;

"(b) After five years after the enactment of the Banking Act of 1933, every such holding company affiliate (1) shall possess, and shall continue to possess during the life of such permit, free and clear of any lien, pledge, or hypothecation of any nature, readily marketable assets other than bank stock in an amount not less than 12 per centum of the aggregate par value of all bank stocks controlled by such holding company affiliate, which amount shall be increased by not less than 2 per centum per annum of such aggregate par value until such assets shall amount to 25 per centum of the aggregate par value of such bank stocks; and (2) shall reinvest in readily marketable assets other than bank stock all net earnings over and above 6 per centum per annum on the book value of its own shares outstanding until such assets shall amount to such 25 per centum of the aggregate par value of all bank stocks controlled by it;

"(c) Notwithstanding the foregoing provisions of this section, after five years after the enactment of the Banking Act of 1933, (1) any such holding company affiliate the shareholders or members of which shall be individually and severally liable in proportion to the number of shares of such holding company affiliate held by them respectively, in addition to amounts invested therein, for all statutory liability imposed on such holding company affiliate by reason of its control of shares of stock of banks, shall be required only to establish and maintain out of net earnings over and above 6 per centum per annum on the book value of its own shares outstanding a reserve of readily marketable assets in an amount of not less than 12 per centum of the aggregate par value of bank stocks controlled by it, and (2) the assets required by this section to be possessed by such holding company affiliate may be used by it for replacement of capital in banks affiliated with it and for losses incurred in such banks, but any deficiency in such assets resulting from such use shall be made up within such period as the Federal Reserve Board may by regulation prescribe;

"(d) Every officer, director, agent, and employee of every such holding company affiliate shall be subject to the same penalties for false entries in any book, report, or statement of such holding company affiliate as are applicable to officers, directors, agents, and employees of member banks under section 5209 of the Revised Statutes, as amended (U.S.C., title 12, sec. 592); and

"(e) Every such holding company affiliate shall, in its application for such voting permit, (1) show that it does not own, control, or have any interest in, and is not participating in the management or direction of, any corporation, business trust, association, or other similar organization formed for the purpose of, or engaged principally in, the issue, flotation, underwriting, public sale, or distribution, at wholesale or retail or through syndicate participation, of stocks, bonds, debentures, notes, or other securities of any sort (hereinafter referred to as 'securities company'); (2) agree that during the period that the permit remains in force it will not acquire any ownership, control, or interest in any such securities company or participate in the management or direction thereof; (3) agree that if, at the time of filing the application for such permit, it owns, controls, or has an interest in, or is participating in the management or direction of, any such securities company, it will, within five years after the filing of such application, divest itself of its ownership, control, and interest in such securities company and will cease participating in the management or direction thereof, and will not thereafter, during the period that the permit remains in force, acquire any further ownership, control, or interest in any such securities company or participate in the management or direction thereof; and (4) agree that thenceforth it will declare dividends only out of actual net earnings.

"If at any time it shall appear to the Federal Reserve Board that any holding company affiliate has violated any of the provisions of the Banking Act of 1933 or of any agreement made pursuant to this section, the Federal Reserve Board may, in its discretion, revoke any such voting permit after giving sixty days' notice by registered mail of its intention to the holding company affiliate and affording it an opportunity to be heard. Whenever the Federal Reserve Board shall have revoked any such voting permit, no national bank whose stock is controlled by the holding company affiliate whose permit is so revoked shall receive deposits of public moneys of the United States, nor shall any such national bank pay any further dividend to such holding company affiliate upon any shares of such bank controlled by such holding company affiliate.

"Whenever the Federal Reserve Board shall have revoked any voting permit as hereinbefore provided, the rights, privileges, and franchises of any or all national banks the stock of which is controlled by such holding company affiliate shall, in the discretion of the Federal Reserve Board, be subject to forfeiture in accordance with section 2 of the Federal Reserve Act, as amended."

Sec. 20. After one year from the date of the enactment of this Act, no member bank shall be affiliated in any manner described in section 2 (b) hereof with any corporation, association, business trust, or other similar organization engaged principally in the issue, flotation, underwriting, public sale, or distribution at wholesale or retail or through syndicate participation of stocks, bonds, debentures, notes, or other securities.

For every violation of this section the member bank involved shall be subject to a penalty not exceeding $1,000 per day for each day during which such violation continues. Such penalty may be assessed by the Federal Reserve Board, in its discretion, and, when so assessed, may be collected by the Federal reserve bank by suit or otherwise.

If any such violation shall continue for six calendar months after the member bank shall have been warned by the Federal Reserve Board to discontinue the same, (a) in the case of a national bank, all the rights, privileges, and franchises granted to it under the National Bank Act may be forfeited in the manner prescribed in section 2 of the Federal Reserve Act, as amended (U.S.C., title 12, secs. 141, 222-225, 281-286, and 502), or, (b) in the case of a State member bank, all of its rights and privileges of membership in the Federal Reserve System may be forfeited in the manner prescribed in section 9 of the Federal Reserve Act, as amended (U.S.C., title 12, secs. 321-332).

Sec. 21. (a) After the expiration of one year after the date of enactment of this Act it shall be unlawful—

(1) For any person, firm, corporation, association, business trust, or other similar organization, engaged in the business of issuing, underwriting, selling, or distributing, at wholesale or retail, or through syndicate participation, stocks, bonds, debentures, notes, or other securities, to engage at the same time to any extent whatever in the business of receiving deposits subject to check or to repayment upon presentation of a passbook, certificate of deposit, or other evidence of debt, or upon request of the depositor; or

(2) For any person, firm, corporation, association, business trust, or other similar organization, other than a financial institution or private banker subject to examination and regulation under state or Federal law, to engage to any extent whatever in the business of receiving deposits subject to check

or to repayment upon presentation of a passbook, certificate of deposit, or other evidence of debt, or upon request of the depositor, unless such person, firm, corporation, association, business trust, or other similar organization shall submit to periodic examination by the Comptroller of the Currency or by the Federal reserve bank of the district and shall make and publish periodic reports of its condition, exhibiting in detail its resources and liabilities, such examination and reports to be made and published at the same time and in the same manner and with like effect and penalties as are now provided by law in respect of national banking associations transacting business in the same locality.

(b) Whoever shall willfully violate any of the provisions of this section shall upon conviction be fined not more than $5,000 or imprisoned not more than five years, or both, and any officer, director, employee, or agent of any person, firm, corporation, association, business trust, or other similar organization who knowingly participates in any such violation shall be punished by a like fine or imprisonment or both.

Sec. 22. The additional liability imposed upon shareholders in national banking associations by the provisions of section 5151 of the Revised Statutes, as amended, and section 23 of the Federal Reserve Act, as amended (U.S.C., title 12, secs. 63 and 64), shall not apply with respect to shares in any such association issued after the date of enactment of this Act.

Sec. 23. Paragraph (c) of section 5155 of the Revised Statutes, as amended (U.S.C., title 12, sec. 36), is amended to read as follows:

"(c) A national banking association may, with the approval of the Comptroller of the Currency, establish and operate new branches: (1) Within the limits of the city, town or village in which said association is situated, if such establishment and operation are at the time expressly authorized to State banks by the law of the State in question; and (2) at any point within the State in which said association is situated, if such establishment and operation are at the time authorized to State banks by the statute law of the State in question by language specifically granting such authority affirmatively and not merely by implication or recognition, and subject to the restrictions as to location imposed by the law of the State on State banks. No such association shall establish a branch outside of the city, town, or village in which it is situated unless it has a paid-in and unimpaired capital stock of not less than $500,000: *Provided,* That in States with a population of less than one million, and which have no cities located therein with a population exceeding one hundred thousand, the capital shall be not less than $250,000: *Provided,* That in States with a population of less than one-half million, and which have no cities located therein with a population exceeding fifty thousand, the capital shall not be less than $100,000."

Paragraph (d) of section 5155 of the Revised Statutes, as amended (U.S.C., title 12, sec. 36), is amended to read as follows:

"(d) The aggregate capital of every national banking association and its branches shall at no time be less than the aggregate minimum capital required by law for the establishment of an equal number of national banking associations situated in the various places where such association and its branches are situated."

Sec. 24. (a) Sections 1 and 3 of the Act entitled "An Act to provide for the consolidation of national banking associations," approved November 7, 1918, as amended (U.S.C., title 12, secs. 33, 34, and 34a), are amended by striking out the words "county, city, town, or village" wherever they occur in each such section, and inserting in lieu thereof the words "State, county, city, town, or village."

(b) Section 3 of such Act of November 7, 1918, as amended, is further amended by striking out the second sentence thereof and inserting in lieu thereof the following: "The capital stock of such consolidated association shall not be less than that required under existing law for the organization of a national banking association in the place in which such consolidated association is located. Upon such a consolidation, or upon a consolidation of two or more national banking associations under section 1 of this Act, the corporate existence of each of the constituent banks and national banking associations participating in such consolidation shall be merged into and continued in the consolidated national banking association and the consolidated association shall be deemed to be the same corporation as each of the constituent institutions. All the rights, franchises, and interests of each of such constituent banks and national banking associations in and to every species of property, real, personal, and mixed, and choses in action thereto belonging, shall be deemed to be transferred to and vested in such consolidated national banking association without any deed or other transfer; and such consolidated national banking association, by virtue of such consolidation and without any order or other action on the part of any court or otherwise, shall hold and enjoy the same and all rights of property, franchises, and interests, including appointments, designations, and nominations and all other rights and interests as trustee, executor, administrator, registrar of stocks and bonds, guardian of estates, assignee, receiver, committee of estates of lunatics and in every other fiduciary capacity, in the same manner and to the same extent as such rights, franchises, and interests were held or enjoyed by any such constituent institution at the time of such consolidation: *Provided, however,* That where any such constituent institution at the time of such consolidation was acting under appointment of any court as trustee, executor, administrator, registrar of stocks and bonds, guardian of estates, assignee, receiver, committee of estates of lunatics or in any other fiduciary capacity, the consolidated national banking association shall be subject to removal by a court of competent jurisdiction in the same manner and to the same extent as was such constituent corporation prior to the consolidation, and nothing herein contained shall be construed to impair in any manner the right of any court to remove such a consolidated national banking association and to appoint in lieu thereof a substitute trustee, executor, or other fiduciary, except that such right shall not be exercised in such a manner as to discriminate against national banking associations, nor shall any such consolidated association be removed solely because of the fact that it is a national banking association."

Sec. 25. The first two sentences of section 5197 of the Revised Statutes (U.S.C., title 12, sec. 85) are amended to read as follows:

"Any association may take, receive, reserve, and charge on any loan or discount made, or upon any notes, bills of exchange, or other evidences of debt, interest at the rate allowed by the laws of the State, Territory, or District where the bank is located, or at a rate of 1 per centum in excess of the discount rate on ninety-day commercial paper in effect at the Federal reserve bank in the Federal reserve district where the bank is located, whichever may be the greater, and no more, except that where by the laws of any State a different rate is limited for banks organized under State laws, the rate so limited shall be allowed for associations organized or existing in any such State under this title. When no rate is fixed by the laws of the State, or Territory, or District, the bank may take, receive, reserve, or charge a rate not exceeding 7 per centum, or 1 per centum in excess of the discount rate on ninety-day commercial paper in effect at the Federal reserve bank in the Federal reserve district where the bank is located, whichever may be the greater, and such interest may be taken in advance, reckoning the days for which the note, bill, or other evidence of debt has to run."

Sec. 26. (a) The second sentence of the first paragraph of section 5200 of the Revised Statutes, as amended (U.S.C., title 12, sec. 84; Supp. VI, title 12, sec. 84) is amended by inserting before the period at the end thereof the following: "and shall include in the case of obligations of a corporation all obligations of all subsidiaries thereof in which such corporation owns or controls a majority interest."

(b) The amendment made by this section shall not apply to such obligations of subsidiaries held by such association on the date this section takes effect.

Sec. 27. Section 5211 of the Revised Statutes, as amended (U.S.C., title 12, sec. 161; Supp. VI, title 12, sec. 161), is amended by adding at the end thereof the following new paragraph:

"Each national banking association shall obtain from each of its affiliates other than member banks and furnish to the Comptroller of the Currency not less than three reports during each year, in such form as the Comptroller may prescribe, verified by the oath or affirmation of the president or such other officer as may be designated by the board of directors of such affiliate to verify such reports, disclosing the information hereinafter provided for as of dates identical with those for which the Comptroller shall during such year require the reports of the condition of the association. For the purpose of this section the term 'affiliate' shall include holding company affiliates as well as other affiliates. Each such report of an affiliate shall be transmitted to the Comptroller at the same time as the corresponding report of the association, except that the Comptroller may, in his discretion, extend such time for good cause shown. Each such report shall contain such information as in the judgment of the Comptroller of the Currency shall be necessary to disclose fully the relations between such affiliate and such bank and to enable the Comptroller to inform himself as to the effect of such relations upon the affairs of such bank. The reports of such affiliates shall be published by the association under the same conditions as govern its own condition reports. The Comptroller shall also have power to call for additional reports with respect to any such affiliate whenever in his judgment the same are necessary in order to obtain a full and complete knowledge of the conditions of the association with which it is affiliated. Such additional reports shall be transmitted to the Comptroller of the Currency in such form as he may prescribe. Any such affiliated bank which fails to obtain and furnish any report required under this section shall be subject to a penalty of $100 for each day during which such failure continues."

Sec. 28. (a) The first paragraph of section 5240 of the Revised Statutes, as amended (U.S.C., title 12, sec. 481), is amended by inserting before the period at the end thereof a colon and the following proviso: "*Provided,* That in making the examination of any national bank the examiners shall include such an examination of the affairs of all its affiliates other than member banks as shall be necessary to disclose fully the relations between such bank and such affiliates and the effect of such relations upon the affairs of such bank; and in the event of the refusal to give any information required in the course of the examination of any such affiliate, or in the event of the refusal to permit such examination, all the rights, privileges, and franchises of the bank shall be subject to forfeiture in accordance with section 2 of the Federal Reserve Act, as amended (U.S.C., title 12, secs. 141, 222-225, 281-286, and 502). The Comptroller of the Currency shall have power, and he is hereby authorized, to publish the report of his examination of any national banking association or affiliate which shall not within one hundred and twenty days after notification of the recommendations or suggestions of the Comptroller, based on said examination, have complied with the same to his satisfaction. Ninety days' notice prior to such publicity shall be given to the bank or affiliate."

(b) Section 5240 of the Revised Statutes, as amended (U.S.C., title 12, sec. 481), is further amended by adding after the first paragraph thereof the following new paragraph:

"The examiner making the examination of any affiliate of a national bank shall have power to make a thorough examination of all the affairs of the affiliate, and in doing so he shall have power to administer oaths and to examine any of the officers, directors, employees, and agents thereof under oath and to make a report of his findings to the Comptroller of the Currency. The expense of examinations of such affiliates may be assessed by the Comptroller of the Currency upon the affiliates examined in proportion to assets or resources held by the affiliates upon the dates of examination of the various affiliates. If any such affiliate shall refuse to pay such expenses or shall fail to do so within sixty days after the date of such assessment, then such expenses may be assessed against the affiliated national bank and, when so assessed, shall be paid by such national bank: *Provided, however,* That, if the affiliation is with two or more national banks, such expenses may be assessed against, and collected from, any or all of such national banks in such proportions as the Comptroller of the Currency may prescribe. The examiners and assistant examiners making the examinations of national banking associations and affiliates thereof herein provided for and the chief examiners, reviewing examiners and other persons whose services may be required in connection with such examinations or the reports thereof, shall be employed by the Comptroller of the Currency with the approval of the Secretary of the Treasury; the employment and compensation of examiners, chief examiners, reviewing examiners, assistant examiners, and of the other employees of the office of the Comptroller of the Currency whose compensation is paid from assessments on banks or affiliates thereof shall be without regard to the provisions of other laws applicable to officers or employees of the United States. The funds derived from such assessments may be deposited by the Comptroller of the Currency in accordance with the provisions of section 5234 of the Revised Statutes (U.S.C., title 12, sec. 192) and shall not be construed to be Government funds or appropriated monies; and the Comptroller of the Currency is authorized and empowered to prescribe regulations governing the computation and assessment of the expenses of examinations herein provided for and the collection of such assessments from the banks and/or affiliates examined. If any affiliate of a national bank shall refuse to permit an examiner to make an examination of the affiliate or shall refuse to give any information required in the course of any such examination, the national bank with which it is affiliated shall be subject to a penalty of not more than $100 for each day that any such refusal shall continue. Such penalty may be assessed by the Comptroller of the Currency and collected in the same manner as expenses of examinations."

Sec. 29. In any case in which, in the opinion of the Comptroller of the Currency, it would be to the advantage of the depositors and unsecured creditors of any national banking association whose business has been closed, for such association to resume business upon the retention by the association, for a reasonable period to be prescribed by the Comptroller, of all or any part of its deposits, the Comptroller is authorized, in his discretion, to permit the association to resume business if depositors and unsecured creditors of the association representing at least 75 per centum of its total deposit and unsecured credit liabilities consent in writing to such retention of deposits. Nothing in this section shall be construed to affect in any manner any powers of the Comptroller under the provisions of law in force on the date of enactment of this Act with respect to the reorganization of national banking associations.

Sec. 30. Whenever, in the opinion of the Comptroller of the Currency, any director of officer of a national bank, or of a bank or trust company doing business in the District of Columbia, or whenever, in the opinion of a Federal reserve agent, any director or officer or a State member bank in his district shall have continued to violate any law relating to such bank or trust company or shall have continued unsafe or unsound practices in conducting the business of such bank or trust company, after having been warned by the Comptroller of the Currency or the Federal reserve agent, as the case may be, to discontinue such violations of law or such unsafe or unsound practices, the Comptroller of the Currency or the Federal reserve agent, as the case may be, may certify the facts to the Federal Reserve Board. In any such case the Federal Reserve Board may cause notice to be served upon such director of officer to appear before such Board to show cause why he should not be removed from office. A copy of such order shall be sent to each director of the bank affected, by registered mail. If after granting the accused director or officer a reasonable opportunity to be heard, the Federal Reserve Board finds that he has continued to violate any law relating to such bank or trust company or has continued unsafe or unsound practices in conducting the business of such bank or trust company after having been warned by the Comptroller of the Currency or the Federal reserve agent to discontinue such violation of law or such unsafe or unsound practices, the Federal Reserve Board, in its discretion, may order that such director or officer be removed from office. A copy of such order shall be served upon such director or officer. A copy of such order shall also be served upon the bank of which he is a director or officer, whereupon such director or officer shall cease to be a director or officer of such bank: *Provided,* That such order and the findings of fact upon which it is based shall not be made public or disclosed to anyone except the director or officer involved and the directors of the bank involved, otherwise than in connection with proceedings for a violation of this section. Any such director or officer removed from office as herein provided who thereafter participates in any manner in the management of such bank shall be fined not more than $5,000, or imprisoned for not more than five years, or both, in the discretion of the court.

Sec. 31. After one year from the date of enactment of this Act, notwithstanding any other provision of law, the board of directors, board of trustees, or other similar governing body of every national banking association and of every State bank or trust company which is a member of the Federal Reserve System shall consist of not less than five nor more than twenty-five members; and every director, trustee, or other member of such governing body shall be the bona fide owner in his own right of shares of stock of such banking association, State bank or trust company having a par value in the aggregate of not less than $2,500, unless the capital of the bank shall not exceed $50,000, in which case he must own in his own right shares having a par value in the aggregate of not less than $1,500, or unless the capital of the bank shall not exceed $25,000, in which case he must own in his own right shares having a par value in the aggregate of not less than $1,000. If any national banking association violates the provisions of this section and continues such violation after thirty days' notice from the Comptroller of the Currency, the said Comptroller may appoint a receiver or conservator therefor, in accordance with the provisions of existing law. If any State bank or trust company which is a member of the Federal Reserve System violates the provisions of this section and continues such violation after thirty days' notice from the Federal Reserve Board, it shall be subject to the forfeiture of its membership in the Federal Reserve System in accordance with the provisions of section 9 of the Federal Reserve Act, as amended.

Sec. 32. From and after January 1, 1934, no officer or director of any member bank shall be an officer, director, or manager of any corporation, partnership, or unincorporated association engaged primarily in the business of purchasing, selling, or negotiating securities, and no member bank shall perform the functions of a correspondent bank on behalf of any such individual, partnership, corporation, or unincorporated association and no such individual, partnership, corporation, or unincorporated association shall perform the functions of a correspondent for any member bank or hold on deposit any funds on behalf of any member bank, unless in any such case there is a permit therefor issued by the Federal Reserve Board; and the Board is authorized to issue such permit if in its judgment it is not incompatible with the public interest, and to revoke any such permit whenever it finds after reasonable notice and opportunity to be heard, that the public interest requires such revocation.

Sec. 33. The Act entitled "An Act to supplement existing laws against unlawful restraints and monopolies, and for other purposes", approved October 15, 1914, as amended (U.S.C., title 15, sec. 19) is hereby amended by adding after section 8 thereof the following new section:

"Sec. 8A. That from and after the 1st day of January 1934, no director, officer, or employee of any bank, banking association, or trust company, organized or operating under the laws of the United States shall be at the same time a director, officer, or employee of a corporation (other than a mutual savings bank) or a member of a partnership organized for any purpose whatsoever which shall make loans secured by stock or bond collateral to any individual, association, partnership, or corporation other than its own subsidiaries."

Sec. 34. The right to alter, amend, or repeal this Act is hereby expressly reserved. If any provision of this Act, or the application thereof to any person or circumstances, is held invalid, the remainder of the Act, and the application of such provision to other persons or circumstances, shall not be affected thereby.

Approved, June 16, 1933, 11:45 a.m.

NATIONAL INDUSTRIAL RECOVERY ACT

Editor's comments: *There are three parts to the National Industrial Recovery Act. Title I of the act deals with overall industrial recovery, Title II provides for the establishment of public works and construction projects, while Title III provides for certain impacts on the existing Reconstruction Finance Corporation and several miscellaneous items.*

Congress recognized widespread unemployment and the disorganization of industry brought on by the depression and considered these problems to constitute a national emergency. The Act is designed to create employment and to promote better organization of industry.

There are two primary features of this legislation that should be highlighted for their overall economic impact. First, trade or industrial associations and groups could ask that codes of fair competition be established as standards for their industries. These codes had to meet specific conditions regarding the rights of employees to participate in union activities and requirements of employers to comply with maximum work hours and minimum rates of pay. Second, a Federal Emergency Administration of Public Works was created with its Administrator directed to prepare a "comprehensive program of public works" that would increase employment quickly by initiating various public works projects.

The total sum appropriated by the Act was $3,300,000,000, of which not less than $400,000,000 was to be used for grants to several State highway departments; not less than $50,000,000 for national forest, national park, and Indian reservation highways, roads, and trails; $25,000,000 for the purchase of subsistence homesteads to aid in the redistribution of the overbalance of population in industrial centers; and not in excess of $100,000,000 for carrying out the purposes, powers, and functions of the Agricultural Adjustment Act as conferred upon the Farm Credit Administration.

An Act to Encourage National Industrial Recovery, to Foster Fair Competition, and to Provide for the Construction of Certain Useful Public Works, and for Other Purposes
June 16, 1933

Be it enacted by the Senate and House of Representatives of the United States of America in Congress assembled,

Title I — Industrial Recovery

Declaration of Policy

Section 1. A national emergency productive of widespread unemployment and disorganization of industry, which burdens interstate and foreign commerce, affects the public welfare, and undermines the standards of living of the American people, is hereby declared to exist. It is hereby declared to be the policy of Congress to remove obstructions to the free flow of interstate and foreign commerce which tend to diminish the amount thereof; and to provide for the general welfare by promoting the organization of industry for the purpose of cooperative action among trade groups, to induce and maintain united action of labor and management under adequate governmental sanctions and supervision, to eliminate unfair competitive practices, to promote the fullest possible utilization of the present productive capacity of industries, to avoid undue restriction of production (except as may be temporarily required), to increase the consumption of industrial and agricultural products by increasing purchasing power, to reduce and relieve unemployment, to improve standards of labor, and otherwise to rehabilitate industry and to conserve natural resources.

Administrative Agencies

Sec. 2. (a) To effectuate the policy of this title, the President is hereby authorized to establish such agencies, to accept and utilize such voluntary and uncompensated services, to appoint, without regard to the provisions of the civil service laws, such officers and employees, and to utilize such Federal officers and employees, and, with the consent of the State, such State and local officers and employees, as he may find necessary, to prescribe their authorities, duties, responsibilities, and tenure, and, without regard to the Classification Act of 1923, as amended, to fix the compensation of any officers and employees so appointed.

(b) The President may delegate any of his functions and powers under this title to such officers, agents, and employees as he may designate or appoint, and may establish an industrial planning and research agency to aid in carrying out his functions under this title.

(c) This title shall cease to be in effect and any agencies established hereunder shall cease to exist at the expiration of two years after the date of enactment of this Act, or sooner if the President shall by proclamation or the Congress shall by joint resolution declare that the emergency recognized by section 1 has ended.

Codes of Fair Competition

Sec. 3. (a) Upon the application to the President by one or more trade or industrial associations or groups, the President may approve a code or codes of fair competition for the trade or industry or subdivision thereof, represented by the applicant or applicants, if the President finds (1) that such associations or groups impose no inequitable restrictions on admission to membership therein and are truly representative of such trades or industries or subdivisions thereof, and (2) that such code or codes are not designed to promote monopolies or to eliminate or oppress small enterprises and will not operate to discriminate against them, and will tend to effectuate the policy of this title: *Provided,* That such code or codes shall not permit monopolies or monopolistic practices: *Provided further,* That where such code or codes affect the services and welfare of persons engaged in other steps of the economic process, nothing in this section shall deprive such persons of the right to be heard prior to approval by the President of such code or codes. The President may, as a condition of his approval of any such code, impose such conditions (including requirements for the making of reports and the keeping of accounts) for the protection of consumers, competitors, employees, and others, and in furtherance of the public interest, and may provide such exceptions to and exemptions from the provisions of such code, as the President in his discretion deems necessary to effectuate the policy herein declared.

(b) After the President shall have approved any such code, the provisions of such code shall be the standards of fair competition for such trade or industry or subdivision thereof. Any violation of such standards in any transaction in or affecting interstate or foreign commerce shall be deemed an unfair method of competition in commerce within the meaning of the Federal Trade Commission Act, as amended; but nothing in this title shall be construed to impair the powers of the Federal Trade Commission under such Act, as amended.

(c) The several district courts of the United States are hereby invested with jurisdiction to prevent and restrain violations of any code of fair competition approved under this title; and it shall be the duty of the several district attorneys of the United States, in their respective districts, under the direction of the Attorney General, to institute proceedings in equity to prevent and restrain such violations.

(d) Upon his own motion, or if complaint is made to the President that abuses inimical to the public interest and contrary to the policy herein declared are prevalent in any trade or industry or subdivision thereof, and if no code of fair competition therefor has theretofore been approved by the President, the President, after such public notice and hearing as he shall specify, may prescribe and approve a code of fair competition for such trade or industry or subdivision thereof, which shall have the same effect as a code of fair competition approved by the President under subsection (a) of this section.

(e) On his own motion, of if any labor organization, or any trade or industrial organization, association, or group, which has complied with the provisions of this title, shall make complaint to the President that any article or articles are being imported into the United States in substantial quantities or increasing ratio to domestic production of any competitive article or articles and on such terms or under such conditions as to render ineffective or seriously to endanger the maintenance of any code or agreement under this title, the President may cause an immediate investigation to be made by the United States Tariff Commission, which shall give precedence to investigations under this subsection, and if, after such investigation and such public notice and hearing as he shall specify, the President shall find the existence of such facts, he shall, in order to effectuate the policy of this title, direct that the article or articles concerned shall be permitted entry into the United

States only upon such terms and conditions and subject to the payment of such fees and to such limitations in the total quantity which may be imported (in the course of any specified period or periods) as he shall find it necessary to prescribe in order that the entry thereof shall not render or tend to render ineffective any code or agreement made under this title. In order to enforce any limitations imposed on the total quantity of imports, in any specified period or periods, of any article or articles under this subsection, the President may forbid the importation of such article or articles unless the importer shall have first obtained from the Secretary of the Treasury a license pursuant to such regulations as the President may prescribe. Upon information of any action by the President under this subsection the Secretary of the Treasury shall, through the proper officers, permit entry of the article or articles specified only upon such terms and conditions and subject to such fees, to such limitations in the quantity which may be imported, and to such requirements of license, as the President shall have directed. The decision of the President as to facts shall be conclusive. Any condition or limitation of entry under this subsection shall continue in effect until the President shall find and inform the Secretary of the Treasury that the conditions which led to the imposition of such condition or limitation upon entry no longer exists.

(f) When a code of fair competition has been approved or prescribed by the President under this title, any violation of any provision thereof in any transaction in or affecting interstate or foreign commerce shall be a misdemeanor and upon conviction thereof an offender shall be fined not more than $500 for each offense, and each day such violation continues shall be deemed a separate offense.

Agreements and Licenses

Sec. 4. (a) The President is authorized to enter into agreements with, and to approve voluntary agreements between and among, persons engaged in a trade or industry, labor organizations, and trade or industrial organizations, associations, or groups, relating to any trade or industry, if in his judgment such agreements will aid in effectuating the policy of this title with respect to transactions in or affecting interstate or foreign commerce, and will be consistent with the requirements of clause (2) of subsection (a) of section 3 for a code of fair competition.

(b) Whenever the President shall find that destructive wage or price cutting or other activities contrary to the policy of this title are being practiced in any trade or industry or any subdivision thereof, and, after such public notice and hearing as he shall specify, shall find it essential to license business enterprises in order to make effective a code of fair competition or an agreement under this title or otherwise to effectuate the policy of this title, and shall publicly so announce, no person shall, after a date fixed in such announcement, engage in or carry on any business, in or affecting interstate or foreign commerce, specified in such announcement, unless he shall have first obtained a license issued pursuant to such regulations as the President shall prescribe. The President may suspend or revoke any such license, after due notice and opportunity for hearing, for violations of the terms or conditions thereof. Any order of the President suspending or revoking any such license shall be final if in accordance with law. Any person who, without such a license or in violation of any condition thereof, carries on any such business for which a license is so required, shall, upon conviction thereof, be fined not more than $500, or imprisoned not more than six months, or both, and each day such violation continues shall be deemed a separate offense. Notwithstanding the provisions of section 2 (c), this subsection shall cease to be in effect at the expiration of one year after the date of enactment of this Act or sooner if the President shall by proclamation or the Congress shall by joint resolution declare that the emergency recognized by section 1 has ended.

Sec. 5. While this title is in effect (or in the case of a license, while section 4 (a) is in effect) and for sixty days thereafter, any code, agreement, or license approved, prescribed, or issued and in effect under this title, and any action complying with the provisions thereof taken during such period, shall be exempt from the provisions of the antitrust laws of the United States.

Nothing in this Act, and no regulation thereunder, shall prevent an individual from pursuing the vocation of manual labor and selling or trading the products thereof; nor shall anything in this Act, or regulation thereunder, prevent anyone from marketing or trading the produce of his farm.

Limitations Upon Application of Title

Sec. 6. (a) No trade or industrial association or group shall be eligible to receive the benefit of the provisions of this title until it files with the President a statement containing such information relating to the activities of the association or group as the President shall by regulation prescribe.

(b) The President is authorized to prescribe rules and regulations designed to insure that any organization availing itself of the benefits of this title shall be truly representative of the trade or industry or subdivision thereof represented by such organization. Any organization violating any such rule or regulation shall cease to be entitled to the benefits of this title.

(c) Upon the request of the President, the Federal Trade Commission shall make such investigations as may be necessary to enable the President to carry out the provisions of this title, and for such purposes the Commission shall have all the powers vested in it with respect of investigations under the Federal Trade Commission Act, as amended.

Sec. 7. (a) Every code of fair competition, agreement, and license approved, prescribed, or issued under this title shall contain the following conditions: (1) That employees shall have the right to organize and bargain collectively through representatives of their own choosing, and shall be free from the interference, restraint, or coercion of employers of labor, or their agents, in the designation of such representatives or in self-organization or in other concerted activities for the purpose of collective bargaining or other mutual aid or protection; (2) that no employee and no one seeking employment shall be required as a condition of employment to join any company union or to refrain from joining, organizing, or assisting a labor organization of his own choosing; and (3) that employers shall comply with the maximum hours of labor, minimum rates of pay, and other conditions of employment, approved or prescribed by the President.

(b) The President shall, so far as practicable, afford every opportunity to employers and employees in any trade or industry or subdivision thereof with respect to which the conditions referred to in clauses (1) and (2) of subsection (a) prevail, to establish by mutual agreement, the standards as to the maximum hours of labor, minimum rates of pay, and such other conditions of employment as may be necessary in such trade or industry or subdivision thereof to effectuate the policy of this title; and the standards established in such agreements, when approved by the President, shall have the same effect as a code of fair competition, approved by the President under subsection (a) of section 3.

(c) Where no such mutual agreement has been approved by the President he may investigate the labor practices, policies, wages, hours of labor, and conditions of employment in such trade or industry or subdivision thereof; and upon the basis of such investigations, and after such hearings as the President finds advisable, he is authorized to prescribe a limited code of fair competition fixing such maximum hours of labor, minimum rates of pay, and other conditions of employment in the trade or industry or subdivision thereof investigated as he finds to be necessary to effectuate the policy of this title, which shall have the same effect as a code of fair competition approved by the President under subsection (a) of section 3. The President may differentiate according to experience and skill of the employees affected and according to the locality of employment; but no attempt shall be made to introduce any classification according to the nature of the work involved which might tend to set a maximum as well as a minimum wage.

(d) As used in this title, the term "person" includes any individual, partnership, association, trust, or corporation; and the terms "interstate and foreign commerce" and "interstate or foreign commerce" include, except where otherwise indicated, trade or commerce among the several States and with foreign nations, or between the District of Columbia or any Territory of the United States and any State, Territory, or foreign nation, or between any insular possessions or other places under the jurisdiction of the United States, or between any such possession or place and any State or Territory of the United States or the District of Columbia or any foreign nation, or

Application of Agricultural Adjustment Act

Sec. 8. (a) This title shall not be construed to repeal or modify any of the provisions of title I of the Act entitled "An Act to relieve the existing national economic emergency by increasing agricultural purchasing power, to raise revenue for extraordinary expenses incurred by reason of such emergency, to provide emergency relief with respect to agricultural indebtedness, to provide for the orderly liquidation of joint-stock land banks, and for other purposes", approved May 12, 1933; and such title I of said Act approved May 12, 1933, may for all purposes be hereafter referred to as the "Agricultural Adjustment Act."

(b) The President may, in his discretion, in order to avoid conflicts in the administration of the Agricultural Adjustment Act and this title, delegate any of his functions and powers under this title with respect to trades, industries, or subdivisions thereof which are engaged in the handling of any agricultural commodity or product thereof, or of any competing commodity or product thereof, to the Secretary of Agriculture.

Oil Regulation

Sec. 9. (a) The President is further authorized to initiate before the Interstate Commerce Commission proceedings necessary to prescribe regulations to control the operations of oil pipe lines and to fix reasonable, compensatory rates for the transportation of petroleum and its products by pipe lines, and the Interstate Commerce Commission shall grant preference to the hearings and determination of such cases.

(b) The President is authorized to institute proceedings to divorce from any holding company any pipe-line company controlled by such holding company which pipe-line company by unfair practices or by exorbitant rates in the transportation of petroleum or its products tends to create a monopoly.

(c) The President is authorized to prohibit the transportation in interstate and foreign commerce of petroleum and the products thereof produced or withdrawn from storage in excess of the amount permitted to be produced or withdrawn from storage by any State law or valid regulation or order prescribed thereunder, by any board, commission, officer, or other duly authorized agency of a State. Any violation of any order of the President issued under the provisions of this subsection shall be punishable by fine of not to exceed $1,000, or imprisonment for not to exceed six months, or both.

Rules and Regulations

Sec. 10. (a) The President is authorized to prescribe such rules and regulations as may be necessary to carry out the purposes of this title, and fees for licenses and for filing codes of fair competition and agreements, and any violation of any such rule or regulation shall be punishable by fine of not to exceed $500, or imprisonment for not to exceed six months, or both.

(b) The President may from time to time cancel or modify any order, approval, license, rule, or regulation issued under this title; and each agreement, code of fair competition, or license approved, prescribed, or issued under this title shall contain an express provision to that effect.

Title II — Public Works and Construction Projects

Federal Emergency Administration of Public Works

Section 201. (a) To effectuate the purposes of this title, the President is hereby authorized to create a Federal Emergency Administration of Public Works, all the powers of which shall be exercised by a Federal Emergency Administrator of Public Works (hereafter referred to as the "Administrator"), and to establish such agencies, to accept and utilize such voluntary and uncompensated services, to appoint, without regard to the civil service laws, such officers and employees, and to utilize such Federal officers and employees, and, with the consent of the State, such State and local officers and employees as he may find necessary, to prescribe their authorities, duties, responsibilities, and tenure, and, without regard to the Classification Act of 1923, as amended, to fix the compensation of any officers and employees so appointed. The President may delegate any of his functions and powers under this title to such officers, agents, and employees as he may designate or appoint.

(b) The Administrator may, without regard to the civil service laws or the Classification Act of 1923, as amended, appoint and fix the compensation of such experts and such other officers and employees as are necessary to carry out the provisions of this title; and may make such expenditures (including expenditures for personal services and rent at the seat of government and elsewhere, for law books and books of reference, and for paper, printing and binding) as are necessary to carry out the provisions of this title.

(c) All such compensation, expenses, and allowances shall be paid out of funds made available by this Act.

(d) After the expiration of two years after the date of the enactment of this Act, or sooner if the President shall by proclamation or the Congress shall by joint resolution declare that the emergency recognized by section 1 has ended, the President shall not make any further loans or grants or enter upon any new construction under this title, and any agencies established hereunder shall cease to exist and any of their remaining functions shall be transferred to such departments of the Government as the President shall designate: *Provided,* That he may issue funds to a borrower under this title prior to January 23, 1939, under the terms of any agreement, or any commitment to bid upon or purchase bonds, entered into with such borrower prior to the date of termination, under this section, of the power of the President to make loans.

Sec. 202. The Administrator, under the direction of the President, shall prepare a comprehensive program of public works, which shall include among other things the following: (a) Construction, repair, and improvement of public highways and parkways, public buildings, and any publicly owned instrumentalities and facilities; (b) conservation and development of natural resources, including control, utilization, and purification of waters, prevention of soil or coastal erosion, development of water power, transmission of electrical energy, and construction of river and harbor improvements and flood control and also the construction of any river or drainage improvement required to perform or satisfy any obligation incurred by the United States through a treaty with a foreign Government heretofore ratified and to restore or develop for the use of any State or its citizens water taken from or denied to them by performance on the part of the United States of treaty obligations heretofore assumed: *Provided*, That no river or harbor improvements shall be carried out unless they shall have heretofore or hereafter been adopted by the Congress or are recommended by the Chief of Engineers of the United States Army; (c) any projects of the character heretofore constructed or carried on either directly by public authority or with public aid to serve the interests of the general public; (d) construction, reconstruction, alteration, or repair under public regulation or control of low-cost housing and slum-clearance projects; (e) any project (other than those included in the foregoing classes) of any character heretofore eligible for loans under subsection (a) of section 201 of the Emergency Relief and Construction Act of 1932, as amended, and paragraph (3) of such subsection (a) shall for such purposes be held to include loans for the construction or completion of hospitals the operation of which is partly financed from public funds, and of reservoirs and pumping plants and for the construction of dry docks; and if in the opinion of the President it seems desirable, the construction of naval vessels within the terms and/or limits established by the London Naval Treaty of 1930 and of aircraft required therefor and construction of heavier-than-air aircraft and technical construction for the Army Air Corps and such Army housing projects as the President may approve, and provision of original equipment for the mechanization or motorization of such Army tactical units as he may designate: *Provided, however,* That in the event of an international agreement for the further limitation of armament, to which the United States is signatory, the President is hereby authorized and empowered to suspend, in whole or in part, any such naval or military construction or mechanization and motorization of Army units: *Provided further,* That this title shall not be applicable to public works under the jurisdiction or control of the Architect of the Capitol or of any commission or committee for which such Architect is the contracting and/or executive officer.

Sec. 203. (a) With a view to increasing employment quickly (while reasonably securing any loans made by the United States) the President is authorized and empowered, through the Administrator or through such other agencies as he may designate or create, (1) to construct, finance, or aid in the construction or financing of any public-works project included in the program prepared pursuant to section 202; (2) upon such terms as the President shall prescribe, to make grants to States, municipalities, or other public bodies for the construction, repair, or improvement of any such project, but no such grant shall be in excess of 30 per centum of the cost of the labor and materials employed upon such project; (3) to acquire by purchase, or by exercise of the power of eminent domain, any real or personal property in connection with the construction of any such project, and to sell any security acquired or any property so constructed or acquired or to lease any such property with or without the privilege of purchase: *Provided,* That all moneys received from any such sale or lease or the repayment of any loan shall be used to retire obligations issued pursuant to section 209 of this Act, in addition to any other moneys required to be used for such purpose; (4) to aid in the financing of such railroad maintenance and equipment as may be approved by the Interstate Commerce Commission as desirable for the improvement of transportation facilities; and (5) to advance, upon request of the Commission having jurisdiction of the project, the unappropriated balance of the sum authorized for carrying out the provisions of the Act entitled "An Act to provide for the construction and equipment of an annex to the Library of Congress", approved June 13, 1930 (46 Stat. 583); such advance to be expended under the direction of such Commission and in accordance with such Act: *Provided,* That in deciding to extend any aid or grant hereunder to any State, county, or municipality the President may consider whether action is in process or in good faith assured therein reasonably designed to bring the ordinary current expenditures thereof within the prudently estimated revenues thereof. The provisions of this section and section 202 shall extend to public works in the several States, Hawaii, Alaska, the District of Columbia, Puerto Rico, the Canal Zone, and the Virgin Islands.

(b) All expenditures for authorized travel by officers and employees, including subsistence, required on account of any Federal public-works projects, shall be charged to the amounts allocated to such projects, notwithstanding any other provisions of law; and there is authorized to be employed such personal services in the District of Columbia and elsewhere as may be required to be engaged upon such work and to be in addition to employees otherwise provided for, the compensation of such additional personal services to be a charge against the funds made available for such construction work.

(c) In the acquisition of any land or site for the purposes of Federal public buildings and in the construction of such buildings provided for in this title, the provisions contained in sections 305 and 306 of the Emergency Relief and Construction Act of 1932, as amended, shall apply.

(d) The President, in his discretion, and under such terms as he may prescribe, may extend any of the benefits of this title to any State, county, or municipality notwithstanding any constitutional or legal restriction or limitation on the right or power of such State, county, or municipality to borrow money or incur indebtedness.

Sec. 204. (a) For the purpose of providing for emergency construction of public highways and related projects, the President is authorized to make grants to the highway departments of the several States in an amount not less than $400,000,000, to be expended by such departments in accordance with the provisions of the Federal Highway Act, approved November 9, 1921, as amended and supplemented, except as provided in this title, as follows:

(1) For expenditure in emergency construction on the Federal aid highway system and extensions thereof into and through municipalities. The amount apportioned to any State under this paragraph may be used to pay all or any part of the cost of surveys, plans, and of highway and bridge construction including the elimination of hazards to highway traffic, such as the separation of grades at crossing, the reconstruction of existing railroad grade crossing structures, the relocation of highways to eliminate railroad crossings, the widening of narrow bridges and roadways, the building of footpaths, the replacement of unsafe bridges, the construction of routes to avoid congested areas, the construction of facilities to improve accessibility and the free flow of traffic, and the cost of any other construction that will provide safer traffic facilities or definitely eliminate existing hazards to pedestrian or vehicular traffic. No funds made available by this title shall be used for the acquisition of any land, right of way, or easement in connection with any railroad grade elimination project.

(2) For expenditure in emergency construction on secondary or feeder roads to be agreed upon by the State highway departments and the Secretary of Agriculture: *Provided,* That the State or responsible political subdivision shall provide for the proper maintenance of said roads. Such grants shall be available for payment of the full cost of surveys, plans, improvement, and construction of secondary or feeder roads, on which projects shall be submitted by the State highway department and approved by the Secretary of Agriculture.

(b) Any amounts allocated by the President for grants under subsection (a) of this section shall be apportioned among the several States seven-eighths in accordance with the provisions of section 21 of the Federal Highway Act, approved November 9, 1921, as amended and supplemented (which Act is hereby further amended for the purposes of this title to include the District of Columbia), and one-eighth in the ratio which the population of each State bears to the total population of the United States, according to the latest decennial census and shall be available on July 1, 1933, and shall remain available until expended; but no part of the funds apportioned to any State need be matched by the State, and such funds may also be used in lieu of State funds to match unobligated balances of previous apportionments of regular Federal-aid appropriations.

(c) All contracts involving the expenditure of such grants shall contain provisions establishing minimum rates of wages, to be predetermined by the State highway department, which contractors shall pay to skilled and unskilled labor, and such minimum rates shall be stated in the invitation for bids and shall be included in proposals for bids for the work.

(d) In the expenditure of such amounts, the limitations in the Federal Highway Act, approved November 9, 1921, as amended and supplemented, upon highway construction, reconstruction, and bridges within municipalities and upon payments per mile which may be made from Federal funds, shall not apply.

(e) As used in this section the term "State" includes the Territory of Hawaii and the District of Columbia. The term "highway" as defined in the Federal Highway Act approved November 9, 1921, as amended and supplemented, for the purposes of this section, shall be deemed to include such main parkways as may be designated by the State and approved by the Secretary of Agriculture as part of the Federal-aid highway system.

(f) Whenever, in connection with the construction of any highway project under this section or section 202 of this Act, it is necessary to acquire rights of way over or through any property or tracts of land owned and controlled by the Government of the United States, it shall be the duty of the proper official of the Government of the United States having control of such property or tracts of land with the approval of the President and the Attorney General of the United States, and without any expense whatsoever to the United States, to perform any acts and to execute any agreements necessary to grant the rights of way so required, but if at any time the land or the property the subject of the agreement shall cease to be used for the purposes of the highway, the title in and the jurisdiction over the land or property shall automatically revert to the Government of the United States and the agreement shall so provide.

(g) Hereafter in the administration of the Federal Highway Act, and Acts amendatory thereof or supplementary thereto, the first paragraph of section 9 of said Act shall not apply to publicly owned toll bridges or approaches thereto, operated by the highway department of any State, subject, however, to the condition that all tolls received from the operation of any such bridge, less the actual cost of operation and maintenance, shall be applied to the repayment of the cost of its construction or acquisition, and when the cost of its construction or acquisition shall have been repaid in full, such bridge thereafter shall be maintained and operated as a free bridge.

Sec. 205. (a) Not less than $50,000,000 of the amount made available by this Act shall be allotted for (A) national forest highways, (B) national forest roads, trails, bridges, and related projects, (C) national park roads and trails in national parks owned or authorized, (D) roads on Indian reservations, and (E) roads through public lands, to be expended in the same manner as provided in paragraph (2) of section 301 of the Emergency Relief and Construction Act of 1932, in the case of appropriations allocated for such purposes, respectively, in such section 301, to remain available until expended.

(b) The President may also allot funds made available by this Act for the construction, repair, and improvement of public highways in Alaska, the Canal Zone, Puerto Rico, and the Virgin Islands.

Sec. 206. All contracts let for construction projects and all loans and grants pursuant to this title shall contain such provisions as are necessary to insure (1) that no convict labor shall be employed on any such project; (2) that (except in executive, administrative, and supervisory positions), so far as practicable and feasible, no individual directly employed on any such project shall be permitted to work more than thirty hours in any one week; (3) that all employees shall be paid just and reasonable wages which shall be compensation sufficient to provide, for the hours of labor as limited, a standard of living in decency and comfort; (4) that in the employment of labor in connection with any such project, preference shall be given, where they are qualified, to ex-service men with dependents, and then in the following order: (A) To citizens of the United States and aliens who have declared their intention of becoming citizens, who are bona fide residents of the political subdivision and/or county in which the work is to be performed, and (B) to citizens of the United States and aliens who have declared their intention of becoming citizens, who are bona fide residents of the State, Territory, or district in which the work is to be performed: *Provided,* That these prefereces shall apply only where such labor is available and qualified to perform the work to which the employment relates; and (5) that the maximum of human labor shall be used in lieu of machinery wherever practicable and consistent with sound economy and public advantage.

Sec. 207. (a) For the purpose of expediting the actual construction of public works contemplated by this title and to provide a means of financial assistance to persons under contract with the United States to perform such construction, the President is authorized and empowered, through the Administrator or through such other agencies as he may designate or create, to approve any assignment executed by any such contractor, with the written consent of the surety or sureties upon the penal bond executed in connection with his contract, to any national or State bank, or his claim against the United States, or any part of such claim, under such contract; and any assignment so approved shall be valid for all purposes, notwithstanding the provisions of sections 3737 and 3477 of the Revised Statutes, as amended.

(b) The funds received by a contractor under any advances made in consideration of any such assignment are hereby declared to be trust funds in the hands of such contractor to be first applied to the payment of claims of subcontractors, architects, engineers, surveyors, laborers, and material men in connection with the project, to the payment of premiums on the penal bond or bonds, and premiums accruing during the construction of such project on insurance policies taken in connection therewith. Any contractor and any officer, director, or agent of any such contractor, who applies, or consents to the application of, such funds for any other purpose and fails to pay any claim or premium hereinbefore mentioned, shall be deemed guilty of a misdemeanor and shall be punished by a fine of not more than $1,000 or by imprisonment for not more than one year, or by both such fine and imprisonment.

(c) Nothing in this section shall be considered as imposing upon the assignee any obligation to see to the proper application of the funds advanced by the assignee in consideration of such assignment.

Subsistence Homesteads

Sec. 208. To provide for aiding the redistribution of the overbalance of population in industrial centers $25,000,000 is hereby made available to the President, to be used by him through such agencies as he may establish and under such regulations as he may make, for making loans for and otherwise aiding in the purchase of subsistence homesteads. The moneys collected as repayment of said loans shall constitute a revolving fund to be administered as directed by the President for the purposes of this section.

Rules and Regulations

Sec. 209. The President is authorized to prescribe such rules and regulations as may be necessary to carry out the purposes of this title, and any violation of any such rule or regulation shall be punishable by fine or not to exceed $500 or imprisonment not to exceed six months, or both.

Issue of Securities and Sinking Fund

Sec. 210. (a) The Secretary of the Treasury is authorized to borrow, from time to time, under the Second Liberty Bond Act, as amended, such amounts as may be necessary to meet the expenditures authorized by this Act, or to refund any obligations previously issued under this section, and to issue therefor bonds, notes, certificates of indebtedness, or Treasury bills of the United States.

(b) For each fiscal year beginning with the fiscal year 1934 there is hereby appropriated, in addition to and as part of, the cumulative sinking fund provided by section 6 of the Victory Liberty Loan Act, as amended, out of any money in the Treasury not otherwise appropriated, for the purpose of such fund, an amount equal to 2½ per centum of the aggregate amount of the

Reemployment and Relief Taxes

Sec. 211. (a) Effective as of the day following the date of the enactment of this Act, section 617 (a) of the Revenue Act of 1932 is amended by striking out "1 cent" and inserting in lieu thereof "1-1/2 cents".

(b) Effective as of the day following the date of the enactment of this Act, section 617 (c) (2) of such Act is amended by adding at the end thereof a new sentence to read as follows: "As used in this paragraph the term 'benzol' does not include benzol sold for use otherwise than as a fuel for the propulsion of motor vehicles, motor boats, or airplanes, and otherwise than in the manufacture or production of such fuel."

Sec. 212. Titles IV and V of the Revenue Act of 1932 are amended by striking out "1934" wherever appearing therein and by inserting in lieu thereof "1935". Section 761 of the Revenue Act of 1932 is further amended by striking out "and on July 1, 1933" and inserting in lieu thereof "and on July 1, 1933, and on July 1, 1934,".

Sec. 213, (a) There is hereby imposed upon receipt of dividends (required to be included in the gross income of the recipient under the provisions of the Revenue Act of 1932) by any person other than a domestic corporation, an excise tax equal to 5 per centum of the amount thereof, such tax to be deducted and withheld from such dividends by the payor corporation. The tax imposed by this section shall not apply to dividends declared before the date of the enactment of this Act.

(b) Every corporation required to deduct and withhold any tax under this section shall, on or before the last day of the month following the payment of the dividend, make return thereof and pay the tax to the collector of the district in which its principal place of business is located, or, if it has no principal place of business in the United States, to the collector at Baltimore, Maryland.

(c) Every such corporation is hereby made liable for such tax and is hereby indemnified against the claims and demands of any person for the amount of any payment made in accordance with the provisions of this section.

(d) The provisions of sections 115, 771 to 774, inclusive, and 1111 of the Revenue Act of 1932 shall be applicable with respect to the tax imposed by this section.

(e) The taxes imposed by this section shall not apply to the dividends of any corporation enumerated in section 103 of the Revenue Act of 1932.

Sec. 214. Section 104 of the Revenue Act of 1932 is amended by striking out the words "the surtax" wherever occurring in such section and inserting in lieu thereof "any internal-revenue tax." The heading of such section is amended by striking out "surtaxes" and inserting in lieu thereof "internal-revenue taxes." Section 13(c) of such Act is amended by striking out "surtax" and inserting in lieu thereof "internal-revenue tax."

Sec. 215. (a) For each year ending June 30 there is hereby imposed upon every domestic corporation with respect to carrying on or doing business for any part of such year an excise tax of $1 for each $1,000 of the adjusted declared value of its capital stock.

(b) For each year ending June 30 there is hereby imposed upon every foreign corporation with respect to carrying on or doing business in the United States for any part of such year an excise tax equivalent to $1 for each $1,000 of the adjusted declared value of capital employed in the transaction of its business in the United States.

(c) The taxes imposed by this section shall not apply—

(1) to any corporation enumerated in section 103 of the Revenue Act of 1932;

(2) to any insurance company subject to the tax imposed by section 201 or 204 of such Act;

(3) to any domestic corporation in respect of the year ending June 30, 1933, if it did not carry on or do business during a part of the period from the date of the enactment of this Act to June 30, 1933, both dates inclusive; or

(4) to any foreign corporation in respect of the year ending June 30, 1933, if it did not carry on or do business in the United States during a part of the period from the date of the enactment of this Act to June 30, 1933, both dates inclusive.

(d) Every corporation liable for tax under this section shall make a return under oath within one month after the close of the year with respect to which such tax is imposed to the collector for the district in which is located its principal place of business or, if it has no principal place of business in the United States, then to the collector at Baltimore, Maryland. Such return shall contain such information and be made in such manner as the Commissioner with the approval of the Secretary may by regulations prescribe. The tax shall, without assessment by the Commissioner or notice from the Collector, be due and payable to the collector before the expiration of the period for filing the return. If the tax is not paid when due, there shall be added as part of the tax interest at the rate of 1 per centum a month from the time when the tax became due until paid. All provisions of law (including penalties) applicable in respect of the taxes imposed by section 600 of the Revenue Act of 1926 shall, in so far as not inconsistent with this section, be applicable in respect of the taxes imposed by this section. The Commissioner may extend the time for making the returns and paying the taxes imposed by this section, under such rules and regulations as he may prescribe with the approval of the Secretary, but no such extension shall be for more than sixty days.

(e) Returns required to be filed for the purpose of the tax imposed by this section shall be open to inspection in the same manner, to the same extent, and subject to the same provisions of law, including penalties, as returns made under title II of the Revenue Act of 1926.

(f) For the first year ending June 30 in respect of which a tax is imposed by this section upon any corporation, the adjusted declared value shall be the value, as declared by the corporation in its first return under this section (which declaration of value cannot be amended), as of the close of its last income-tax taxable year ending at or prior to the close of the year for which the tax is imposed by this section (or as of the date of organization in the case of a corporation having no income-tax taxable year ending at or prior to the close of the year for which the tax is imposed by this section). For any subsequent year ending June 30, the adjusted declared value in the case of a domestic corporation shall be the original declared value plus (1) the cash and fair market value of property paid in for stock or shares, (2) paid-in surplus and contributions to capital, and (3) earnings and profits, and minus (A) the value of property distributed in liquidation to shareholders, (B) distributions of earnings and profits, and (C) deficits, whether operating or nonoperating; each adjustment being made for the period from the date as of which the original declared value was declared to the close of its last income-tax taxable year ending at or prior to the close of the year for which the tax is imposed by this section. For any subsequent year ending June 30, the adjusted declared value in the case of a foreign corporation shall be the original declared value adjusted, in accordance with regulations prescribed by the Commissioner with the approval of the Secretary, to reflect increases or decreases (for the period specified in the preceding sentence) in the capital employed in the transaction of its business in the United States.

(g) The terms used in this section shall have the same meaning as when used in the Revenue Act of 1932.

Sec. 216. (a) There is hereby imposed upon the net income of every corporation, for each income-tax taxable year ending after the close of the first year in respect of which it is taxable under section 215, an excess-profits tax equivalent to 5 per centum of such portion of its net income for such income-tax taxable year as is in excess of 12½ per centum of the adjusted declared value of its capital stock (or in the case of a foreign corporation the adjusted declared value of capital employed in the transaction of its business in the United States) as of the close of the preceding income-tax taxable year (or as of the date of organization if it had no preceding income-tax taxable year) determined as provided in section 215. The terms used in this section shall have the same meaning as when used in the Revenue Act of 1932.

(b) The tax imposed by this section shall be assessed, collected, and paid in the same manner, and shall be subject to the same provisions of law (including penalties), as the taxes imposed by title I of the Revenue Act of 1932.

Sec. 217. (a) The President shall proclaim the date of—

(1) the close of the first fiscal year ending June 30 of any year after the year 1933, during which the total receipts of the United States (excluding public-debt receipts) exceed its total expenditures (excluding public-debt expenditures other than those chargeable against such receipts), or

(2) the repeal of the eighteenth amendment to the Constitution, whichever is earlier.

(b) Effective as of the 1st day of the calendar year following the date so proclaimed section 617(a) of the Revenue Act of 1932, as amended, is amended by striking out "1½ cents" and inserting in lieu thereof " 1 cent".

(c) The tax on dividends imposed by section 213 shall not apply to any dividends declared on or after the 1st day of the calendar year following the date so proclaimed.

(d) The capital-stock tax imposed by section 215 shall not apply to any taxpayer in respect of any year beginning on or after the 1st day of July following the date so proclaimed.

(e) The excess-profits tax imposed by section 216 shall not apply to any taxpayer in respect of any taxable year after its taxable year during which the date so proclaimed occurs.

Sec. 218. (a) Effective as of January 1, 1933, sections 117, 23 (i), 169, 187, and 205 of the Revenue Act of 1932 are repealed.

(b) Effective as of January 1, 1933, section 23(r) (2) of the Revenue Act of 1932 is repealed.

(c) Effective as of January 1, 1933, section 23(r) (3) of the Revenue Act of 1932 is amended by striking out all after the word "Territory" and inserting a period.

(d) Effective as of January 1, 1933, section 182(a) of the Revenue Act of 1932 is amended by inserting at the end thereof a new sentence as follows: "No part of any loss disallowed to a partnership as a deduction by section 23(r) shall be allowed as a deduction to a member of such partnership in computing net income."

(e) Effective as of January 1, 1933, section 141(c) of the Revenue Act of 1932 is amended by striking out "except that for the taxable years 1932 and 1933 there shall be added to the rate of tax prescribed by sections 13(a), 201(b), and 204(a), a rate of three fourths of 1 per centum" and inserting in lieu thereof the following: "except that for the taxable years 1932 and 1933 there shall be added to the rate of tax prescribed by sections 13(a), 201(b), and 204(a), a rate of three fourths of 1 per centum and except that for the taxable years 1934 and 1935 there shall be added to the rate of tax prescribed by sections 13(a), 201(b), and 204(a), a rate of 1 per centum".

(f) No interest shall be assessed or collected for any period prior to September 15, 1933, upon such portion of any amount determined as a deficiency in income taxes as is attributable solely to the amendments made to the Revenue Act of 1932 by this section.

(g) In cases where the effect of this section is to require for a taxable year ending prior to June 30, 1933, the making of an income-tax return not otherwise required by law, the time for making the return and paying the tax shall be the same as if the return was for a fiscal year ending June 30, 1933.

(h) Section 55 of the Revenue Act of 1932 is amended by inserting before the period at the end thereof a semicolon and the following: "and all returns made under this Act after the date of enactment of the National Industrial Recovery Act shall constitute public records and shall be open to public examination and inspection to such extent as shall be authorized in rules and regulations promulgated by the President".

Sec. 219. Section 500 (a) (1) of the Revenue Act of 1926, as amended, is amended by striking out the period at the end of the second sentence thereof and inserting in lieu thereof a comma and the following: "except that no tax shall be imposed in the case of persons admitted free to any spoken play (not a mechanical reproduction), whether or not set to music or with musical parts or accompaniments, which is a consecutive narrative interpreted by a single set of characters, all necessary to the development of the plot, in two or more acts, the performance consuming more than 1 hour and 45 minutes of time."

Appropriation

Sec. 220. For the purposes of this Act, there is hereby authorized to be appropriated, out of any money in the Treasury not otherwise appropriated, the sum of $3,300,000,000. The President is authorized to allocate so much of said sum, not in excess of $100,000,000, as he may determine to be necessary for expenditures in carrying out the Agricultural Adjustment Act and the purposes, powers, and functions heretofore and hereafter conferred upon the Farm Credit Administration.

Sec. 221. Section 7 of the Agricultural Adjustment Act, approved May 12, 1933, is amended by striking out all of its present terms and provisions and substituting therefor the following:

"Sec. 7. The Secretary shall sell the cotton held by him at his discretion, but subject to the foregoing provisions: *Provided,* That he shall dispose of all cotton held by him by March 1, 1936: *Provided further,* That notwithstanding the provisions of section 6, the Secretary shall have authority to enter into option contracts with producers of cotton to sell to the producers such cotton held by him, in such amounts and at such prices and upon such terms and conditions as the Secretary may deem advisable, in combination with rental or benefit payments provided for in part 2 of this title.

"Notwithstanding any provisions of existing law, the Secretary of Agriculture may in the administration of the Agricultural Adjustment Act make public such information as he deems necessary in order to effectuate the purposes of such Act."

Title III—Amendments to Emergency Relief and Construction Act and Miscellaneous Provisions

Section 301. After the expiration of ten days after the date upon which the Administrator has qualified and taken office, (1) no application shall be approved by the Reconstruction Finance Corporation under the provisions of subsection (a) of section 201 of the Emergency Relief and Construction Act of 1932, as amended, and (2) the Administrator shall have access to all applications, files, and records of the Reconstruction Finance Corporation relating to loans and contracts and the administration of funds under such subsection: *Provided,* That the Reconstruction Finance Corporation may issue funds to a borrower under such subsection (a) prior to January 23, 1939, under the terms of any agreement or any commitment to bid upon or purchase bonds entered into with such borrower pursuant to an application approved prior to the date of termination, under this section, of the power of the Reconstruction Finance Corporation to approve applications.

Decrease of Borrowing Power of Reconstruction Finance Corporation

Sec. 302. The amount of notes, debentures, bonds, or other such obligations which the Reconstruction Finance Corporation is authorized and empowered under section 9 of the Reconstruction Finance Corporation Act, as amended, to have outstanding at any one time is decreased by $400,000,000.

Separability Clause

Sec. 303. If any provision of this Act, or the application thereof to any person or circumstances, is held invalid, the remainder of the Act, and the application of such provision to other persons or circumstances, shall not be affected thereby.

Short Title

Sec. 304. This Act may be cited as the "National Industrial Recovery Act."

Approved, June 16, 1933, 11:55 a.m.

EMERGENCY RAILROAD TRANSPORTATION ACT

Editor's comments: *Under section 2 of Title I of the Emergency Railroad Transportation Act, the office of the Federal Coordinator of Transportation was created. The Coordinator, appointed by the President, was to, among other things, "foster and protect interstate commerce in relation to railroad transportation ... in order to safeguard and maintain a national system of transportation...."*

Section 3 of Title I provided for the railroad lines to be divided into an eastern group, a southern group, and a western group. Each group was to be placed under one of three regional coordinating committees.

The purposes of Title I were to encourage the railroads to (1) avoid duplication of services and facilities and wasteful practices, (2) promote financial reorganization, and (3) provide for the study of various ways of improving overall transportation conditions.

Title II of the Act primarily amended the Interstate Commerce Act.

An Act to Relieve the Existing National Emergency in Relation to Interstate Railroad Transportation, and to Amend Sections 5, 15a, and 19a of the Interstate Commerce Act, as Amended
June 16, 1933

Be it enacted by the Senate and House of Representatives of the United States of America in Congress assembled, That this Act may be cited as the "Emergency Railroad Transportation Act, 1933."

Title I — Emergency Powers

Section 1. As used in this title —

(a) The term "Commission" means the Interstate Commerce Commission.

(b) The term "Coordinator" means the Federal Coordinator of Transportation hereinafter provided for.

(c) The term "committee" means any one of the regional coordinating committees hereinafter provided for.

(d) The term "carrier" means any common carrier by railroad subject to the provisions of the Interstate Commerce Act, as amended, including any receiver or trustee thereof.

(e) The term "subsidiary" means any company which is directly or indirectly controlled by, or affiliated with, any carrier or carriers. For the purpose of the foregoing definition a company shall be deemed to be affiliated with a carrier if so affiliated within the meaning of paragraph (8) of section 5 of the Interstate Commerce Act, as amended by this Act.

(f) The term "employee" includes every person in the service of a carrier (subject to its continuing authority to supervise and direct the manner of rendition of his service) who performs any work defined as that of an employee or subordinate official in accordance with the provisions of the Railway Labor Act.

(g) The term "State commission" means the commission, board, or official, by whatever name designated, exercising power to regulate the rates or service of common carriers by railroad under the laws of any State.

Sec. 2. In order to foster and protect interstate commerce in relation to railroad transportation by preventing and relieving obstructions and burdens thereon resulting from the present acute economic emergency, and in order to safeguard and maintain an adequate national system of transportation, there is hereby created the office of Federal Coordinator of Transportation, who shall be appointed by the President, by and with the advice and consent of the Senate, or be designated by the President from the membership of the Commission. If so designated, the Coordinator shall be relieved from other duties as Commissioner during his term of service to such extent as the President may direct; except that the Coordinator shall not sit as a member of the Commission in any proceedings for the review or suspension of any order issued by him as Coordinator. The Coordinator shall have such powers and duties as are hereinafter set forth and prescribed, and may, with the approval of the President, and without regard to the civil service laws and the Classification Act of 1923, as amended, appoint and fix the compensation of such assistants and agents, in addition to the assistance provided by the Commission, as may be necessary to the performance of his duties under this Act. The office of the Coordinator shall be in Washington, District of Columbia, and the Commission shall provide such office space, facilities, and assistance as he may request and it is able to furnish. The Coordinator shall receive such compensation as the President shall fix, except that if designated from the Commission, he shall receive no compensation in addition to that which he receives as a member of the Commission.

Sec. 3. The Coordinator shall divide the lines of the carriers into three groups, to wit, an eastern group, a southern group, and a western group, and may from time to time make such changes or subdivisions in such groups as he may deem to be necessary or desirable. At the earliest practicable date after the Coordinator shall have initially designated such groups, three regional coordinating committees shall be created, one for each group, and each committee shall consist of five regular members and two special members. The carriers in each group, acting each through its board of directors or its receiver or receivers or trustee or trustees or through an officer or officers designated for the purpose by such board, shall select the regular members of the committee representing that group, and shall prescribe the rules under which such committee shall operate; but no railroad system shall have more than one representative on any such committee. In such selection each carrier shall have a vote in proportion to its mileage lying within the group. The two special members of each committee shall be selected in such manner as the Coordinator may approve, one to represent the steam railroads within the group which had in 1932 railway operating revenues of less than $1,000,000 and the other to represent electric railways within the group not owned by a steam railroad or operated as a part of a general steam railroad system of transportation. Each such special member shall have reasonable notice of all meetings of his committee at which any matter affecting any carrier which he represents is to be considered, and may participate in the consideration and disposition of such matter. Members of the committees may be removed from office and vacancies may be filled in like manner.

Sec. 4. The purposes of this title are (1) to encourage and promote or require action on the part of the carriers and of subsidiaries subject to the Interstate Commerce Act, as amended, which will (a) avoid unnecessary duplication of services and facilities of whatsoever nature and permit the joint use of terminals and trackage incident thereto or requisite to such joint use: *Provided,* That no routes now existing shall be eliminated except with the consent of all participating lines or upon order of the Coordinator, (b) control allowances, accessorial services and the charges therefor, and other practices affecting service or operation, to the end that undue impairment of net earnings may be prevented, and (c) avoid other wastes and preventable expense; (2) to promote financial reorganization of the carriers, with due regard to legal rights, so as to reduce fixed charges to the extent required by the public interest and improve carrier credit; and (3) to provide for the immediate study of other means of improving conditions surrounding transportation in all its forms and the preparation of plans therefor.

Sec. 5. It shall be the duty of the committees on their own initiative, severally within each group and jointly where more than one group is affected, to carry out the purposes set forth in subdivision (1) of section 4, so far as such action can be voluntarily accomplished by the carriers. In such instances as the committees are unable, for any reason, legal or otherwise, to carry out such purposes by such voluntary action, they shall recommend to the Coordinator that he give appropriate directions to the carriers or subsidiaries subject to the Interstate Commerce Act, as amended, by order; and the Coordinator is hereby authorized and directed to issue and enforce such orders if he finds them to be consistent with the public interest and in furtherance of the purposes of this title.

Sec. 6. (a) The Coordinator shall confer freely with the committees and give them the benefit of his advice and assistance. At his request, the committees, the carriers, the subsidiaries, and the Commission shall furnish him, or his assistants and agents, such information and reports as he may desire in investigating any matter within the scope of his duties under this title; and the Coordinator, his assistants, and agents, and the Commission, shall at all times have access to all accounts, records, and memoranda of the carriers and subsidiaries. If, in any instance, a committee has not acted with respect to any matter which the Coordinator has brought to its attention and upon which he is of the opinion that it should have acted, under the provisions of section 5, he is hereby authorized and directed to issue and enforce such order, giving appropriate directions to the carriers and subsidiaries subject to the Interstate Commerce Act, as amended, with respect to such matter, as he shall find to be consistent with the public interest.

(b) Insofar as may be necessary for the purposes of this title, the Commission and the members and examiners thereof shall have the same power to administer oaths and require by subpena the attendance and testimony of witnesses and the production of books, papers, tariffs, contracts, agreements, and documents and to take testimony by deposition, relating to any matter under investigation, as though such matter arose under the Interstate Commerce Act, as amended and supplemented; and any person subpenaed or testifying in connection with any matter under investigation under this title shall have the same rights, privileges, and immunities and be subject to the same duties, liabilities, and penalties as are provided in the case of persons subpenaed or testifying in connection with any matter under investigation under the Interstate Commerce Act, as amended.

Sec. 7. (a) A labor committee for each regional group of carriers may be selected by those railroad labor organizations which, as representatives duly designated and authorized to act in accordance with the requirements of the Railway Labor Act, entered into the agreements of January 31, 1932, and December 21, 1932, with duly authorized representatives of the carriers, determining the wage payments of the employees of the carriers. A similar labor committee for each regional group of carriers may be selected by such other railroad labor organizations as may be duly designated and authorized to represent employees in accordance with the requirements of the Railway Labor Act. It shall be the duty of the regional coordinating committees and the Coordinator to give reasonable notice to, and to confer with, the appropriate regional labor committee or committees upon the subject matter prior to taking any action or issuing any order which will affect the interest of the employees, and to afford the said labor committee or committees reasonable opportunity to present views upon said contemplated action or order.

(b) The number of employees in the service of a carrier shall not be reduced by reason of any action taken pursuant to the authority of this title below the number as shown by the pay rolls of employees in service during the month of May, 1933, after deducting the number who have been removed from the pay rolls after the effective date of this Act by reason of death, normal retirements, or resignation, but not more in any one year than 5 per centum of said number in service during May, 1933; nor shall any employee in such service be deprived of employment such as he had during said month of May or be in a worse position with respect to his compensation for such employment, by reason of any action taken pursuant to the authority conferred by this title.

(c) The Coordinator is authorized and directed to establish regional boards of adjustment whenever and wherever action taken pursuant to the authority conferred by this title creates conditions that make necessary such boards of adjustment to settle controversies between carriers and employees. Carriers and their employees shall have equal representation on such boards of adjustment for settlement of such controversies, and said boards shall exercise the functions of boards of adjustment provided for by the Railway Labor Act.

(d) The Coordinator is authorized and directed to provide means for determining the amount of, and to require the carriers to make just compensation for, property losses and expenses imposed upon employees by reason of transfers of work from one locality to another in carrying out the purposes of this title.

(e) Carriers, whether under control of a judge, trustee, receiver, or private management, shall be required to comply with the provisions of the Railway Labor Act and with the provisions of section 77, paragraphs (o), (p), and (q), of the Act approved March 3, 1933, entitled "An Act to amend an Act entitled 'An Act to establish a uniform system of bankruptcy throughout the United States', approved July 1, 1898, and Acts amendatory thereof and supplementary thereto."

Sec. 8. Any order issued by the Coordinator pursuant to this title shall be made public in such reasonable manner as he may determine and shall become effective as of such date, not less than twenty days from the date of such publication, as the Coordinator shall prescribe in the order; and such order shall remain in effect until it is vacated by him or suspended or set aside by the Commission or other lawful authority, as hereinafter provided, and such order may include provision for the creation and administration of such just pooling arrangements or for such just compensation for the use of property or for carrier services as he may deem necessary or desirable and in furtherance of the purposes of this title.

Sec. 9. Any interested party, including, among others, any carrier, subsidiary, shipper, or employee, or any group of carriers, shippers, or employees, or any State commission, or the Governor of any State, or the official representative or representatives of any political subdivision thereof, dissatisfied with any order of the Coordinator may, at any time prior to the effective date of the order, file a petition with the Commission asking that such order be reviewed and suspended pending such review, and stating fully the reasons therefor. Such petitions shall be governed by such general rules as the Commission may establish. If the Commission, upon considering such petition and any answer or answers thereto, finds reason to believe that the order may be unjust to the petitioner or inconsistent with the public interest, the Commission is hereby authorized to grant such review and, in its discretion, the Commission may suspend the order if it finds immediate enforcement thereof would result in irreparable damage to the petitioner or work grave injury to the public interest, but if the Commission suspends an order, it shall expedite the hearing and decision on that order as much as possible. Thereupon the Commission shall, after due notice and a public hearing, review the order and take such action in accord with the purposes of this title as it finds to be just and consistent with the public interest, either confirming the order or setting it aside or reissuing it in modified form, and any order so confirmed or reissued shall thereafter remain in effect until vacated or modified by the Commission.

Sec. 10. (a) The carriers or subsidiaries subject to the Interstate Commerce Act, as amended, affected by any order of the Coordinator or Commission made pursuant to this title shall, so long as such order is in effect, be, and they are hereby, relieved from the operation of the antitrust laws, as designated in section 1 of the Act entitled "An Act to supplement existing laws against unlawful restraints and monopolies, and for other purposes", approved October 15, 1914, and of all other restraints or prohibitions by law, State or Federal, other than such as are for the protection of the public health or safety, in so far as may be necessary to enable them to do anything authorized or required by such order made pursuant to this title: *Provided, however,* That nothing herein shall be construed to repeal, amend, suspend, or modify any of the requirements of the Railway Labor Act or the duties and obligations imposed thereunder or through contracts entered into in accordance with the provisions of said Act.

(b) The Coordinator shall issue no order which shall have the effect of relieving any carrier or subsidiary from the operation of the law of any State or of any order of any State commission until he has advised the State commission of said State, or the Governor of said State if there be no such commission, that such order is in contemplation, and shall afford the State commission or Governor so notified reasonable opportunity to present views and information bearing upon such contemplated order, nor unless such order is necessary, in his opinion, to prevent or remove an obstruction to or a burden upon interstate commerce.

Sec. 11. Nothing in this title shall be construed to relieve any carrier from any contractual obligation which it may have assumed, prior to the enactment of this Act, with regard to the location or maintenance of offices, shops, or roundhouses at any point.

Sec. 12. The willful failure or refusal of any carrier or subsidiary or of any officer or employee of any carrier or subsidiary to comply with the terms of any order of the Coordinator or of the Commission made pursuant to this title shall be a misdemeanor, and upon conviction thereof the carrier, subsidiary, or person offending shall be subject to a fine of not less than $1,000 or more than $20,000 for each offense, and each day during which such carrier, subsidiary, or person shall willfully fail or refuse to comply with the terms of such order shall consitute a separate offense. It shall be the duty of any district attorney of the United States to whom the Coordinator or the Commission may apply to institute in the proper court and to prosecute under the direction of the Attorney General of the United States all necessary proceedings for the enforcement of the provisions of this title and for the punishment of all violations thereof, and the costs and expenses of such prosecution shall be paid out of the appropriation for the expense of the courts of the United States: *Provided,* That nothing in this title shall be construed to require any employee or officer of any carrier to render labor or service without his consent, or to authorize the issuance of any orders requiring such service, or to make illegal the failure or refusal of any employee individually, or any number of employees collectively, to render labor or services.

Sec. 13. It shall further be the duty of the Coordinator, and he is hereby authorized and directed, forthwith to investigate and consider means, not provided for in this title, of improving transportation conditions throughout the country, including cost finding in rail transportation and the ability, financial or otherwise, of the carriers to improve their properties and furnish service and charge rates which will promote the commerce and industry of the country and including, also, the stability of railroad labor employment and other improvement of railroad labor conditions and relations; and from time to time he shall submit to the Commission such recommendations calling for further legislation to these ends as he may deem necessary or desirable in the public interest. The Commission shall promptly transmit such recommendations, together with its comments thereon, to the President and to the Congress.

Sec. 14. The expenses of the Coordinator except so far as they are borne by the Commission in accordance with the provisions of section 2, but not including the expenses of the coordinating committees, shall be allowed and paid, on the presentation of itemized vouchers therefor approved by the Coordinator, out of a fund obtained from assessments on the carriers, and said fund is hereby appropriated for the payment of such expenses. It shall be the duty of each carrier, within thirty days after the date of enactment of this Act, to pay into this fund, for the first year of the operation of this title, one and one-half dollars for every mile of road operated by it on December 31, 1932, as reported to the Commission, and to pay into said fund within thirty days after the expiration of such year a proportional amount covering any period of extension of this title by proclamation of the President under section 17, and it shall be the duty of the Secretary of the Treasury to collect such assessments. Any amount remaining in the fund when this title ceases to have effect shall be returned by the Secretary of the Treasury to the carriers in proportion to their contributions. The carriers and the Pullman Company shall be permitted, anything in the Interstate Commerce Act, as amended, to the contrary notwithstanding, to provide free transportation and other carrier service to the Coordinator and his assistants and agents and to the employees of the Commission when engaged in the service of the Coordinator.

Sec. 15. The Commission shall not approve a loan to a carrier under the Reconstruction Finance Corporation Act, as amended, if it is of the opinion that such carrier is in need of financial reorganization in the public interest: *Provided, however,* That the term "carrier" as used in this section shall not include a receiver or trustee.

Sec. 16. Any final order made under this title shall be subject to the same right of relief in court by any party in interest as is now provided in respect to orders of the Commission made under the Interstate Commerce Act, as amended. The provisions of the Urgent Deficiencies Appropriation Act of October 22, 1913 (38 Stat. L. 219), shall be applicable to any proceeding in court brought to suspend or set aside any order of the Coordinator or of the Commission entered pursuant to the provisions of this title.

Sec. 17. This title shall cease to have effect at the end of one year after the effective date, unless extended by a proclamation of the President for one year or any part thereof, but orders of the Coordinator or of the Commission made thereunder shall continue in effect until vacated by the Commission or set aside by other lawful authority, but notwithstanding the provisions of section 10 no such order shall operate to relieve any carrier from the effect of any State law or of any order of a State commission enacted or made after this title ceases to have effect.

Title II — Amendments to Interstate Commerce Act

Section 201. Section 5 of the Interstate Commerce Act, as amended (U.S.C., title 49, sec. 5), is amended by striking out paragraphs (2) and (3) and by renumbering paragraphs (4) and (5) as paragraphs (2) and (3), respectively, and by striking out the last sentence of the paragraph so renumbered as paragraph (3).

Sec. 202. Such section 5 is further amended by striking out paragraphs (6) and (7), and (8), and by inserting in lieu thereof the following paragraphs:

"(4) (a) It shall be lawful, with the approval and authorization of the Commission, as provided in subdivision (b), for two or more carriers to consolidate or merge their properties, or any part thereof, into one corporation for the ownership, management, and operation of the properties theretofore in separate ownership; or for any carrier, or two or more carriers jointly, to purchase, lease, or contract to operate the properties, or any part thereof, of another; or for any carrier, or two or more carriers jointly, to acquire control of another through purchase of its stock; or for a corporation which is not a carrier to acquire control of two or more carriers through ownership of their stock; or for a corporation which is not a carrier and which has control of one or more carriers to acquire control of another carrier through ownership of its stock.

"(b) Whenever a consolidation, merger, purchase, lease, operating contract, or acquisition of control is proposed under subdivision (a), the carrier or carriers or corporation seeking authority therefor shall present an application to the Commission, and thereupon the Commission shall notify the Governor of each State in which any part of the properties of the carriers involved in the proposed transaction is situated, and also such carriers and the applicant or applicants, of the time and place for a public hearing. If after such hearing the Commission finds that, subject to such terms and conditions and such modifications as it shall find to be just and reasonable, the proposed consolidation, merger, purchase, lease, operating contract, or acquisition of control will be in harmony with and in furtherance of the plan for the consolidation of railway properties established pursuant to paragraph (3), and will promote the public interest, it may enter an order approving and authorizing such consolidation, merger, purchase, lease, operating contract, or acquisition of control, upon the terms and conditions and with the modifications so found to be just and reasonable.

"(5) Whenever a corporation which is not a carrier is authorized, by an order entered under paragraph (4), to acquire control of any carrier or of two or more carriers, such corporation thereafter shall, to the extent provided by the Commission, for the purposes of paragraphs (1) to (10), inclusive, of section 20 (relating to reports, accounts, and so forth, of carriers), including the penalties applicable in the case of violations of such paragraphs, be considered as a common carrier subject to the provisions of this Act, and for the purposes of paragraphs (2) to (11), inclusive, of section 20a (relating to issues of securities and assumptions of liability of carriers), including the penalties applicable in the case of violations of such paragraphs, be considered as a 'carrier' as such term is defined in paragraph (1) of such section, and be treated as such by the Commission in the administration of the paragraphs specified. In the application of such provisions of section 20a in the case of any such corporation the Commission shall authorize the issue or assumption applied for only if it finds that such issue or assumption is consistent with the proper performance by each carrier which is under the control of such corporation of its service to the public as a common carrier, will not impair the ability of any such carrier to perform such service, and is otherwise compatible with the public interest.

"(6) It shall be unlawful for any person, except as provided in paragraph

(4), to accomplish or effectuate, or to participate in accomplishing or effectuating, the control or management in a common interest of any two or more carriers, however such result is attained, whether directly or indirectly, by the use of common directors, officers, or stockholders, a holding or investment company or companies, a voting trust or trusts, or in any other manner whatsoever. It shall be unlawful to continue to maintain control or management accomplished or effectuated after the enactment of this amendatory paragraph and in violation of its provisions. As used in this paragraph and paragraph (7), the words 'control or management' shall be construed to include the power to exercise control or management.

"(7) For the purposes of paragraphs (6) and (11), but not in anywise limiting the application thereof, any transaction shall be deemed to accomplish or effectuate the control or management in a common interest of two carriers—

"(a) If such transaction is by a carrier, and if the effect of such transaction is to place such carrier and persons affiliated with it, taken together, in control of another carrier.

"(b) If such transaction is by a person affiliated with a carrier, and if the effect of such transaction is to place such carrier and persons affiliated with it, taken together, in control of another carrier.

"(c) If such transaction is by two or more persons acting together, one of whom is a carrier or is affiliated with a carrier, and if the effect of such transaction is to place such persons and carriers and persons affiliated with any one of them and persons affiliated with any such affiliated carrier, taken together, in control of another carrier.

"(8) For the purposes of paragraph (7) a person shall be held to be affiliated with a carrier if, by reason of the relationship of such person to such carrier (whether by reason of the method of, or circumstances surrounding organization or operation, or whether established through common directors, officers, or stockholders, a voting trust or trusts, a holding or investment company or companies, or any other direct or indirect means), it is reasonable to believe that the affairs of any carrier of which control may be acquired by such person will be managed in the interest of such other carrier.

"(9) For the purposes of paragraphs (6), (7), (8), and (11), wherever reference is made to control it is immaterial whether such control is direct or indirect. As used in this paragraph and paragraphs (7), (8), and (11) the term 'control' shall be construed to include the power to exercise control.

"(10) The Commission is hereby authorized, upon complaint or upon its own initiative without complaint, but after notice and hearing, to investigate and determine whether any person is violating the provisions of paragraph (6). If the Commission finds after such investigation that such person is violating the provisions of such paragraph, it shall by order require such person to take such action as may be necessary, in the opinion of the Commission, to prevent continuance of such violation.

"(11) For the proper protection and in furtherance of the plan for the consolidation of railway properties established pursuant to paragraph (3) and the regulation of interstate commerce in accordance therewith, the Commission is hereby authorized, upon complaint or upon its own initiative without complaint, but after notice and hearing, to investigate and determine whether the holding by any person of stock or other share capital of any carrier (unless acquired with the approval of the Commission) has the effect (a) of subjecting such carrier to the control of another carrier or to common control with another carrier, and (b) of preventing or hindering the carrying out of any part of such plan or of impairing the independence, one of another, of the systems provided for in such plan. If the Commission finds after such investigation that such holding has the effects described, it shall by order provide for restricting the exercise of the voting power of such person with respect to such stock or other share capital (by requiring the deposit thereof with a trustee, or by other appropriate means) to the extent necessary to prevent such holding from continuing to have such effects.

"(12) If in the course of any proceeding under this section before the Commission, or of any proceeding before a court in enforcement of an order entered by the Commission under this section, it appears that since the beginning of such proceeding the plan for consolidation has been reopened under paragraph (3) for changes or modifications with respect to the allocation of the properties of any carrier involved in such proceeding, then such proceeding may be suspended.

"(13) The district courts of the United States shall have jurisdiction upon the application of the Commission, alleging a violation of any of the provisions of this section or disobedience of any order issued by the Commission thereunder by any person, to issue such writs of injunction or other proper process, mandatory or otherwise, as may be necessary to restrain such person from violation of such provision or to compel obedience to such order.

"(14) The Commission may from time to time, for good cause shown, make such orders, supplemental to any order made under paragraph (1), (4), (10), or (11), as it may deem necessary or appropriate.

"(15) The carriers and any corporation affected by any order made under the foregoing provisions of this section shall be, and they are hereby, relieved from the operation of the antitrust laws as designated in section 1 of the Act entitled 'An Act to supplement existing laws against unlawful restraints and monopolies, and for other purposes', approved October 15, 1914, and of all other restraints or prohibitions by or imposed under authority of law, State or Federal, insofar as may be necessary to enable them to do anything authorized or required by such order.

"(16) If any provision of the foregoing paragraphs of this section, or the application thereof to any person or circumstances, is held invalid, the other provisions of such paragraphs, and the application of such provision to any other person or circumstances, shall not be affected thereby.

"(17) As used in paragraphs (4) to (16), inclusive, the term 'person' includes an individual, partnership, association, joint-stock company, or corporation, and the term 'carrier' means a carrier by railroad subject to this Act."

Sec. 203. Such section 5 is further amended by renumbering as paragraph (18) the paragraph added by the Act entitled "An Act to amend section 407 of the Transportation Act of 1920," approved June 10, 1921, and by renumbering the remaining three paragraphs as paragraphs (19), (20), and (21), respectively.

Sec. 204. The provisions of the Interstate Commerce Act, as amended, and of all other applicable Federal statutes, as in force prior to the enactment of this title, shall remain in force, as though this title had not been enacted, with respect to the acquisition by any carrier, prior to the enactment of this title, of the control of any other carrier or carriers.

Sec. 205. Section 15a of the Interstate Commerce Act, as amended (U.S.C., title 49, sec. 15a), is amended to read as follows:

"Sec. 15a. (1) When used in this section, the term 'rates' means rates, fares, and charges, and all classifications, regulations, and practices relating thereto.

"(2) In the exercise of its power to prescribe just and reasonable rates the Commission shall give due consideration, among other factors, to the effect of rates on the movement of traffic; to the need, in the public interest, of adequate and efficient railway transportation service at the lowest cost consistent with the furnishing of such service; and to the need of revenues sufficient to enable the carriers, under honest, economical, and efficient management, to provide such service."

Sec. 206. (a) All moneys which were recoverable by and payable to the Interstate Commerce Commission, under paragraph (6) of section 15a of the Interstate Commerce Act, as in force prior to the enactment of this title, shall cease to be so recoverable and payable; and all proceedings pending for the recovery of any such moneys shall be terminated. The general railroad contingent fund established under such section shall be liquidated and the Secretary of the Treasury shall distribute the moneys in such fund among the carriers which have made payments under such section, so that each such carrier shall receive an amount bearing the same ratio to the total amount in such fund that the total of amounts paid under such section by such carrier bears to the total of amounts paid under such section by all carriers; except that if the total amount in such fund exceeds the total of amounts paid under such section by all carriers such excess shall be distributed among such carriers upon the basis of the average rate of earnings (as determined by the Secretary of the Treasury) on the investment of the moneys in such fund and differences in dates of payments by such carriers.

(b) The income, war-profits, and excess-profits tax liabilities for any taxable period ending after February 28, 1920, of the carriers and corporations whose income, war-profits, or excess-profits tax liabilities were affected by section 15a of the Interstate Commerce Act, as in force prior to the enactment of this Act, shall be computed as if such section had never been enacted, except that, in the case of carriers or corporations which have made payments under paragraph (6) of such section, an amount equal to such payments shall be excluded from gross income for the taxable periods with respect to which they were made. All distributions made to carriers in accordance with subdivision (a) of this section shall be included in the gross income of the carriers for the taxable period in which this Act is enacted. The provisions of this subdivision shall not be held to affect (1) the statutes of limitations with respect to the assessment, collection, refund, or credit of income, war-profits or excess-profits taxes or (2) the liabilities for such taxes of any carriers or corporations if such liabilities were determined prior to the enactment of this Act in accordance with section 1106 (b) of the Revenue Act of 1926 or section 606 of the Revenue Act of 1928, or in accordance with a final judgment of a court, an order of the Board of Tax Appeals which had become final, or an offer in compromise duly accepted in accordance with law.

Sec. 207. Paragraph (a) of section 19a of the Interstate Commerce Act, as amended (U.S.C., title 49, sec. 19a (a)), is amended to read as follows:

"(a) That the Commission shall, as hereinafter provided, investigate, ascertain, and report the value of all the property owned or used by every common carrier subject to the provisions of this Act, except any street, suburban, or interurban electric railway which is not operated as a part of a general steam railroad system of transportation; but the Commission may in its discretion investigate, ascertain, and report the value of the property owned or used by any such electric railway subject to the provisions of this Act whenever in its judgment such action is desirable in the public interest. To enable the Commission to make such investigation and report, it is authorized to employ such experts and other assistants as may be necessary. The Commission may appoint examiners who shall have power to administer oaths, examine witnesses, and take testimony. The Commission shall, subject to the exception hereinbefore provided for in the case of electric railways, make an inventory which shall list the property of every common carrier subject to the provisions of this Act in detail, and show the value thereof as hereinafter provided, and shall classify the physical property, as nearly as practicable, in conformity with the classification of expenditures for road and equipment, as prescribed by the Interstate Commerce Commission."

Sec. 208. Paragraphs (f) and (g) of such section 19a, as amended (U.S.C., title 49, sec. 19a (f), (g)), are amended to read as follows:

"(f) Upon completion of the original valuations herein provided for, the Commission shall thereafter keep itself informed of all new construction, extensions, improvements, retirements, or other changes in the condition, quantity, use, and classification of the property of all common carriers as to which original valuations have been made, and of the cost of all additions and betterments thereto and of all changes in the investment therein, and may keep itself informed of current changes in costs and values of railroad properties, in order that it may have available at all times the information deemed by it to be necessary to enable it to revise and correct its previous inventories, classifications, and values of the properties; and when deemed necessary, may revise, correct, and supplement any of its inventories and valuations.

"(g) To enable the Commission to carry out the provisions of the preceding paragraph, every common carrier subject to the provisions of this Act shall make such reports and furnish such information as the Commission may require."

Sec. 209. If any provision of this Act, or the application thereof to any person or circumstances, is held invalid, the other provisions of this Act or the application of such provision to any other person or circumstances shall not be affected thereby.

Approved, June 16, 1933, 12:05 p.m.

FARM CREDIT ACT

Editor's comments: The Farm Credit Act authorized the Governor of the Farm Credit Administration to "organize and charter twelve corporations to be known as Production Credit Corporations and twelve banks known as Banks for Cooperatives." Further, the Governor was authorized to charter "Production Credit Associations," and a "Central Bank for Cooperatives." These organizations, while differing in function and regulation, all focused on providing loans for the production and marketing of agricultural products. Annual examinations, by examiners designated by the Governor, were to be made for each of the organizations.

This Act also amended various sections of the Federal Farm Loan Act and the Agricultural Marketing Act.

An Act to Provide for Organizations Within the Farm Credit Administration to Make Loans for the Production and Marketing of Agricultural Products, to Amend the Federal Farm Loan Act, to Amend the Agricultural Marketing Act, to Provide a Market for Obligations of the United States, and for Other Purposes
June 16, 1933

Be it enacted by the Senate and House of Representatives of the United States of America in Congress assembled,

Title I

Section 1. This Act shall be known as the "Farm Credit Act of 1933."

Establishment of Production Credit Corporations and Banks for Cooperatives

Sec. 2. The Governor of the Farm Credit Administration, hereinafter in this Act referred to as the "governor", is authorized and directed to organize and charter twelve corporations to be known as "Production Credit Corporations" and twelve banks to be known as "Banks for Cooperatives." One such corporation and one such bank shall be established in each city in which there is located a Federal land bank. The directors of the several Federal land banks shall be ex officio the directors of the respective Production Credit Corporations and Banks for Cooperatives. Such directors shall have power, subject to the approval of the governor, to employ and fix the compensation of such officers and employees of such corporations and banks as may be necessary to carry out the powers and duties conferred upon such corporations and banks under this Act.

Charters and Bylaws

Sec. 3. The charters of the Production Credit Corporations and the Banks for Cooperatives shall be granted by the governor upon application of the directors of the Federal land bank of the proper district, and applications and charters shall be in such form as the governor shall prescribe. The directors shall have power, subject to the approval of the governor, to adopt such bylaws as may be necessary for the conduct of the business of the corporations and banks.

Capital of Production Credit Corporations

Sec. 4. The capital stock of each Production Credit Corporation shall be in such amount as the governor determines is required for the purpose of meeting the credit needs of the district to be served by such corporation, and such amount may be increased or decreased from time to time by the governor in accordance with such credit needs. Such capital stock shall be divided into shares of $100 each. The initial capital stock of each such corporation shall be $7,500,000, which shall be subscribed for by the governor and held by him on behalf of the United States. Payments on subscriptions to stock by the governor shall be subject to call in whole or in part by the board of directors of the corporation with the approval of the governor. The governor shall make such payments out of the revolving fund created in section 5. The stock ownership of the United States in such corporation shall be evidenced by such means as the governor shall determine.

Revolving Fund and Appropriation

Sec. 5. (a) There is hereby created a revolving fund of not to exceed $120,000,000 which shall be made up as follows:

(1) The Reconstruction Finance Corporation is authorized and directed to make available to the Governor of the Farm Credit Administration all unobligated balances of the following funds and all sums heretofore returned or released to the corporation from such funds:

(A) Any balance of funds for, and for all collections on loans by, the Secretary of Agriculture pursuant to section 2 of the Reconstruction Finance Corporation Act as amended;

(B) All collections on loans made or to be made pursuant to the Act of February 4, 1933 (Public, Numbered 327, Seventy-second Congress);

(C) All balances of funds authorized and directed to be made available to the Secretary of Agriculture by such Act and not used for loans pursuant thereto; and

(D) Any balances of the funds originally directed to be allocated and made available to the Secretary of Agriculture by such Acts except as expended pursuant to subsection (e) of section 201 of the Emergency Relief and Construction Act of 1932.

(2) There are hereby made available to the Governor of the Farm Credit Administration all unobligated balances of appropriations and funds available thereunder to enable the Secretary of Agriculture to make advances or

loans under the following Acts and resolutions, and all repayments of such advances and loans: March 3, 1921 (41 Stat. 1347), March 20, 1922 (42 Stat. 467), April 26, 1924 (43 Stat. 110), February 28, 1927 (44 Stat. 1251), February 25, 1929 (45 Stat. 1306), as amended May 17, 1929 (46 Stat. 3), March 3, 1930 (46 Stat. 78, 79), December 20, 1930 (46 Stat. 1032), as amended February 14, 1931 (46 Stat. 1160), and February 23, 1931 (46 Stat. 1276), and Public Resolution Numbered 11, Seventy-second Congress, approved March 3, 1932.

(3) There is hereby authorized to be appropriated the sum of $40,000,000 out of any money in the Treasury not otherwise appropriated.

(b) There is hereby authorized to be appropriated the sum of $2,000,000, which shall remain available until expended, for all necessary administrative expenses in connection with the establishment and supervision of the Production Credit Corporations and the Production Credit Associations.

(c) The authority of the Governor of the Farm Credit Administration to allocate and expend out of the funds covered by subsection (a) of this section such amounts as he shall deem necessary for salaries, expenses, and all other administrative expenditures in the execution of the functions for which such funds have hitherto been available shall not be deemed to be restricted by this section.

(d) The authority to make loans during the calendar year 1933 pursuant to the Act of February 3, 1933 (Public Numbered 327, Seventy-second Congress) as amended, out of funds made available by that Act shall not be deemed to be restricted by this section.

Stock Ownership of Production Credit Corporations in Production Credit Associations

Sec. 6. (a) Each Production Credit Corporation shall have power to invest its funds in stock of production credit associations as provided in this section. Such corporation is authorized to subscribe and pay for class A stock in each Production Credit Association located in the district served by such corporation in amounts sufficient to maintain the amount of class A stock held by it and other holders of class A stock equal, as nearly as may be, to 20 per centum of the volume of loans made or to be made by such associaton, as estimated by the corporation, but at no time shall the amount of class A stock outstanding be less than $5,000 except with the consent of the association. Notwithstanding the provisions of the preceding sentence, (1) the governor, under rules and regulations prescribed by him, may permit a Production Credit Corporation to maintain the class A holdings of stock by the corporation and other investors at such amount, in excess of 20 per centum of such loans, as may be necessary, and (2) the corporation may at any time require the association to retire and cancel stock held by the corporation in such association, if, in the judgment of the corporation, the association has resources available therefor.

(b) Under such rules and regulations as may be prescribed by the governor and subject to such restrictions and limitations as he may prescribe, each Production Credit Corporation is authorized to subscribe and pay for stock in production credit associations not organized under this Act if such associations are controlled by cooperative associations as defined in section 55. Only stock which is preferred as to assets on liquidation and is entitled to participate in dividend distributions without discrimination may be subscribed for. The amount of the stock subscribed for by any Production Credit Corporation in any such association shall not at any one time exceed 75 per centum of the total paid-in capital of such association.

(c) The amount of the excess of earnings on stock held by the corporation above amounts above amounts necessary to pay operating expenses and restore losses and impairment of capital, if any, of the corporation shall be devoted to the creation and maintenance of a surplus equal to at least 25 per centum of the paid-in capital of the corporation. The amount of the surplus shall be invested as the governor shall prescribe in direct obligations of the United States or in class A stock of Production Credit Associations, or both.

(d) The amount of such excess of earnings not required in order to comply with the provisions of subsection (c) shall be paid into the revolving fund heretofore authorized. Stock held by the governor in the Production Credit Corporation shall be retired upon such payment in an amount equal to the amount of such payment.

Title II — Production Credit Associations

Establishment of Production Credit Associations

Section 20. The governor is authorized and directed to organize and charter corporations to be known as "Production Credit Associations." Such associations may be organized by ten or more farmers desiring to borrow money under the provisions of this title. Such individuals shall enter into articles of incorporation which shall specify in general terms the objects for which the association is formed and the powers to be exercised by it in carrying out the functions conferred upon it by this Act. Such articles shall be signed by the individuals uniting to form the association and a copy thereof shall be forwarded to the Production Credit Corporation of the district, and such copy shall be filed and preserved in its office. The governor may, for good cause shown, deny a charter to such individuals. Upon the approval of such articles by the governor, the association shall become as of the date of such approval a body corporate. The governor shall have power, under rules and regulations prescribed by him, or by prescribing the terms of the charter of the association, or both, to provide for the organization, management, and conduct of the business of the association; and the power of the governor shall extend to prescribing the amount of the stock of such association; fixing the territory within which its operations may be carried on; fixing the method of election and appointment of, and the amount and payment of the compensation of, directors, officers, and employees; fixing the maximum amount of individual loans which may be made; prescribing the conditions under which the stock may be retired; and providing for the consolidation of two or more such associations. The governor may, at any time, direct such changes in the charter of any such association as he finds necessary in accomplishing the purposes of this title. Bylaws of any such association may be adopted by the directors but shall not be valid unless approved by the governor.

Stock of Production Credit Associations

Sec. 21. The stock of such associations shall be divided into shares of $5 each; and there shall be two classes of such stock: (1) Class A stock which is to be held by Production Credit Corporations, and which may be purchased and held by investors, and (2) class B stock which may be purchased only by farmer borrowers from the association and individuals eligible to become borrowers. Class B stock only shall be entitled to voting rights but each holder of such stock shall be entitled to no more than one vote. No class B stock, or any interest therein or right to receive dividends thereon, shall be transferred by act of parties or operation of law except to another farmer borrower or an individual eligible to become a borrower, and then only with the approval of the directors of the association. Each holder of class B stock, within two years after he has ceased to be a borrower, shall exchange such class B stock at the fair book value (not to exceed par) thereof, as determined by the association, for class A stock. All stock shall share in dividend distributions without preference, but the directors of the association may, in their discretion, apply the amount of any dividend payable to a holder of class B stock to any indebtedness of such holder to the association. Class A stock shall be preferred as to assets of the association upon liquidation. During such time as any Production Credit Corporation is a holder of any stock of any such association, the appointment or election of directors, the secretary-treasurer, and the loan committee of such association shall be subject to the approval of the president of the Production Credit Corporation and during such time any such director, secretary-treasurer, or other officer may, at any time, be removed by the president of the Production Credit Corporation.

Earnings of Production Credit Associations

Sec. 22. Each Production Credit Association shall, at the end of its fiscal year, apply the amount of its earnings in excess of operating expenses during such fiscal year, first, to making up any losses in excess of its reserve for bad and doubtful debts; second, to the restoration of the amount of the impairment, if any, of capital; third, to the creation and maintenance of a reserve account for bad and doubtful debts, the amount of which account shall be prescribed by the Production Credit Corporation; and fourth, to the creation and maintenance of a guaranty fund equal to at least 25 per centum of the paid-in capital of the association. Any sums remaining may, with the approval of the Production Credit Corporation, be devoted to the payment of dividends but no rate of dividend in excess of 7 per centum per annum shall be paid. Sums in the guaranty fund herein provided for shall be invested subject to such rules and regulations as may be prescribed by the Production Credit Corporation.

Sec. 23. Each Production Credit Association shall, under such rules and regulations as may be prescribed by the Production Credit Corporation of the district with the approval of the governor, invest its funds and make loans to farmers for general agricultural purposes, but such part of its funds as is represented by the guaranty fund provided for in section 22 shall not be devoted to making loans to farmers. Such loans shall be made on such terms and conditions, at such rates of interest, and with such security as may be prescribed by the Production Credit Corporation. No loan shall be made for a less amount than $50, nor shall any one borrower be indebted to the association at any one time in an amount in excess of 20 per centum of the capital and guaranty fund of the association or, if the loan is secured by collateral approved by the Corporation, in an amount in excess of 50 per centum of the capital and guaranty fund, but loans may be made to any borrower in an amount in excess of 50 per centum of the capital and guaranty fund if the loan is approved by the Production Credit Commissioner of the Farm Credit Administration. Borrowers shall be required to own, at the time the loan is made, class B stock in an amount equal in fair book value (not to exceed par), as determined by the association, to $5 per $100 or fraction thereof of the amount of the loan. Such stock shall not be canceled or retired upon payment of the loan, but may be transferred or exchanged as provided in section 21.

Sec. 24. Production Credit Associations doing business under this Act are authorized to borrow from, and rediscount paper with, Federal Intermediate Credit Banks subject to the restrictions, limitations, and conditions applicable under title II of the Federal Farm Loan Act, as amended (U.S.C., title 12, ch. 8). Except with the approval of the Governor, Production Credit Associations shall not have the power to borrow from or rediscount paper with any other bank or agency.

Title III — Central Bank for Cooperatives

Establishment of Bank

Section 30. The governor is authorized and directed to organize and charter a corporation to be known as the "Central Bank for Cooperatives" with its principal office in the District of Columbia and such other offices as in the opinion of the governor may be necessary.

Board of Central Bank

Sec. 31. (a) The board of directors of the Central Bank for Cooperatives shall consist of seven members, one of whom shall be the Cooperative Bank Commissioner of the Farm Credit Administration, who shall be chairman of the board of directors. The other six directors shall be appointed by the governor, of whom the successors of three first appointed shall be appointed from nominees selected by borrowers as provided in subsection (b). The terms of the directors first appointed shall be for one, two, and three years as designated by the governor at the time of appointment and their successors shall hold their offices during a term of three years, but a director appointed to fill a vacancy shall hold his office for the unexpired term of the director whose place he is selected to fill. Any appointed director may at any time be removed for cause by the governor. No compensation shall be paid any director as a director of the corporation but the corporation, subject to the approval of the governor, may allow directors a reasonable per diem and expenses.

(b) The successors of three of the directors first appointed shall be selected one each year by the governor from among individuals nominated by borrowers (except Banks for Cooperatives). The governor shall, not less than sixty days prior to the end of the term of any director whose successor is to be appointed from among nominees as herein provided, or as soon as practicable after a vacancy occurs in the office of such director other than by the expiration of his term, cause notice of the vacancy to be sent to each borrower eligible to vote for nominees. Each such borrower shall be eligible to cast one vote. The governor shall not count any ballot received after the expiration of thirty days after the sending of notice. From those (not exceeding three) receiving the highest number of votes, as shown by his count, the governor shall appoint the director.

Powers of Chairman and Board

Sec. 32. The chairman of the board of the corporation shall be the executive officer of the corporation and the powers of the board of directors shall be such powers as may be prescribed in the charter and bylaws.

Capital Stock of Central Bank

Sec. 33. The capital stock of the central bank shall be in such amount as the governor determines is required for the purpose of meeting the credit needs of eligible borrowers from the bank under this title, and the governor may from time to time increase or decrease such amount, subject to the limitations contained in sections 35 and 37, in accordance with such needs.

The stock of such bank shall be divided into shares of $100 each. Out of the revolving fund created under section 6 of the Agricultural Marketing Act, as amended, the governor, on behalf of the United States, shall subscribe for and make payments for stock in the Central Bank and such payments shall be subject to call in whole or in part by the chairman of the board of the Central Bank with the approval of the governor.

Lending Power of Central Bank

Sec. 34. The Central Bank is authorized to make loans to cooperative associations, as defined in the Agricultural Marketing Act, as amended, including amendments made in Title V of this Act, for any of the purposes and subject to the conditions and limitations set forth in such Act, as so amended, and to make loans, by way of discount or otherwise and subject to such terms and conditions as may be prescribed by the chairman of the board of the Central Bank, to Banks for Cooperatives established under section 2 of this Act.

Stock Subscriptions of Borrowers from Central Bank

Sec. 35. (a) Cooperative associations borrowing from the Central Bank shall be required to own, at the time the loan is made, an amount of stock of the bank equal in fair book value (not to exceed par), as determined by the bank, to $100 per $2,000 or fraction thereof of the amount of the loan. Upon discharge of the loan the stock held by the borrowing association shall be retired and canceled and the association shall be paid therefor, or in case the stock subscription is included in the amount of the loan there shall be credited on the final payment of the loan, an amount equal to the amount paid for the stock or loaned to subscribe for the stock, as the case may be, minus the pro rata impairment, if any, of capital and guaranty fund of the Central Bank, as determined by the chairman of the board of the Central Bank.

(b) In any case in which a cooperative association applying for a loan is not authorized, under the law of the State in which it is organized, to subscribe for stock in the Central Bank, the bank shall, in lieu of stock subscription, require the borrowing association to pay into a guaranty fund, or the bank may retain out of the amount of the loan and credit to the guaranty fund, an amount equal to the amount which the borrowing association would have been required to own in stock if such association had been authorized to hold such stock. Upon discharge of its loan, the provisions of the last sentence of subsection (a) shall apply with respect to sums of such association in the guaranty fund in the same manner as if such sums were represented by stock.

Earnings and Reserves of Central Bank

Sec. 36. The Central Bank for Cooperatives shall, at the end of its fiscal year, apply the amount of its earnings in excess of operating expenses during such fiscal year, first, to making up losses incurred; second, to the restoration of the amount of the impairment, if any, of capital and guaranty fund as determined by the chairman of the board; and at least 25 per centum of the remainder of such excess of earnings shall be applied to the creation and maintenance of a surplus equal to at least 25 per centum of the amount of the capital and guaranty fund. Any sums remaining may, with the approval of the chairman of the board, be devoted to the payment of dividends. Subscribers to the guaranty fund shall be entitled to dividends in the same amounts as subscribers to stock. No rate of dividend in excess of 7 per centum per annum shall be paid. Dividends on stock held by the governor, when paid, shall be credited to the revolving fund created under section 6 of the Agricultural Marketing Act, as amended.

Debentures of Central Bank

Sec. 37. The Central Bank is authorized to issue debentures, but the amount of debentures which may be outstandng may not exceed at any one time five times the paid-in capital and surplus of the bank. Such debentures shall be issued at such times and subject to such terms and conditions as the board of directors shall determine but shall bear such interest rates as may be fixed by the chairman of the board. Such debentures shall be secured by collateral which shall be at least equal in value to the amount of debentures outstanding and which shall consist of cash, direct obligations of the United States, or notes or other obligations discounted or purchased or representing loans made under section 34. The provisions of law applicable to the preparation and issue of Federal intermediate credit bank debentures shall, so far as applicable, govern the preparation and issue of debentures issued under this section. The governor shall appoint a custodian of such collateral who shall have power subject to such rules and regulations as the governor may prescribe to approve and accept substitutions of collateral.

Division of Lending Authority
of Central and Regional Banks for Cooperatives

Sec. 38. The governor shall, by regulation or by prescribing the terms of the charters issued to the Central Bank for Cooperatives and the Banks for Cooperatives, or both, provide such limitations, as between the two types of banks, on the classes of borrowers to which loans may be made and the amount of the loans which may be made to individual borrowers, as will best insure the absence of duplication of effort by the two types of banks and will secure the greatest efficiency in extending the benefits of this title and Title IV to borrowers.

Title IV — Banks for Cooperatives

Stock of Banks

Section 40. The capital stock of each Bank for Cooperatives established under section 2 shall be in such amount as the governor determines is required for the purpose of meeting the credit needs of eligible borrowers from the bank under this title, and such amount may be increased or decreased from timt to time by the governor in accordance with such needs. Such stock shall be divided into shares of $100 each. Out of the revolving fund created under section 6 of the Agricultural Marketing Act, as amended, the governor, on behalf of the United States, shall make payments for stock in the banks and such payments, shall be subject to call in whole or in part by the board of directors of the bank with the approval of the governor.

Lending Power of Banks for Cooperatives

Sec. 41. The Banks for Cooperatives are authorized to make loans to cooperative associations for any of the purposes and subject to the conditions and limitations set forth in the Agricultural Marketing Act, as amended, including amendments made by Title V of this Act, and subject to such terms and conditions as may be prescribed by the board of the bank with the approval of the governor.

Stock Subscriptions and Earnings and Reserves

Sec. 42. The provisions of sections 35 and 36 shall apply in the case of Banks for Cooperatives in the same manner and to the same extent as such provisions are applicable to the Central Bank for Cooperatives, except that powers conferred on the chairman of the board of the Central Bank shall be exercised by the boards of directors of the Banks for Cooperatives, subject to the approval of the governor.

Retirement of Stock

Sec. 43. The governor may at any time require any such bank to retire and cancel stock held by the governor in such bank, if, in the judgment of the governor, the bank has resources available therefor, and amounts received by the governor in any such case shall be credited to the revolving fund created under section 6 of the Agricultural Marketing Act, as amended.

Title V — Amendments to Agricultural Marketing Act

Section 50. (a) The following provisions of the Agricultural Marketing Act, as amended, are hereby repealed:

(1) Section 3 (relating to Advisory Commodity Committees);

(2) Paragraph (4) of section 5 (relating to powers of the Farm Board to investigate overproduction);

(3) Paragraph (5) of section 5 (relating to miscellaneous investigations by the Farm Board);

(4) Paragraph (3) of subsection (a) of section 7 (relating to loans to assist in forming clearing house associations);

(5) Paragraph (4) of subsection (a) of section 7 (relating to education in the advantages of cooperative marketing);

(6) Paragraph (5) of subsection (a) of section 7 (relating to loans to enable cooperatives to advance a greater share of the market price of commodities than is practicable under other credit facilities);

(7) Section 10 (authorizing the Farm Board to assist in forming clearing house associations); and

(8) Section 11 (authorizing the Farm Board to enter into price insurance agreements).

(b) The repeal of section 7 (a) (5) shall not be construed to prohibit the extension, renewal, or refinancing of any loan made thereunder and outstanding on the date of the enactment of this Act, but loans to extend, renew, or refinance any such loan shall bear interest rates as determined under section 8 (a) of the Agricultural Marketing Act as amended by section 54 of this Act.

Sec. 51. Paragraph (1) of subsection (a) of section 7 of the Agricultural Marketing Act, as amended, is amended to read as follows:

"(1) the effective merchandising of agricultural commodities and food products thereof and the financing of its operations;"

Sec. 52. Paragraph (2) of subsection (a) of section 7 of the Agricultural Marketing Act, as amended, is amended to read as follows:

"(2) the construction or acquisition by purchase or lease, or refinancing the cost of such construction or acquisition, of physical marketing facilities for preparing, handling, storing, processing, or merchandising agricultural commodities or their food products;"

Sec. 53. Subsection (c) of section 7 of the Agricultural Marketing Act, as amended, is amended to read as follows:

"(c) Loans for the construction or acquisition by purchase or lease of physical facilities, or for refinancing the cost of such construction or acquisition,[1] shall be subject to the following conditions:

"(1) No such loan shall be made in an amount in excess of 60 per centum of the value of the facilities.

"(2) No loan for the purchase or lease of such facilities shall be made unless the Governor of the Farm Credit Administration finds that the purchase price or rent to be paid is reasonable."

Sec. 54. Subsection (a) of section 8 of the Agricultural Marketing Act is amended to read as follows:

---

[1] *So in original.*

"(a) Loans to any cooperative association shall bear such rates of interest as the Governor of the Farm Credit Administration shall by regulation prescribe, but in no case shall the rate be less than 3 per centum per annum or more than 6 per centum per annum on the unpaid principal. In fixing such rates of interest, the governor shall fix such rates as he deems the needs of the lending agencies require and in the case of loans made for the purposes of section 7 (a) (1) the rate shall, as nearly as practicable, conform to a rate 1 per centum per annum in excess of the Federal Intermediate Credit Bank discount rate at the time the loan is made, and in the case of loans made for the purposes of section 7 (a) (2) the rate of interest shall, as nearly as practicable, conform to the prevailing rate on mortgage loans made to members of national farm-loan associations at the time the loan is made."

Sec. 55. Subsection (a) of section 15 of the Agricultural Marketing Act, as amended, is amended to read as follows:

"(a) As used in this Act the term 'cooperative association' means any association in which farmers act together in collectively processing, preparing for market, handling and/or marketing the farm products of persons so engaged and also means any association in which farmers act together in collectively purchasing, testing, grading, and/or processing their farm supplies: *Provided, however,* That such associations are operated for the mutual benefit of the members thereof as such producers or purchasers and conform to one or both of the following requirements:

"First. That no member of the association is allowed more than one vote because of the amount of stock or membership capital he may own therein; and

"Second. That the association does not pay dividends on stock or membership capital in excess of 8 per centum per annum.

"And in any case to the following:

"Third. That the association shall not deal in the products of or supplies for non-members to an amount greater in value than such as are handled by it for members."

Title VI — Provisions Common to Corporations Created Under Act

General Corporate Powers

Section 60. The Central Bank for Cooperatives, and the Production Credit Corporations, the Production Credit Associations, and the Banks for Cooperatives, organized under this Act, shall have succession, until dissolved in accordance with this or any other Act of Congress; shall have power to sue and be sued in any court, to adopt and use a corporate seal, to make contracts, to acquire, hold, and dispose of real and personal property necessary and incident to the conduct of their business, to prescribe fees and charges (which in any case shall be subject to the rules and regulations prescribed by the governor) for loans and other services; and shall have such other powers necessary and incident to carrying out their powers and duties under this or any other Act of Congress as may be provided by the governor in their charters or in any amendments thereto. Each such bank, association, or corporation shall, for the purposes of jurisdiction, be deemed a citizen of the State or District within which its principal office is located. No district court of the United States shall have jurisdiction of any action or suit by or against any Production Credit Corporation or Production Credit Association upon the ground that it was incorporated under this Act or that the United States owns a majority of the stock in it, nor shall any district court of the United States within the land bank district served by such association or corporation have jurisdiction by removal or otherwise of any suit by or against any such association or corporation except in cases by or against the United States or by or against any officer of the United States and except in cases by or against any receiver of any such corporation or association appointed in accordance with section 65.

Examinations

Sec. 61. At least once each year and at such other times as the governor deems necessary, the Central Bank for Cooperatives, and each Production Credit Corporation, Production Credit Association, and Bank for Cooperatives, organized under this Act, shall be examined by examiners designated by the governor. The governor shall assess the cost of such examinations against the bank, association, or corporation examined, which shall pay such costs to the governor. The amounts so assessed and unpaid shall be a prior lien on all assets of the bank, association, or corporation examined except on assets pledged to secure loans.

Fiscal Agents of United States

Sec. 62. The Central Bank for Cooperatives, the Production Credit Corporations, Production Credit Associations, and Banks for Cooperatives, organized under this Act, when designated for that purpose by the Secretary of the Treasury, shall act as fiscal agents of the United States Government and when acting as such shall perform such duties as shall be prescribed by the Secretary of the Treasury.

Sec. 63. The Central Bank for Cooperatives, and the Production Credit Corporations, Production Credit Associations, and Banks for Cooperatives, organized under this Act, and their obligations, shall be deemed to be instrumentalities of the United States, and as such, any and all notes, debentures, bonds, and other such obligations issued by such banks, associations, or corporations shall be exempt both as to principal and interest from all taxation (except surtaxes, estate, inheritance, and gift taxes) now or hereafter imposed by the United States or by any State, Territorial, or local taxing authority. Such banks, associations, and corporations, their property, their franchises, capital, reserves, surplus, and other funds, and their income, shall be exempt from all taxation now or hereafter imposed by the United States or by any State, Territorial, or local taxing authority; except that any real property and any tangible personal property of such banks, associations, and corporations shall be subject to Federal, State, Territorial, and local taxation to the same extent as other similar property is taxed. The exemption provided herein shall not apply with respect to any Production Credit Association or its property or income after the stock held in it by the Production Credit Corporation has been retired, or with respect to the Central Bank for Cooperatives, or any Production Credit Corporation or Bank for Cooperatives, or its property or income after the stock held in it by the United States has been retired.

Unlawful Acts and Penalties

Sec. 64. (a) Whoever makes any material representation knowing it to be false, or whoever willfully overvalues any property or security, for the purpose of influencing in any way the action of the Farm Credit Administration or any division, officer, or employee thereof, or of any corporation organized under this Act, or in which a Production Credit Corporation organized under this Act holds stock, or of any regional agricultural credit corporation established pursuant to subsection (e) of section 201 of the Emergency Relief and Construction Act of 1932, upon any application, advance, discount, purchase or repurchase agreement, or loan, or any change or extension of any of the same, by renewal, deferment of action or otherwise, or the acceptance, release, or substitution of security therefor, shall be punished by a fine of not more than $5,000, or by imprisonment for not more than two years, or both.

(b) Whoever (1) falsely makes, forges, or counterfeits any note, debenture, bond, or other obligation, coupon, or paper in imitation of or purporting to be a note, debenture, bond, or other obligation, coupon, or paper issued by the Farm Credit Administration or by any corporation referred to in subsection (a) of this section; or (2) passes, utters, or publishes, or attempts to pass, utter, or publish, any false, forged, or counterfeited note, debenture, bond, or other obligation, coupon, or paper, purporting to have been issued by the Farm Credit Administration or by any such corporation, knowing the same to be false, forged, or counterfeited; or (3) falsely alters any note, debenture, bond, or other obligation, coupon, or paper issued or purporting to have been issued by the Farm Credit Administration or by any such corporation; or (4) passes, utters, or publishes, or attempts to pass, utter, or publish, any of the same as true, knowing it to be falsely altered or spurious, shall be punished by a fine of not more than $10,000, or by imprisonment for not more than five years, or both.

(c) Whoever, being an employee, officer, or agent of the Farm Credit Administration or connected in any capacity with any corporation referred to in subsection (a) of this section, (1) embezzles, abstracts, purloins, or willfully misapplies any moneys, funds, securities, or other things of value, whether belonging to the Farm Credit Administration or such corporation or pledged or otherwise intrusted to the same; or (2) with intent to defraud the United States, or any such corporation, or any other body politic or corporate, or any individual, or to deceive any officer, auditor, or examiner of the Farm Credit Administration or of any such corporation, makes any false entry in any book, report, or statement of or to the Farm Credit Administration or any such corporation, or draws any order, or issues, puts forth, or assigns any note, debenture, bond, or other obligation, or draft, mortgage, judgment, or decree thereof; or (3) with intent to defraud the United States or any corporation referred to in subsection (a) of this section, participates or shares in or receives directly or indirectly any money, profit, property, or benefits through any transaction, loan, commission, contract, or any other act of any such corporation, shall be punished by a fine of not more than $10,000, or by imprisonment for not more than five years, or both.

(d) Whoever knowingly, with intent to defraud the United States or any corporation referred to in subsection (a) of this section, shall conceal, remove, dispose of, or convert, to his own use or to that of another, any property mortgaged or pledged to, or held by, the Farm Credit Administration, or any such corporation, as security for any obligation, shall be punished by a fine of not more than $5,000, or by imprisonment for not more than two years, or both.

(e) The provisions of sections 112, 113, 114, 115, 116, and 117 of the Criminal Code of the United States (U.S.C., title 18, secs. 202 to 207, inclusive), in so far as applicable, are extended to apply to contracts or agreements made by the Farm Credit Administration, its divisions, officers, and employees, and by the corporations referred to in subsection (a) of this section, which, for the purposes hereof, shall be held to include advances, loans, discounts, and purchase and repurchase agreements; extensions and renewals thereof; and acceptances, releases, and substitutions of security therefor.

(f) Whoever conspires with another to accomplish any of the acts made unlawful by the preceding provisions of this section shall, on conviction thereof, be subject to the same fine or imprisonment, or both, as is applicable in the case of conviction for doing such unlawful act.

Liquidation

Sec. 65. Upon default of any obligation of any Production Credit Corporation, Production Credit Association, or regional Bank for Cooperatives, such bank, association, or corporation may be declared insolvent and placed in the hands of a receiver by the governor and proceedings shall thereupon be had in accordance with the provisions of law relating to the insolvency of national farm-loan associations. Any such bank, association, or corporation may, with the consent of the governor, liquidate voluntarily, but only in accordance with such rules and regulations as the governor may prescribe.

Sec. 66. No director, officer, or employee of the Central Bank for Cooperatives, or of any Production Credit Corporation, Production Credit Association, or Bank for Cooperatives shall be paid compensation at a rate in excess of $10,000 per annum. No officer or employee of the Farm Credit Administration engaged in carrying out the provisions of titles I to VI, inclusive, of this Act shall be paid compensation at a rate in excess of $10,000 per annum.

Title VII — Amendments to Federal Farm Loan Act

Section 70. Effective January 1, 1934, the fourteenth paragraph of section 4 of the Federal Farm Loan Act, as amended (U.S.C., title 12, sec. 683), is amended by adding after the first sentence the following: "Not more than one director of a Federal land bank may serve the bank or the Farm Credit Administration as an officer or employee. Except with the approval of the Farm Loan Commissioner, no director (other than the director who may be an officer or employee) shall receive compensation or allowances for any services rendered any Federal land bank in his capacity as director for more than thirty days in any one calendar year exclusive of the period for which compensation is paid for attendance at directors' meetings."

Sec. 70a. (a) Effective one year after the enactment of this Act, section 4 of the Federal Farm Loan Act, as amended, is amended as follows:

(1) The ninth paragraph of such section (U.S.C., title 12, sec. 678) is amended to read as follows:

"The board of directors of every Federal land bank shall be selected as hereinafter specified and shall consist of seven members. Three of said directors shall be known as local directors of whom one shall be chosen by and be representative of national farm-loan associations and borrowers through agencies, one shall be chosen by and be representative of Production Credit Associations organized under the Farm Credit Act of 1933, and one shall be chosen by and be representative of borrowers from regional Banks for Cooperatives organized under the Farm Credit Act of 1933. Three of the seven directors shall be known as district directors and shall be appointed by the Governor of the Farm Credit Administration of whom two shall represent the public interest and one shall represent national farm-loan associations and borrowers through agencies and such director shall be a borrower from a Federal land bank. The terms of office of local and district directors shall be three years."

(2) The tenth paragraph of such section (U.S.C., title 12, sec. 679) is amended to read as follows:

"At least two months before an election of a local director the Land Bank Commissioner shall cause notice in writing to be sent to those entitled to nominate candidates for such local director. In the case of an election of a director to represent national farm-loan associations and borrowers through agencies, such notice shall be sent to all national farm-loan associations and borrowers through agencies in the district; in the case of an election to represent Production Credit Associations, such notice shall be sent to all Production Credit Associations in the district; and in the case of a director to represent borrowers from Banks for Cooperatives, such notice shall be sent to all cooperatives which are borrowers at the time of sending notice. Within ten days of receipt of such notice those entitled to nominate the director shall forward nominations of residents of the district to the Land Bank Commissioner. The Land Bank Commissioner shall, from such nominations, then prepare a list of candidates for such local director consisting of the ten nominees receiving the highest number of votes."

(3) The eleventh paragraph of such section (U.S.C., title 12, sec. 680) is amended to read as follows:

"At least one month before the election of a local director the Land Bank Commissioner shall mail to each person or organization entitled to elect the local director the list of the ten candidates nominated in accordance with the tenth paragraph of this section. In the case of an election of a director to represent national farm-loan associations and borrowers through agencies, the directors of each farm-loan association shall cast the vote of such association for one of the candidates on the list. In voting under this section each such association shall be entitled to cast a number of votes equal to the number of stockholders of such association and each borrower through agencies shall be entitled to cast one vote. In voting under this section each Production Credit Association shall be entitled to case a number of votes equal to the number of the class B stockholders of such associations. In voting under this section each cooperative which is a holder of stock in a Bank for Cooperatives (except the Governor of the Farm Credit Administration) shall be entitled to cast one vote. The votes shall be forwarded to the Land Bank Commissioner and no vote shall be counted unless forwarded to him within ten days after the list of candidates is received. In case of a tie the Land Bank Commissioner shall determine the choice. The nominations from which the list of candidates is prepared, and the votes of the respective voters, as counted, shall be tabulated and preserved and shall be subject to examination by any candidate for at least one year after the results of the election is announced."

(4) The sixth and seventh sentences of the twelfth paragraph of such section (U.S.C., title 12, sec. 681) are amended to read as follows: "The Governor of the Farm Credit Administration shall select a director at large for the

district who shall hold his office during a term of three years. Such seventh director may be removed by the Governor of the Farm Credit Administration at any time."

(b) Subsection (a) shall apply only to the appointment or election of the successors of directors of land banks whose regular terms expire after the effective date of such subsection. The successors of the first local director whose regular term so expires shall be elected by and be representative of Production Credit Associations and the successors of the second local director whose regular term so expires shall be elected by and be representative of borrowers from Banks for Cooperatives. The successors of the third local director whose regular term so expires shall be elected by and be representative of national farm-loan associations and borrowers through agencies.

Sec. 71. Paragraph "Sixth" of section 14 of the Federal Farm Loan Act, as amended, is amended to read as follows:

"Sixth. To accept as additional security for any loan to any borrower under this Act, or any installment of any such loan, any personal property which is exempt from execution upon judgment under the laws of the State in which the land with respect to which the mortgage is given is situated."

Sec. 72. Notwithstanding the provisions of the fourth paragraph of section 9 of the Federal Farm Loan Act, as amended (U.S.C., title 12, sec. 744), the shareholders of national farm-loan associations shall not be held individually responsible for any contract, debt, or engagement of such association entered into after the date of the enactment of this Act, but this section shall not be construed to relieve any other liability with respect to stock held by such shareholders.

Sec. 73. Paragraph "Second" of section 12 of the Federal Farm Loan Act, as amended (U.S.C., title 12, sec. 771), is amended to inserting after "exceeding" where it appears the second time a comma and the following: "except with the approval of the Governor of the Farm Credit Administration,".

Sec. 74. The first sentence of paragraph "Sixth" of section 12 of the Federal Farm Loan Act, as amended (U.S.C., title 12, sec. 771), is amended to read as follows:

"No such loan shall be made to any person who is not at the time, or shortly to become, engaged in farming operations or to any other person unless the principal part of his income is derived from farming operations."

Sec. 75. (a) Paragraph "Fourth" of section 14 of the Federal Farm Loan Act, as amended (U.S.C., title 12, sec. 791) is amended by inserting after "bonds" the following: "(including consolidated bonds issued on its behalf)".

(b) Section 21 of the Federal Farm Loan Act, as amended, is amended by striking out the fourth and tenth paragraphs thereof (U.S.C., title 12, secs. 874 and 880) the word "indorsed" wherever the same appears in said paragraphs.

Sec. 76. (a) Section 201(b) of the Federal Farm Loan Act, as amended (U.S.C., title 12, sec. 1022), is amended to read as follows:

"(b) Such institutions shall be established in the same cities as the twelve Federal Land Banks. The directors of the several Federal Land Banks shall be ex officio directors of the several Federal Intermediate Credit Banks hereby provided for and shall have power, subject to the approval of the Governor of the Farm Credit Administration, to employ and fix the compensation of such officers and employees of such Federal Intermediate Credit Banks as may be necessary to carry on the business authorized by this title."

(b) Paragraph (1) of subsection (a) of section 202 of the Federal Farm Loan Act, as amended (U.S.C., title 12, sec. 1031), is amended to read as follows:

"(1) To discount for, or purchase from, any national bank, and/or any State bank, trust company, agricultural credit corporation, incorporated livestock loan company, savings institution, cooperative bank, credit union, cooperative association of agricultural producers, organized under the laws of any State or of the Government of the United States, and/or any other Federal Intermediate Credit Bank, with its endorsement, any note, draft, bill of exchange, debenture, or other such obligation the proceeds of which have been advanced or used in the first instance for any agricultural purpose or for the raising, breeding, fattening, or marketing of livestock; and to make loans or advances direct to any such organization, secured by such obligations; and to discount for, or purchase from, any Production Credit Association organized under the Farm Credit Act of 1933 or any production credit association in which a Production Credit Corporation organized under such Act holds stock, with its endorsement, any note, draft, bill of exchange, debenture, or other such obligation presented by such association, and to make loans and advances direct to any such association secured by such collateral as may be approved by the Governor of the Farm Credit Administration";

(c) Paragraph (3) of subsection (a) of section 202 of the Federal Farm Loan Act, as amended (U.S.C., title 12, sec. 1031), is amended to read as follows:

"(3) To make loans or advances direct to any cooperative association organized under the laws of any State and composed of persons engaged in producing, or producing and marketing, staple agricultural products, or livestock, if the notes or other such obligations representing such loans are secured by warehouse receipts, and/or shipping documents covering such products, and/or mortgages on livestock, and/or such other collateral as may be approved by the Governor of the Farm Credit Administration: *Provided,* That no such loan or advance, when secured only by warehouse receipts and/or shipping documents, and/or mortgages on livestock, shall exceed 75 per centum of the market value of the products covered by said warehouse receipts and/or shipping documents, or of the livestock covered by said mortgages; and to accept drafts or bills of exchange issued or drawn by any such association when secured by warehouse receipts and/or shipping documents covering staple agricultural products as herein provided."

Sec. 77. After the date of the enactment of this Act, no national agricultural credit corporation shall be formed under the provisions of the title II of the Agricultural Credits Act of 1923.

Sec. 78. Section 31 of the Federal Farm Loan Act, as amended (U.S.C., title 12, sec. 986), is amended by adding at the end thereof a new paragraph, as follows:

"Any mortgagee who shall knowingly make any false statement in any paper, proposal, or letter, relating to the sale of any mortgage, to any Federal land bank under the provisions of section 13 of this Act, as amended, or any appraiser provided for in this Act who shall willfully overvalue any land securing such mortgage, shall be punished by a fine of not exceeding $5,000 or by imprisonment not exceeding one year, or both."

Sec. 79. Section 13 of the Federal Farm Loan Act, as amended (U.S.C., title 12, sec. 781), is amended by adding at the end thereof the following new paragraph:

"Fourteenth. To enter into agreements with national farm-loan associations of the district under the terms of which losses incurred and gains realized on account of the disposition of lands covered by a defaulted mortgage indorsed by such association will be shared equally by the bank and the association."

Title VIII — Miscellaneous

Section 80. (a) After the date of the enactment of this Act, the office of Farm Loan Commissioner shall be known as the office of the Land Bank Commissioner and the Farm Loan Commissioner shall be known as the Land Bank Commissioner. The provisions of the third paragraph of section 3 of the Federal Farm Loan Act, as amended (U.S.C., title 12, sec. 653), prescribing a term of office of eight years shall not apply to incumbents hereafter appointed to the office of Land Bank Commissioner.

(b) There shall be in the Farm Credit Administration three commissioners who shall be known, respectively, as the Production Credit Commissioner, the Cooperative Bank Commissioner, and the Intermediate Credit Commissioner. Such commissioners shall be appointed by the President, by and with the advice and consent of the Senate. They shall receive an annual salary of $10,000, payable monthly, together with actual necessary traveling expenses. Such commissioners shall perform such duties as may be assigned to them by law or by the governor of the Farm Credit Administration.

Sec. 81. The signature of the Land Bank Commissioner on Federal farm-loan bonds shall be attested by any Deputy Land Bank Commissioner.

Sec. 82. The authority and powers conferred upon the governor under this Act shall not be construed to be in substitution for authority and powers conferred upon him under existing law but shall be construed to be supplementary to such authority and powers.

Sec. 83. This Act shall not be construed to repeal subsection (e) of section 201 of the Emergency Relief and Construction Act of 1932.

Sec. 84. The Reconstruction Finance Corporation is authorized, with the approval of the Governor of the Farm Credit Administration, to reduce the capital of any Regional Agricultural Credit Corporation by such action as may be suitable for the purpose. The funds made available by any such reduction shall constitute a revolving fund, all or any part of which shall be available for use from time to time by the Reconstruction Finance Corporation for the purpose of increasing, with the approval of the Governor of the Farm Credit Administration, the capital of any Regional Agricultural Credit Corporation.

Sec. 85. The Farm Credit Administration shall have a seal, as adopted by the governor, which shall be judicially noticed.

Sec. 86. Subdivision (a) of section 10 of the Act entitled "An Act to relieve the existing national economic emergency by increasing agricultural purchasing power, to raise revenue for extraordinary expenses incurred by reason of such emergency, to provide emergency relief with respect to agricultural indebtedness, to provide for the orderly liquidation of joint-stock land banks, and for other purposes," approved May 12, 1933, is amended by inserting before the period at the end of the first sentence a colon and the following: "*And provided further,* That the State Administrator appointed to administer this Act in each State shall be appointed by the President, by and with the advice and consent of the Senate."

Sec. 87. If any provision of this Act, or the application thereof to any person or circumstances, is held invalid, the remainder of the Act, and the application of such provisions to other persons or circumstances, shall not be affected thereby.

Sec. 88. The right to alter, amend, or repeal this Act is hereby expressly reserved.

Approved, June 16, 1933, 1:10 p.m.

Tables

United States Population (Estimated) — 000

Age Group (in years)

Year	Total	Under 5	5-14	15-24	25-34	35-44	45-54	55 and Over
1946	141,389	13,244	21,844	23,382	22,954	20,073	16,820	23,072
1945	139,928	12,979	21,599	23,705	22,734	19,787	16,642	22,482
1944	138,397	12,524	21,573	23,999	22,511	19,505	16,419	21,866
1943	136,739	12,016	21,699	24,065	22,194	19,226	16,199	21,339
1942	134,860	11,301	21,823	24,093	21,911	18,950	15,976	20,804
1941	133,402	10,850	22,089	24,074	21,691	18,692	15,759	20,247
1940	132,122	10,579	22,363	24,033	21,446	18,422	15,555	19,725
1939	130,880	10,418	22,701	23,819	21,176	18,178	15,336	19,251
1938	129,825	10,176	23,146	23,655	20,953	18,001	15,077	18,818
1937	128,825	10,009	23,564	23,487	20,723	17,866	14,785	18,390
1936	128,053	10,044	23,942	23,309	20,505	17,783	14,495	17,976
1935	127,250	10,170	24,213	23,130	20,275	17,712	14,208	17,543
1934	126,374	10,331	24,402	22,963	20,022	17,640	13,933	17,084
1933	125,579	10,612	24,531	22,820	19,750	17,569	13,684	16,612
1932	124,840	10,903	24,614	22,716	19,484	17,504	13,481	16,139
1931	124,040	11,179	24,629	22,617	19,242	17,412	13,296	15,663
1930	123,077	11,372	24,631	22,487	19,039	17,270	13,096	15,182
1929	121,767	11,734	24,470	22,151	18,941	16,921	12,761	14,789
1928	120,509	11,978	24,320	21,811	18,953	16,540	12,430	14,477
1927	119,035	12,111	24,152	21,430	18,948	16,172	12,092	14,130
1926	117,397	12,189	23,906	21,037	18,867	15,847	11,786	13,765

International Migration—Immigrants to the United States

YEAR	ALL COUNTRIES	EUROPE Total	North-western	Central	Eastern	Southern	ASIA	AMERICA	AFRICA	AUSTRALASIA[1]	ALL OTHER COUNTRIES
1946	108,721	52,852	45,297	3,444	251	3,860	2,108	46,066	1,516	6,106	73
1945	38,119	5,943	4,045	573	195	1,130	461	29,646	406	1,663	—
1944	28,551	4,509	2,333	846	266	1,064	231	23,084	112	615	—
1943	23,725	4,920	2,909	848	213	950	342	18,162	141	160	—
1942	28,781	11,153	6,983	2,889	314	967	615	16,377	473	163	—
1941	51,776	26,541	18,132	5,265	964	2,180	1,971	22,445	564	255	—
1940	70,756	50,454	16,000	25,850	1,389	7,215	2,050	17,822	202	228	—
1939	82,998	63,138	10,639	41,921	1,641	8,937	2,281	17,139	218	222	—
1938	67,895	44,495	8,092	24,797	1,502	10,104	2,492	20,486	174	248	—
1937	50,244	31,863	5,740	15,870	1,162	9,091	1,149	16,903	155	174	—
1936	36,329	23,480	4,145	9,938	802	8,595	793	11,786	105	165	—
1935	34,956	22,778	4,363	9,062	871	8,482	682	11,174	118	141	63
1934	29,470	17,210	3,575	6,846	954	5,835	597	11,409	104	147	3
1933	23,068	12,383	2,873	4,232	810	4,468	552	9,925	71	137	—
1932	35,576	20,579	5,092	5,715	1,228	8,544	1,931	12,577	186	303	—
1931	97,139	61,909	23,979	18,505	2,588	16,837	3,345	30,816	417	652	—
1930	241,700	147,438	70,549	44,984	4,931	26,974	4,535	88,104	572	1,051	—
1929	279,678	158,598	67,718	63,834	4,603	22,443	3,758	116,177	509	636	—
1928	307,255	158,513	70,489	61,264	4,428	21,972	3,380	144,281	475	606	—
1927	335,175	168,368	78,208	64,283	4,641	21,236	3,669	161,872	520	746	—
1926	304,488	155,562	76,016	63,567	4,919	11,060	3,413	144,393	529	591	—

[1] Australia, New Zealand, and other Pacific Islands.

Vital Statistics

Year	Marriages (000)	Divorces (000)[1]	Birth Rate Live Births per 1,000 Total Population	Expectation of Life (in years) at Birth			Death Rate per 100,000 Population	
				Both Sexes	Male	Female	Accidental Falls	Suicide
1946	2,291	610	24.1	66.7	64.4	69.4	16.1	11.5
1945	1,613	485	20.4	65.9	63.6	67.9	17.7	11.2
1944	1,452	400	21.2	65.2	63.6	66.8	17.0	10.0
1943	1,577	359	22.7	63.3	62.4	64.4	18.0	10.2
1942	1,772	321	22.2	66.2	64.7	67.9	16.6	12.0
1941	1,696	293	20.3	64.8	63.1	66.8	16.7	12.8
1940	1,596	264	19.4	62.9	60.8	65.2	17.2	14.4
1939	1,404	251	18.8	63.7	62.1	65.4	17.5	14.1
1938	1,331	244	19.2	63.5	61.9	65.3	19.5	15.3
1937	1,451	249	18.7	60.0	58.0	62.4	20.4	15.0
1936	1,369	236	18.4	58.5	56.6	60.6	20.8	14.3
1935	1,327	218	18.7	61.7	59.9	63.9	19.2	14.3
1934	1,302	204	19.0	61.1	59.3	63.3	18.8	14.9
1933	1,098	165	18.4	63.3	61.7	65.1	15.1	15.9
1932	982	164	19.5	62.1	61.0	63.5	14.8	17.4
1931	1,061	188	20.2	61.1	59.4	63.1	14.6	16.8
1930	1,127	196	21.3	59.7	58.1	61.6	14.7	15.6
1929	1,233	206	21.2	57.1	55.8	58.7	14.5	13.9
1928	1,182	200	22.2	56.8	55.6	58.3	14.1	13.5
1927	1,201	196	23.5	60.4	59.0	62.1	14.0	13.2
1926	1,203	185	24.2	56.7	55.5	58.0	14.0	12.6

[1] Includes reported annulments.

Social Welfare Expenditures Under Public Programs ($000,000)

Year	Total	Percent of Gross National Product	Social Insurance	Public Aid	Health and Medical Programs	Education	Veterans Programs	Housing	Other Social Welfare
1946	12,798	6.1	3,652	1,151	1,904	3,297	2,403	159	233
1945	9,205	4.4	1,409	1,031	2,354	3,076	1,126	11	198
1944	8,228	4.1	1,256	1,032	2,225	2,800	720	13	182
1943	8,283	4.7	1,259	1,550	1,886	2,793	623	14	159
1942	8,609	6.1	1,376	2,777	949	2,694	645	14	154
1941	8,953	8.0	1,330	3,524	724	2,617	613	9	136
1940	8,795	9.2	1,272	3,597	616	2,561	629	4	116
1939	9,213	10.5	1,181	4,230	575	2,504	606	3	114
1938	7,924	9.0	849	3,233	540	2,563	627	4	108
1937	7,858	9.1	545	3,436	500	2,376	893	3	105
1936	10,184	13.2	456	3,079	454	2,228	3,826[1]	42	101
1935	6,548	9.5	406	2,998	427	2,008	597	13	99
1934	5,832	9.7	362	2,531	400	1,914	530	[2]	96
1933	4,462	7.9	344	689	418	2,104	819	—	89
1932	4,303	6.4	355	256	435	2,352	825	—	81
1931	4,201	5.1	368	154	406	2,440	744	—	79
1930	4,085	4.2	361	78	378	2,523	668	—	78
1929	3,921	3.9	342	50	351	2,434	658	—	76
1928	—	—	—	—	—	—	—	—	—
1927	—	—	—	—	—	—	—	—	—
1926	—	—	—	—	—	—	—	—	—

[1] Of the 3,826 total, 3,241 was welfare and other. [2] Less than $500,000. Note: For some years the sum of the parts do not equal the Total Expenditures.

Recreation (000)

Year	Visits to National Parks[1]	Visits to National Monuments[1]	American League Baseball Attendance	National League Baseball Attendance
1946	8,991	3,603	9,621	8,902
1945	4,538	2,512	5,580	5,261
1944	2,646	1,851	4,798	3,975
1943	2,054	1,578	3,697	3,769
1942	3,815	1,832	4,200	4,353
1941	8,459	3,745	4,912	4,778
1940	7,358	2,817	5,434	4,390
1939	6,854	2,592	4,271	4,707
1938	6,619	2,364	4,446	4,561
1937	6,705	1,966	4,736	4,204
1936	5,791	1,681	4,179	3,904
1935	4,056	1,332	3,688	3,657
1934	3,517	1,386	3,764	3,200
1933	2,867	523	2,926	3,163
1932	2,949	406	3,133	3,841
1931	3,153	392	3,883	4,584
1930	2,775	472	4,686	5,447
1929	2,757	491	4,662	4,926
1928	2,569	456	4,221	4,881
1927	2,381	417	4,613	5,310
1926	1,942	373	4,913	4,920

[1] For years ending September 30 prior to 1941; thereafter, for years ending December 31, or as of January 1 of the following year. Includes areas in Alaska, Hawaii, Virgin Islands, and Puerto Rico.

Education

Year	Enrollment-Public Day Schools (000)				Institutions of Higher Learning-Degrees Conferred			
	Total	Kindergarten	Elementary	Secondary	Total All Degrees	Bachelor's or First Professional	Master's or Second Professional	Doctor's or Equivalent
1946	23,300	773	16,905	5,622	157,349	136,174	19,209	1,966
1945	—	—	—	—	—	—	—	—
1944	23,267	697	17,016	5,554	141,582	125,863	13,414	2,305
1943	—	—	—	—	—	—	—	—
1942	24,562	626	17,549	6,388	213,491	185,346	24,648	3,497
1941	—	—	—	—	—	—	—	—
1940	25,434	595	18,237	6,601	216,521	186,500	26,731	3,290
1939	—	—	—	—	—	—	—	—
1938	25,975	607	19,141	6,227	189,503	164,943	21,628	2,932
1937	—	—	—	—	—	—	—	—
1936	26,367	607	19,786	5,975	164,197	143,125	18,302	2,770
1935	—	—	—	—	—	—	—	—
1934	26,434	602	20,163	5,669	157,279	136,156	18,293	2,830
1933	—	—	—	—	—	—	—	—
1932	26,275	701	20,434	5,140	160,084	138,063	19,367	2,654
1931	—	—	—	—	—	—	—	—
1930	25,678	723	20,556	4,399	139,752	122,484	14,969	2,299
1929	—	—	—	—	—	—	—	—
1928	25,180	695	20,573	3,911	124,995	111,161	12,387	1,447
1927	—	—	—	—	—	—	—	—
1926	24,741	673	20,311	3,757	108,407	97,263	9,735	1,409

Crime and Correction

Year	Homicides Number	Homicides Rate[1]	Suicides Number	Suicides Rate[1]	Prisoners Present (at end of year) Total	Prisoners Present (at end of year) Federal Institutions	Prisoners Present (at end of year) State Institutions
1946	8,913	6.4	16,152	11.5	140,079	17,622	122,457
1945	7,547	5.7	14,782	11.2	133,649	18,638	115,011
1944	6,675	5.0	13,231	10.0	132,456	18,139	114,317
1943	6,823	5.1	13,725	10.2	137,220	16,113	121,107
1942	7,890	5.9	16,117	12.0	150,384	16,623	133,761
1941	8,048	6.0	17,102	12.8	165,439	18,465	146,974
1940	8,329	6.3	18,907	14.4	173,706	19,260	154,446
1939	8,394	6.4	18,511	14.1	179,818	19,730	160,088
1938	8,799	6.8	19,802	15.3	159,382	17,083	142,299
1937	9,811	7.6	19,294	15.0	149,357	15,309	134,048
1936	10,232	8.0	18,294	14.3	143,573	15,373	128,200
1935	10,587	8.3	18,214	14.3	144,665	14,777	129,888
1934	12,055	9.5	18,828	14.9	138,220	12,080	126,140
1933	12,124	9.7	19,993	15.9	136,947	10,851	126,096
1932	10,722	9.0	20,646	17.4	137,183	12,282	124,901
1931	10,862	9.2	19,807	16.8	137,082	12,964	124,118
1930	10,331	8.8	18,323	15.6	127,495	12,181	115,314
1929	9,637	8.4	16,045	13.9	120,496	12,964	107,532
1928	9,780	8.6	15,390	13.5	116,626	8,204	108,422
1927	8,997	8.4	14,096	13.2	106,517	7,722	98,795
1926	8,740	8.4	13,082	12.6	96,125	6,803	89,322

[1] Rates per 100,000 of resident population.

Unemployed
(14 years and older — annual averages)

Year	Total Civilian (000)	Percent of Civilian Labor Force
1946	2,270	3.9
1945	1,040	1.9
1944	670	1.2
1943	1,070	1.9
1942	2,660	4.7
1941	5,560	9.9
1940	8,120	14.6
1939	9,480	17.2
1938	10,390	19.0
1937	7,700	14.3
1936	9,030	16.9
1935	10,610	20.1
1934	11,340	21.7
1933	12,830	24.9
1932	12,060	23.6
1931	8,020	15.9
1930	4,340	8.7
1929	1,550	3.2
1928	1,982	4.2
1927	1,519	3.3
1926	801	1.8

Earnings in Current Dollars

Year	Agriculture, Forestry, and Fisheries[1]	Manufacturing	Mining	Construction	Transportation	Communications and Public Utilities
1946	1,200	2,517	2,719	2,537	2,973	2,582
1945	1,125	2,517	2,621	2,600	2,734	2,446
1944	1,021	2,517	2,499	2,602	2,679	2,275
1943	860	2,349	2,162	2,503	2,493	2,098
1942	669	2,023	1,796	2,191	2,183	1,891
1941	496	1,653	1,579	1,635	1,885	1,766
1940	407	1,432	1,388	1,330	1,756	1,717
1939	385	1,363	1,367	1,268	1,723	1,691
1938	369	1,296	1,282	1,193	1,676	1,673
1937	360	1,376	1,366	1,278	1,644	1,600
1936	308	1,287	1,263	1,178	1,582	1,520
1935	288	1,216	1,154	1,027	1,492	1,483
1934	253	1,153	1,108	942	1,393	1,424
1933	232	1,086	990	869	1,334	1,351
1932	250	1,150	1,016	907	1,373	1,440
1931	315	1,369	1,221	1,233	1,549	1,514
1930	388	1,488	1,424	1,526	1,610	1,499
1929	401	1,543	1,526	1,674	1,643	1,478
1928	385	1,534	1,478	1,719	1,607	1,474
1927	387	1,502	1,590	1,708	1,579	1,440
1926	386	1,476	1,597	1,664	1,562	1,427

[1] *Prior to 1929, agriculture only.*

Earnings in Current Dollars, *continued*

Year	Wholesale and Retail Trade	Finance, Insurance, and Real Estate	Services	Total	Government State and Local[1]	Government Public Education	Government Federal Civilian[2]
1946	2,378	2,570	1,863	2,351	2,117	2,025	2,801
1945	2,114	2,347	1,688	2,052	1,962	1,882	2,646
1944	1,946	2,191	1,538	1,924	1,822	1,730	2,677
1943	1,781	2,041	1,347	1,777	1,713	1,608	2,628
1942	1,608	1,885	1,132	1,623	1,592	1,512	2,226
1941	1,478	1,777	1,020	1,388	1,534	1,462	1,970
1940	1,382	1,725	953	1,344	1,502	1,435	1,894
1939	1,360	1,729	952	1,337	1,476	1,403	1,843
1938	1,352	1,731	942	1,336	1,472	1,406	1,832
1937	1,352	1,788	938	1,355	1,441	1,367	1,797
1936	1,295	1,713	898	1,279	1,402	1,329	1,896
1935	1,279	1,632	873	1,292	1,290	1,293	1,759
1934	1,228	1,601	857	1,284	1,295	1,265	1,717
1933	1,183	1,555	854	1,328	1,338	1,300	1,673
1932	1,315	1,652	918	1,477	1,432	1,399	1,824
1931	1,495	1,858	1,008	1,547	1,500	1,463	1,895
1930	1,569	1,973	1,066	1,553	1,521	1,455	1,768
1929	1,594	2,062	1,079	1,551	1,504	1,445	1,933
1928	1,573	2,043	1,065	1,550	1,500	1,433	1,916
1927	1,480	2,019	1,046	1,531	1,488	1,393	1,907
1926	1,416	2,008	1,005	1,482	1,422	1,342	1,888

[1] *Prior to 1929, general government only.* [2] *Prior to 1929, includes work relief.*

Index of Employee Output
1958 = 100

Year	Total[1]	Output per Man-hour		Farm
		Nonfarm[2]	Manufacturing	
1946	68.7	73.3	65.8	51.4
1945	70.7	76.8	71.5	47.9
1944	67.2	72.7	72.5	47.6
1943	63.0	67.4	73.4	47.9
1942	62.0	66.7	72.4	49.9
1941	61.8	67.2	71.2	47.7
1940	58.5	66.1	68.7	42.7
1939	56.9	63.6	65.4	44.2
1938	54.7	61.4	59.9	43.3
1937	53.1	59.7	60.7	40.3
1936	53.2	60.2	61.6	37.0
1935	50.6	57.7	61.2	39.2
1934	49.0	55.9	57.4	36.2
1933	44.5	50.4	54.9	38.9
1932	45.4	51.6	50.5	39.8
1931	47.2	53.3	54.0	39.5
1930	46.8	52.5	52.3	35.6
1929	48.6	54.1	52.0	37.3
1928	46.5	52.0	49.7	36.3
1927	46.5	51.6	47.6	37.2
1926	45.7	51.4	46.5	34.8

[1] *For total private domestic economy.*
[2] *For nonfarm business economy.*

Wholesale Price Indexes, by Major Product Groups
1967 = 100

Year	All Commodities	Industrial Commodities	Farm Products	Fuels and Related Products and Power	Lumber and Wood Products	Metals and Metal Products	Furniture and Household Durables	Motor Vehicles and Equipment
1946	62.3	58.0	90.9	64.4	47.2	44.3	67.1	56.0
1945	54.6	53.0	78.5	60.1	41.2	39.6	63.2	48.3
1944	53.6	52.3	75.5	59.5	40.6	39.0	63.1	47.5
1943	53.3	51.5	75.0	57.8	37.7	39.0	61.4	47.2
1942	50.9	50.7	64.8	56.2	35.6	39.1	61.8	47.2
1941	45.1	47.3	50.3	54.6	32.7	38.5	57.2	43.2
1940	40.5	44.0	41.4	51.4	27.4	37.8	53.8	40.4
1939	39.8	43.3	40.0	52.3	24.8	37.6	52.6	39.1
1938	40.5	43.4	42.0	54.6	24.1	38.0	52.8	39.9
1937	44.5	45.2	52.9	55.5	26.5	39.4	54.1	37.4
1936	41.7	42.2	49.5	54.5	22.4	34.5	48.8	34.9
1935	41.3	41.4	48.1	52.6	21.4	33.8	48.1	35.2
1934	38.6	41.6	40.0	52.4	22.3	33.9	48.5	36.7
1933	34.0	37.8	31.4	47.6	19.0	30.7	44.6	34.8
1932	33.6	37.3	29.5	50.3	16.0	29.9	44.5	36.5
1931	37.6	39.9	39.7	48.3	18.6	32.6	50.5	37.5
1930	44.6	45.2	54.2	56.2	22.9	36.2	54.9	39.4
1929	49.1	48.6	64.1	59.4	25.0	40.2	55.8	41.9
1928	50.0	49.3	64.8	60.4	24.1	38.8	56.3	40.7
1927	49.3	50.0	60.8	63.2	25.0	38.8	57.7	40.2
1926	51.6	53.2	61.3	71.5	26.5	41.4	59.1	41.9

Wholesale Prices of Selected Commodities
(in Dollars per Unit)

Year	Wheat bu.	Sugar lb.	Wool lb.	Steel Rails gross ton	Nails 100 lbs.
1946	1.895	.064	1.025	47.90	3.477
1945	1.664	.054	1.192	42.94	2.850
1944	1.604	.055	1.188	40.00	2.550
1943	1.440	.055	1.183	40.00	2.550
1942	1.189	.055	1.195	40.00	2.550
1941	.992	.049	1.091	40.00	2.550
1940	.871	.044	.966	40.00	2.550
1939	.755	.046	.823	40.00	2.461
1938	.777	.045	.691	41.79	2.575
1937	1.201	.047	.971	41.89	2.773
1936	1.123	.048	.881	36.63	2.229
1935	1.040	.049	.723	36.38	2.628
1934	.932	.044	.817	36.38	2.623
1933	.724	.043	.663	39.33	2.089
1932	.494	.040	.459	42.38	2.050
1931	.606	.044	.621	43.00	1.978
1930	.900	.047	.763	43.00	2.191
1929	1.180	.051	.987	43.00	2.667
1928	1.324	.056	1.159	43.00	2.676
1927	1.372	.058	1.107	43.00	2.638
1926	1.496	.055	1.152	43.00	2.750

Consumer Price Indexes
(1967 = 100)

Year	All Items	Food at Home	Housing — Rent	Housing — House Furnishings	Apparel
1946	58.5	58.1	59.2	80.0	67.5
1945	53.9	50.7	58.8	73.3	61.5
1944	52.7	49.6	58.6	68.6	58.5
1943	51.8	50.3	58.5	63.1	54.6
1942	48.8	45.1	58.5	61.4	52.3
1941	44.1	38.4	57.2	54.0	44.8
1940	42.0	35.2	56.2	50.5	42.8
1939	41.6	34.6	56.0	50.9	42.4
1938	42.2	35.6	56.0	52.0	43.0
1937	43.0	38.4	54.2	52.4	43.2
1936	41.5	36.9	51.9	48.4	41.1
1935	41.1	36.5	50.6	47.6	40.8
1934	40.1	34.1	50.7	46.6	40.4
1933	38.8	30.6	54.1	42.4	36.9
1932	40.9	31.5	62.8	42.9	38.2
1931	45.6	37.8	70.0	49.3	43.2
1930	50.0	45.9	73.9	54.7	47.5
1929	51.3	48.3	76.0	56.2	48.5
1928	51.3	47.7	77.8	56.8	49.0
1927	52.0	48.2	79.7	58.2	49.7
1926	53.0	50.0	81.0	59.6	50.8

Retail Prices of Selected Foods in U.S. Cities
(in Cents per Unit Indicated)

Year	Flour 5 lb.	Bread lb.	Coffee lb.	Sugar 5 lb.	Meats			
					Round Steak lb.	Chuck Roast lb.	Pork Chops lb.	Bacon lb.
1946	35.4	10.4	34.4	38.4	52.1	36.6	48.5	53.3
1945	32.1	8.8	30.5	33.4	40.6	28.1	37.1	41.1
1944	32.4	8.8	30.1	33.6	41.4	28.8	37.3	41.1
1943	30.6	8.9	30.0	34.2	43.9	30.2	40.3	43.1
1942	26.4	8.7	28.3	34.1	43.5	29.3	41.4	39.4
1941	22.6	8.1	23.6	28.6	39.1	25.5	34.3	34.3
1940	21.5	8.0	21.2	26.0	36.4	23.5	27.9	27.3
1939	19.0	7.9	22.4	27.2	36.0	23.4	30.4	31.9
1938	19.8	8.6	23.2	26.6	34.9	22.8	32.9	36.7
1937	24.0	8.6	25.5	28.2	39.1	25.7	36.7	41.3
1936	23.8	8.2	24.3	27.9	34.1	22.3	34.1	40.7
1935	25.3	8.3	25.7	28.2	36.0	24.0	36.1	41.3
1934	24.5	8.3	26.9	27.5	28.1	17.5	25.5	29.1
1933	19.5	7.1	26.4	26.5	25.7	16.0	19.8	22.6
1932	16.0	7.0	29.4	25.0	29.7	18.5	21.5	24.2
1931	18.0	7.7	32.8	28.0	35.4	22.7	29.6	36.6
1930	23.0	8.6	39.5	30.5	42.6	28.6	36.2	42.5
1929	25.5	8.8	47.9	32.0	46.0	31.4	37.5	43.9
1928	26.5	8.9	48.2	34.5	43.7	29.6	35.2	44.4
1927	27.5	9.2	47.4	36.0	38.7	25.2	37.2	47.8
1926	30.0	9.3	50.2	34.0	37.1	23.7	39.9	50.8

Retail Prices of Selected Foods in U.S. Cities, *continued*
(in Cents per Unit Indicated)

	Dairy Products and Eggs			Fruits and Vegetables			
Year	Butter lb.	Eggs Doz.	Milk Delivered ½ gal.	Oranges Doz.	Potatoes 10 lb.	Tomatoes Canned 303 can	Navy Beans lb.
1946	71.0	58.6	35.2	49.9	46.8	12.6	14.0
1945	50.7	58.1	31.2	48.5	49.3	10.3	11.4
1944	50.0	54.5	31.2	46.0	46.5	10.1	10.7
1943	52.7	57.2	31.0	44.3	45.6	10.6	10.1
1942	47.3	48.4	30.0	35.7	34.2	9.9	9.0
1941	41.1	39.7	27.2	31.0	23.5	7.7	7.4
1940	36.0	33.1	25.6	29.1	23.9	7.2	6.6
1939	32.5	32.1	24.4	28.9	24.7	7.2	6.2
1938	34.7	35.5	25.0	26.7	21.3	7.5	6.3
1937	40.7	36.2	25.0	38.9	27.9	7.9	9.6
1936	39.5	37.1	24.0	33.6	31.9	8.0	6.7
1935	36.0	37.6	23.4	22.0	19.1	8.6	6.2
1934	31.5	32.5	22.4	31.9	23.0	8.8	6.1
1933	27.8	28.8	20.8	27.3	23.0	7.7	5.3
1932	27.8	30.2	21.4	30.2	17.0	7.8	5.2
1931	35.8	35.0	25.2	35.0	24.0	8.5	8.1
1930	46.4	44.5	28.2	57.1	36.0	10.2	11.7
1929	55.5	52.7	28.8	44.7	32.0	10.8	14.1
1928	56.9	50.3	28.4	58.6	27.0	9.9	11.8
1927	56.3	48.7	28.2	52.0	38.0	10.0	9.4
1926	53.6	51.9	28.0	51.6	49.0	9.9	9.4

Apparent Civilian per Capita Consumption of Foods
(in Pounds, Except Eggs)

Year	Beef and Veal (Carcass Weight)	Pork excluding Lard (Carcass Weight)	Fish (Edible Weight)	Lard	Apples	Potatoes (Farm Weight)	Fresh Vegetables (Farm Weight)	Melons (Farm Weight)
1946	71.6	75.8	12.8	11.8	23.0	123	129.9	30.6
1945	71.3	66.6	11.9	11.7	22.9	122	134.3	29.7
1944	68.0	79.5	10.7	12.3	25.5	136	123.9	28.0
1943	61.5	78.9	9.9	13.0	24.9	125	116.7	21.8
1942	69.4	63.7	10.7	12.8	28.1	127	119.0	22.5
1941	68.5	68.4	13.2	13.8	31.7	128	113.8	24.5
1940	62.3	73.5	13.0	14.4	29.7	123	116.9	26.5
1939	62.3	64.7	12.7	12.7	30.7	122	116.6	25.4
1938	62.0	58.2	12.8	11.1	28.2	129	114.5	27.2
1937	63.8	55.8	13.8	10.5	33.6	126	111.0	28.8
1936	68.9	55.1	13.7	11.3	27.6	130	112.5	26.4
1935	61.7	48.4	12.5	9.6	32.9	142	111.2	27.2
1934	73.2	64.4	11.2	13.0	25.3	135	115.2	25.6
1933	58.6	70.7	10.7	14.0	40.0	132	104.5	25.3
1932	53.3	70.7	10.4	14.4	39.2	134	108.8	27.1
1931	55.2	68.4	10.8	13.6	51.7	136	108.3	32.8
1930	55.3	67.0	12.2	12.7	42.1	132	111.9	33.0
1929	56.0	69.6	13.9	12.7	39.7	159	112.6	32.1
1928	55.2	70.9	14.1	13.2	48.9	147	104.2	30.6
1927	61.9	67.7	14.2	12.7	37.4	141	106.0	30.8
1926	68.5	64.1	13.4	12.2	62.3	128	100.6	36.4

Apparent Civilian per Capita Consumption of Foods, *continued*
(in Pounds, Except Eggs)

DAIRY PRODUCTS

Year	Dry Beans (Cleaned Basis)	Total Milk for Human Consumption	Cheese	Eggs (Number)	Chicken and Turkey[1]	Wheat Flour	Corn Flour and Meal	Coffee (Green Bean Basis)
1946	8.7	786	6.7	379	23.1	156	15.2	20.1
1945	7.8	788	6.7	403	25.1	161	17.6	16.4
1944	8.1	763	4.9	354	23.1	149	19.2	15.8
1943	8.9	750	4.9	347	25.7	163	20.5	12.9
1942	11.1	832	6.4	318	20.7	157	19.8	13.6
1941	8.8	803	5.9	311	18.3	156	20.6	15.9
1940	8.4	818	6.0	319	17.0	155	21.8	15.5
1939	9.3	824	6.0	313	16.6	158	21.7	14.9
1938	9.6	796	5.9	310	15.0	160	22.1	14.9
1937	7.8	797	5.5	308	15.9	159	22.8	13.3
1936	9.0	792	5.4	289	15.9	163	24.2	13.7
1935	8.4	800	5.3	280	14.8	158	24.7	13.4
1934	9.1	813	4.9	289	15.3	157	25.3	12.3
1933	7.1	814	4.6	296	16.7	162	25.7	12.8
1932	7.4	832	4.4	313	16.0	170	26.5	12.4
1931	8.8	838	4.5	333	15.5	169	26.6	13.0
1930	9.5	819	4.7	331	17.2	171	28.3	12.5
1929	7.8	811	4.7	334	15.7	177	30.5	12.2
1928	8.6	804	4.4	338	14.6	179	29.9	11.9
1927	8.7	813	4.6	342	15.2	181	28.8	12.2
1926	7.6	818	4.6	339	14.2	182	28.9	12.4

[1] *Chicken only, 1926–1928, but turkey consumption was very small during those years.*

Gross National Product

	Current Prices		1958 Prices	
Year	Total Bil. Dollars	Per Capita Dollars	Total Bil. Dollars	Per Capita Dollars
1946	208.5	1,475	312.6	2,211
1945	211.9	1,515	355.2	2,538
1944	210.1	1,518	361.3	2,611
1943	191.6	1,401	337.1	2,465
1942	157.9	1,171	297.8	2,208
1941	124.5	934	263.7	1,977
1940	99.7	754	227.2	1,720
1939	90.5	691	209.4	1,598
1938	84.7	651	192.9	1,484
1937	90.4	701	203.2	1,576
1936	82.5	643	193.0	1,506
1935	72.2	567	169.5	1,331
1934	65.1	514	154.3	1,220
1933	55.6	442	141.5	1,126
1932	58.0	465	144.2	1,154
1931	75.8	611	169.3	1,364
1930	90.4	734	183.5	1,490
1929	103.1	847	203.6	1,671
1928	97.0	805	190.9	1,584
1927	94.9	797	189.8	1,594
1926	97.0	826	190.0	1,619

Agriculture — Farms

Year	Farm Population Total (000)	Farm Population Percent of Total Population	Value of Farm Property ($000) Implements and Machinery	Value of Farm Property ($000) Livestock	Farm Employment (000) Total	Farm Employment (000) Family Workers	Farm Employment (000) Hired Workers	Wage Rate per Day Without Board and Room ($)
1946	25,403	18.0	5,174	8,072	10,295	8,106	2,189	4.80
1945	24,420	17.5	6,474	7,281	10,000	7,881	2,119	4.35
1944	24,815	18.0	5,346	7,687	10,219	7,988	2,231	3.95
1943	26,186	19.2	4,906	7,754	10,446	8,010	2,436	3.30
1942	28,914	21.5	3,981	5,552	10,504	7,949	2,555	2.55
1941	30,118	22.6	3,254	3,877	10,669	8,017	2,652	1.95
1940	30,547	23.2	3,060	3,540	10,979	8,300	2,679	1.60
1939	30,840	23.6	3,036	3,359	11,338	8,611	2,727	1.55
1938	30,980	23.9	2,998	3,164	11,622	8,815	2,807	1.55
1937	31,266	24.3	2,648	3,036	11,978	9,054	2,924	1.65
1936	31,737	24.8	2,359	3,145	12,331	9,350	2,981	1.45
1935	32,161	25.3	2,217	1,837	12,733	9,855	2,878	1.35
1934	32,305	25.6	2,168	1,743	12,627	9,765	2,862	1.25
1933	32,393	25.8	2,464	1,787	12,739	9,874	2,865	1.15
1932	31,388	25.2	2,915	2,264	12,816	9,922	2,894	1.20
1931	30,845	24.9	3,217	3,337	12,745	9,642	3,103	1.65
1930	30,529	24.9	3,302	4,598	12,497	9,307	3,190	2.15
1929	30,580	25.2	3,178	4,672	12,763	9,360	3,403	2.30
1928	30,548	25.4	3,088	4,139	12,691	9,340	3,351	2.30
1927	30,530	25.7	3,126	3,653	12,642	9,278	3,364	2.35
1926	30,979	26.5	3,042	3,421	12,976	9,526	3,450	2.40

Farm Income and Expenses
($000,000)

Year	Realized Gross Farm Income	Cash Receipts from Marketings			Government Payments	Value of Farm Products Consumed in Farm Households	Gross Rental Value of Farm Dwellings
		Total	Crops	Livestock and Livestock Products			
1946	29,539	24,802	11,016	13,786	772	2,662	1,303
1945	25,813	21,663	9,655	12,008	742	2,356	1,052
1944	24,448	20,536	9,185	11,351	776	2,181	955
1943	23,397	19,620	8,127	11,493	645	2,253	879
1942	18,794	15,565	6,526	9,039	650	1,758	821
1941	13,851	11,111	4,619	6,492	544	1,429	767
1940	11,059	8,382	3,469	4,913	723	1,210	744
1939	10,585	7,872	3,336	4,536	763	1,209	741
1938	10,149	7,723	3,200	4,523	446	1,235	745
1937	11,367	8,864	3,924	4,940	336	1,434	733
1936	10,756	8,391	3,649	4,742	278	1,394	693
1935	9,696	7,120	2,977	4,143	573	1,320	683
1934	8,568	6,357	3,021	3,336	446	1,125	640
1933	7,107	5,332	2,486	2,846	131	1,030	614
1932	6,405	4,748	1,996	2,752	—	993	664
1931	8,421	6,381	2,540	3,841	—	1,265	775
1930	11,472	9,055	3,868	5,187	—	1,552	865
1929	13,938	11,312	5,130	6,182	—	1,713	913
1928	13,598	10,991	4,956	6,035	—	1,724	883
1927	13,336	10,733	5,125	5,608	—	1,725	878
1926	13,302	10,558	4,875	5,683	—	1,875	869

Indexes of Prices Received and Paid by Farmers
(1967 = 100)

	Prices Received by Farmers			Prices Paid by Farmers	
Year	All Farm Products	Crops	Livestock and Products	Living	Production
1946	93	104	87	63	67
1945	81	92	76	57	61
1944	78	87	71	54	60
1943	76	85	71	52	57
1942	63	70	62	46	52
1941	49	55	50	40	45
1940	39	44	39	38	43
1939	37	42	39	37	42
1938	38	43	40	38	43
1937	48	54	45	40	46
1936	45	50	43	39	43
1935	43	48	41	39	43
1934	35	40	29	38	40
1933	28	31	25	34	34
1932	26	29	26	33	34
1931	34	38	35	39	39
1930	49	55	48	45	47
1929	58	65	57	48	51
1928	58	65	56	48	52
1927	55	62	53	48	49
1926	57	64	55	49	49

Agriculture — Crops
(Season Average Price)

Year	Corn for All Purposes ($ per Bushel)	Wheat for Grain ($ per Bushel)	Oats for Grain ($ per Bushel)	Barley for Grain ($ per Bushel)	Soybeans for Beans ($ per Bushel)	Sweet Potatoes ($ per 100 lb.)	Rice ($ per 100 lb.)	Cotton (Cents per lb.)
1946	1.53	1.90	.81	1.38	2.57	3.87	5.00	32.64
1945	1.23	1.49	.67	1.01	2.08	3.64	3.98	22.52
1944	1.03	1.41	.71	1.01	2.05	3.40	3.93	20.73
1943	1.12	1.36	.72	.99	1.81	3.85	3.96	19.90
1942	.92	1.10	.49	.63	1.61	2.22	3.61	19.05
1941	.75	.94	.41	.53	1.55	1.71	3.01	17.03
1940	.62	.68	.30	.40	.90	1.59	1.80	9.89
1939	.57	.69	.31	.41	.81	1.35	1.62	9.09
1938	.49	.56	.24	.37	.67	1.31	1.42	8.60
1937	.52	.96	.30	.54	.85	1.41	1.46	8.41
1936	1.04	1.02	.45	.78	1.27	1.70	1.85	12.36
1935	.66	.83	.26	.38	.73	1.25	1.60	11.09
1934	.82	.85	.48	.69	.99	1.41	1.76	12.36
1933	.52	.74	.34	.43	.94	1.29	1.73	10.17
1932	.32	.38	.16	.22	.54	.86	.93	6.52
1931	.32	.39	.21	.33	.50	1.21	1.08	5.66
1930	.60	.67	.32	.41	1.37	2.02	1.74	9.46
1929	.80	1.04	.42	.54	1.88	2.15	2.22	16.78
1928	.84	1.00	.41	.57	1.88	2.07	2.03	17.98
1927	.85	1.19	.47	.69	1.81	1.93	2.02	20.20
1926	.74	1.22	.40	.58	2.01	2.07	2.51	12.49

Agriculture—Livestock, Poultry, and Eggs

	Meat Slaughtering—$ per 100 lb.[1]				Prices Received by Farmers		
Year	Beef[2]	Veal[2]	Pork[3]	Lamb and Mutton	Chickens (Cents per lb.)	Turkeys (Cents per lb.)	Eggs (Cents per Dozen)
1946	19.16	16.87	18.40	18.40	27.6	36.3	37.6
1945	16.18	15.12	14.66	14.90	25.9	33.7	37.7
1944	15.44	14.86	13.57	14.52	23.7	33.9	32.5
1943	15.30	15.18	14.31	14.91	24.3	32.7	37.1
1942	13.79	14.48	13.70	13.82	18.7	27.5	30.0
1941	11.33	12.18	9.45	11.28	15.6	19.9	23.5
1940	10.43	10.61	5.71	9.66	13.0	15.2	18.0
1939	9.75	9.82	6.57	9.33	13.2	15.7	17.4
1938	9.39	9.00	8.09	8.50	14.8	17.5	20.3
1937	11.47	10.07	10.02	10.78	16.0	18.1	21.3
1936	8.82	9.30	9.89	9.91	15.0	15.6	21.8
1935	10.26	8.88	9.27	9.02	14.9	20.1	23.4
1934	6.76	6.10	4.65	8.01	11.1	15.1	17.0
1933	5.42	5.88	3.94	6.65	9.5	11.6	13.8
1932	6.70	6.21	3.83	5.92	11.7	12.8	14.2
1931	8.06	8.33	6.16	7.26	15.8	19.3	17.6
1930	10.95	11.51	9.47	9.69	18.4	20.2	23.7
1929	13.43	14.76	10.16	14.62	22.8	24.5	29.8
1928	13.91	14.56	9.22	14.99	21.4	—	28.1
1927	11.36	12.90	9.95	14.12	20.2	—	25.1
1926	9.47	11.61	12.34	14.26	22.1	—	28.9

[1] At Chicago. [2] Excludes cattle and calves purchased for slaughter for the Federal Surplus Relief Corporation (FSRC) from June 1934–February 1935, and for August 1936. Also excludes cattle for the FSRC for September 1936. [3] Excludes purchases on the Governments account for the Emergency Hog Production Control Program from August 22–October 7, 1933.

Agriculture — Dairy Products

Year	Prices Received by Farmers		Whole Milk		Wholesale Prices	
	Butter (Cents per lb.)	Milkfat in Cream (Cents per lb.)	Wholesale ($ per 100 lb.)	Retail (Cents per Quart)	Cheese, American Twins (Cents per lb.)	Butter at New York (Cents per lb.)
1946	58.3	64.3	3.99	15.2	34.8	62.8
1945	45.3	50.3	3.19	13.4	23.2	42.8
1944	43.8	50.3	3.21	13.2	23.2	42.2
1943	43.7	49.9	3.12	12.7	23.2	44.8
1942	35.2	39.6	2.58	11.8	21.6	40.1
1941	30.4	34.2	2.19	10.8	19.4	34.3
1940	26.6	28.0	NA	10.3	14.3	29.5
1939	25.0	23.9	1.69	10.3	12.8	26.0
1938	26.6	26.3	1.73	10.3	12.6	28.0
1937	29.6	33.3	1.99	10.5	15.9	34.4
1936	28.8	32.2	1.88	10.1	15.3	33.1
1935	26.7	28.1	1.72	9.8	14.3	29.8
1934	22.7	22.7	1.55	9.4	11.8	25.7
1933	20.1	18.8	1.30	8.6	10.2	21.6
1932	20.8	17.9	1.28	8.9	10.0	21.0
1931	27.2	24.8	1.69	10.1	12.5	28.3
1930	36.3	34.5	2.21	11.3	16.4	36.5
1929	42.2	45.2	2.53	11.5	20.2	45.0
1928	42.6	46.1	2.52	11.5	22.1	47.4
1927	41.5	44.5	2.51	11.3	22.7	47.3
1926	40.9	41.6	2.38	11.3	20.1	44.4

Forest Products

Wholesale Price Indexes (1967 = 100)

Year	Lumber	Woodpulp	Paper	Paper Board
1946	44.7	59.5	50.2	54.8
1945	38.9	53.8	45.9	49.9
1944	38.5	53.3	45.5	47.9
1943	35.5	49.3	44.5	46.8
1942	33.4	49.3	43.4	43.4
1941	30.8	47.4	42.3	42.2
1940	25.8	43.0	40.3	37.6
1939	23.4	28.2	38.5	32.9
1938	22.0	32.8	39.4	32.0
1937	25.1	44.6	38.6	37.8
1936	21.9	28.8	36.4	32.1
1935	20.6	27.7	36.2	32.0
1934	21.2	30.0	36.0	36.6
1933	17.8	25.0	34.5	31.9
1932	14.8	24.6	36.2	24.3
1931	17.5	30.7	38.6	24.4
1930	21.5	33.1	39.9	28.8
1929	23.6	33.9	40.0	34.4
1928	22.7	34.0	40.7	37.7
1927	23.5	35.4	41.1	40.8
1926	25.2	38.3	45.0	38.8

Minerals — Price

Year	Pig Iron F.O.B. Valley Furnaces ($ per Long Ton)	Copper New York Electrolytic F.O.B. Refinery (Cents per lb.)	Pig Lead New York (Cents per lb.)	Slab Zinc New York (Cents per lb.)
1946	27.13	13.92	8.11	9.15
1945	24.52	11.87	6.50	8.65
1944	23.50	11.87	6.50	8.65
1943	23.50	11.87	6.50	8.66
1942	23.50	11.87	6.48	8.66
1941	23.50	11.87	5.79	7.87
1940	22.50	11.40	5.18	6.73
1939	21.10	11.07	5.05	5.51
1938	21.71	10.10	4.74	4.99
1937	22.99	13.27	6.01	6.87
1936	19.10	9.58	4.71	5.28
1935	18.17	8.76	4.06	4.70
1934	17.70	8.53	3.86	4.51
1933	15.44	7.15	3.87	4.40
1932	14.25	5.67	3.18	3.25
1931	15.88	8.24	4.24	3.99
1930	17.99	13.11	5.52	4.91
1929	18.20	18.23	6.83	6.84
1928	16.56	14.68	6.31	6.38
1927	17.71	13.05	6.75	6.60
1926	18.55	13.95	8.42	7.72

Construction — Value and Cost Indexes

Private Construction ($000,000)

Year	Residential Including Farm	Nonresidential Excluding Farm	Farm Nonresidential	Construction Costs Indexes (1967 = 100)[1]
1946	4,752	3,341	447	45
1945	1,376	1,020	167	39
1944	923	351	175	37
1943	1,006	233	163	38
1942	1,850	635	125	35
1941	3,692	1,482	128	31
1940	3,130	1,025	95	29
1939	2,786	786	106	28
1938	2,069	764	92	30
1937	1,975	1,085	107	30
1936	1,641	713	85	28
1935	1,071	472	65	27
1934	661	456	30	28
1933	499	406	20	25
1932	654	502	13	23
1931	1,624	1,099	38	27
1930	2,182	2,003	86	29
1929	3,772	2,694	160	30
1928	4,926	2,573	175	30
1927	5,320	2,534	195	30
1926	5,737	2,513	160	30

[1] *Department of Commerce composite.*

Rail and Highway Transportation

Year	Revenue Freight-All Tonnage (000)[1]	Total Railroad Operating Revenue ($000)	Railroad Employees Number (000)	Railroad Employees Compensation ($000,000)	Passenger Car Sales, Number (000)
1946	1,366,617	7,709,171	1,378	4,214	2,148.6
1945	1,424,913	8,986,954	1,439	3,901	69.5
1944	1,491,491	9,524,628	1,434	3,898	.6
1943	1,481,225	9,138,419	1,375	3,556	.1
1942	1,421,187	7,547,826	1,291	2,966	222.8
1941	1,227,650	5,413,972	1,159	2,360	3,779.6
1940	1,009,421	4,354,712	1,046	1,991	3,717.3
1939	901,669	4,050,047	1,007	1,889	2,888.5
1938	771,862	3,616,072	958	1,771	2,019.5
1937	1,015,586	4,226,325	1,137	2,014	3,929.2
1936	958,830	4,108,658	1,086	1,874	3,679.2
1935	789,627	3,499,126	1,014	1,666	3,273.8
1934	765,296	3,316,861	1,027	1,541	2,160.8
1933	698,943	3,138,186	991	1,424	1,560.5
1932	646,223	3,168,537	1,052	1,535	1,103.5
1931	894,186	4,246,385	1,283	2,125	1,948.1
1930	1,153,197	5,356,484	1,517	2,589	2,787.4
1929	1,339,091	6,373,004	1,694	2,940	4,455.1
1928	1,285,943	6,212,464	1,692	2,874	3,775.4
1927	1,281,611	6,245,716	1,776	2,963	2,936.5
1926	1,336,142	6,508,679	1,822	3,002	3,692.3

[1] *In tons of 2000 pounds.*

Telephones

Year	Number (000)	Per 1,000 Population	Households with (Percent)	Residence (000)	Business (000)
1946	31,611	221.3	51.4	21,239	10,372
1945	27,867	198.1	46.2	18,409	9,458
1944	26,859	192.9	45.1	17,791	9,068
1943	26,381	191.6	45.0	17,706	8,675
1942	24,919	183.4	42.2	16,619	8,300
1941	23,521	175.3	39.3	15,453	8,068
1940	21,928	165.1	36.9	14,271	7,657
1939	20,831	158.3	35.6	13,446	7,385
1938	19,953	153.0	34.6	12,727	7,226
1937	19,453	150.4	34.3	12,341	7,112
1936	18,433	143.5	33.1	11,654	6,779
1935	17,424	136.4	31.8	11,003	6,421
1934	16,869	133.0	31.4	10,683	6,186
1933	16,628	132.0	31.3	10,475	6,153
1932	17,341	138.5	33.5	11,054	6,287
1931	19,602	157.5	39.2	12,754	6,848
1930	20,103	162.6	40.9	13,153	6,950
1929	19,970	163.1	41.6	13,135	6,835
1928	19,256	158.9	40.8	12,645	6,611
1927	18,446	153.9	39.7	12,086	6,360
1926	17,680	149.5	39.2	11,689	5,991

Average Annual Earnings per Full-Time Employee in Distribution and Selected Service Industries ($)

Year	Wholesale Trade	Retail Trade[1]	Hotels and Other Lodging	Personal Services	Miscellaneous Business Services	Miscellaneous Repair Services	Motion Pictures	Amusement and Recreation exc. Movies
1946	3,021	2,141	1,745	1,854	2,861	2,766	2,978	2,185
1945	2,751	1,879	1,612	1,709	2,739	2,810	2,567	1,888
1944	2,600	1,709	1,455	1,570	2,584	2,901	2,379	1,663
1943	2,416	1,555	1,269	1,384	2,332	2,641	2,250	1,461
1942	2,177	1,395	1,097	1,196	2,072	2,152	2,124	1,328
1941	1,943	1,299	1,025	1,075	1,967	1,891	2,016	1,292
1940	1,754	1,236	997	1,042	1,889	1,579	1,948	1,280
1939	1,698	1,224	958	1,034	1,886	1,603	1,971	1,277
1938	1,686	1,217	946	992	1,899	1,552	1,942	1,270
1937	1,693	1,218	941	978	1,966	1,544	1,972	1,269
1936	1,652	1,159	897	940	1,915	1,456	1,896	1,232
1935	1,640	1,139	878	915	1,884	1,429	1,892	1,193
1934	1,550	1,102	863	905	1,709	1,339	1,844	1,190
1933	1,477	1,066	816	889	1,653	1,286	1,891	1,185
1932	1,672	1,173	908	996	1,844	1,464	1,959	1,218
1931	1,934	1,324	1,030	1,136	2,255	1,684	2,179	1,244
1930	2,039	1,384	1,097	1,200	2,412	1,793	2,175	1,268
1929	2,072	1,409	1,098	1,219	2,274	1,814	2,169	1,273
1928	—	—	—	—	—	—	—	—
1927	—	—	—	—	—	—	—	—
1926	—	—	—	—	—	—	—	—

[1] Includes automobile repair, services, and garages.

Average Annual Earnings per Full-Time Employee in Distribution and Selected Service Industries ($), *continued*

Year	Medical and Other Health Services	Legal Services	Educational Services	Miscellaneous Professional Services	Nonprofit Membership Organizations
1946	1,605	1,757	1,802	3,280	1,984
1945	1,401	1,856	1,641	3,258	1,876
1944	1,262	1,653	1,562	3,237	1,795
1943	1,127	1,423	1,469	3,063	1,679
1942	1,036	1,324	1,344	2,654	1,482
1941	955	1,265	1,264	2,245	1,379
1940	927	1,224	1,240	1,902	1,408
1939	908	1,198	1,234	1,973	1,546
1938	899	1,205	1,228	1,909	1,529
1937	876	1,231	1,211	1,774	1,497
1936	851	1,200	1,180	1,759	1,465
1935	829	1,163	1,162	1,600	1,435
1934	801	1,160	1,175	1,609	1,440
1933	810	1,168	1,189	1,619	1,442
1932	865	1,260	1,279	1,714	1,545
1931	919	1,333	1,323	1,897	1,653
1930	933	1,394	1,329	2,027	1,698
1929	925	1,378	1,312	2,314	1,712
1928	—	—	—	—	—
1927	—	—	—	—	—
1926	—	—	—	—	—

Electric Production, and Residential Service

Year	Total Util. and Ind.	Net Production[1] (000,000 kW-hr) Electric Utilities	Industrial Establishments	Annual Use per Customer (kW-hr)	Residential Service Percentage of Dwelling Units with Electric Service All Dwellings	Farm
1946	269,609	223,178	46,431	1,329	85.5	53.3
1945	271,255	222,486	48,769	1,229	85.0	48.0
1944	279,525	228,189	51,336	1,151	84.0	42.2
1943	267,540	217,759	49,781	1,070	81.3	40.0
1942	233,146	185,979	47,167	1,022	81.2	37.8
1941	208,306	164,788	43,518	986	80.0	35.0
1940	179,907	141,837	38,070	952	78.7	32.6
1939	161,308	127,642	33,666	897	77.3	27.4
1938	141,955	113,812	28,143	853	74.9	23.9
1937	146,476	118,913	27,563	805	73.1	18.3
1936	136,006	109,316	26,690	735	70.3	14.5
1935	118,935	95,287	23,648	677	68.0	12.6
1934	110,404	87,258	23,146	629	67.1	12.1
1933	102,655	81,740	20,915	600	66.7	11.8
1932	99,359	79,393	19,966	601	67.0	11.2
1931	109,373	87,350	22,023	583	67.4	10.7
1930	114,637	91,112	23,525	547	68.2	10.4
1929	116,747	92,180	24,567	502	67.9	9.2
1928	108,069	82,794	25,275	463	65.0	7.3
1927	101,390	75,418	25,972	446	63.1	5.9
1926	94,222	69,353	24,869	430	57.9	4.8

[1] Net production data include generation by manufacturing and extracting industries and by electric railroads and railways. Excluded are nonutility generating plants of less than 100 kW; plants operated by hotels, apartment houses, office buildings, or other commercial, transport, or service establishments; and plants in military installations.

Value of Exports and Imports
($000,000)

Total Merchandise, Gold, and Silver

Year	Exports	Imports	Excess of Exports (+) or Imports (−)
1946	9,996	5,533	+ 4,464
1945	10,097	4,280	+ 5,816
1944	15,345	4,066	+ 11,279
1943	13,028	3,511	+ 9,517
1942	8,081	3,113	+ 4,968
1941	5,153	4,375	+ 778
1940	4,030	7,433	− 3,403
1939	3,192	5,978	− 2,786
1938	3,107	4,170	− 1,063
1937	3,407	4,807	− 1,400
1936	2,495	3,750	− 1,254
1935	2,304	4,143	− 1,839
1934	2,202	2,944	− 742
1933	2,061	1,703	+ 358
1932	2,434	1,706	+ 729
1931	2,918	2,731	+ 186
1930	4,013	3,500	+ 514
1929	5,441	4,755	+ 686
1928	5,776	4,328	+ 1,448
1927	5,142	4,447	+ 695
1926	5,017	4,714	+ 303

Retail Stores Sales by Kind of Store
($000,000)

	Total Durable and Nondurable Goods Stores	Total Sales[1] of Durable Goods	Durable Goods Stores			
			Furniture, Home Furnishings Stores	Household Appliance Stores	Hardware Stores	Jewelry Stores
Year						
1946	102,488	27,570	3,264	1,575	1,911	1,260
1945	78,034	16,026	2,101	639	1,237	997
1944	70,208	13,942	1,848	462	1,030	909
1943	63,235	12,221	1,692	415	903	894
1942	57,212	12,320	1,776	594	973	710
1941	55,274	17,213	1,780	796	905	566
1940	46,375	13,576	1,386	625	712	422
1939	42,042	11,312	1,200	533	629	362
1938	38,053	9,475	1,014	476	563	299
1937	42,150	12,048	1,254	592	651	347
1936	38,339	10,751	1,082	533	576	297
1935	32,791	8,321	852	438	467	235
1934	—	—	—	—	—	—
1933	24,517	5,384	646	313	311	175
1932	—	—	—	—	—	—
1931	—	—	—	—	—	—
1930	—	—	—	—	—	—
1929	48,459	15,610	1,813	942	706	536
1928	—	—	—	—	—	—
1927	—	—	—	—	—	—
1926	—	—	—	—	—	—

[1] Includes subclasses not shown separately.

Retail Stores Sales by Kind of Store, *continued*
($000,000)

Nondurable Goods Stores

Year	Total Sales[1] of Nondurable Goods	Apparel Stores	Drug and Proprietary Stores	Eating and Drinking Places	Grocery Stores	General Merchandise Stores
1946	74,918	8,880	3,723	10,619	18,640	14,724
1945	62,008	7,689	3,155	9,575	14,593	11,802
1944	56,266	6,704	2,924	8,305	13,665	11,076
1943	51,014	6,158	2,628	7,216	12,481	10,162
1942	44,892	5,089	2,213	5,699	11,368	9,204
1941	38,061	4,137	1,847	4,570	9,312	7,973
1940	32,799	3,451	1,636	3,787	8,169	6,859
1939	30,730	3,259	1,563	3,529	7,722	6,475
1938	28,578	2,998	1,474	3,188	7,187	6,145
1937	30,102	3,323	1,527	3,293	7,266	6,673
1936	27,588	3,102	1,409	2,748	6,850	6,366
1935	24,470	2,656	1,233	2,395	6,352	5,730
1934	—	—	—	—	—	—
1933	19,133	1,930	1,066	1,434	5,004	4,982
1932	—	—	—	—	—	—
1931	—	—	—	—	—	—
1930	—	—	—	—	—	—
1929	32,849	4,241	1,690	2,132	7,353	9,015
1928	—	—	—	—	—	—
1927	—	—	—	—	—	—
1926	—	—	—	—	—	—

[1] *Includes subclasses not shown separately.*

Business

		Business Failures		
Year	Total Concerns in Business (000)	Total Number of Failures	Total Current Liabilities ($000,000)	Business Failure Rate[1]
1946	2,142	1,129	67	5
1945	1,909	809	30	4
1944	1,855	1,222	32	7
1943	2,023	3,221	45	16
1942	2,152	9,405	101	45
1941	2,171	11,848	136	55
1940	2,156	13,619	167	63
1939	2,116	14,768	183	70
1938	2,102	12,836	247	61
1937	2,057	9,490	183	46
1936	2,010	9,607	203	48
1935	1,983	12,244	311	62
1934	1,974	12,091	334	61
1933	1,961	19,859	458	100
1932	2,077	31,822	928	154
1931	2,125	28,285	736	133
1930	2,183	26,355	668	122
1929	2,213	22,909	483	104
1928	2,199	23,842	490	109
1927	2,172	23,146	520	106
1926	2,158	21,773	409	101

[1] *Per 10,000 enterprises.*

Indexes of National Productivity

Real Gross Private Domestic Product
(per Man-Hour) 1958 = 100

Year	Total Economy	Farm	Nonfarm
1946	68.7	51.4	73.3
1945	70.7	47.9	76.8
1944	67.2	47.6	72.7
1943	63.0	47.9	67.4
1942	62.0	49.9	66.7
1941	61.8	47.7	67.2
1940	58.5	42.7	66.1
1939	56.9	44.2	63.6
1938	54.7	43.3	61.4
1937	53.1	40.3	59.7
1936	53.2	37.0	60.2
1935	50.6	39.2	57.7
1934	49.0	36.2	55.9
1933	44.5	38.9	50.4
1932	45.4	39.8	51.6
1931	47.2	39.5	53.3
1930	46.8	35.6	52.5
1929	48.6	37.3	54.1
1928	—	—	—
1927	—	—	—
1926	—	—	—

Net Public and Private Debt
(Billions of Dollars)

Year	Total Public and Private	Total Public	Total Corporate, Individual and Noncorporate	Private Corporate	Private Individual and Noncorporate
1946	396.6	243.2	153.4	93.5	59.9
1945	405.9	265.9	140.0	85.3	54.7
1944	370.6	225.8	144.8	94.1	50.7
1943	313.2	168.9	144.3	95.5	48.8
1942	258.6	117.1	141.5	91.6	49.9
1941	211.4	72.4	139.0	83.4	55.6
1940	189.8	61.2	128.6	75.6	53.0
1939	183.3	59.0	124.3	73.5	50.8
1938	179.9	56.6	123.3	73.3	50.0
1937	182.2	55.3	126.9	75.8	51.1
1936	180.6	53.9	126.7	76.1	50.6
1935	175.0	50.5	124.5	74.8	49.7
1934	171.6	46.3	125.3	75.5	49.8
1933	168.5	40.6	127.9	76.9	51.0
1932	175.0	37.9	137.1	80.0	57.1
1931	182.9	34.5	148.4	83.5	64.9
1930	192.3	31.2	161.1	89.3	71.8
1929	191.9	30.1	161.8	88.9	72.9
1928	186.3	30.2	156.1	86.1	70.0
1927	177.9	30.3	147.6	81.2	66.4
1926	169.2	30.3	138.9	76.2	62.7

Currency Stock and Currency in Circulation — as of June 30
($000)

			Currency Outside Treasury	
Year	Total Currency in U.S.[1]	Currency Held in Treasury[2]	In Federal Reserve Banks	In Circulation
1946	49,648,011	17,539,072	3,863,941	28,244,997
1945	48,009,400	17,517,449	3,745,512	26,746,438
1944	44,805,301	18,489,163	3,811,797	22,504,342
1943	40,868,266	19,676,674	3,770,331	17,421,260
1942	35,840,908	19,937,577	3,520,465	12,382,866
1941	32,774,611	19,781,266	3,380,914	9,612,432
1940	28,457,960	17,124,764	3,485,695	7,847,501
1939	23,754,736	13,271,527	3,436,467	7,046,743
1938	20,096,865	10,132,397	3,503,576	6,460,891
1937	19,376,690	9,475,429	3,454,205	6,447,056
1936	17,402,493	7,800,438	3,360,854	6,241,200
1935	15,113,035	8,398,521	1,147,422	5,567,093
1934	13,634,381[3]	6,953,734	1,305,985	5,373,470
1933	10,078,417	2,085,971	2,271,682	5,720,764
1932	9,004,505	1,513,985	1,795,349	5,695,171
1931	9,079,624	2,031,632	2,226,059	4,821,933
1930	8,306,564	2,043,489	1,741,087	4,521,988
1929	8,538,796	1,935,513	1,856,986	4,746,297
1928	8,118,091	1,738,889	1,582,576	4,796,626
1927	8,667,282	2,062,851	1,753,110	4,851,321
1926	8,428,971	2,070,588	1,473,118	4,885,266

[1] *Excludes gold certificates, silver certificates, since the gold and silver held as security against them are included.*
[2] *Includes coin, bullion, and paper money. Includes the following categories of currency: Reserves held against U.S. notes and Treasury notes of 1890, held for Federal Reserve banks and agents, and all other money. Excludes amount held as security against gold and silver certificates since the certificates and notes are included elsewhere; for 1860–1933 they are included as currency outside the Treasury, and beginning in 1934 they were included either as currency outside the Treasury or as amounts held in Treasury for Federal Reserve banks and agents payable in gold certificates.*
[3] *Agrees with source; however, figures for components do not add to total shown.*

Interest Rates, Stocks Volume, Consumer Credit, and Banks

Year	U.S. Government Bonds Interest Rates (Percent per Annum)	Stocks Volume—NYS (000,000)	Total Credit Outstanding	Short— and Intermediate—Term Credit ($000,000) Installment Credit Outstanding	Non-Installment Credit Outstanding	Number of Banks (as of June 30)
1946	2.19	364	8,384	4,172	4,212	14,685
1945	2.37	378	5,665	2,462	3,203	14,660
1944	2.48	263	5,111	2,176	2,935	14,674
1943	2.47	279	4,901	2,136	2,765	14,734
1942	2.46	126	5,983	3,166	2,817	14,891
1941	2.05	171	9,172	6,085	3,087	14,975
1940	2.26	208	8,338	5,514	2,824	15,076
1939	2.41	262	7,222	4,503	2,719	15,210
1938	2.61	297	6,370	3,686	2,684	15,419
1937	2.74	409	6,948	4,118	2,830	15,646
1936	2.69	496	6,375	3,747	2,628	15,884
1935	2.79	382	5,190	2,817	2,373	16,047
1934	3.12	324	4,218	1,999	2,219	15,913
1933	3.31	655	3,885	1,723	2,162	14,771
1932	3.68	425	4,026	1,672	2,354	19,317
1931	3.34	577	5,315	2,463	2,852	22,242
1930	3.29	810	6,351	3,022	3,329	24,273
1929	3.60	1,125	7,116	3,524	3,592	25,568
1928	3.33	920	6,258	2,935	3,323	26,401
1927	3.34	577	5,344	2,319	3,025	27,255
1926	3.68	451	5,227	2,363	2,864	28,350

Life Insurance Companies and Sales

Year	Number of Companies (as of Dec. 31)	Sales of Life Insurance, by U.S. Companies ($000,000)			
		Total	Ordinary	Group	Industrial
1946	514	22,805	16,244	2,152	4,409
1945	473	15,391	10,577	1,302	3,512
1944	451	14,124	9,184	1,621	3,319
1943	437	13,281	8,022	1,924	3,335
1942	435	11,888	7,041	1,657	3,190
1941	438	12,564	7,935	1,197	3,432
1940	444	11,087	7,022	747	3,318
1939	446	10,935	6,886	844	3,205
1938	435	11,045	6,745	507	3,793
1937	436	12,572	7,593	800	4,179
1936	372	12,165	7,314	626	4,225
1935	373	12,298	7,550	715	4,033
1934	371	11,928	7,363	534	4,031
1933	375	10,846	6,786	427	3,633
1932	392	12,305	7,896	720	3,689
1931	413	15,066	10,161	927	3,978
1930	438	17,265	11,905	1,381	3,979
1929	438	17,755	12,305	1,379	4,071
1928	433	16,942	11,654	1,508	3,780
1927	407	15,582	10,777	1,008	3,797
1926	396	15,217	10,508	1,174	3,535

Federal Government Employment and Finances

Finances ($000) (Years Ending June 30)

Year	Total Paid Civilian Employees (as of June 30)	Receipts[1]	Expenditures[2]	Surplus or Deficit(−)[3]	Total Gross Debt[4]
1946	2,696,529	39,771,404	60,447,574	−20,676,171	269,422,099
1945	3,816,310	44,475,304	98,416,220	−53,940,916	258,682,187
1944	3,332,356	43,635,315	95,058,708	−51,423,393	201,003,387
1943	3,299,414	21,986,701	79,407,131	−57,420,430	136,696,090
1942	2,296,384	12,555,436	34,045,679	−21,490,243	72,422,445
1941	1,437,682	7,102,931	13,262,204	−6,159,272	48,961,444
1940	1,042,420	5,144,013	9,062,032	−3,918,019	42,967,531
1939	953,891	4,966,300	8,858,458	−3,862,158	40,439,532
1938	882,226	5,615,221	6,791,838	−1,176,617	37,164,740
1937	895,993	4,978,601	7,756,021	−2,777,421	36,424,614
1936	867,432	4,068,937	8,493,486	−4,424,549	33,778,543
1935	780,582	3,729,914	6,520,966	−2,791,052	28,700,893
1934	698,649	3,064,268	6,693,900	−3,629,632	27,053,141
1933	603,587	2,021,213	4,622,865	−2,601,652	22,538,673
1932	605,496	1,923,913	4,659,203	−2,735,290	19,487,002
1931	609,746	3,115,557	3,577,434	−461,877	16,801,281
1930	601,319	4,177,942	3,440,269	737,673	16,185,310
1929	579,559	4,033,250	3,298,859	734,391	16,931,088
1928	560,772	4,042,348	3,103,265	939,083	17,604,293
1927	547,127	4,129,394	2,974,030	1,155,365	18,511,907
1926	548,713	3,962,756	3,097,612	865,144	19,643,216

[1] Excludes receipts from borrowing. Prior to 1931, total receipts; thereafter, net receipts. [2] Excludes debt repayment. Prior to 1931, total expenditures; thereafter, net expenditures. [3] Receipts compared with expenditures. [4] As of end of period.

[p. 293] Various Social and Economic Data for Selected Years Pre-, Post-, and During the Great Depression

ITEMS	NUMERICAL VALUES					PERCENTAGE CHANGE			
	1926	1929	1933	1937	1946	1929–33	1933–37	1937–46	1926–46
United States Pop.(Est.)—000 Total	117,397	121,767	125,579	128,825	141,389	3.1	2.6	9.8	20.4
Age Group (in years)									
Under 5	12,189	11,734	10,612	10,009	13,244	−9.6	−5.7	32.3	8.7
5–14	23,906	24,470	24,531	23,564	21,844	0.2	−3.9	−7.3	−8.6
15–24	21,037	22,151	22,820	23,487	23,382	3.0	2.9	−0.4	11.1
25–34	18,867	18,941	19,750	20,723	22,954	4.3	4.9	10.8	21.7
35–44	15,847	16,921	17,569	17,866	20,073	3.8	1.7	12.4	26.7
45–54	11,786	12,761	13,684	14,785	16,820	7.2	8.0	13.8	42.7
55 and over	13,765	14,789	16,612	18,390	23,072	12.3	10.7	25.5	67.6
International Migration—Immigrants to the United States									
All Countries	304,488	279,678	23,068	50,244	108,721	−91.8	117.8	116.4	−64.3
Europe									
Total	155,562	158,598	12,383	31,863	52,852	−92.2	157.3	65.9	−66.0
Northwestern	76,016	67,718	2,873	5,740	45,297	−95.8	99.8	689.1	−40.4
Central	63,567	63,834	4,232	15,870	3,444	−93.4	275.0	−78.3	−94.6
Eastern	4,919	4,603	810	1,162	251	−82.4	43.5	−78.4	−94.9
Southern	11,060	22,443	4,468	9,091	3,860	−80.1	103.5	−57.5	−65.1
Asia	3,413	3,758	552	1,149	2,108	−85.3	108.2	83.5	−38.2
America	144,393	116,177	9,925	16,903	46,066	−91.5	70.3	172.5	−68.1
Africa	529	509	71	155	1,516	−86.1	118.3	878.1	186.6
Australasia[1]	591	636	137	174	6,106	−78.5	27.0	3,409.2	933.2
All Other Countries	—	—	—	—	73	—	—	—	—

[1] *Australia, New Zealand, and other Pacific Islands.*

[p. 294] **Various Social and Economic Data for Selected Years Pre-, Post-, and During the Great Depression,** *continued*

ITEMS	NUMERICAL VALUES					PERCENTAGE CHANGE			
	1926	1929	1933	1937	1946	1929–33	1933–37	1937–46	1926–46
Vital Statistics									
Marriages (000)	1,203	1,233	1,098	1,451	2,291	−10.9	32.1	57.9	90.4
Divorces (000)[1]	185	206	165	249	610	−19.9	50.9	145.0	229.7
Birth Rate-Live Births per 1000 Total Population	24.2	21.2	18.4	18.7	24.1	−13.2	1.6	28.9	−0.4
Expectation of Life (In Years) at Birth									
Both Sexes	56.7	57.1	63.3	60.0	66.7	10.9	−5.2	11.2	17.6
Male	55.5	55.8	61.7	58.0	64.4	10.6	−6.0	11.0	16.0
Female	58.0	58.7	65.1	62.4	69.4	10.9	−4.1	11.2	19.7
Death Rate per 100,000 Population									
Accidental Falls	14.0	14.5	15.1	20.4	16.1	4.1	35.1	−21.1	15.0
Suicide	12.6	13.9	15.9	15.0	11.5	14.4	−5.7	−23.3	−8.7
Social Welfare Expenditures Under Public Programs ($000,000)									
Total Expenditures									
Total	—	3,921	4,462	7,858	12,798	13.8	76.1	62.9	—
Percent of Gross National Product	—	3.9	7.9	9.1	6.1	102.6	15.2	−33.0	—
Social Insurance	—	342	344	545	3,652	0.1	58.4	570.1	—
Public Aid	—	60	689	3,436	1,151	1,048.3	398.7	−66.5	—
Health and Medical Programs	—	351	418	500	1,904	19.1	19.6	280.8	—
Education	—	2,434	2,104	2,376	3,297	−13.6	12.9	38.8	—
Veterans Programs	—	658	819	893	2,403	24.5	9.0	169.1	—
Housing	—	—	—	3	159	—	—	5,200.0	—
Other Social Welfare	—	76	89	105	233	17.1	18.0	121.9	—

[1] *Includes reported annulments.*

[p. 295] Various Social and Economic Data for Selected Years Pre-, Post-, and During the Great Depression, *continued*

ITEMS	NUMERICAL VALUES					PERCENTAGE CHANGE			
	1926	1929	1933	1937	1946	1929–33	1933–37	1937–46	1926–46
Recreation (000)									
Visits to National Parks[1]	1,942	2,757	2,867	6,705	8,991	4.0	133.9	34.1	363.0
Visits to National Monuments[1]	373	491	523	1,966	3,603	6.5	275.9	83.3	866.0
American League Baseball Attendance	4,913	4,662	2,926	4,736	9,621	−37.2	61.9	103.1	95.8
National League Baseball Attendance	4,920	4,926	3,163	4,204	8,902	−35.8	32.9	111.8	80.9
Education									
Enrollment-Public Day Schools (000)									
Total	24,741	—	—	—	23,300	—	—	—	−5.8
Kindergarten	673	—	—	—	773	—	—	—	14.9
Elementary	20,311	—	—	—	16,905	—	—	—	−16.8
Secondary	3,757	—	—	—	5,622	—	—	—	49.6
Institutions of Higher Learning— Degrees Conferred									
Total All Degrees	108,407	—	—	—	157,349	—	—	—	45.1
Bachelor's or First Professional	97,263	—	—	—	136,174	—	—	—	40.0
Master's or Second Professional	9,735	—	—	—	19,209	—	—	—	97.3
Doctor's or Equivalent	1,409	—	—	—	1,966	—	—	—	39.5

1. *For years ending September 30 prior to 1941; thereafter, for years ending December 31, or as of January 1 of the following year. Includes areas in Alaska, Hawaii, Virgin Islands and Puerto Rico.*

[p. 296] **Various Social and Economic Data for Selected Years Pre-, Post-, and During the Great Depression,** *continued*

ITEMS	NUMERICAL VALUES					PERCENTAGE CHANGE			
	1926	1929	1933	1937	1946	1929–33	1933–37	1937–46	1926–46
Crime and Correction									
Homicides									
Number	8,740	9,637	12,124	9,811	8,913	25.8	–19.1	–9.2	2.0
Rate[1]	8.4	8.4	9.7	7.6	6.4	15.5	–21.6	–15.8	–23.8
Suicides									
Number	13,802	16,045	19,993	19,294	16,152	24.6	–3.5	–16.3	17.0
Rate[1]	12.6	13.9	15.9	15.0	11.5	14.4	–5.7	–23.3	–8.7
Prisoners Present (at End of Year)									
Total	96,125	120,496	136,947	149,357	140,079	13.7	9.1	–6.2	45.7
Federal Institutions	6,803	12,964	10,851	15,309	17,622	–16.3	41.1	15.1	159.0
State Institutions	89,322	107,532	126,096	134,048	122,457	17.3	6.3	–8.6	37.1
Unemployed—14 years and older—annual averages									
Total Civilian (000)	801	1,550	12,830	7,700	2,270	727.7	–40.0	–70.5	183.4
Percent of Civilian Labor Force	1.8	3.2	24.9	14.3	3.9	678.1	–42.6	–72.7	116.7

[1] *Rates per 100,000 of resident population.*

[p. 297] **Various Social and Economic Data for Selected Years Pre-, Post-, and During the Great Depression,** *continued*

ITEMS	NUMERICAL VALUES					PERCENTAGE CHANGE			
	1926	1929	1933	1937	1946	1929–33	1933–37	1937–46	1926–46
Indexes of Employee Output 1958 = 100									
Output per Man-Hour									
Total[1]	45.7	48.6	44.5	53.1	68.7	− 8.4	19.3	29.4	50.3
Nonfarm[2]	51.4	54.1	50.4	59.7	73.3	− 6.8	18.5	22.8	42.6
Manufacturing	46.5	52.0	54.9	60.7	65.8	5.6	10.6	8.4	41.5
Farm	34.8	37.3	38.9	40.3	51.4	4.3	3.6	27.5	47.7
Earnings (in Current Dollars)									
Agriculture, Forestry, and Fisheries[3]	386	401	232	360	1,200	−42.1	55.2	233.3	210.9
Manufacturing	1,476	1,543	1,086	1,376	2,517	−29.6	26.7	82.9	70.5
Mining	1,597	1,526	990	1,366	2,719	−35.1	38.0	99.0	70.3
Construction	1,664	1,674	869	1,278	2,537	−48.1	47.1	98.5	52.5
Transportation	1,562	1,643	1,334	1,644	2,973	−18.8	23.2	80.8	90.3
Communications and Public Utilities	1,427	1,478	1,351	1,600	2,582	− 8.6	18.4	61.4	80.9
Wholesale and Retail Trade	1,416	1,594	1,183	1,352	2,378	−25.8	14.3	75.9	67.9
Finance, Insurance, and Real Estate	2,008	2,062	1,555	1,788	2,570	−24.6	15.0	43.7	28.0
Services	1,005	1,079	854	938	1,863	−20.9	9.8	98.6	85.4
Government									
Total	1,482	1,551	1,328	1,355	2,351	−14.4	2.0	73.5	58.6
State and Local[4]	1,422	1,504	1,338	1,441	2,117	−11.0	7.7	46.9	48.9
Public Education	1,342	1,445	1,300	1,367	2,025	−10.0	5.2	48.1	50.9
Federal Civilian[5]	1,888	1,933	1,673	1,797	2,801	−13.5	7.4	55.9	48.4

[1] *For total private domestic economy.* [2] *For nonfarm business economy.* [3] *Prior to 1929, agriculture only.* [4] *Prior to 1929, general government only.* [5] *Prior to 1929, includes work relief.*

[p. 298] **Various Social and Economic Data for Selected Years Pre-, Post-, and During the Great Depression,** *continued*

ITEMS	NUMERICAL VALUES					PERCENTAGE CHANGE			
	1926	1929	1933	1937	1946	1929–33	1933–37	1937–46	1926–46
Wholesale Price Indexes, by Major Product Groups (1967 = 100)									
All Commodities	51.6	49.1	34.0	44.5	62.3	−30.8	30.9	40.0	20.7
Industrial Commodities	53.2	48.6	37.8	45.2	58.0	−22.2	19.6	28.3	9.0
Farm Products	61.3	64.1	31.4	52.9	90.9	−51.0	68.5	71.8	48.3
Fuels & Related Products & Power	71.5	59.4	47.6	55.5	64.4	−19.9	16.6	16.0	−9.9
Lumber and Wood Products	26.5	25.0	19.0	26.5	47.2	−24.0	39.5	78.1	78.1
Metals and Metal Products	41.4	40.2	30.7	39.4	44.3	−23.6	28.3	12.4	7.0
Furniture and Household Durables	59.1	55.8	44.6	54.1	67.1	−20.1	21.3	24.0	13.5
Motor Vehicle and Equipment	41.9	41.9	34.8	37.4	56.0	−16.9	7.5	49.7	33.7
Wholesale Prices of Selected Commodities (in Dollars per Unit)									
Wheat – bu.	1.496	1.180	.724	1.201	1.895	−38.6	65.9	57.8	26.7
Sugar – lb.	.055	.051	.043	.047	.064	−15.7	9.3	36.2	16.4
Wool – lb.	1.152	.987	.663	.971	1.025	−32.8	46.5	5.6	−11.0
Steel Rails – gross ton	43.00	43.00	39.33	41.89	47.90	−8.5	6.5	14.3	11.4
Nails – 100 lbs.	2.750	2.667	2.089	2.773	3.477	−21.7	32.7	25.4	26.4
Consumer Price Indexes (1967 = 100)									
All Items	53.0	51.3	38.8	43.0	58.5	−24.4	10.8	36.0	10.4
Food at Home	50.0	48.3	30.6	38.4	58.1	−36.6	25.5	51.3	16.2
Housing									
Rent	81.0	76.0	54.1	54.2	59.2	−28.8	0.2	9.2	−26.9
House furnishings	59.6	56.2	42.4	52.4	80.0	−24.6	23.6	52.7	34.2
Apparel	50.8	48.5	36.9	43.2	67.5	−23.9	17.1	56.3	32.9

[p. 299] **Various Social and Economic Data for Selected Years Pre-, Post-, and During the Great Depression,** *continued*

	NUMERICAL VALUES					PERCENTAGE CHANGE			
ITEMS	1926	1929	1933	1937	1946	1929–33	1933–37	1937–46	1926–46
Retail Prices of Selected Foods in U.S. Cities (In Cents per Unit Indicated)									
Flour – 5 lb.	30.0	25.5	19.5	24.0	35.4	–23.5	23.1	47.5	18.0
Bread – lb.	9.3	8.8	7.1	8.6	10.4	–19.3	21.1	20.9	11.8
Coffee – lb.	50.2	47.9	26.4	25.5	34.4	–44.9	–3.4	34.9	–31.5
Sugar – 5 lb.	34.0	32.0	26.5	28.2	38.4	–17.2	6.4	36.2	12.9
Meats									
Round Steak – lb.	37.1	46.0	25.7	39.1	52.1	–44.1	52.1	33.2	40.4
Chuck Roast – lb.	23.7	31.4	16.0	25.7	36.6	–49.0	60.6	42.4	54.4
Pork Chops – lb.	39.9	37.5	19.8	36.7	48.5	–47.2	85.4	32.2	21.6
Bacon – lb.	50.8	43.9	22.6	41.3	53.3	–48.5	82.7	29.1	4.9
Dairy Products									
Butter – lb.	53.6	55.5	27.8	40.7	71.0	–49.9	46.4	74.4	32.5
Eggs – doz.	51.9	52.7	28.8	36.2	58.6	–45.4	25.7	61.9	12.9
Milk Delivered – ½ gal.	28.0	28.8	20.8	25.0	35.2	–27.8	20.2	40.8	25.7
Fruits and Vegetables									
Oranges – doz.	51.6	44.7	27.3	38.9	49.9	–38.9	42.5	28.3	–3.3
Potatoes – 10 lb.	49.0	32.0	23.0	27.9	46.8	–28.1	21.3	67.7	–4.5
Tomatoes Canned – 303 can	9.9	10.8	7.7	7.9	12.6	–28.7	2.6	59.5	27.3
Navy Beans – lb.	9.4	14.1	5.3	9.6	14.0	–62.4	81.1	45.8	48.9

[p. 300] Various Social and Economic Data for Selected Years Pre-, Post-, and During the Great Depression, *continued*

ITEMS	NUMERICAL VALUES					PERCENTAGE CHANGE			
	1926	1929	1933	1937	1946	1929–33	1933–37	1937–46	1926–46
Apparent Civilian per Capita Consumption of Foods (in Pounds, Except Eggs)									
Beef and Veal (Carcass Weight)	68.5	56.0	58.6	63.8	71.6	4.6	8.9	12.2	4.5
Pork Excluding Lard (Carcass Weight)	64.1	69.6	70.7	55.8	75.8	1.6	−21.1	35.8	18.3
Fish (Edible Weight)	13.4	13.9	10.7	13.8	12.8	−23.0	29.0	−7.2	−4.5
Lard	12.2	12.7	14.0	10.5	11.8	10.2	−25.0	12.4	−3.3
Apples	62.3	39.7	40.0	33.6	23.0	0.8	−16.0	−31.5	−63.1
Potatoes (Farm Weight)	128	159	132	126	123	−17.0	−4.5	−2.4	−3.9
Fresh vegetables (Farm Weight)	100.6	112.6	104.5	111.0	129.9	−7.2	6.2	17.0	29.1
Melons (Farm Weight)	36.4	32.1	25.3	28.8	30.6	−21.2	13.8	6.3	−15.9
Dry Beans (Cleaned Basis)	7.6	7.8	7.1	7.8	8.7	−9.0	9.9	11.5	14.5
Dairy Products									
Total Milk for Human Consumption	818	811	814	797	786	0.4	−2.1	−1.4	−3.9
Cheese	4.6	4.7	4.6	5.5	6.7	−2.1	19.6	21.8	45.7
Eggs (Number)	339	334	296	308	379	−11.4	4.1	23.1	11.8
Chicken and Turkey[1]	14.2	15.7	16.7	15.9	23.1	6.4	−4.8	45.3	62.7
Wheat Flour	182	177	162	159	156	−8.5	−1.9	−1.9	−14.3
Corn Flour and Meal	28.9	30.5	25.7	22.8	15.2	−15.7	−11.3	−33.3	−47.4
Coffee (Green Bean Basis)	12.4	12.2	12.8	13.3	20.1	4.9	3.9	51.1	62.1

[1] *Chicken only, 1926–28, but turkey consumption was very small during those years.*

[p. 301] **Various Social and Economic Data for Selected Years Pre-, Post-, and During the Great Depression,** *continued*

ITEMS	NUMERICAL VALUES					PERCENTAGE CHANGE			
	1926	1929	1933	1937	1946	1929–33	1933–37	1937–46	1926–46
Gross National Product									
Current Prices									
Total (Billion Dollars)	97.0	103.1	55.6	90.4	208.5	−46.1	62.6	130.6	114.9
per Capita ($)	826	847	442	701	1,475	−47.8	58.6	110.4	78.6
1958 Prices									
Total (Billion Dollars)	190.0	203.6	141.5	203.2	312.6	−30.5	43.6	53.8	64.5
per Capita ($)	1,619	1,671	1,126	1,576	2,211	−32.6	40.0	40.3	36.6
Agriculture—Farms									
Farm Population									
Total (000)	30,979	30,580	32,393	31,266	25,403	5.9	−3.5	−18.8	−18.0
Percent of Total Population	26.5	25.2	25.8	24.3	18.0	2.4	−5.8	−25.9	−32.1
Value of Farm Property ($000)									
Implements and Machinery	3,042	3,178	2,464	2,648	5,174	−22.5	7.5	95.4	70.1
Livestock	3,421	4,672	1,787	3,036	8,072	−61.8	69.9	165.9	136.0
Farm Employment (000)									
Total	12,976	12,763	12,739	11,978	10,295	−0.2	−6.0	−14.1	−20.7
Family Workers	9,526	9,360	9,874	9,054	8,106	−5.5	−8.3	−10.5	−14.9
Hired Workers	3,450	3,403	2,865	2,924	2,189	−15.8	2.1	−25.1	−36.6
Wage Rate per Day without Board or Room ($)	2.40	2.30	1.15	1.65	4.80	−50.0	43.5	190.9	100.0

[p. 302] Various Social and Economic Data for Selected Years Pre-, Post-, and During the Great Depression, *continued*

ITEMS	NUMERICAL VALUES					PERCENTAGE CHANGE			
	1926	1929	1933	1937	1946	1929–33	1933–37	1937–46	1926–46
Farm Income and Expenses ($000,000)									
Realized Gross Farm Income	13,302	13,938	7,107	11,367	29,539	−49.0	59.9	159.9	122.1
Cash Receipt from Marketing									
Total	10,558	11,312	5,332	8,864	24,802	−52.9	66.2	179.8	134.9
Crops	4,875	5,130	2,486	3,924	11,016	−51.5	57.8	180.7	126.0
Livestock and Livestock Products	5,683	6,182	2,846	4,940	13,786	−54.0	73.6	179.1	142.6
Government Payments	—	—	131	336	772	—	156.5	129.8	—
Value of Farm Products Consumed in Farm Households	1,875	1,713	1,030	1,434	2,662	−39.9	39.2	85.6	42.0
Gross Rental Value of Farm Dwellings	869	913	614	733	1,303	−32.7	19.4	77.8	49.9
Indexes of Prices Received and Paid by Farmers (1967 = 100)									
Prices Received by Farmers									
All Farm Products	57	58	28	48	93	−51.7	71.4	93.8	63.2
Crops	64	65	31	54	104	−52.3	74.2	92.6	62.5
Livestock and Products	55	57	25	45	87	−56.1	80.0	93.3	58.2
Prices Paid by Farmers									
Living	49	48	34	40	63	−29.2	17.6	57.5	28.6
Production	49	51	34	46	67	−33.3	35.3	45.7	36.7

[p. 303] Various Social and Economic Data for Selected Years Pre-, Post-, and During the Great Depression, *continued*

ITEMS	NUMERICAL VALUES					PERCENTAGE CHANGE			
	1926	1929	1933	1937	1946	1929–33	1933–37	1937–46	1926–46
Agriculture—Crops (Season Avg. Price)									
Corn for All Purposes ($ per bu.)	.74	.80	.52	.52	1.53	−35.0	0.0	194.2	106.8
Wheat for Grain ($ per bu.)	1.22	1.04	.74	.96	1.90	−28.8	29.7	97.9	55.7
Oats for Grain ($ per bu.)	.40	.42	.34	.30	.81	−19.0	−11.8	170.0	102.5
Barley for Grain ($ per bu.)	.58	.54	.43	.54	1.38	−20.4	25.6	155.6	137.9
Soybeans for Beans ($ per bu.)	2.01	1.38	.94	.85	2.57	−50.0	−9.6	202.4	27.9
Sweet Potatoes ($ per 100 lb.)	2.07	2.15	1.29	1.41	3.87	−40.0	9.3	174.5	87.0
Rice ($ per 100 lb.)	2.51	2.22	1.73	1.46	5.00	−22.1	−15.6	242.5	99.2
Cotton (¢ per lb.)	12.49	16.78	10.17	8.41	32.64	−39.4	−17.3	288.1	161.3
Agriculture—Livestock, Poultry, and Eggs									
Meat Slaughtering ($ per 100 lb.)[1]									
Beef	9.47	13.43	5.42	11.47	19.16	−59.6	111.6	67.0	102.3
Veal	11.61	14.76	5.88	10.07	16.87	−60.2	71.3	67.5	45.3
Pork[2]	12.34	10.16	3.94	10.02	18.40	−61.2	154.3	83.6	49.1
Lamb and Mutton	14.26	14.62	6.65	10.78	18.40	−54.5	62.1	70.7	29.0
Prices Received by Farmers									
Chickens (¢ per lb.)	22.1	22.8	9.5	16.0	27.6	−58.3	68.4	72.5	24.9
Turkeys (¢ per lb.)	—	24.5	11.6	18.1	36.3	−52.7	56.0	100.6	—
Eggs (¢ per doz.)	28.9	29.8	13.8	21.3	37.6	−53.7	54.3	76.5	30.1

[1] At Chicago. [2] Excludes purchases on the Government's account for the Emergency Hog Production Control Program from August 22–October 7, 1933.

[p. 304] Various Social and Economic Data for Selected Years Pre-, Post-, and During the Great Depression, *continued*

ITEMS	NUMERICAL VALUES					PERCENTAGE CHANGE			
	1926	1929	1933	1937	1946	1929–33	1933–37	1937–46	1926–46
Agriculture—Dairy Products									
Prices Received by Farmers									
Butter (¢ per lb.)	40.9	42.2	20.1	29.6	58.3	−52.4	47.3	97.0	42.5
Milkfat in Cream (¢ per lb.)	41.6	45.2	18.8	33.3	64.3	−58.4	77.1	93.1	54.6
Whole Milk									
Wholesale ($ per 100 lb.)	2.38	2.53	1.30	1.99	3.99	−48.6	53.1	100.5	67.6
Retail (¢ per qt.)	11.3	11.5	8.6	10.5	15.2	−25.2	22.1	44.8	34.5
Wholesale Prices									
Cheese, American Twins (¢ per lb.)	20.1	20.2	10.2	15.9	34.8	−49.5	55.9	118.9	73.1
Butter at New York (¢ per lb.)	44.4	45.0	21.6	34.4	62.8	−52.0	59.3	82.6	41.4
Forest Products									
Wholesale Price Indexes (1967 = 100)									
Lumber	25.2	23.6	17.8	25.1	44.7	−24.6	41.0	78.1	77.4
Woodpulp	38.3	33.9	25.0	44.6	59.5	−26.3	78.4	33.4	55.4
Paper	45.0	40.0	34.5	38.6	50.2	−13.7	11.9	30.1	11.6
Paper Board	38.8	34.4	31.9	37.8	54.8	−7.3	18.5	45.0	41.2
Minerals—Price									
Pig Iron, F.O.B. Valley Furnaces ($ per Long Ton)	18.55	18.20	15.44	22.99	27.13	−15.2	48.9	18.0	46.3
Copper, New York Electrolytic, F.O.B. Refinery (¢ per lb.)	13.95	18.23	7.15	13.27	13.92	−60.8	85.6	4.9	−0.2
Pig Lead, New York (¢ per lb.)	8.42	6.83	3.87	6.01	8.11	−43.3	55.3	34.9	−3.7
Slab Zinc, New York (¢ per lb.)	7.72	6.84	4.40	6.87	9.15	−35.7	56.1	33.2	18.5

[p. 305] Various Social and Economic Data for Selected Years Pre-, Post-, and During the Great Depression, *continued*

ITEMS	NUMERICAL VALUES					PERCENTAGE CHANGE			
	1926	1929	1933	1937	1946	1929–33	1933–37	1937–46	1926–46
Construction—Value and Cost Indexes									
Private Construction ($000,000)									
Residential Including Farm	5,737	3,772	499	1,975	4,752	−86.8	295.8	140.6	−17.2
Nonresidential Excluding Farm	2,513	2,694	406	1,085	3,341	−84.9	167.2	207.9	33.0
Farm Nonresidential	160	160	20	107	447	−87.5	435.0	317.8	179.4
Construction Costs Indexes (1967 = 100)[1]	30	30	25	30	45	−16.7	20.0	50.0	50.0
Rail and Highway Transportation									
Revenue Freight—All Tonnage (000)[2]	1,336,142	1,339,091	698,943	1,015,586	1,366,617	−47.8	45.3	34.6	2.3
Total Railroad Operating Revenue ($000)	6,508,679	6,373,004	3,138,186	4,226,325	7,709,171	−50.8	34.7	82.4	18.4
Railroad Employees									
Number (000)	1,822	1,694	991	1,137	1,378	−41.5	14.7	21.2	−24.4
Compensation ($000,000)	3,002	2,940	1,424	2,014	4,214	−51.6	41.4	109.2	40.4
Passenger Car Sales, Number (000)	3,692.3	4,455.1	1,560.5	3,929.2	2,148.6	−65.0	151.8	−45.3	−41.8
Telephones									
Total									
Number (000)	17,680	19,970	16,628	19,453	31,611	−16.7	17.0	62.5	78.8
Per 1000 Population	149.5	163.1	132.0	150.4	221.3	−19.1	13.9	47.1	48.0
Household with (Percent)	39.2	41.6	31.3	34.3	51.4	−24.8	9.6	49.9	31.1
Residence (000)	11,689	13,135	10,475	12,341	21,239	−20.3	17.8	72.1	81.7
Business (000)	5,991	6,835	6,153	7,112	10,372	−10.0	15.6	45.8	73.1

[1] *Department of Commerce composite.* [2] *In tons of 2000 pounds.*

[p. 306] Various Social and Economic Data for Selected Years Pre-, Post-, and During the Great Depression, *continued*

ITEMS	NUMERICAL VALUES					PERCENTAGE CHANGE			
	1926	1929	1933	1937	1946	1929–33	1933–37	1937–46	1926–46
Electric Production, and Residential Service									
Net Production (000,000 kW-hr)[1]									
Total Utility and Industrial	94,222	116,747	102,655	146,476	269,609	−12.1	42.7	84.1	186.1
Electric Utilities	69,353	92,180	81,740	118,913	223,178	−11.3	45.5	87.7	221.8
Industrial Establishments	24,869	24,567	20,915	27,563	46,431	−14.9	31.8	68.5	86.7
Residential Service									
Annual Use per Customer (kW-hr)	430	502	600	805	1,329	19.5	34.2	65.1	209.1
Percentage of Dwelling Units with Electric Service									
All Dwellings	57.9	67.9	66.7	73.1	85.5	−1.8	9.6	17.0	47.7
Farm	4.8	9.2	11.8	18.3	53.3	28.3	55.1	191.3	1,010.4

[1] *Net production data include generation by manufacturing and extracting industries and by electric railroads and railways. Excluded are nonutility generating plants of less than 100kW; plants operated by hotels, apartment houses, office buildings, or other commercial, transport, or service establishments; and plants in military installations.*

[p. 307] Various Social and Economic Data for Selected Years Pre-, Post-, and During the Great Depression, *continued*

ITEMS	NUMERICAL VALUES					PERCENTAGE CHANGE			
	1926	1929	1933	1937	1946	1929-33	1933-37	1937-46	1926-46
Average Annual Earnings per Fulltime Employee in Distribution and Selected Service Industries ($)									
Wholesale Trade	—	2,072	1,477	1,693	3,021	−28.7	14.6	78.4	—
Retail Trade[1]	—	1,409	1,066	1,218	2,141	−24.3	14.3	75.8	—
Hotels and Other Lodging Places	—	1,098	816	941	1,745	−25.7	15.3	85.4	—
Personal Services	—	1,219	889	978	1,854	−27.1	10.0	89.6	—
Miscellaneous Business Services	—	2,274	1,653	1,966	2,861	−27.3	18.9	45.5	—
Miscellaneous Repair Services	—	1,814	1,286	1,544	2,766	−29.1	20.1	79.1	—
Motion Pictures	—	2,169	1,891	1,972	2,978	−12.8	4.3	51.0	—
Amusement and Recreation, Except Motion Pictures	—	1,273	1,185	1,269	2,185	−6.9	7.1	72.2	—
Medical and Other Health Services	—	925	810	876	1,605	−12.4	8.1	83.2	—
Legal Services	—	1,378	1,168	1,231	1,757	−15.2	5.4	42.7	—
Educational Services	—	1,312	1,189	1,211	1,802	−9.4	1.9	48.8	—
Miscellaneous Professional Services	—	2,314	1,619	1,774	3,280	−30.0	9.6	84.9	—
Nonprofit Membership Organizations	—	1,712	1,442	1,497	1,984	−15.8	3.8	32.5	—

[1] Includes *automobile repair, services, and garages.*

[p. 308] Various Social and Economic Data for Selected Years Pre-, Post-, and During the Great Depression, *continued*

ITEMS	NUMERICAL VALUES					PERCENTAGE CHANGE			
	1926	1929	1933	1937	1946	1929–33	1933–37	1937–46	1926–46
Retail Store Sales by Kind of Store ($000,000)									
Total Durable and Nondurable Goods Stores	—	48,459	24,517	42,150	102,488	−49.4	71.9	143.2	—
Durable Goods Stores									
Total Sales of Durable Goods[1]	—	15,610	5,384	12,048	27,570	−65.5	123.8	128.8	—
Furniture, Home Furnishing Stores	—	1,813	646	1,254	3,264	−64.4	94.1	160.3	—
Household Appliance Store	—	942	313	592	1,575	−66.8	89.1	166.0	—
Hardware Stores	—	706	311	651	1,911	−55.9	109.3	193.5	—
Jewelry Stores	—	536	175	347	1,260	−67.4	98.3	263.1	—
Nondurable Goods Stores									
Total Sales of Nondurable Goods[1]	—	32,849	19,133	30,102	74,918	−41.7	57.3	148.9	—
Apparel Stores	—	4,241	1,930	3,323	8,880	−54.5	72.2	167.2	—
Drug and Proprietary Stores	—	1,690	1,066	1,527	3,723	−36.9	43.3	143.8	—
Eating and Drinking Places	—	2,132	1,434	3,293	10,619	−32.7	129.6	222.5	—
Grocery Stores	—	7,353	5,004	7,266	18,640	−31.9	45.2	156.5	—
General Merchandise Stores	—	9,015	4,982	6,673	14,724	−44.7	33.9	120.7	—
Value of Exports and Imports ($000,000)									
Total Merchandise, gold, and silver									
Exports	5,017	5,441	2,061	3,407	9,996	−62.1	65.3	193.4	99.2
Imports	4,714	4,755	1,703	4,807	5,533	−64.2	182.3	15.1	17.4
Excess of Exports (+) or Imports (−)	+303	+686	+358	−1,400	+4,464	−47.8	−391.1	318.9	1,373.3

[1] *Includes subclasses not shown separately.*

[p. 309] **Various Social and Economic Data for Selected Years Pre-, Post-, and During the Great Depression,** *continued*

ITEMS	NUMERICAL VALUES					PERCENTAGE CHANGE			
	1926	1929	1933	1937	1946	1929–33	1933–37	1937–46	1926–46
Business									
Total Concerns in Business (000)	2,158	2,213	1,961	2,057	2,142	−11.4	4.9	4.1	−0.7
Business Failures									
Total Number of Failures	21,773	22,909	19,859	9,490	1,129	−13.3	−52.2	−88.1	−94.8
Total Current Liabilities ($000,000)	409	483	458	183	67	−5.2	−60.0	−63.4	−83.6
Business Failure Rate[1]	101	104	100	46	5	−3.8	−54.0	−89.1	−95.0
Indexes of National Productivity Real Gross Private Domestic Product (per Man-Hr) 1958 = 100									
Total Economy	—	48.6	44.5	53.1	68.7	−8.4	19.3	29.4	—
Farm	—	37.3	38.9	40.3	51.4	4.3	3.6	27.5	—
Nonfarm	—	54.1	50.4	59.7	73.3	−6.8	18.5	22.8	—
Net Public and Private Debt (Billions of Dollars)									
Total Public and Private	169.2	191.9	168.5	182.2	396.6	−12.2	8.1	117.7	134.4
Total Public	30.3	30.1	40.6	55.3	243.2	34.9	36.2	339.8	702.6
Private									
Total Corporate, Individual and Noncorporate	138.9	161.8	127.9	126.9	153.4	−20.9	0.8	20.9	10.4
Corporate	76.2	88.9	76.9	75.8	93.5	−13.5	−1.4	23.4	22.7
Individual and Noncorporate	62.7	72.9	51.0	51.1	59.9	−30.0	0.2	17.2	−4.5

[1] *Per 10,000 enterprises.*

[p. 310] **Various Social and Economic Data for Selected Years Pre-, Post-, and During the Great Depression,** *continued*

ITEMS	NUMERICAL VALUES					PERCENTAGE CHANGE			
	1926	1929	1933	1937	1946	1929–33	1933–37	1937–46	1926–46
Currency Stock and Currency in Circulation—As of June 30 ($000)	8,428,971	8,538,796	10,078,417	19,376,690	49,648,011	18.0	92.3	156.2	489.0
Total Currency in U.S.[1]	2,070,588	1,935,513	2,085,971	9,475,429	17,539,072	7.8	354.2	85.1	747.1
Currency Held in Treasury[2]	1,473,118	1,856,986	2,271,682	3,454,205	3,863,941	22.3	52.1	11.9	162.3
Currency Outside Treasury in Federal Reserve Banks in Circulation	4,885,266	4,746,297	5,720,764	6,447,056	28,244,997	20.5	12.7	338.1	478.2
Interest Rates, Stock Volume, Consumer Credit, and Banks	3.68								
U.S. Government Bonds Interest Rates (Percent per Annum)	451	3.60	3.31	2.74	2.19	–8.1	–17.2	–20.1	–40.5
Stocks Volume—NYS (000,000)	5,227	1,125	655	409	364	–41.8	–37.6	–11.0	–19.3
Short- and Intermediate-Term Credit ($000,000)	2,363	7,116	3,885	6,948	8,384	–45.4	78.8	20.7	60.4
Total Credit Outstanding	2,864	3,524	1,723	4,118	4,172	–51.1	139.0	1.3	76.6
Installment Credit Outstanding	28,350								
Non-Installment Credit Outstanding		3,592	2,162	2,830	4,212	–39.8	30.9	48.8	47.1
Number of Banks (as of June 30)		25,568	14,771	15,646	14,685	–42.2	5.9	–6.1	–48.2

[1] Excludes gold certificates, silver certificates, since the gold and silver held as security against them are included. Includes the following categories of currency: Reserves held against U.S. notes and Treasury notes of 1890, held for Federal Reserve banks and agents, and all other money. Excludes amount held as security against gold and silver certificates since the certificates and notes are included elsewhere; for 1860–1933 they are included as currency outside the Treasury, and beginning in 1934 they were included either as currency outside the Treasury or as amounts held in Treasury for Federal Reserve banks and agents payable in gold certificates. [2] Includes coin, bullion, and paper money.

[p. 311] **Various Social and Economic Data for Selected Years Pre-, Post-, and During the Great Depression,** *continued*

ITEMS	NUMERICAL VALUES					PERCENTAGE CHANGE			
	1926	1929	1933	1937	1946	1929–33	1933–37	1937–46	1926–46
Life Insurance Companies and Sales									
Number of Companies (as of Dec. 31)	396	433	375	436	514	–14.4	16.3	17.9	29.8
Sales of Life Insurance by U.S. Companies ($000,000)									
Total	15,217	17,755	10,846	12,572	22,805	–38.9	15.9	81.4	49.9
Ordinary	10,508	12,305	6,786	7,593	16,244	–44.9	11.9	113.9	54.6
Group	1,174	1,379	427	800	2,152	–69.0	87.4	169.0	83.3
Industrial	3,535	4,071	3,633	4,179	4,409	–10.8	15.0	5.5	24.7
Federal Government Employment and Finances									
Total Paid Civilian Employees (as of June 30)	548,713	579,559	603,587	895,993	2,696,529	4.2	48.4	201.0	391.4
Finances ($000) (Years Ending June 30)									
Receipts[1]	3,962,756	4,033,250	2,021,213	4,978,601	39,771,404	–49.9	146.3	698.9	903.6
Expenditures[2]	3,097,612	3,298,859	4,622,865	7,756,021	60,447,574	40.1	67.8	679.4	1,851.4
Surplus or Deficit (–)[3]	865,144	734,391	–2,601,652	–2,777,421	–20,676,171	–354.3	–6.8	–644.4	2,389.9
Total Gross Debt[4]	19,643,216	16,931,088	22,538,673	36,424,614	269,422,099	33.1	61.6	639.7	1,271.6

[1] *Excludes receipts from borrowing. Prior to 1931, total receipts; thereafter, net receipts.*   [2] *Excludes debt repayment. Prior to 1931, total expenditures; thereafter, net expenditures.*   [3] *Receipts compared with expenditures.*   [4] *As of end of period.*

Bibliography

Galbraith, John Kenneth. *The Great Crash: 1929*. New York: Time Inc., 1962.
Lightner, Otto C. *The History of Business Depressions*. 1922; reprint, New York: Burt Franklin, 1970.
Mitchell, Broadus. *Depression Decade: From New Era through New Deal, 1929-1941*. Volume IX, *The Economic History of the United States*. New York: Harper & Row, 1947.
Shannon, David A. *The Great Depression*. Englewood Cliffs, N.J.: Prentice-Hall, 1960.

Index

Administrator of Veterans Affairs 49, 50, 51, 53
Advisory Commodity Committees 237
Agricultural Adjustment Act (1933) viii, 194, 200, 212
Agricultural Adjustment Administration 68
Agricultural Appropriations Act (1932) 25
Agricultural Credit Act (1923) 247
Agricultural Marketing Act 228, 235, 236, 237, 238, 239
Alabama Power Company 98
Albrook Field 26, 30
architect of the Capitol 202
attorney general 32, 69, 125, 196, 205, 220

Bank Conservation Act 39, 41
bank holiday 35, 37
Banking Act (1933) 153, 157, 164, 182, 183
Bankruptcy Act (1898) 82
Bankruptcy Act (1933) 14
Banks for Cooperatives 228, 234, 236, 237, 239, 240, 241, 243, 244, 245
Barksdale Field 26, 30
Benton Field 30
Board of Tax Appeals 226
Bolling Field 27, 30
Boulder Canyon Project Act (1928) 26
Boxer Rebellion 49, 50, 52
Budget Statement No. 9 56
Bureau of Internal Revenue 73
Bureau of Yards and Docks 26

Camp Devens 27
Camp Gaillard 31
Camp Knox 28
Canal Zone 26, 30, 41, 68, 111, 203, 206
Carlisle Barracks 27

Central Bank for Cooperatives 228, 233, 234, 235, 236, 237, 239, 240, 241, 243
Chanute Field 27, 30
chief of engineers of the United States Army 202
Civil War 49, 50
Classification Act (1923) 68, 90, 139, 195, 201, 215
clerk of the House of Representatives 19, 91
Clinch River 103, 104
Coast and Geodetic Survey 26, 54
Coast Guard 53, 54
commissioner of patents 105
comptroller general of the United States 99, 100
comptroller of the currency 6, 22, 41, 42, 43, 44, 45, 46, 48, 158, 160, 161, 162, 165, 167, 170, 179, 180, 181, 186, 188, 189, 190, 191, 192
Congress vii, 2, 4, 9, 11, 15, 16, 26, 39, 40, 47, 49, 54, 57, 58, 59, 61, 65, 84, 89, 90, 93, 99, 100, 105, 106, 110, 113, 135, 137, 139, 140, 144, 194, 195, 201, 202, 214, 220, 228, 239, 240
Constitution 54, 56, 58, 99, 211
cooperative bank commissioner of the Farm Credit Administration 234, 247
Corporation of Foreign Security Holders 133, 136
Cotton Stabilization Corporation 20
Court of Appeals, District of Columbia 118
Cove Creek Dam 102, 103, 104
Credit Act 49
Criminal Code of the United States 11, 44, 152, 173, 242

dam numbered 2 99, 102, 103, 104
Department of Agriculture 67, 68
Department of Commerce 26

315

Department of Labor 139
Department of the Interior 25
deputy land bank commissioner 247
director of the Bureau of the Budget 56
Duncan Field 27, 30

Edgewood Arsenal 27
Eighteenth Amendment 211
electric power 94, 97, 98, 101, 102, 103, 107, 202
Emergency Farm Mortgage Act (1933) 78, 85
Emergency Railroad Transportation Act 214
Emergency Relief and Construction Act (1932) ix, 13, 16, 21, 22, 89, 202, 204, 206, 213, 229, 241, 248
Emergency Relief Appropriations Act (1935) ix, 19
Employment Stabilization Act (1931) 24
Employment Stabilization Board 26

Fair Labor Standards Act (1938) x
Farm Board 237, 238
Farm Credit Act 228, 243, 246
Farm Credit Administration 85, 194, 212, 241, 242, 243, 246, 247, 248
farm loan commissioner 3, 73, 74, 75, 76, 77, 78, 79, 80, 81, 82, 84, 243, 247
Farm Security Administration ix
Farm Tenant Act (1937) ix
Federal Advisory Council 142
Federal Coordinator of Transportation 214, 215
Federal Deposit Insurance Corporation 153, 160, 172, 173
Federal Emergency Administration of Public Works 194, 201
Federal Emergency Relief Act (1933) 89, 92
Federal Emergency Relief Administration 89, 90
Federal Emergency Relief Administrator 90
Federal Farm Board 20, 62
Federal Farm Loan Act 61, 73, 74, 75, 76, 77, 78, 79, 81, 82, 181, 228, 233, 243, 245, 246, 247
Federal Farm Loan Board 6, 22, 78
Federal Highway Act 24, 31, 204, 205
Federal Home Loan Bank Act 144, 145, 150
Federal Home Loan Bank Board 144
federal home loan banks 148, 149, 151, 178, 179, 181

federal intermediate credit banks 233, 236, 239, 246
federal land banks 246
Federal Open Market Committee 160
Federal Power Commission ix
Federal Reserve Act 23, 39, 40, 45, 46, 47, 78, 86, 88, 153, 154, 155, 158, 159, 160, 174, 176, 177, 178, 179, 181, 185, 186, 189, 192
Federal Reserve Board ix, 3, 6, 22, 23, 44, 47, 86, 88, 154, 156, 157, 158, 159, 160, 162, 175, 176, 177, 179, 182, 183, 184, 185, 191, 192
Federal Reserve System ix, 38, 39, 40, 154, 155, 156, 158, 160, 161, 162, 163, 164, 169, 170, 173, 174, 175, 185, 192
federal savings and loan associations 144, 149, 151
Federal Trade Commission ix, 110, 111, 133, 196, 198
Federal Trade Commission Act 69, 196, 198
Fitzsimmons General Hospital 27
Foreign Services of the United States 56
Forest Products Laboratory 60
Fort Benjamin Harrison 27
Fort Benning 26, 30
Fort Bliss 27, 30
Fort Bragg 27
Fort Douglas 27
Fort DuPont 27
Fort Francis E. Warren 29
Fort George G. Meade 28
Fort George Wright 29
Fort Hamilton 27
Fort Holye 27
Fort Howard 27
Fort Huachuca 27
Fort Humphreys 27
Fort Jay 27
Fort Lawton 28
Fort Leavenworth 28
Fort Lewis 28
Fort Logan 28
Fort McClellan 28
Fort McPherson 28
Fort Mason 28
Fort Meade 28
Fort Monmouth 28
Fort Myer 28
Fort Oglethorpe 28
Fort Ontario 28
Fort Sam Houston 27
Fort Sill 29
Fort Snelling 29
Fort Totten 29
Fort Wadsworth 29
Fort Winfield Scott 29

Index

Gamboa Reach 31
General Accounting Office 100
governor of the Farm Credit Administration 228, 229, 230, 238, 239, 243, 244, 245, 246, 248
governor, production credit associations 233

Hamilton Field 27, 30
Hatbox Field 30
Hensley Field 27
Holabird Quartermaster Depot 27
Home Owners' Loan Act (1933) 144
Home Owners' Loan Corporation 144, 145, 151, 152, 178, 179, 181
Hoover, Herbert viii
Hoover Dam 25
House document numbered 788 26
House of Representatives 2, 11, 15, 16, 19, 39, 47, 49, 54, 57, 59, 61, 89, 91, 93, 95, 110, 137, 139, 144, 194, 214, 228
Hull, Cordell 36, 37, 38

intermediate credit commissioner 247
Interstate Commerce Act 113, 214, 216, 217, 221, 225, 226
Interstate Commerce Commission 2, 5, 6, 21, 22, 200, 203, 214, 225
interstate commerce commissioner 247

Jefferson Barracks 28
Judicial Code 118, 125

land bank commissioner 244, 247
Langley Field 28, 30
Legislative Appropriation Act (1933) 55, 56, 57, 58, 84, 85
Letterman General Hospital 28
Library of Congress 203
Lighthouse Service 26, 54
London Naval Treaty (1930) 202
Luke Field 30

March Field 28, 30
Maxwell Field 28, 30
Mississippi River 104
Mississippi River Basin 93
Mitchel Field 28, 31
Morris Plan banks 155
Muscle Shoals 93, 94, 96, 98, 99, 100, 101, 103

National Bank Act 181
National Banking System 40
National Cooperative Employment Service Act 139
National Forest Administration 25
National Housing Act (1937) x
National Industrial Recovery Act 194, 212, 213
National Labor Relations Act (1935) ix
nitrate plant numbered 2 97, 98

Panama Canal Zone 31, 56, 57, 103
Panama Railroad Company 57
Patent Office of the United States 105
Patterson Field 31
Pay Act (1922) 55
Philippine Insurrection 49, 50, 52
Plattsburg Barracks 28
Pope Field 29, 31
Post Field 29, 31
Post Office Department 55
Postal Savings 177
postmaster general 26, 34, 143, 177
president viii, 3, 5, 19, 23, 35, 36, 37, 38, 39, 40, 41, 44, 45, 47, 49, 50, 51, 53, 54, 55, 56, 58, 59, 60, 70, 85, 86, 87, 89, 90, 91, 93, 94, 97, 98, 99, 102, 103, 104, 106, 107, 136, 139, 158, 160, 165, 173, 195, 196, 197, 198, 199, 200, 201, 202, 203, 204, 205, 206, 207, 211, 212, 215, 220, 247, 248
Presidio of San Francisco 29
production credit associations 228, 230, 231, 232, 233, 239, 240, 241, 242, 243, 244, 245, 246
production credit commissioner of the Farm Credit Administration 223, 247
production credit corporations 228, 229, 230, 231, 232, 233, 239, 240, 241, 242, 243, 246
Public Health Service 54
Public Utility Holding Company Act (1935) ix
Pullman Company 221

Railway Labor Act 215, 217, 218, 219
Randolph Field 29, 31
Raritan Arsenal 29
Reconstruction Finance Act (1932) viii
Reconstruction Finance Corporation ix, 2, 5, 6, 11, 12, 13, 14, 16, 18, 19, 20, 22, 23, 45, 63, 65, 73, 78, 79, 81, 83, 84, 89, 90, 91, 92, 135, 145, 194, 213, 229, 248

Reconstruction Finance Corporaton Act (1932) 2, 12, 14, 15, 20, 21, 22, 23, 65, 73, 83, 84, 89, 145, 229
Regional Agricultural Credit Corporation 248
regional banks for cooperatives 236, 242
Reorganization Act (1939) ix
Representatives in Congress 54
Revenue Act (1926) 73, 209, 210, 212, 226
Revenue Act (1928) 226
Revenue Act (1932) 66, 73, 113, 208, 209, 210, 211, 212
Revenue Act (1935) ix
revised statutes 6, 32, 44, 60, 157, 167, 170, 180, 181, 182, 184, 186, 188, 189, 206
rice 67, 69
Rock Island Arsenal 29
Rockwell Field 29, 31
Roosevelt, Franklin D. vii, ix, 35, 36, 37, 38
Rural Electrification Administration ix
Rural Electrification Administration Act (1936) ix

Schoen Field 31
Scott Field 31
Second Library Bond Act 7, 207
Secret Service Division of the Treasury Department 173
secretary of agriculture 2, 3, 20, 22, 24, 25, 61, 62, 63, 64, 65, 66, 67, 68, 69, 70, 71, 200, 204, 205, 212, 229
secretary of commerce 26
secretary of labor 95, 142, 143
secretary of state 36, 37, 38
secretary of the interior 25, 84, 103, 104
secretary of the Navy 97
secretary of the Senate 19, 91
secretary of the treasury 3, 7, 8, 9, 11, 12, 23, 26, 27, 32, 33, 34, 36, 38, 39, 40, 41, 44, 45, 46, 57, 68, 69, 70, 72, 73, 74, 75, 76, 85, 86, 87, 88, 103, 141, 145, 146, 150, 158, 159, 161, 170, 171, 173, 190, 197, 207, 208, 220, 221, 225, 226, 240
secretary of war 97, 103, 104
Securities Act (1933) 110
Selfridge Field 29, 31
Senate 2, 3, 11, 15, 16, 19, 39, 47, 49, 54, 59, 61, 89, 91, 93, 95, 110, 137, 139, 144, 160, 194, 214, 228, 247, 248
senators 54, 57
Sheffield, Alabama 98
silver 35, 36, 40, 87, 88
silver certificates 88

Social Security Act (1935) ix
Spanish-American War 49, 52, 53
Speaker of the House of Representatives 54
Supreme Court vii, 118, 125

Temporary Federal Deposit Insurance Fund 173
Tennessee River 93, 96, 102, 104, 106
Tennessee River Basin 93, 106
Tennessee Valley 93, 104
Tennessee Valley Authority 93
Tennessee Valley Authority Act (1933) 93
tobacco 62, 67, 69
transmission line 96, 98, 100, 101, 104
Transportation Act (1920) 225
treasurer 2, 6, 7, 8, 9, 22, 46, 47, 55, 57, 69, 70, 71, 73, 74, 75, 86, 87, 88, 109, 146, 148, 151, 161, 170, 171, 175, 207, 212, 230
Treasury and Post Office Appropriation Act (1934) 56, 58
treasury bills 207

under secretary of the treasury 3, 23
Unemployment Relief-Public Works Act 59
United States Code 103
United States Court of Claims 105
United States Employment Service 139, 140, 141, 142, 143
United States Housing Authority x
United States Tariff Commission 196
Urgent Deficiencies Appropriation Act (1913) 221

Veterans' Administration 50, 51
vice president 54, 57
Victory Liberty Loan Act 34, 207
Virgin Islands 68, 72, 92, 111, 151, 203, 206

Waco Quarry 98, 99
Walter Reed General Hospital 29
War Department 56, 97
War Finance Corporation Act 6
West Point 29
wheat 67, 69
Wheeler Field 31
William Beaumont General Hospital 26
Work Progress Administration ix
Work Projects Administration ix
World War I 49, 50, 51, 52
World War II vii

www.ingramcontent.com/pod-product-compliance
Lightning Source LLC
Chambersburg PA
CBHW051209300426
44116CB00006B/483